St. Elisabeth of Thuringia

Hagiography beyond Tradition

The study of sanctity in medieval Europe is starting to elicit cutting-edge, innovative and genuinely interdisciplinary scholarship that destabilizes what people have conventionally considered to be hagiography. This is demonstrated in the topic range of panels sponsored by the Hagiography Society at recent landmark medievalist conferences. While hagiography has traditionally been understood only in religious terms, recent scholarship moves beyond such frameworks to consider alternate ways of identifying and representing exemplary people. So doing, such research emphasises modern cultural analogies and resonances with medieval figures.

It is not enough, however, to approach saints' lives with a "sexy" modern framework. The best scholarship is rooted in analytical rigour, close attention to context(s), and a keen awareness of the potential pitfalls of anachronism, all the while accepting that anachronism can often be productive. This series provides a home for the kind of work that negotiates that border between the traditional and the contemporary and encourages scholarship enhanced by interventions drawn from celebrity studies, trans studies, crip theory, animal and monster studies, the history of senses and the emotions, media studies, and beyond. Rather than considering hagiography as a single genre, the series is open to expanding the ways in which we imagine how people come to be offered for veneration, as well as the media and genres in which they are fashioned, represented, and celebrated.

St. Elisabeth of Thuringia

A Psychological Study (1931)

Elisabeth Busse-Wilson

Translated, with notes and an introduction by
Ulrike Wiethaus

Amsterdam University Press

Originally published as *Das Leben der Heiligen Elisabeth von Thüringen. Das Abblid einer mittelalterlichen Seele*. München: C.H. Beck 1931.

Translated from German by Ulrike Wiethaus

Cover illustration: Master i e, *Saint Elizabeth of Hungary*, end of the 15th century. Engraving. Collection of the Birmingham Museum of Art, Alabama; Museum purchase with funds provided by the European Art Society.Photo: Sean Pathasema

Cover design: Coördesign, Leiden
Lay-out: Crius Group, Hulshout

ISBN	978 94 6372 580 4
e-ISBN	978 90 4854 358 8
DOI	10.5117/9789463725804
NUR	684

Elisabeth Johanna Auguste Busse-Wilson (1890-1974) was a German historian and public intellectual. She was one of the first generation of German women to receive a university education. Undated Photo. Copyright: Busse-Wilson descendants.

Table of Contents

Introduction to the Translation

Ulrike Wiethaus

In 1931, 700 years after the saint's death, the cultural historian and social critic Elisabeth Busse-Wilson (1890–1974) published a book-length study of Elisabeth of Thuringia (1207–1231) with a curious subtitle, literally translated as "The Life of St. Elisabeth of Thuringia: Portrait of a Medieval Soul" (*Das Leben der Heiligen Elisabeth von Thüringen. Das Abbild einer mittelalterlichen Seele*).[1] The subtitle suggests an emphasis on interiority, individuality, and emotional dynamics while simultaneously creating a distance to formulaic definitions of sanctity. The biography mined new critical editions of primary sources and was written with an educated lay audience in mind. While other publications commemorated the 700-year anniversary with conservative decorum and pious devotion, Busse-Wilson's book burst on the scene with the intent to demonstrate that the cult of Germany's most popular female had covered up male clerical and aristocratic abuse in a medieval case of violence against women. In the absence of a critical feminist discourse, which would not emerge until several generations later, Busse-Wilson leveraged the language of psychology to make her case.

As M. W. Bychowski has argued in his study of St. Marinos, early twentieth-century German cultural historians, such as sexologist and political activist Magnus Hirschfeld, employed the term *Seele* (soul) to denote personal authenticity and self-directed inner wisdom.[2] Busse-Wilson's deliberate

---

1   Elisabeth Busse-Wilson, *Das Leben der Heiligen Elisabeth von Thüringen: Das Abbild einer mittelalterlichen Seele* (Munich: C.H. Beck, 1931). She published two additional essays about St. Elisabeth after 1931: Busse-Wilson, "Eine Franziskanerin des Nordens: Zur Heiligsprechung der heiligen Elisabeth Pfingsten 1235," *Die Wartburg* 34 (1935): 203–206, and "Die Wunder am Grabe der Heiligen Elisabeth in Marburg: Ein Beitrag zur Erhebung ihrer Gebeine im Jahre 1236," *Beiträge zur Hessischen Kirchengeschichte* 11 (1939): 184–209.

2   M. W. Bychowski, "The Authentic Lives of Transgender Saints: Imago Dei and Imitatio Christi in the Life of St Marinos the Monk," in *Trans and Genderqueer Subjects in Medieval Hagiography*, ed. Alicia Spencer-Hall and Blake Gutt (Amsterdam: Amsterdam University Press, 2021). For a German example of psychoanalytic interpretations, see Oskar Pfister, "Hysterie und Mystik bei Margaretha Ebner (1291–1351)," *Zentralblatt für Psychoanalyse* 1 (1911): 468–85. For the Spanish

Busse-Wilson, E., *St. Elisabeth of Thuringia: A Psychological Study (1931)*. Amsterdam: Amsterdam University Press, 2025

DOI 10.5117/9789463725804_INTRO

choice of subtitle propagated values and esteem that the medico-clinical term *Psyche* lacked, while keeping her psychological focus. Moving her analysis and methodology into a discursive domain beyond psychoanalytic parlance, she refused to follow popular psychoanalytic trends that defined medieval religious women as sexually frustrated hysterics. [2] Instead, the subtitle signaled the author's commitment to foreground Elisabeth's full personhood, individuality, and autonomous choices within the gendered constraints of medieval society. The book became an immediate sensation and garnered polarized reviews from across the cultural, religious, and political spectrum. An English translation of her study was planned from the beginning, but it took nearly another century until the author's goal to reach an international audience would be realized.[3]

While historical and cultural aspects of St. Elisabeth's cult continue to be studied in the United States and Europe, American biographies of the saint are still scarce.[4] The reasons for such scarcity are difficult to identify. Biographies generally tend to straddle the fence between literature, scholarly research, and trends in popular culture. Biographies of saints specifically are lionized by religious institutions through liturgical remembrance and hagiographic literature. Busse-Wilson's study thus invites reflection on the charged relationship between the biographical genre's attractiveness to the literary marketplace, the institutionalized devotion of a saint, and the academy. With only few exceptions, no academic studies of the saint or her cult have replicated Busse-Wilson's focus on the gender violence that shaped Elisabeth's short life as a religious lay woman.[5] This should

---

context, see Jennifer Smith's recent study, *Women, Mysticism, and Hysteria in Fin-de-Siècle Spain* (Nashville: Vanderbilt University, 2021).

3   Impressed by the initial sales of the book, C.H. Beck'sche Verlagshandlung contacted an interested translator, but the contract with the publisher Knopf in the United States fell through. See Britt Großmann, *Elisabeth Busse-Wilson (1890-1974): Eine Werk- und Netzwerkanalyse* (Weinheim: Benz Juventa, 2017), 314 n. 96, and Regina Marianne Illemann, *"Abbild einer mittelalterlichen Seele"? Das Bild der heiligen Elisabeth bei Busse-Wilson*, unpublished *Diplomarbeit* (Katholische-Theologische Fakultät, Rheinische Friedrich-Wilhelm-Universität Bonn, 2008), 91. I thank the author for providing me with a copy of her thoughtful study.

4   Lori Pieper, *The Greatest of These is Love: The Life of St. Elizabeth of Hungary*, 2nd rev. ed. (New York: Tau Cross Books and Media, 2013); Lori Pieper, *The Voice of a Medieval Woman: St. Elizabeth of Hungary as a Franciscan Penitent in the Early Sources for Her Life*, 2nd ed. (New York: Tau Cross Books and Media, 2016); Nesta De Robeck, *Elizabeth of Hungary: A Story of Twenty-four Years* (Milwaukee: Bruce Publishing Company, 1954).

5   See Dyan Elliott, "Elisabeth of Hungary: Between Men," in id., *Proving Woman: Female Spirituality and Inquisitional Culture in the Later Middle Ages* (Princeton: Princeton University Press, 2004).; Julie B. Miller, "Eroticized Violence in Medieval Women's Mystical Literature: A Call for a Feminist Critique," *Journal of Feminist Studies in Religion* 15, no. 2 (1999).; Ulrike Wiethaus,

come as a surprise. As documented in the canonization files, four women in the saint's entourage described her mistreatment and identified it as such.[6] Remarkably, historians like Busse-Wilson could thus rely on women's eyewitness accounts as much as the perpetrator's version of events, and study dynamics of ecclesiastical cover-up in the unfolding of the hagiographic narrativization of Elisabeth's suffering. Her analysis thus marks the forgotten genesis point of a new discursive field and analytical method in the study of gender violence that has been all too slow to gain momentum. Equally important, Busse-Wilson situated the young woman's life in a larger social context and refrained from painting her as a passive victim. Her proposition that the saint elected self-destruction as the means to protect her autonomy was and perhaps still is controversial. It was another contemporary, the Russian psychoanalyst Sabina Spielrein (1885–1942), who also dared to articulate the choice of self-destruction as an expression of individuation and the affirmation of authentic personhood. After an initial rejection, Sigmund Freud eventually adopted and reinterpreted Spielrein's insight as death instinct.[7]

As scholars have demonstrated, clerical and lay male abuse has consistently been concealed and normalized through a religious language

"The Punishments of St. Elisabeth," in id., *German Mysticism and the Politics of Culture* (New York: Peter Lang, 2014). On the refusal of many male scholars to grasp her feminist reading of male violence, see Ulrike Wiethaus, "Feminist Historiography as Pornography: St. Elisabeth of Thuringia in Nazi Germany," in *Medieval Feminist Newsletter* 24 (1997), and Ulrike Wiethaus, "Naming and Un-naming Violence against Women: German Historiography and the Cult of St. Elisabeth of Thuringia," in *Studies in Medievalism*, vol. 1, IX (1997). Busse-Wilson's stark analysis of Elisabeth of Thuringia's destructive dependency on Konrad of Marburg was preceded by only one other psychological demythologization of the saint. In his medical and cultural history of sadism and masochism, published in 1902, the neurologist Albert Eulenburg noted that Elisabeth's acquiescence to Konrad's authoritarian excesses was widely known. Albert Eulenburg, *Sadismus und Masochismus* (Wiesbaden: Verlag von J.F. Bergmann, 1902), 64. On the tensions between biographical and historiographical methodologies, see Levke Harders, "Legitimizing Biography: Critical Approaches to Biographical Research," in *Bulletin of the German Historical Institute* 55 (Fall 2014). Großmann notes the fashionable German trend of writing and reading historical biographies in the twenties as a reaction against the trauma of World War One. See Großmann, *Elisabeth Busse-Wilson*, 291–93.

6   The testimonies, which were edited and redacted by scribes in 1235, are also available in scholarly English translations. See Lori Pieper, *The Greatest of the These is Love,* op. cit., 119–49; Kenneth Baxter Wolf, *The Life and Afterlife of St. Elizabeth of Hungary: Testimony from Her Canonization Hearings* (Oxford: Oxford University Press, 2011); and Nesta de Robeck, op.cit., 202–34.

7   See Sabina Spielrein, "Die Destruktion als Ursache des Werdens," *Jahrbuch für Psychoanalytische und Psychopathologische Forschungen* 4 (1912).

of female heroic suffering and martyrdom.[8] The ideal of female heroic suffering is central to a definition of female sanctity and makes it especially difficult for female survivors of abuse to speak up.[8] The canonization of Maria Goretti (1890–1902), a twelve-year-old girl who was murdered in an attempted rape but forgave the rapist on her deathbed, serves as a contemporary example of concealing violence against women through religious rhetoric and the promotion of the victim's veneration. The strategy provides a sacrosanct haven for male abusers and glorifies the toleration of abuse as a path to sainthood.[9] The centuries-old silence surrounding St. Elisabeth's case is especially poignant, since her abuser was a high-ranking cleric. Preacher of the sixth crusade and inquisitor Konrad of Marburg (ca. 1180–1233) attended to her spiritual and economic needs as her confessor and guardian.

As a married Landgravine, the Hungarian-born Elisabeth of Thuringia enjoyed rare privileges, which included access to significant material resources. Once widowed, however, she was subjected to a religious regime that trumped her aristocratic advantages. As a foreigner and young widow with children, her life choices became increasingly circumscribed by her guardian confessor. Fanned by his propaganda and her husband's kin, her lucrative cult was set in motion immediately after her death at the age of twenty-four. Idolized as a selfless young princess and mother to the poor, Elisabeth's life became increasingly sanitized as her cultic resonance increased. Her cult's value as an ideological tool extended to the political arena. Nationalist celebrations of a Germanic Christian Middle Ages during the nineteenth and twentieth centuries conjoined St. Elisabeth with playwright Hrotsvit of Gandersheim (935–1002) and polymath Hildegard of Bingen (1098–1179) as preeminent medieval emblems of Germanic womanhood.[10]

---

8   Beverly Mayne Kienzle and Nancy Nienhuis, "Battered Women and the Construction of Sanctity," *Journal of Feminist Studies in Religion* 17, no. 1 (2001); Dyan Elliott, "Sexual Scandal and the Clergy: A Medieval Blueprint," in *Why the Middle Ages Matter. Medieval Light on Modern Injustice*, ed. Celia Chazelle, Simon Doubleday, Felice Lifshitz, and Amy G. Riemensnyder (London: Routledge, 2012); Ianere Angulo, "The Unnamed Presence: Abuse of Power in Consecrated Life," *Magistra* 28, no. 1 (2022).

9   Kathleen Zuanich Young, "The Imperishable Virginity of St. Maria Goretti," *Gender and Society* 3, no. 4 (1989). The case of Blessed Elizabeth Canori (1774–1825) is another modern example of a battered woman who was beatified, and her abuser forgiven. Canori was beatified in 1994. Goretti was canonized in 1950.

10   On Hrotsvit's genealogy as an icon of Germanic female genius, see Ulrike Wiethaus, "Who is Hrotsvit of Gandersheim?" in *German Mysticism,* op.cit., 57–75. On Hildegard's elevated place in the genealogy of German humanism, see Joseph Bernhart, "Hildegard of Bingen," *Archiv für Kulturgeschichte* (December 1930), 249–60.

Elisabeth Busse-Wilson, a public intellectual trained in the avantgarde field of interdisciplinary humanities, brought a keen feminist lens to the hagiographic obfuscation of her medieval namesake's short and tragic life. Published on the eve of the Nazi regime's rise to power, her fiery study shocked traditionally trained medievalists and Christian lay readers alike, who regarded St. Elisabeth's carefully curated cultic image as historical truth. Nonetheless, Busse-Wilson's biography of St. Elisabeth came to be viewed, at least by some notable historians at the time, as the most significant scholarly contribution to St. Elisabeth Studies in the twentieth century.[11]

Busse-Wilson could draw on new manuscript editions by the eminent expert on St. Elisabeth's medieval source materials, Catholic historian Albert Huyskens (1879–1956). Huyskens applauded Busse-Wilson, noting that she had set out to correct "naïve" and "sentimental" Catholic and scholarly representations of St. Elisabeth as a kind nurse and generous alms provider of royal lineage.[12] As theologian Regina Marianne Illemann's analysis of over forty book reviews at the time of publication reveals, female readers generally judged Busse-Wilson's work more positively than male readers. The author had hit a raw nerve, and some Germans were willing to listen.[13]

As one of only a handful of female German academics and public intellectuals in her generation, Busse-Wilson chose to be trained by some of the most

11 Hans-Jürgen Scholz, "Elisabethforscher von Justi bis Busse-Wilson," in *St. Elisabeth – Kult, Kirche, Konfessionen*, ed. Brigitte Rechberg (Marburg: J.A. Koch, 1983), 152.

12 Scholz, ibid.; for a discussion of Huysken's review, see also Großmann, op.cit., 304. In later years, Huyskens leveraged his expertise in critical source studies to provide genealogical research for the Nazi regime. See Stefan Krebs and Werner Tschacher, "Im Sinne der rassischen Erneuerung unseres Volkes: Albert Huyskens, die Westdeutsche Gesellschaft für Familienkunde und das Aachener Stadtarchiv im Nationalsozialismus," *Zeitschrift des Aachener Geschichtsvereins* 109 (2007). Huysken's studies of primary sources concerning Elisabeth's life comprise *Quellenstudien zur Geschichte der Heiligen Elisabeth* (Marburg: N.G. Elwert, 1908); *Der sogenannte Libellus de dictis ancillarum s. Elisabeth confectus* (Kempten and Munich: Verlag der Josef Kösel'schen Buchhandlung, 1911); and *Die Schriften des Caesarius von Heisterbach über die heilige Elisabeth von Thüringen* (Bonn: Publikationen der Gesellschaft für Rheinische Geschichtskunde 43, 1937). Huyskens (and by implication Busse-Wilson) were not yet aware of an at the time undiscovered Franciscan biography of St. Elisabeth, which adds nuanced perspectives of St. Elisabeth's Franciscan values and relationships. See Lori Pieper, "A New Life of St. Elizabeth of Hungary: The Anonymous Franciscan," *Archivum Franciscanum historicum* 93 (2000). Matthias Werner's analysis of the pastoral and caritative interplay between Franciscan ideals, Konrad's elite status as a representative of the Roman see, and Elisabeth's innovations as a lay religious (soror in saeculo) offers a positive interpretation of Konrad's religious agenda. Werner, "Elisabeth of Thüringen, Franziskus of Assisi und Konrad von Marburg," in *Elisabeth von Thüringen: Eine Europäische Heilige. Aufsätze*, ed. Dieter Blume and Matthias Werner (Petersberg: Michael Imhof Verlag, 2007).

13 Illemann, op.cit., 91–95.

innovative minds at German universities. She began her graduate work in
interdisciplinary humanities and social studies at the Institute for the Study
of Culture and Global History (Institut für Kultur und Universalgeschichte)
in Leipzig, founded in 1909 by the historian Karl Lamprecht (1856 – 1915).[14]

Lamprecht, a medievalist, developed groundbreaking methodologies
to link culture, art, and economic analyses in historical perspective that
influenced, among others, Chinese philosopher and educational reformer
Cai Yuanpei (1868–1940) and French medievalist Marc Bloch (1886–1944), a
co-founder of the Annales school. The institute's goal was to identify patterns
of historic change that could be applied universally. Driven by her interest
in comparative historical studies, Busse-Wilson also studied the work of
Wilhelm Wundt (1832– 1920), the founder of experimental psychology and a
pioneering proponent of comparative cultural psychology at the University
of Leipzig.[15] Likely because of Wundt, Busse-Wilson was introduced to the
innovative work of American philosopher and psychologist William James
(1842–1910).

Still widely read today, James' study of the subjective dimensions of
religious experience contributed significantly to her analysis of St. Elisabeth.[16] James was the first who utilized empirical biographical data in an
array of case studies to generate a theoretical model of religiosity. James
advanced the concepts of healthy-mindedness and morbid-mindedness to
account for the influence of adverse life experiences and personal suffering
in the construction of religious identity. Of all criticisms launched against
Busse-Wilson's radical departure from hagiographic tradition, it was her use
of psychological categories of analysis that provoked the most polemical
and often ill-informed responses; these include judgments of her book such
as "a pseudo-scientific, tendentious work"; "the false book of a rational
psychoanalyst"; "how else could one write about saints if one wishes that
they would not exist?" "Her dishonoring of the saint must hurt any sensitive
religious feeling." It is "an unscrupulous concoction."[17]

---

14   See Roger Chickering, *Karl Lamprecht: A German Academic Life (1856-1915)* (Atlantic Highlands,
NJ: Humanities Press, 1993). I thank Robert Beachy for alerting me to Chickering's study. For a
contemporaneous American evaluation, see Arley Barthlow Show's highly critical essay, "The
New Culture-History in Germany," *History Teacher's Magazine* 4 (1913).

15   On Wundt's status at the University of Leipzig and his alliance with Lamprecht, see Chickering, op.cit., 195–201.

16   Busse-Wilson cites the German translation as William James, *Die religiöse Erfahrung in
ihrer Mannigfaltigkeit*, 1907.

17   The comments are documented in Scholz, "Elisabethforscher," 154–56, and expanded upon
in Illemann, op.cit., 99–102.

Busse-Wilson's graduate training in interdisciplinary historical studies culminated in a dissertation in the field of comparative art history, for which she won second prize in a competition organized by Wilhelm Wundt. Completed in Leipzig in 1914, it is still considered a valuable typological overview of motifs in early decorative arts.[18] Having received her doctorate several years before German women gained suffrage, women's status as second-class citizens affected her standing in the academy and sharpened her analysis of gender discrimination. Busse-Wilson remarked that after she had passed her dissertation exams, "none [of the professors] congratulated me. I felt again that the leaders of the university only saw us academic women as an increase of their own workload... They took very little personal interest in us, not even [expressed] curiosity."[19] Such lack of personal mentoring and attention was especially detrimental to female students, since the German university system fostered academic careers through intense attachments to a dissertation adviser (Doktorvater), whose responsibility it was to place his favorite students in desirable academic positions.[20] As she reminisced much later in life, "To have been an academic then meant a lot, to have been a woman nothing."[21]

Her graduate training in comparative cultural analysis enabled her to assess and juxtapose medieval and modern social relationships, family configurations, status-dependent and class-specific behaviors and norms, and patterns of gendered identity formation. For each chapter of Elisabeth's

18 Großmann, op.cit., 60. The topic of her dissertation was "The Ornament in Ethnological and Prehistorical Perspective" (*Das Ornament auf ethnologischer und prähistorischer Grundlage*). See Scholz, "Elisabethforscher," op.cit., 152, and Großmann, op.cit, 55–64. Franz Boas praised her dissertation as an "excellent review" of ornament studies in his work, *Primitive Art* (Oslo: Instituttet for Sammenlignende Kulturforskning, 1927), 16.

19 "Keiner [der Professoren] gratulierte mir. Ich spürte wieder, die Führer der Universität sahen in uns akademischen Frauen nur eine Vergrößerung der Arbeitsanforderung an sie... Aber persönliches Interesse nahm man wenig an uns, nicht einmal Neugierde." Quoted in Musial, op.cit., 238.

20 In 1932, German universities employed seventy-four female professors and lecturers (*Privat-dozentinnen*) vis-à-vis approximately 7,000 male professors and lecturers. See Rita Thalmann, *Frausein im Dritten Reich* (Munich: Carl Hanser Verlag, 1984), 101. The proportion was the same for enrolled students at Leipzig University in 1909, with forty-four female students out of a student body of more than 4,400. See Franz Eulenburg, *Die Entwicklung der Universität Leipzig in den letzten hundert Jahren: Statistische Untersuchungen* (Leipzig: S. Hirzel, 1909), 194. Cited in Chickering, op.cit., 369. See also Ulrike Wiethaus, "The German Historian Elisabeth Busse-Wilson (1890-1974): Academic Feminism and Medieval Hagiography 1914-1931," in *Women Medievalists and the Academy*, ed. Jane Chance (Madison: University of Wisconsin Press, 2005). The biographical study forms the foundation for some of the sections in this chapter.

21 Musial, op.cit., 241.

biography, Busse-Wilson identified modern and medieval similarities and differences organized around themes of a specific social and psychological phenomenon's emergence, maturation, decline and survival across a span of time. A feminist methodology of comparative cultural analysis left no discursive space for a nationalist or religious glorification of the medieval past, and brought the challenges faced by a medieval woman to bear on a critical discussion of gender discrimination in contemporary society and religion. It is in the comparative method that her dual identities as a public intellectual and historian intersected. In some ways, her biography of St. Elisabeth also continued her journalistic and activist work related to the contemporary German Youth Movement (Jugendbewegung) and women's status.[22] By choosing a popular literary genre and medieval culture as a preeminent marker of German identity at the time, she extended and grounded her life-long thematic focus on women's rights and demonstrated its significance across a wide span of time. It also guaranteed a wide and diverse readership.

Her graduate interest in the intersections of psychology, culture, and history deepened in the twenties, when she encountered the work of social psychologist Alfred Adler (1870–1937).[23] A member of Sigmund Freud's inner circle, Adler eventually broke with Freud to establish his own psychological school. Adler and his collaborators deemphasized childhood sexuality in favor of a study of wider networks of social relationships. The Adlerian emphasis on social dynamics enabled a sustained critique of sexism and stereotypical gender roles.[23] Adler's social network theories provided Busse-Wilson with additional analytical tools to dissect both the saint's cult and the fraught relationships between Elisabeth of Thuringia, her aristocratic kin, and her papally backed confessor.

Left-leaning and incisive, her criticism of contemporary German anti-feminism and sexism won her wide acclaim and lasting recognition.[24] When she turned her attention to a near ubiquitous German icon of femininity

---

22 Großmann, op. cit., 280–81.

23 Adler's model of the interdependence between individual mental health and social well-being also influenced American humanistic psychologist Abraham Maslow's theory of human development and self-actualization. See Erik Mansager and Marina Bluvshtein, "Adler and Maslow in Collaboration: Applied Therapeutic Creativity," *Journal of Humanistic Psychology* 60, no. 6 (2020).

24 See Großmann, op.cit., for a nuanced analysis of Busse-Wilson's political views across her life span. On her reputation at the time, see Irmgard Klönne, "Nachwort," in *Elisabeth Busse-Wilson: Die Frau und die Jugendbewegung*, ed. Irmgard Klönne (Hamburg: Freideutscher Jugendverlag Saal, 1920, repr. Münster: Lit Verlag, 1989).

who served to mythologize and as such obfuscate female oppression and acquiescence to such oppression, Busse-Wilson was forty-one and could boast an impressive publication record to her name.[25] Since most of her publications between 1914 and 1931 had analyzed contemporary feminist and social reform issues, Busse-Wilson was better equipped than her traditionally trained male medievalist colleagues to bring fresh perspectives to the primary source materials that could articulate medieval gender disparities, but also questions of female subjectivity and authenticity. Her unconventional training and post-graduate work had freed her from nationalist biases and the quest for a fictitious Germanic heroic past that was popular at the time. Importantly, Busse-Wilson's choice of topic also marks a critical departure from models of cultural history that focused on the achievements of male genius, whether in politics, religion, the history of states, or the arts.[26]

However, her academic training and subsequent professional work did not free her from her own unexamined bias against medieval and contemporary rural culture and an evolutionary view of religion as a developmental stage sandwiched between magic and science. The au courant evolutionary approach to world cultures that she studied during her graduate school years forms the basis of such bias and was amplified by her own identification with the German bourgeoisie.[27]

Since 1869, the city of Leipzig housed a substantial ethnographical collection, which grew into the Leipzig Museum of Ethnography under German colonial expansion. To absorb the growth of ethnographic museum collections on the scholarly level, the University of Leipzig created a new professorship of Anthropology, Ethnography, and Pre-History in 1901, and another chair for Colonial Geography and Colonial Policy in 1915. Busse-Wilson thus enjoyed privileged access to an extraordinary collection of artefacts for her dissertation research, which was at the same time leveraged as proof for theories that framed Western imperialism as evolutionary progress. Western European societies were granted the most advanced civilization status, at the evolutionary apex, and colonized peoples at the evolutionary bottom, defined as the "primitive" and "savage" stage. As David Chidester put it, "raw religious materials" of the Global South were turned

---

25 Busse-Wilson regularly wrote for the journals *Philosophie und Leben, Die Tat, Die Erziehung*, and *Zeitschrift für Völkerpsychologie und Soziologie*. See Magdalena Musial, "Jugendbewegung und Emanzipation der Frau: Ein Beitrag zur Rolle der weiblichen Jugend in der Jugendbewegung bis 1933" (PhD Diss., Universität Essen, 1982), 241. Großmann, op.cit., 447–79.

26 Busse-Wilson, *St. Elisabeth*, 8 (German original). English Translation: p. 24.

27 See Großmann, 332–36, passim.

into "intellectual manufactured goods" in the Global North.[28] As cultural evolution was imagined as progressing from primitivism and savagery through barbarism to civilization, humanity was envisioned to advance intellectually through the early stages of magic and religion to achieve its highest mental accomplishment in the modern West in secular science and rational thought. It was further posited that so-called primitive cultural stages and magic survived ontogenetically in childhood, and phylogenetically in medieval and modern folk culture and the working class.[29]

In her dissertation, Busse-Wilson created her own taxonomy to suggest that the historic fabrication of ornaments worldwide followed evolutionary stages. Older stages of ornament decorations survived in more "advanced" cultures among rural populations and in religious folk art, which consequently were labelled "primitive," "archaic," or "atavistic." Transferring an evolutionary taxonomy to religious mentalities and practices, Busse-Wilson posited that the Catholic veneration of relics and the belief in miracles worked by saints were nothing but a survival of earlier "primitive" stages of human evolution. Her evolutionary classification put any ideological claim of medieval saints as the apex of Christian faith and piety to the lie. Medieval as much as modern believers in St. Elisabeth's relics and miracles were European primitives and savages amid rational post-religious actors at the apex of civilization. Busse-Wilson thus turned an imperial rhetorical register of cultural denigration against the colonizing culture itself, but without undoing the implicit harmful hierarchy of status these terms superimposed on rural medieval populations and the Catholic faithful.[30]

Busse-Wilson chose the publication date of her critical interdisciplinary study with initial luck on her side. As noted above, 1931 marked the 700-year anniversary of St. Elisabeth's death. The anniversary was widely celebrated and raised interest in Busse-Wilson's work. After an initial wave of success, evidenced by the public debates her book engendered and the large number of reviews, conservative Catholicism as well as the Nazi regime's repressive gender ideology and politics negatively impacted the sale of

---

28   David Chidester, "'Classify and Conquer': Friedrich Max Müller, Indigenous Religious Traditions, and Imperial Comparative Religion" in *Beyond Primitivism: Indigenous Religious Traditions and Modernity*, ed. Jacob K. Olupona (New York: Routledge, 2004), 71–72.

29   Busse-Wilson dedicated a separate chapter of her dissertation to a discussion of ontogenetic survivals in childhood drawings. Busse-Wilson, *The Ornament*, 157–63. On her identification of working-class women with earlier cultural stages, see Großmann, op.cit., 406–8.

30   On the global stage, it was not until the International Labour Organization's Indigenous and Tribal Populations Convention in 1957 that the term Indigenous began to replace earlier derogatory comparative ethnographic designations.

her book. Her career faltered after National Socialism's overwhelming success at the voting booth.[31] German scholar Britt Großmann uncovered that Busse-Wilson colluded with the new regime at least twice before the outbreak of World War II. Her political choices placed Busse-Wilson into a professional borderland of neither outright persecution nor sanctioned inclusion into the fascist system. Her legally required application to the Reich's Office for Publications (Reichsschrifttumkammer) for a permit to publish and to be registered as a professional writer was initially granted, but the license was soon withdrawn. The Reich's Office for Publications was created as a branch of the Reich's Ministry for Public Information and Propaganda (Reichsministerium für Volksaufklärung und Propaganda). It was founded by Joseph Goebbels, secretary of education and propaganda, as a bureaucratic follow-up to the infamous book burning campaigns of 1933. Elisabeth Busse-Wilson fought for several years to regain her permit, yet without success. Perhaps as a form of silent protest, she never officially returned her license card.[32]

Her studies of Wundt, James, and Adler provided the basis for an attempt to build a second career as a psychotherapist. Busse-Wilson took advantage of a new German law that permitted the practice of psychotherapy without a medical background and enrolled in the only training institution available at the time, the German Institute for Psychological Research and Psychotherapy (Deutsches Institut für psychologische Forschung und Psychotherapie) in Berlin, also known as the Göring Institute. The institute's director and founder, Matthias H. Göring (1879–1945), actively promoted Nazi ideology. He was a cousin of Hermann Göring, Hitler's second in command.[33] After one year, the effort ended in a debacle, with Busse-Wilson threatening to publicize widespread incompetence at the institute.

Unsuccessful in continuing her academic work during the Third Reich, Busse-Wilson appears to have at least privately compromised her intellectual integrity by adopting antisemitic stereotypes. Fearing for her family's safety by her husband's refusal to let go of his Jewish employees, she noted in a diary entry dated August 15, 1935, "I have become an antisemite."[34] Her concerns for her family were somewhat justified. Six years later, in 1941, her husband, a publisher, was denounced to the Reich's Office for Publications

31 Großmann, op.cit., 345–50.
32 Großmann, op. cit. 359–62.
33 On the institute's collusion with the Nazi regime, see Geoffrey Cocks, "Repressing, Remembering, Working Through: German Psychiatry, Psychotherapy, Psychoanalysis, and the 'Missed Resistance' in the Third Reich," *Journal of Modern History* 64 (1992).
34 Großmann, op.cit., 348.

as lacking in loyalty to the regime.[35] Her circle of notable female friends
and supporters spanned the gamut of the political spectrum, and it appears
that well-connected female friends on the right protected Busse-Wilson to
some degree. For example, the populist writer Lulu von Strauss und Torney
(1873–1956), a friend since Busse-Wilson's early years as a graduate student,
was a Nazi favorite. Embracing St. Elisabeth's Germanic cult image, she had
published a biography and edited a collection of legends about the saint in 1926
and 1927 respectively.[36] In 1933, von Strauss und Torney signed the infamous
Writers' Pledge of Most Faithful Allegiance (Gelöbnis treuester Gefolgschaft)
in support of the new regime. She endorsed Busse-Wilson's initial application
to the Office for Publications as a reference.[37] A likely National Socialist
sympathizer and widely published female literary author, Gertrud Bäumer
(1873–1954), secured much-needed funding for Elisabeth Busse-Wilson's new
biographical project, a study of the German romantic author Annette von
Droste-Hülshoff (1797–1848).[38] Gertrud Bäumer, life partner and collaborator
of feminist activist Helene Lange, had medievalist credentials. Busse-Wilson
especially appreciated Bäumer's 1936 novel about German empress Adelheid
(931–999), which she said to have read and reread multiple times.[39]

In 1933, two years after the publication of her St. Elisabeth study, Busse-
Wilson was denied an academic position in the History Department at the
Dortmunder Pädagogische Akademie. Her license to publish her work was
revoked, and her effort at a new career as psychotherapist derailed. Although
she continued to engage in research after World War II, her career as a
public intellectual and historian of women's *Kulturgeschichte* was over by
the beginning of World War II. Busse-Wilson was unable to reenter German
academic life after the war, and her study of St. Elisabeth was forgotten.

Although radical in its emphasis on gender violence, Elisabeth Busse-
Wilson's contributions to feminist historiography did not occur in a vacuum.
Writing the biography of a striking female figure such as St. Elisabeth
of Thuringia was a common strategy female historians used at the time

---

35 Großmann, ibid.

36 Lulu von Strauss und Torney, *Das Leben der heiligen Elisabet. Nach den alten Quellen erzählt*
(Jena: Eugen Diederichs Verlag, 1926); von Strauss und Torney (ed.), *Volksbuch von der Heiligen
Elisabeth* (Jena: Eugen Diederichs Verlag, 1927).

37 Großmann, op.cit., 373.

38 The study was completed in 1948, but never published. Großmann, op.cit., 355–56.

39 Gertrud Bäumer, *Adelheid, Mutter der Königreiche* (Tübingen: Rainer Wunderlich Verlag
Hermann Leins, 1936). See Großmann, op.cit., 423. On divergent views of Bäumer's Nazi sympathies and the immense success of her Adelheid biography, see Christina Stange-Fayos, "Die
erste Kaiserin: Ein Mythos zum 'geistigen Zusammenhalt' der Frauenbewegung," in *Cahiers
d'Études Germaniques* 76 (2019).

to "write women back into history." Historian Billie Melman notes that the proper subject for nineteenth-century historical scholarship was the male propertied citizen as he engaged in diplomacy and war.[40] Reclaiming individual women as historical agents simultaneously legitimized female scholars' growing presence in history departments, a presence strengthened by reforms in women's secondary education during the second half of the nineteenth century.[41] Female suffrage conveyed a public presence in social and civic terms, and to that end, women's history provided a rationale and a vocabulary that could name and demarcate newly won extra-domestic visibility. In a 1927 essay, for example, abbess Hildegard of Bingen was celebrated as "the first female German natural scientist and doctor"; also in 1927, in the series Source Notebooks on Women's Lives in History (Quellenhefte zum Frauenleben in der Geschichte), historians Emmy Beckmann and Irma Stoss published primary sources on the public and private roles of German medieval women that highlighted women's ubiquitous presence in both domestic and public domains, as Hausfrau, as member of guilds, and of the noble class.[42] Busse-Wilson's study of St. Elisabeth was thus part of a larger, oftentimes nationalistic trend to recapture medieval women's economic and social status; it differed, though, in its bleak assessment of a medieval religious past for religious women.[43]

While cultural history, ethnography, psychology, and the archival labors of German medievalists offered a toolbox for sketching Elisabeth's medieval social context, the Weimar Republic's high culture generated a visual and literary discourse that paralleled and possibly influenced Busse-Wilson's efforts to find a language capable of naming gendered violence.[44] Artists and writers such as Yvan Goll (1891–1950), Otto Dix (1891–1969), Max

40 Billie Melman, "Gender, History and Memory: The Invention of Women's Past in the Nineteenth and Early Twentieth Centuries," *History and Memory. Studies in Representation of the Past* 5, no. 1 (1993), 8–10.

41 Melman, op.cit.,19–21.

42 Hermann Fischer, *Die heilige Hildegarde von Bingen, die erste deutsche Naturforscherin und Ärztin: Ihr Leben und Werk* (Munich: C.H. Beck, 1927); *Quellenhefte zum Frauenleben in der Geschichte*, vol. 2, ed. Emmy Beckmann and Irma Stoss (Berlin: F.A. Herbig, 1927).

43 In 1925, Busse-Wilson presented a public lecture on women's cultural history. She credited the secular medieval phenomenon of courtly love as an incisive cultural shift that advanced women's opportunities for self-determination and individuation. Her view of medieval secular progress makes her criticism of St. Elisabeth's religious environment even more poignant. Großmann, op.cit., 241.

44 The common cultural denominator was a fascination with male sexual crime, the so-called *Lustmord*. See Maria Tatar, *Lustmord: Sexual Murder in Weimar Germany* (Princeton: Princeton University Press, 1995).

Beckmann (1884–1950), and George Grosz (1893–1959), and the art movement New Objectivity (Neue Sachlichkeit) articulated an unvarnished view of male brutality and female objectification.[44] As radical and powerful as the literature and art of New Objectivity was in naming violence against women, it would take second-wave feminism in the second half of the twentieth century to replicate and expand Busse-Wilson's critique of patriarchal religion, male privilege, and gender violence in academic and public contexts. It was not until the critical work of Kimberlé Crenshaw and others on intersectionality replaced second-wave feminism that interlocking systems of power, privilege, and marginality in women's lives began to be named and dismantled analytically and on a large scale.[45]

In the genealogy of European women's history and the history of Medieval Studies, Elisabeth Busse-Wilson thus has earned her place as a trenchant early critic of what Dyan Elliott has called out as "strategic hypocrisy" and "corporate narcissism" among church elites.[46] Busse-Wilson summarized her approach in a letter to the historian of religion Friedrich Heiler (1892–1967): "Perhaps you felt nonetheless that I loved St. Elisabeth very much – even though the portrait turned out to be different from the norm."[47] The scholar Busse-Wilson insisted on writing the life history of a soul, not of a myth. It is up to us to recognize her as the forgotten progenitor of a critical analysis of violence against women, to recognize the strengths and weaknesses of her analysis and methodology, and to build on her commitment to trust witnesses of gender violence and amplify their voices.

45   Patricia Hill Collins and Sirma Bilge, *Intersectionality*, 2nd ed. (Cambridge: Polity Press, 2020).
46   Dyan Elliott, "Sexual Scandal" 92, 101.
47   Großmann, op.cit., 313.

1 Research Objectives and Categories of Analysis

St. Elisabeth's Life as a Legend and Moral Cliché

The story of St. Elisabeth of Thuringia (1207–1231) has come down to us as a saint's legend. For a contemporary reader, the effort and devotion with which the legend narrates her life appear almost childlike. Her legend generates neither admiration nor outrage. Situated between fairy tales and moral treatise, legends belong to an intellectual and cultural era that a twentieth-century audience might find difficult to comprehend fully. Theologians and church historians barely tolerate Christian legends as a subcategory of theology. Even conservative Catholics find little general educational value in them. The problem is simple: a legend's story line is dependent on a fallacious belief in the non-empirical and the miraculous. Entirely fictitious, the world of legends brims with capriciousness and mystery. Contemporary readers thus need guidance to fully appreciate the moral and very human action of its heroes. A legend's narrative arc should be best approached as emblematic of a "magical" epoch with its own laws of logic.

It would be wrong to judge the popular heroic stories of early and medieval Christianity as mere historical waste and rubbish. Legends offer a treasure trove of non-official historiography, psychology, and character analysis. Literary scholars and psychologists, often with considerable effort, relish extracting character traits buried in literary works to draw an individual's intimate portrait. In a similar manner, it is possible for us to mine legends for little-known personal dimensions that may add up to a human destiny. Time and again, we may discover the course of an anguished human life underneath the cover of a fabricated causality and, for us, an importune morality.

In our century, saints' legends emerged from church history's dusty corners into the realm of literature proper. It is to his great merit that Richard

Busse-Wilson, E., *St. Elisabeth of Thuringia: A Psychological Study (1931)*. Amsterdam: Amsterdam University Press, 2025
DOI 10.5117/9789463725804_CH01

Benz translated and published this half-forgotten, yet formidable cultural legacy of the Middle Ages for a wide audience.[1]

Unfortunately, however, saints' legends are still approached as mere literary curiosity with an enjoyably naïve style and a seemingly awkward solemnity. For an educated audience, legends thus perhaps rank on a par with Romanesque sculptures: partly primitive and partly an intimation of an archaic but magnificent art form to come.[2]

Yet the aesthetic appeal of saints' legends, as strong as it may be, is but a thin veil that covers a spiritual world of much deeper religious power. The subject of all saints' legends, whether profound or naïve, whether medieval or early Christian, is human struggle. Not the struggle found in the formidable acts of grand history, but the fight between a human will and its environment, a psyche's war with both secret and public enemies, and the defeats and victories on a battlefield, which exists only within a human being.[3] Princes and maidservants, monks and ladies, warriors and virgins are all actors in the long history of saints' legends. The legend transforms each one of them into a hero or heroine. The legend does not make distinctions based on gender or nation. Scintillating figures of world history are not taken more seriously than nameless men and women. As told by a legend, the psyche of an unknown and unsung human being who has suffered and struggled is as holy as the monumental impact of a renowned statesman or church leader. For the Christian genre of legends, heroic suffering is the only standard.

Every saint's legend constitutes a cosmology and a gigantomachy. Saints were notorious dualists whose lives encompassed the world of the senses and the world of the supernatural, God and the devil. In every legend, ego and alter-ego fight each other. Shocked by the breakthrough experience of new insights, some saints became secret heretics. They paid for such rare mental courage with debilitating and destabilizing doubt. Their contemporaries

---

1   Translator's note: The reference is to the German historian Richard Benz's (1884–1966) translation *Die Legenda Aurea des Jacobus de Voragine* (Berlin: Union Verlag, 1912).

2   Translator's note: Busse-Wilson draws here on her graduate research in art history with its emphasis on the evolution from simpler ("primitive") to more complex forms. See Busse-Wilson, *Das Ornament auf ethnologischer und prähistorischer Grundlage: Ein Abschnitt aus den Anfängen der Kunst* (Erfurt: J.G. Cramer's Buchdruckerei, 1914). Transferring the taxonomy to literary genres, legends are posited to exist between the earlier, more "primitive" genre of fairytales and the more "developed" morality treatise. Subverting the scale, however, Busse-Wilson defends the genre of legends as a valuable source of historical truth.

3   Translator's note: As discussed in the introduction, Busse-Wilson makes an argument against the common historiographical choice to write history through the lens of "grand history" made by famous men.

were not always partial to their company, since all saints, at some point, stepped beyond norms. For this reason, saints were in even greater need of legitimization in an epoch ruled by authoritarian norms. Many were declared saints only long after their deaths with the intent to rewrite their extraordinary and provocative lives as a teleologically reframed support for the global community of Catholic Christianity.

Brilliant minds and hearts, intellectual and religious innovators, wretched and weak human beings alike received such distinction in equal measure. This is the paradox of the complex dignity of sainthood. It is the hidden power of creativity at work in legends, yet such creativity may turn into a dangerous enemy of truth: legends also perform the unrecognized and unclaimed self-idealization processes of an era. When an era's self-idealization aligns with a specific person or action, the legend imperceptibly and incomprehensibly discolors and displaces the original biographical likeness. The compulsion toward self-idealization is as forceful in the scientific era as it was in epochs of prescientific world views. Wrapped in the cloak of scientific rationality, it still can generate a persuasive simulacrum. The historiography of the nineteenth and twentieth centuries is undeniably no less one-sided and transient as what seems to us the naïve glorification of a Christian hero in medieval literature. Both are naïve in their own fashion.[4]

The interpretation and comprehension of St. Elisabeth of Thuringia by authors of the nineteenth and twentieth centuries is thus precisely the kind of mythmaking usually associated with premodern epochs. Despite their knowledge of the earliest primary sources, and despite every critical analysis of these sources, contemporary authors adopt the traditional narratives with a guileless impartiality and without truly sensing what lies underneath. Undeterred— comparable to a child that believes every clear liquid to be water—they retell the medieval stories as they are written down in the *Libellus* and in the *Epistola*.[5]

Landgravine Elisabeth of Thuringia is one of only a handful of saints, perhaps the only one of the Middle Ages proper, whose sainthood survived the Reformation. Contemporary Church liturgy still celebrates her as the "Patrona Thuringiae." In tandem with Martin Luther, she is revered at the Wartburg castle near Eisenach; the force of folk tradition thus joined a greatly mismatched couple in the service of a cult of remembrance.

4 Translator's note: In her opening salvo, Busse-Wilson once again subverts evolutionary cultural models. She challenges proponents of the superiority of modern rational thought by pointing out their capacity for self-delusion, which she deems as powerful a force now as in earlier epochs.

5 For more on the primary sources, see "The Value of the Primary Sources" below.

Church historians of both confessions claim St. Elisabeth today. She plays a significant role in the history of Thuringia. The Hohenstaufen dynasty's grand political history forms the luminous backdrop of her short life. St. Elisabeth only became truly popular, however, as the representative and protective patroness of Christian charity in the service of the poor, the sick, and the orphaned. As a symbol of social assistance and care, the Catholic Church still honors her in the present day. The Protestant churches did not let go of her during the Reformation's assault on saints. Catholic service organizations for the poor prefer to be named after her, and Protestant services claim her as a model.

Fashioned into an inflexible stereotype, Elisabeth appears in new literary texts as a pious benefactress and as a representative of the most feminine vocation of all, that of helping and healing charity. In this view, the true secret of our saint's universal calling and boundless popularity lies in a rare amalgamation of the noblest human and highest Christian virtues. According to this formula, Elisabeth will continue to live in the memory of all good and noble human beings. As the feminine, exquisite, and graceful woman painted by Moritz of Schwind, the image reemerges even in contemporary scholarly studies.[6]

Ever since Franz Wegele, the earliest critical Elisabeth scholar, reproduced the Elisabeth stereotype of the late Romantic period, it has been nearly impossible to replace it even in academic circles. Her image thus perfected, all scholarly studies, even those of the medieval sources, celebrate the "loveliest and most feminine figure of the Middle Ages." Even clearheaded historians have persistently clung to this image, although the medieval sources should have compelled all subsequent interpreters to draw a very different character portrait. The sources do not offer any clues to a saccharine diminution of the saint into a pious do-gooder. The reason for these ahistorical distortions lies in specific dynamics of depth psychology.

All aspects of Elisabeth's stereotype have been generated and controlled by an unambiguously and inevitably masculine fantasy. The iconic saint represents the feminine ideal of a feminine psychology created by men. Consequently, Elisabeth as ideal female type was placed on a pedestal to signify motherhood and maternal care. Landgravine Elisabeth's life was forcefully repurposed to perform the representational work for the Middle

---

6   Translator's note: The Viennese artist Moritz of Schwind (1804–1871) painted the renowned romantic Wartburg frescoes of scenes from Elisabeth's life.

Ages that Queen Luise's cult staged for the nineteenth century.[7] Scientific objectivity could not demolish this idealization. Although scientific ethics and moral standards today are not considered the "handmaiden" of theology or moral convention, they still do not operate as autonomously as they perhaps proclaim. Hence, a wishful fantasy anchored in the subconscious of a masculinist social order generated the cliché of the pious and maternal national benefactress; St. Elisabeth's figure evolved into a conventional female moral prototype and beauty ideal of the bourgeoisie. As such, her legend is indefensible, and, therefore, our first task shall be to destroy the modern legend for the sake of an Elisabeth image of greater authenticity.

Despite all glorification, the saint has been misunderstood and underestimated. The extent and magnitude of her suffering will only emerge truthfully if we attempt to understand the genuine human distress she had to endure. If viewed without bias, even her acts of charity cannot be salvaged by Protestant or Catholic moral sentiment. The Christian effort at interpreting her charity as standardized loving action only diminishes her greatness. No doubt, Elisabeth cultivated the impulse toward care, helping, and healing others in a highly unusual manner, even during periods of deepest personal humiliation. Yet, at her core, she was motivated by a formidable sense of being in the world that is not ours today. Her acts of charity carried meaning that we need to assess anew, and that we can access anew in its factual holiness. In this sense, the numinous aspects of her suffering, pointless in a rational sense, but heroic and full of pathos in a religious sense, mark her as a saint and can be felt as such.

Elisabeth's sainthood consists of absolute self-renunciation, even self-annihilation with the goal of reaching a more exalted state of religious existence. What a biographer of St. Elisabeth's contemporary St. Clare of Assisi had to say about St. Clare's motivation also holds true for the former: "to break the alabaster vessel of her body with the penitential scourge, blow by blow, so that the house of the Church will be filled with the scent of her soul." Medieval Christianity granted spiritual dignity to a drive toward self-humiliation and self-annihilation. Elisabeth's short life became heroic and her character commanding precisely because of her determination to choose illness and even death.[8]

---

7   Translator's note: Queen Louise of Preussen (1776–1810) was Germany's version of a "people's princess" myth, not unlike Britain's cult of Princess Diana.
8   Translator's note: As discussed in the introduction, Busse-Wilson's psychoanalytically trained contemporary Sabina Spielrein (1885-1942) developed a similarly positive psychological

Elisabeth was a disciple of Franciscan poverty. Her Seven Works of Mercy, however, are very different from that of a Samaritan.[9] Her demanding and uncompromising poverty is the precise opposite of aristocratic charity and amicability. Elisabeth's acts of dressing like a maidservant, working like a maidservant, and leaving the court to live in a wretched hovel are nothing but symbols of a bold determination to break free of expected norms. With great force, Elisabeth attempted to abscond from her 'bourgeois' milieu, the feudal-aristocratic social class into which she was born. Her acts of charity never amounted to a maternal idyll. Fueled by religious passion, she stepped into unusual territory without being able to sustain its impact.

Elisabeth also failed in her transpersonal goal, the practice of radical Franciscan poverty, because she could not overcome the constraints of her social rank and patriarchal family structures. Her saintly virtues were purchased at a high price: the tragedy of her unhappy life circumstances and her futile efforts to devote her female existence fully to a religious ideal unfit for her circumstances. Unable to live by herself outside society, she ended up in disgraceful dependence on her confessor Konrad of Marburg, who ruled over her until her early death in terrifying sexual as well as asexual tyranny. Elisabeth is a tragic historical figure solely because of her undignified passive stance and enslavement to the owner of her soul. The second half of her life alternated between destruction and humiliation, which she tried to preempt through self-destruction but was able to evade only through death. We interpret her early death in the twenty-fourth year of her unusually short life as an intentional act of self-annihilation. Death became life's final protest. Lacking any alternative, self-preservation as self-destruction remained the only possible free choice.

Her failures—and her whole life ultimately consists only of failures—are, however, more valuable than her "heroic deeds" when viewed through the lens of medieval sensibilities. Embracing suffering with religious determination, she could turn humiliating experiences into triumphs. She developed an "art of suffering," a concept we may use to describe the content of her life. An acceptance of suffering is the medieval attitude toward life par excellence.

view of self-annihilation as the desire for transcending personal limitations. See Spielrein, "Die Destruktion als Ursache des Werdens," *Jahrbuch für Psychoanalytische und Psychopathologische Forschungen* 4 (1912).

9   Translator's note: The Seven Works of Mercy include feeding the hungry, giving water to the thirsty, clothing the naked, sheltering the homeless, visiting the sick and imprisoned, and burying the dead. The biblical source is found in Matthew 25.

As we shall see, it is a form of bargaining to make the unavoidable tolerable. In this way, Elisabeth lightened the burden of an anguished and partially unmoored existence through freely willed suffering. She turned constraint into freedom. Elisabeth's moral, spiritual, and paradigmatic achievement is to have made this shift under duress. Compared to such internal attainment, her external accomplishments, such as the two hospitals that she built and where she worked, are merely good-natured episodes. Until now, however, only these episodes garnered attention.

Scholars, as much as contemporary popular authors, thus reworked the image of this genuine martyr, who was determined to experience suffering at its very extreme into that of an affectionate healer and helper. Once forced into the cliché of the Samaritan servant of a nation, her icon became increasingly sentimental. Her physical existence, imprinted by the distinctly medieval fear of death, became covered and thus distorted with the mask of courtly love, or *Minne*. The seemingly inaccessible opacity of the past invited the temptation of romantic idealized distortion and the seemingly unhindered projection of contemporary desires and fantasies. Over time, the erstwhile authentic icon received not just an ostentatiously hefty crown, but a heavy layering of gold from head to toe that was spun from lopsided fantasy and desire.

To free the original likeness from such patina, we gathered fragments from primary sources, which were ignored in the process of falsification, either because they did not fit the new model or because they were deemed unimportant. Our analysis reveals the glorified feminine ideal of a royal nurse as a cloying historical lie and an inadequate bourgeois appropriation of Gothic greatness. We discard the wishful fantasy of a German national saint. Beneath the palimpsest of multiple reinterpretations, we find instead the terrifying but truthful face of a medieval predisposition to suffering. Protestantism glorified Elisabeth's care for the poor and ill. Catholicism honored her choice of Franciscan poverty and asceticism. We propose, however, that Elisabeth's authentic yet covert sainthood rests solely in her personal martyrdom.

As noted above, Protestantism, as much as Catholicism, contrived the bourgeois adaptation of a conventional feminine stereotype. Both buried the heartbreak of her human life. It is telling that Catholic authors always followed Protestantism in clinging to the image of Elisabeth as a nurse. Modern Catholics find such a view most convenient since they are closer to today's Protestantism than to their own medieval religious ancestors. Even though exemplars of medieval religiosity are conscientiously collected and bravely defended, Catholic spiritual pedagogy does not endorse a contemporary imitation of the deeds of medieval saints. A Protestant St. Elisabeth is thus perfectly suited to salvage the Catholicism of the Middle Ages. "Look! Our Middle Ages could produce feminine benefactresses and charitable sisters of such caliber!"

The Catholic eagerness to sanitize the female saint makes sense only as a salvaging act. Yet neither religious profession can ignore that the most popular German saint was not a figure of monumental greatness. Compared to eminent religious personalities of her era, including consummate spiritual leaders such as Mechthild of Magdeburg and St. Clare of Assisi, Elisabeth of Thuringia seems rather insignificant. Authors used this fact as reason to feminize Elisabeth even more emphatically. In contrast, a psychologically skilled critic will approach Landgravine Elisabeth's personality precisely because of her lack of genius, and precisely because it offers an extraordinarily valuable object lesson in the discovery of an authentically lived rhythm of medieval daily life and religiosity. Prodigious medieval personalities such as St. Hildegard, St. Clare, and St. Bernard are much less useful in this regard since their religious virtuosity broke with all conventions. Historians of medieval religion have preferred the study of exceptional men and women who created a Catholic worldview such as successful abbots, and mystics of high literary achievements. And it is generally true that until recently, all historiography and all cultural history was written as a history of exceptional accomplishments. Only the most prominent representatives could signify a nation, politics, or art. This led to a distorted view of medieval mentalities, culture, and history. The life and impact of non-exceptional characters explicate medieval mindsets and religiosity with much greater accuracy.

Elisabeth's new biography will reveal that the woman who generated the modern paradigm of a heroic nurse garnered little respect during her lifetime. Elisabeth made numerous scurrilous choices. Her pursuit of Franciscan goals disrupted the habitual rhythms of her social environment. There was also the matter of her peculiar relationship with her confessor. Her choice to transgress religious and social conventions was unforgivable. Her swift canonization was an accident of family politics. As we will demonstrate, her contemporaries were astonished, if not angered about this highest of ecclesiastical honors. It is precisely in the publicly abject turn of events that the true face of medieval society comes into view. Its judgmental attitude toward religious men and women, its disregard for holiness, and the severity of its moral conventions surface clearly during Elisabeth's life. Elisabeth was broken by medieval society's rigidity and rejection. It is why she died a martyr's death at a young age.

Legend and History

By necessity, all historiography, except universal historiography and the philosophy of history, must be partial.[10] Such natural and unavoidable bias is especially true for national and religious historiography. In the domain of religious historiography, it is hagiography that inevitably exhibits such bias at its most extreme. Hagiography is always limited to the story of heroes; furthermore, its function is specific in that it must shore up the renown and glory of the Christian-Catholic Church and secure a particular ideological morality formed in the early Christian and medieval era.

The story of Landgravine Elisabeth of Thuringia is just such a saint's legend. Everything that is communicated about her person is selected and told in view of the distinctive character of a religious life defined as sainthood. To prove her saintliness, the first statements about her life were not composed until four years after her death. Her reputation as a representative of extraordinary Christian virtues was secured and dispersed based on legendary narratives and accounts created throughout the medieval period. There is not a single statement about Landgravine Elisabeth penned by lay people, that is, by people who saw and experienced her as a human being rather than a saint, for example, her closest relatives, peers, fellow citizens, or neutral observers. Verified and unverified reports alike were penned instead by religious authors. A Cistercian monk was Elisabeth's first biographer, and a Dominican wrote the most popular medieval memoir. Her biographers measured Elisabeth's character and morals with the yardstick of medieval piety and medieval Christian virtue. In short, all medieval sources of St. Elisabeth's life are typical examples of special interest historiography.

Several nineteenth-century scholars applied a thorough historical critique to the tendentious religious genealogy of biographical texts about Elisabeth. Sifting through legendary source materials, scholars separated anecdotes and miracle stories to create an uncontaminated core of verifiable biographical

---

10   Translator's note: Busse-Wilson's use of the terms "universal history" and "philosophy of history" references Karl Lamprecht's innovative interdisciplinary work at his Institut für Kultur und Universalgeschichte at the University of Leipzig. As discussed in the introduction, Lamprecht, his students, and his colleagues tried to develop a classificatory system that could map all of history and prehistory in a global, i.e., universal context. Postcolonial studies have disavowed such efforts as masking imperial heuristic privilege and bias. However, Lamprecht's approach enabled Busse-Wilson to critique religious and nationalistic hegemonic discourse in her own culture by relativizing its truth claims.

source materials.[11] One is a letter, the so-called *Epistola*, composed by Magister Konrad von Marburg, Elisabeth's confessor, and sent to the Pope as a
canonization proposal. The other is a transcript of biographical statements
by four women, the so-called *Libellus* or *Libellus de dictis quatuor ancillarum*.

These two original sources form the bedrock of our study. They comprise
no more than thirty printed pages of Latin text. Yet even these doubtlessly
authentic sources are once more tendentious renderings of the highest
caliber. All that was written down was intended for the distinct purpose
of justifying the deceased Landgravine's canonization. The four female
witnesses were interrogated according to the ecclesiastical requirements
for qualifying a candidate for sainthood, including evidence of Christian
heroic virtues such as charity, foresight, justice, humility, and piety. The
psychological content of the *Libellus* demonstrates how easily answers could
be predetermined by certain questions, and how interrogative expectations
could shape the judgment of witnesses aware of such expectations. It goes
without saying that all comments and stories were repressed that did not
fit the format and goals of the *Libellus*. To compensate, other traits were
emphasized and moved into the foreground that could guarantee Elisabeth's
ascent to the status of a saint according to the standards of the medieval
church. Everything was suppressed that revealed Elisabeth as an ordinary,
even erring human being. Furthermore, the *Libellus* was compiled in haste.
No interviews with close relatives of Elisabeth, all members of her aristocratic
family, took place—certainly intentionally so.[12]

A historian intent on writing the psychological biography of a woman
who lived during the High Middle Ages, as will be attempted in this study,
can thus only draw from a meagre and narrow set of primary sources that
are acceptable as an authentic selection of traits and actions, yet which
do not shed light on her personality as a whole. However, we attempt this
new biography precisely for that reason. Because of their partialities, the
biased primary sources reveal more than they intended. To a modern reader,
they expose actions and situations with more objective truthfulness than
sources that were committed to biographical veracity as defined by medieval
standards. Studying medieval accounts of the heroine's virtues and deeds
today, we employ a perspective that differs from people living 700 years
ago. For this reason, her character and fate frequently emerge more honestly

11   Translator's note: These scholars are Gustav Börner and Hellmut Mielke (ca. 1888), Albert
Huyskens and Karl Wenck (ca. 1907). Their work is cited and discussed in Busse-Wilson's annotated
bibliography in the appendix.
12   See the section "Achieving Sanctity Through Politics" in Chapter Four below.

and authentically than intended by the medieval scribes. Unknowingly, the female witnesses revealed patterns of behavior and character traits which are rarely and barely saintly when measured by the moral standards of the nineteenth and twentieth century. For example, they expose the terrifying and tormented interior life of an unwilling recluse and nun and thus prove the opposite of what they intended to prove.

The finest modern source could not generate episodes such as the scene of a beating in the Altenberg monastery, which uncovers the cruel psychological depth connection between Konrad von Marburg and his ward St. Elisabeth. Intended to glorify the saint, the story of her encounter with the beautiful Hildegund depicts an Elisabeth who cuts Hildegund's hair against her will. Ostensibly, her purpose was to recruit Hildegund for a life devoted to religion. Given that she had no right to do so, however, the story instead exposes Elisabeth's impulsiveness, bitterness, and loss of happiness. Narrated to depict Elisabeth's extraordinary humility, the incident of the female beggar who pushes her benefactress Elisabeth into the filth of the gutter exposes medieval society's disregard for saintly men and women more clearly than a bundle of objective biographical data.

Told with great attention to detail, numerous anecdotes in the primary sources reveal a perspective that is of little interest to us today—such as proving the miraculous power of Elisabeth's prayer—yet they uncover an abundance of distinctive details about the heroine's lifestyle and individuality. We can draw on statements by Guda, the saint's childhood companion. It is obvious that Guda intended to communicate something about St. Elisabeth's precocious childhood religiosity with singlemindedness and vehemence. Unwittingly, the tendentious statements of an artless person reveal very different traits that are germane to establishing the saint's biographical context. According to Guda, Elisabeth refused to leave the castle's chapel and only pretended to participate in the children's games so she could swiftly return to her prayers. For us, Guda's story conveys the early onset of a habit of self-isolation and a girl's sense of loneliness when left bereft of her parents. Later in life, these traits developed into an attitude of protest against her feudal environment.

The primary sources thus provide various opportunities for reading between the lines. A critical interpreter may also learn a great deal from historical omissions. Not mentioning specific issues reveals them all. If only one sentence covers decisive biographical turning points, then one must assume that a particular life phase has been so problematic as to force the medieval narrators to quickly pass over it. In this regard, we merely posit that a comparison between a specific life story and the general historical outline of an era offers the possibility of revealing value standards for narrating an individual saint's character and actions. Elisabeth lived during the era of the Hohenstaufen rule.[13] This age generated a rich cultural and moral history accessible to us today, including an abundantly nuanced religious and secular body of literature. The task of a twentieth-century critic will be to note both common and uncommon features of Elisabeth's life and uncover what caused appreciation and what caused rejection at the time. We will thus understand how she fared in the judgment of her contemporaries rather than in the wishful thinking of the nineteenth century's smoke and mirrors.

The scant pages of the *Libellus* and the *Epistola*, both official canonization documents, are not the only sources at our disposal that describe the saint's life. The truly legendary and anecdotal medieval traditions, most of them not contemporaneous with Elisabeth, are loquacious and informative, yet historical research has treated them with an exaggerated selectivity. What seems to us today sentimental and romantic are perspectives and themes that have been overused, watered down, and rendered bourgeois over time. Yet, 700 years ago, during Elisabeth's era, these very same perspectives and motives might have had the appeal of something original and unusual. For example, all accounts of the affectionate relationship between Elisabeth and her husband could well be approached as authentic even when they seem a bit too sentimental for our taste. If a high-spirited youthful marriage bond appears unremarkable to us today, it references medieval exceptionality and an early prototype for things to come.[14]

Inversely, critical Elisabeth scholars frequently reject biographical stories with the argument that they are "improbable" or "strange." But this is precisely what accounts for their authenticity. We must necessarily expect, first and foremost, that personalities and life stories will strike us as alien if 700 years have passed between them and us. Taking them with a grain of salt, we may rather state that the more alien and even the more "stupid"

---

13   Translator's note: Busse-Wilson continues to make her argument for the use of the biographic genre as a valid historiographic method above and beyond the common feminist strategy at the time of using biography to "write women back into history" (see Introduction). The dominating value system of a specific era becomes most visible when studying biographical narratives with their omissions in light of epoch-specific narrative emphases. The Hohenstaufen, or Staufer, dynasty (1079-1254) produced three German emperors and is considered an era of high cultural achievement in literature and the arts.

14   Translator's note: This is another example of Busse-Wilson's deft use of comparativist academic training to undo romantic stereotypes and make Elisabeth's experiences come to life with as much authenticity as the primary sources seem to be able to convey.

a story sounds, the higher the probability becomes that the story is close to the spirit of the personality and her fate. Whatever medieval religious biographers and the narrators of legends put into writing is intended to place the heroine into an interesting and virtuous light; indeed, her life's ordinariness, which is our concern, does not get recorded. The reverse is true as well: what seems commonplace to us today—and which is, therefore, left unmentioned and unrecorded by modern historians—likely would not have been a quotidian matter 700 years ago.

Apart from retroactive and false causal connections, legends reflect truthful circumstances in need of analysis. Take the little miracle stories about the pitcher, which never emptied when poured out as a gift to the needy, and the provisions, which never ran out when pious Elisabeth lived as the benefactress to her people on the Wartburg castle. The objective cause for choosing to tell of a miraculous increase in loaves of bread are times when provisions are short in supply and thus cause widespread want. Subjectively, however, the populace experienced Elisabeth's donations as too lavish to be explained rationally. The miracle story authenticates Elisabeth's overly generous home and hearth economics and her addictive recklessness as a spendthrift. Her family had good reason to be offended by her generosity. Elisabeth's charitable actions are among the chief conflicts that led to her expulsion.

Whereas historians have proven the lack of credible narrative evidence of a malicious relative who banished her, the legend insists on the existence of an "evil brother-in-law" by her side. Long after Elisabeth's death, her only son, Hermann, then eighteen years old, died suddenly and unexpectedly. The legend's accusation that Heinrich Raspe, Elisabeth's brother-in-law, was intent on claiming the throne for himself, and thus was guilty of Hermann's demise, cannot be proven by existing historical sources. Yet Raspe is recorded to have made an enigmatic and, therefore, highly intriguing remark. Raspe expressed his wish that Elisabeth's son should not be buried next to his mother, so she would not be able to raise him from the dead. Heinrich Raspe thus reveals—in truly medieval fashion—not only his fear of the reappearance of the dead Elisabeth, but also his displeasure in thinking of his nephew as alive. If no other historical circumstances exist to point to his guilt about Hermann's death, such minor and apparently unimportant yet biographically plausible vignettes prove that at its deepest core, the legend rarely lies.

If historical research tends to expunge all persecutions that the pious young woman might have endured as mere literary additions, it is nothing but extreme compensation, and understandably so. The reason for such editorial work can be found in the hagiographers' skewed drive to depict the saint as an innocent victim. The truth can be uncovered halfway between both positions. Medieval historiography generally, including legends, shunned an obligation to tell the truth objectively and without any self-interest. For the medieval psyche, the intellectual and ethical aptitude to write *sine ira et studio* did not yet exist.[15] With a certain subjective innocence, most of both oral and written accounts spread good and bad news alike about a personality. It all depended on whether the information could augment the moral and economic reputation of religious institutions such as a monastery.[16] Thus Kloster Reinhardsbrunn, the favorite monastery of the Thuringian landgraves, and especially beloved and generously endowed by Landgrave Ludwig, became the source of the majority of stories about Landgravine Elisabeth and her spouse. The Reinhardsbrunn chronicles are filled with praise for Landgrave Ludwig and Landgravine Elisabeth. Precisely because of their bias, these records are easier to sort through than sources with unknown and unperceivable preconceptions.

To conclude, all narrative sources rejected by scholars as "unhistorical" in a narrow sense are of excellent use as either primary sources or as supplements. They often tend to be more valuable historically than sober files packed with certified information. Some of St. Elisabeth's legends and anecdotes characterize an action or characteristic with such brilliance that they ought to be invented if they would not be authentic in the sense described above. Indeed, a legend may be based on gossip and rumors. Yet, the channels and tracks through which rumors run carry in and of themselves elements of psychological truth. Even if facts reported as such by legends are false, legends nonetheless demonstrate how a medieval person could have acted. We propose that legend and anecdote are indeed indispensable in creating standards for the proper interpretation of bare facts in medieval history. Medieval people's mentality and morality, their ways of viewing and judging the world find their clearest expression not in the factual course of events as such, but in the unrealistic and wishful invented scenarios of a legend. Historiography communicates that which is correct. Legends communicate that which is true. Legends are historiography at work underground and in secret. They are always true, even if they assert what cannot be proven historically.

---

15   Translator's note: The Latin phrase translates into English as "without anger and zealousness."
16   By some estimates, at least fifty percent of medieval charters written between the ninth and thirteenth centuries are frauds.

The Value of Primary Sources about St. Elisabeth

Only one question remains if we accept all written traditions, even legends, biased remembrances, and anecdotes, as useful for the construction of a biography: how to rank such traditions according to their age. Serendipitously, the foundation of the undoubtedly authentic traditions, that is, the canonization files, was created by five persons who knew St. Elisabeth personally, and who shared their knowledge about her as early as four years after her death. This constitutes an unusually favorable research situation for an official document that dates to the thirteenth century. Konrad of Marburg's Epistola was composed in 1232, one year after Elisabeth's death. Konrad of Marburg spent the last three years of her life in close contact with his protégée, the former Landgravine of Thuringia. Two of the exclusive four witnesses of the *Libellus*, Guda and Isentrud, were maids of honor who had served Elisabeth since her youth. The remaining two witnesses were the sisters Irmingard and a woman also named Elisabeth, who worked as her retainers from the time that Elisabeth held court on the Marburg castle. Additional biographical information was also processed soon after her death. As a type of Festschrift celebrating the canonization, Caesarius of Heisterbach wrote the first vita and biographical sermon as early as 1236, that is, five years after Elisabeth's death. Besides the sources mentioned above, Caesarius also drew from supplementary information that he must have obtained from other highly qualified observers of her life. Furthermore, Caesarius of Heisterbach visited Marburg, Elisabeth's final residence and the location of her death. Equally reliable seems the earliest editor of the *Libellus*, according to Huyskens possibly a monk by the name of Nikolaus. This editor visited Marburg a few years after the saint's death. Whatever he added to the original four testimonies was thus gleaned more or less directly from Elisabeth's contemporaries generally or her companions specifically.

The Dominican monk Dietrich of Apolda composed the most popular Elisabeth biography between 1289 and 1297 and constitutes a different case. Dietrich wrote the saint's vita sixty years after Elisabeth had died. All other medieval and younger sources rely on his oeuvre. Dietrich of Apolda includes oral traditions in his sources. But how rapidly an event changes when repeated by word of mouth. Within a few months, sometimes even within a few weeks, the original news is barely recognizable due to numerous mutations. Yet, there is nothing more reliable and more conservative than oral traditions if they are preserved among populations whose pace of change is slower than the furious speed of modernity. This condition holds true for medieval men and women and guarantees a stability of information transfer hard to find today, even in relatively isolated rural communities.

The often-criticized passion for confabulation characteristic of medieval chroniclers and their lack of a sense of obligation to objective truth is thus corrected by the impressive constancy of medieval mentalities, a medieval faith in authority, and an immense reverence for the so rarely transcribed word. Medieval audiences generally refrained from adding little that might be personal or new. Today, it is de rigeur for scholarly works to critique in 1910 what was written in 1900, and to render it obsolete in 1920. With some caution, we may claim the reverse for medieval intellectual processes due to a very different cultural rhythm and the stability of a peasant culture's mentality. Even among the wealthier classes, illiteracy ruled. Therefore, what was spoken in 1400 is barely being criticized in 1500 and is accepted as truth with humility and faithfulness.

Information passed on by later medieval accounts thus does not lose much credibility when compared to information available on the ground at the time when an event occurred. Therefore, we can use information about St. Elisabeth recorded sixty years after her death in Dietrich of Apolda's *Vita* and parts of the *Life of St. Ludwig* as if they originated from Elisabeth's decades. The *Life of St. Ludwig* was added to the *Vita* about seventy years later in the Kloster Reinhardsbrunn. It cannot be traced back to Ludwig's companion, Chaplain Berthold. Even Johannes Rothe, who penned the *Thuringian Chronicle* of around 1435 and committed to writing all that could be known at the time about the saintly Landgravine Elisabeth, confirms our hypothesis. He barely dares to diverge from Dietrich of Apolda, the oldest and most widely referenced biographer. Whatever might be new in his account surely traveled across generations in Thuringia's oral traditions. Johannes Rothe might possibly also be hiding in the epithet "auctor rhythmicus," an otherwise unknown author who composed a verse poem about the life of the popular Thuringian saint.

Despite the partiality and biases of a tendentious and comparatively scarce tradition and the unsteady character of later legends, we dare to embark on writing the story of a medieval soul. Church historian Hauck thought it to be an impossible undertaking yet hoped for the possibility of an accurate portrait of the medieval spirit of her era.[17] However, even if we

17   Translator's note: The Protestant Albert Hauck (1845–1918) was a highly regarded church historian at the University of Leipzig. He was esteemed for his deep erudition, including Christian archaeology, but refrained from taking sides in the controversies surrounding Karl Lamprecht's Institut. Citing Hauck in her methodological argumentation might have served as a signal that Busse-Wilson was intent on forging her own methodological approach even though applying some of the tools of Lamprecht's comparative analysis. See Hermann Hempel, "Hauck, Albert," *Neue*

choose courage in daring to interpret these sparse testimonials, and even if we attempt a search for truth in mere anecdotes and sterile protocols, the saint as a type and an expression of the life of a community cannot always be sharply distinguished from Elisabeth of Thuringia's personal fate. By comparison, the dominant modern portrait of Elisabeth is likewise not a historical image, but a collective wished-for representation. In our case, a tragic female life will replace the official saintly icon.

The Religious Character – A Neurosis?

Sentimental historiographical revisionism bent the sorrowful female exist-ence which Elisabeth endured under the tyrannical rule of a sadistic monk into a sappy career as a religious nurse at a hospital. We equally reject another type of revisionism, which casts her life and fate as the object of psychopathological studies.[18] Slight propensities toward this view can already be found among all scholars who studied the primary sources more thoroughly. They discovered that visions and penitential practices occupied a more substantial part of her life than charity and asceticism. These uncom-fortable surprises were summarily dismissed as "hysterical" traits—a typical solution for not having to explain certain peculiar phenomena of religious life.[19] Even empathetic psychiatric scholars branded as heavy psychoses those manifestations of an intensive religious existence that include the habit of hermits and penitents, a hypersensitive conscience, incurable feelings of guilt, and regular prayer and mortification practices. The same label holds for visions and ecstasies. If not directly cast as fraudulent maneuvers, they were pigeon-holed as emotional and imaginative aberrations, which, by their very nature, would poison a person's character. The truth of the matter, however, is that all the above are merely an expression of the entirely

Deutsche Biographie 8 (1969): 75–76 [Online-Version]; URL: https://www.deutsche-biographie. de/pnd118773410.html#ndbcontent. Accessed December 2023.

18   Translator's note: The tendency to pathologize medieval female saints and mystics is discussed in the introduction. Critics of Busse-Wilson's work apparently refused to engage with her nuanced psychological analysis by situating her squarely in the field of psychoanalysis. More recent psychological studies of medieval female mystics apply diagnostic rubrics such as eating disorders, childhood abuse, and self-harm. See Rudolph Bell, *Holy Anorexia* (Chicago: University of Chicago Press, 1985); Ralph Frenken, "Childhood and Fantasies of Medieval Mystics," *Journal of Psychohistory* 28, no. 2 (2000): 150–72; Jerome Kroll and Bernard Bachrach, *The Mystic Mind: The Psychology of Medieval Mystics and Ascetics* (London: Taylor & Francis Group, 2005).

19   E.g., Wenck and Kühn.

different mentality of medieval men and women. A medieval person does not dare to say "I think." She would be deeply frightened of her own individual thoughts, perhaps indeed considering them the devil's work. Yet, this very same person might well receive a vision of the Virgin Mary or a saint, who will communicate with her. This clever presentation of original ideas is therefore a perfectly sane process.

Asceticism is equally misunderstood. As we will demonstrate below, asceticism is generally not a medieval response to sexual deprivation experienced later in life, but rather a reaction to sexual experiences that took place too early. Asceticism functioned as self-protection against "too early" and "too much" sexuality, and, as such, as a rebalancing act of the psyche. In this framework, asceticism, seemingly life-negating and repressive, is not a perverse but indeed a very healthy choice. It is entirely possible that asceticism turned retroactively into a means to minimize a sexuality, then became exaggerated to an intolerable extreme by monastic celibacy and thus resulted in psychic self-destruction. Yet, we consider this a secondary development.

Unfortunately, even the most educated interpreters stopped at a diagnosis of pathology. For this reason, either anxious theologians guarded knowledge about medieval religious life as a secret science, or secularized scholars committed to the ideas of the Enlightenment profaned it, according to their own fashion. The newest branch of psychiatry, psychoanalytic method, is of greatest heuristic value when examining the inner working of the human mind to enhance humankind's growth toward self-awareness. It is our duty, in the service of advancing objectivity, to detach with precision the domain of pure instinct—which poses frequently in the disguise of religion or spirituality—from the sphere of intellect, and vice versa. In the final analysis, such psychoanalytical probing serves only to enhance reverence for intellectual achievements. Taken as a whole, psychoanalysis preserves a scientific-rationalistic teleology. Within the parameters of a history of epistemology, psychoanalysis constitutes a secular discovery. As a practice of psychotherapy, it is dominated by dogmatic philistinism. The fit and prim person with a "normal" sex life—in this context, a sex life without tragedy; the man or woman able to aim for feasible love objects; the human being who marries rather than committing suicide—that human being is the a priori moral compass of psychoanalysis.

The beneficiaries of the research results generated by the in and of itself indispensable psycho-dynamic method of inquiry still produce conclusions in line with the scientific naturalism of the nineteenth century. As soon as they have revealed its manifold causal origin or the physio-kinetic conditions of its growth, members of the psychoanalytic school consider an idea or ideal, even a political or religious conviction, as proven wrong and irrelevant.

Psychoanalysts were done with the medieval worldview when they recognized that many of its representatives disclosed psychotic and neurotic traits. This contemporary "mode of thought" is rooted in socio-historical ground. The psychoanalytic examination of religious and intellectual life generally still serves as a tool of the Enlightenment era, although the historical goal of the Enlightenment to dislodge authoritative customs and beliefs as well as "privileged classes" has become obsolete. Still, the scientific-genetic perspective in the service of truth remains a great blessing when tasked to reduce the cult of heroes in outsized historiographical endeavors.

In an areligious era, such as our modern epoch, morality becomes synonymous with religion because a sensibility for the core of religiosity has been lost. As a necessary consequence, religiosity in its most basic preternatural sense is to be experienced as something alien. Nonetheless, even if an authentically religious person should display psychotic or neurotic traits, or even if his or her era and environment in its entirety display mildly pathological characteristics, we should not need to lose respect for a specific religious or spiritual act. Quite the contrary, a "neurosis" frequently remains the best aspect of such human beings and serves as the cause of their extraordinary mental abilities and ethical predisposition. Generally, an anxious and unstable mindset characterizes a religiously productive personality type; a partially psycho-pathological disposition may be linked to exceptionally rare religious aptitude. "Ordinary" men and women are never gripped by the power of a quintessentially religious experience.[20]

Several humanities-trained psychiatric experts have conceded the interdependency between pathological disposition and cultural achievement, and, reversely, the cultural productivity of mental disabilities.[21] Yet nobody dares to name the true relationship between the forces of anxious impulses and mild psychopathology and those of genuine, productive spiritual achievements of the highest order. William James admits that,

> In the psychopathic temperament we have the emotionality which is the sine qua non of moral perception; we have the intensity and tendency to

---

20   Translator's note: In this section, Busse-Wilson relies heavily on William James' model of morbid-mindedness to challenge bourgeois notions of normality and yet another, in this case secular, stereotype. It constitutes another layer of her effort to reconstitute Elisabeth's personhood as an authentically lived existence, which includes Elisabeth's freely chosen religious path.
21   K. Birnbaum, *Kulturpsychopathologie,* 1924.

emphasis which are the essence of practical moral vigor; and we have the
love of metaphysics and mysticism which carry one's interests beyond the
surface of the sensible world. What, then, is more natural than that this
temperament should introduce one to regions of religious truth, to corners
of the universe, which your robust Philistine type of nervous system [...]
would be sure to hide forever from its self-satisfied possessors?[22]

Yet it remains a question which force contributes the most in generating religious and spiritual strengths. Are pathology or anxiousness mere
catalysts in producing a thought or an idea? Or is religious genius pure
contrariness and, as such, can only manifest with psychotic features? Is a
bent toward illness the mark of the creative mind as such?

In contemporary culture, a positive valuation of psychopathological
traits is generally not possible, yet it applies to a large swath of the history
of medieval mentalities. In any case, were we to define the creative impulse
as fundamentally dependent upon psychological and mental health, we
would need to label all medieval religious life as culturally inferior. The
characterology of medieval saints, especially those of exemplary spiritual
rank, reads as a clinical textbook of mental states which we would experience
as abnormal today. Historians of religion "excuse" these states if they are
accompanied by remarkable spiritual achievements. It does not have to be
an axiomatic decision to accept what seems pathological today only as the
exception to the rule. Historians, psychologists, and sociologists are usually
caught up in naïve cultural subjectivity when defining their own era's
emotional landscape as healthy but reject divergent mentalities as unhealthy.
It is an undeniable truth that contemporary virtues and capabilities such as
a disciplined work ethic, an unruffled composure, and a valiant loneliness,
often endured without the comforts of religion, are bought for the price of
a no less neurotic and pathological culture.[23]

One may label St. Elisabeth's short life as one long neurosis. Due to
its tragic disposition, hers was a personality type made for a sorrowful
life's journey. A lack of realism and social good sense despite a passionate
devotion to charitable duties, combined with a certain inflexibility in her

22   Translator's note: William James, *The Varieties of Religious Experience: A Study in Human
Nature* (London: Longmans, Green, & Co, 1902; reprint, London: Collier Books, 1961), 38. German
translation Leipzig 1907.
23   Translator's note: Busse-Wilson vigorously rejects the evolutionary scheme of rational
civilization as the apex of human evolution and makes a case for the modern presence of a
falsely labelled "earlier stage" of religious mentalities as a preferable choice. She will return to
her criticism of modernity several times throughout her study of Elisabeth.

own convictions, formed an interior life emblematic of a numerically well represented religious type. Hard blows of fate dealt to her at a young age and premature physical and psychic exhaustion generated a predictably neurotic mindset, which oscillated between exaltation and despair, between untimely resignation and rejoicing. Based on a purely psychophysiological interpretation and the results of our biographical study, we could count the royal Landgravine Elisabeth among those personalities who chose religion as an escape, an eradication and rebalancing of external mishaps and a lack of talent. Yet for Elisabeth, religiosity did not function as this kind of hyper-compensation. She was talented and beautiful, a lady of high nobility who lacked nothing. It is true, however, that her uncompromising religiosity emerged from the striking power of despair.[24]

At the beginning, Elisabeth of Thuringia embarked on the customary life pattern as wife of a medieval feudal lord. At the time, it was a natural and appropriate form of female existence to enter engagement as planned for by a woman's relatives and to approach this event as a political transaction. It was equally natural and appropriate that Elisabeth experienced an early separation from her parents, that she married as an adolescent, and that she lost her spouse early on—twice resulting in an experience of homelessness. The ability to endure varied turns of fate, especially at a young age, is defined as one of several characteristics of mental health. Every psychological and cultural epoch is in its own way "unhealthy," yet a healthy psychological constitution generates such an abundance of healing ferment that it can ward off an external assault on the psyche. A person can acquire a resistance to external stimuli either by focusing on their work, as is true today, or as was the case in the Middle Ages, by escaping into asceticism and world-renouncing piety. A neurosis develops if such resiliency fails to develop. This was Elisabeth's lot. The social conditions and general lifestyle around 1200—Elisabeth was born in 1207—were the perfect breeding ground for neurotic and anxiety-driven personalities. The lives of all those who belonged to Elisabeth's social class were caught in the tension between a refined courtly cultural milieu and the constant life-threatening realities of war, feuds, and political circumstance. The onslaught of life's challenges in modernity, today's "age of anxiety," is still lighter than in the cultural epoch that belonged to Elisabeth. She never experienced childhood. She was lonely and beleaguered when she should have been cared for and protected. She became an adult woman at an age when we today still shower human beings with caring attention and shield

24 See the section "The Art of Suffering" below.

them from life's interferences. Yet the particularity of her transition from what is natural to what is "unnatural," and what saturates her life as a saint cannot be solely understood by the standards of rational psychodynamic research or sociology. Her neurosis remains her best trait even if her life's circumstances can be explained as its cause. Other female contemporaries could endure what triggered her break-down. She lacked resiliency for her era's ordinary life rhythms because her psychic structures were arranged too delicately. All anxieties of her time assaulted her psyche. The thoughtless-ness, the mix of impulsive coarseness and cultural hyper refinement typical of her class and generation thickened into a fear of life and a fear of the world. Whatever her environment experienced as normal became an occasion for her to criticize, to doubt, and to reject all worldly matters. Originally vague, a sense of guilt about the medieval aristocratic world germinated within; in just a few years, the seedling pushed into the open as a radical rejection of her courtly milieu. At that point, she discovered the frail, the poor, and the neglected, whose existence did not cause concern for her peers. Her "psycho-emotional" weakness became her greatest ethical strength. She was driven on an "unnatural" path and level of religious action which demands other goals than a wish for a placid, "normal" life. The reasons lie in the restlessness of her intellectual doubt and protest of her social surroundings. There exists no virtue and no intellectual labor for which a human being does not need to pay the price in some way. It is usually a high price.

Even though St. Elisabeth experienced religious visions and ecstasies only in small measure, her religious and ethical ideals as such were destructive when measured by the ethos of our own bourgeois era. Her charity did not concern suffering humankind, but her desire for a mystical convergence with Christ. Most of her adult life was spent in a psychically harrowing depend-ency on her confessor. Yet she consciously endured her brutal oppressor as a form of penitence and a relay to heaven. At the age of twenty-four, she succeeded in escaping through death. From the contemporary perspec-tive of a rational ethic, all her efforts were misguided. Nonetheless, the "psychopathological" traits of this saint are nothing but the "standard" psychopathology of her culture and epoch. Her heroic acts of desperation, her opposition against secular culture, and her religious development were propelled by the historical distinctiveness of the social order into which she was born and by the random circumstances of her personal fortunes. This does not make them any less idealistic, heroic, or intellectual, even if their foundation should be understood as cultural pathology.

Elisabeth's constitutional anxiety was psychically productive. Since her religious impulse chanced upon early external stimulation, Elisabeth embraced suffering and asceticism organically and deliberately. Her life as a saint is the result of a collision between a psychically rich and supple constitution unfit for medieval life and the demands and pretensions of her society.

St. Elisabeth's decisive exploits and actions took place between the age of sixteen and twenty-four. Considering contemporary concepts of life's stages and rhythms, the study of her character and aspirations thus qualifies as a topic of adolescent psychology. This approach is certainly an option, yet it would capture nothing but a collective social modulation at work in the Middle Ages. In Elisabeth's time, the early onset of adulthood was a given. A medieval person entered the state of full adulthood at a point which we today would define as early adolescence.[25] It has been common to address the onset of strongly religious tendencies as a typical sign of puberty. Yet despite their otherwise valuable findings, scholars of adolescent psychology and the psychology of religion lack a value-oriented perspective.

Could the age of puberty perhaps be a stage of life that deserves greater appreciation and esteem precisely because the noblest expressions of the human mind prefer to be concentrated in this period?[26] Or, inversely, might religious life be merely a transitory phenomenon that ends with life's more "mature" subject matters? This latter interpretation is more frequent than the former. In any case, religious passion, if at all tied to specific life phases, is never diminished in its time-transcendent appeal and value. Were this not the case, we would have to label all medieval religiosity as an adolescent neurosis. A simple way out. Elisabeth's contemporaries never praised or excused the Landgravine's' activities as those of a youth. Elisabeth pursued actions and decisions strictly matter-of-factly and, as such, in an adult rather than a childlike and coy manner. Elisabeth's type of responses were not intended to draw the reactions of others. She lacked the craving for recognition that is typical of hysterics. A smug display of many quasi- and semi-mature talents intended to arouse attention and admiration was entirely alien to her. She suffered on behalf of her choice of an interior religious life, yet never used it to draw attention to herself. Her private religiosity and flight from the world had been reported since her childhood. It suggests an introverted personality and a common religious type, as does her catastrophic failure to meet life's exigencies.

25 See the chapter "Christian Asceticism and its Modern Misinterpretation" below.
26 Translator's note: Busse-Wilson's considerable theoretical emphasis on St. Elisabeth's youth is buoyed by her professional interests as a historian of the German Youth Movement. See Großmann, op.cit., 68–86.

However, some of Elisabeth's other traits testify to typically youthful attitudes and feelings. Characteristic expressions of early adolescence might be found in the unconditional and unreserved manner, even lack of inhibition, with which she dedicated herself to the realization of Franciscan ideals from the unqualified care of the sick to aiding lepers with a mystically inclined assistance. It is evident in her stubbornness and in her lack of realism, diplomacy, and political savvy, all of which eventually led to her demise. Since we cannot get the sense that she learned anything from the harsh blows of fate, Elisabeth seems to have preserved a certain perpetual childlike quality. A superficial psychology of religion might perceive the character of Elisabeth's peculiar ethic-religious temper to be preconfigured in a "masochistic" predisposition. St. Elisabeth lived in extreme bondage to her spiritual foster father Konrad. In this most pivotal of her relationships, the religious agenda of self-denigration and self-abandonment as the core of her ethic-religious goals could indeed be devalued as the ideological self-justification of a disastrous psychological disposition.[27]

However, these traits are not simply an individual's pathology. Maxims and statements of self-reflection such as the following earmark them as general ethical demands of her times:

> If you are being offered honor, feel shame; if you are made to suffer, rejoice; if you receive anything good, be afraid…. When I, the poorest of all humanity, go to pray, I adorn myself with the baseness of my being and dress myself with the scum that is me. Then I put on the shoes of the noble time that I have lost in all my days and gird myself with the pain caused by my guilt. I cover myself in a coat of perdition which fills me to the brim. I crown my head with a crown of secret disrepute with which I violated the Divine. Then my hand will grasp a mirror of true insight and I shall see in it who I am. Alas, I will not see anything else.[28]

27 Translator's note: This is likely a reference to neurologist Albert Eulenburg's historiography of sadism and masochism, which briefly mentions St. Elisabeth.

28 Mechthild of Magdeburg, *The Book of Contemplation*. Translator's note: It is more common today to refer to Mechthild's books in their entirety as *The Flowing Light of the Godhead*, a phrase Mechthild chose to describe the content of her writings. Sharmain van Blommestein has astutely noted the confluence of a female mystical pursuit of pain and medieval patriarchal expectations of wives' submission to their husbands. See Sharmain van Blommestein, "Medieval Redemptive Suffering: Female Mystical Expressions of Pain and Pleasure and Medieval Society's Influence on Mystical Spirituality," *International Journal of Religion and Spirituality in Society* 4, no. 2 (2014): 39–53. For a later period, see Ulrike Wiethaus, "'For This I Ask You, Punish Me': Norms of Spiritual Orthopraxis in the Work of Maria van Hout (d. 1547)," *Ons Geestelijk Erf* 68, no. 3 (1994): 253–70.

Such truisms were not devised by Elisabeth, who was addicted to authority, who let herself be thrashed by her confessor, who threw herself at the feet of lepers. They were devised by her independent, self-confident, passionate, and keen contemporary Mechthild of Magdeburg. A yearning for self-abasement must be counted among a medieval religious psyche's most stable experiences of desire, whether expressed in contemplation or in action. Elisabeth's conscious choice of remaining in a hopeless condition of suffering unto self-annihilation and her inner preparedness to remain in a state that was ordained for her by Konrad and which amounted to psychological torture— all this is not simply the necessary evil of a feminine-passive disposition. Rather, all her religious endeavors and physical chastisements, even though augmented by her individual constitution, are always the ethical substance and the spiritual force of her era. These were laid out before her. Indeed, the saint does not display a single behavior, action, and emotion that seems odd to us today, which did not already exist in the collective consciousness of her time. To understand the life of St. Elisabeth is to understand a medieval attitude toward life as lived across a long swath of time.

2   Elisabeth's Life

A Lonely Childhood

In the year 1208, at the Bamberg bishopric's imperial palace, the Hohen-staufen dynasty's destiny took a turn for the worse. The rival King Otto IV of Braunschweig instigated the murder of Emperor Philipp of Swabia with the full knowledge of Bamberg's Bishop Ekbert of Bamberg.[1] The political crime unleashed chaos and anarchy. The poet Walther von der Vogelweide repeatedly returned to the catastrophic events in his secular songs. Bishop Ekbert was forced to leave the country in response to an escalation of suspicion and resentment. He fled to his sister and mother of his future niece, Queen Gertrud of Hungary.

Landgrave Hermann von Thuringia stood by his father-in-law Otto IV and intervened on behalf of Bishop Ekbert, who returned to Germany after three years of exile. As a compensation for his efforts at mediation, the bishop placed his social network at Hermann's disposal and arranged an advantageous engagement for the landgrave's house. One of the daughters of the Hungarian royal couple with whom he had lived during his exile, a girl by the name of Elisabeth, was chosen as a bride for the Thuringian landgrave's son. With this move, the Bishop of Bamberg formed family ties with his closest territorial neighbor. Through Gertrude, the mother of the bride, the Thuringian house consolidated good relations with the preeminent noble family in Southern Germany, the house of Andechs-Meran. These political negotiations created the historical conditions for the future St. Elisabeth's arrival in Germany.

The family politics driving her engagement were typical of medieval society. Marriage was not a matter of love, but a task to be tackled by the extended family. Following custom, Elisabeth's parents removed the four-year-old girl to the landgrave's Thuringian family in Germany. Legends focus at great length on the young Hungarian princess's relocation. Especially

---

[1]   Translator's note: The author mistakenly identifies Otto IV as a member of the house of Wittelsbach. The English translation has corrected the German original.

Busse-Wilson, E., *St. Elisabeth of Thuringia: A Psychological Study* (1931). Amsterdam: Amsterdam University Press, 2025

DOI 10.5117/9789463725804_CH02

popular are folktales about the presence of the Hungarian magician Klingsor at the so-called minstrels' contest on the Wartburg castle and his relationship with the Hungarian child bride. It is likely that the arrival of the diminutive exotic transplant and her bridal treasure elicited notice at the Thuringian court. Her dowry in particular became the focus of attention. It included choice jewelry, precious fabrics from the East, and a silver bathtub.

Elisabeth was born in Pressburg in 1207; alternative birth places as recorded in the sources include Sárospatak.[2] Nothing is known about her father Andreas II, king of Hungary and Croatia, other than that he led a politically inglorious life. A volatile king, he was dominated by his wife. Upon reaching adulthood, his son Béla IV demanded his resignation. In contrast to her spouse, Gertrude was praised as a woman endowed with "manly, joyous courage." She was unusually assertive. Her great vice was boundless extravagance and acquisitiveness. Elisabeth inherited characteristics from both parents that contributed to her unhappy life: from her father, an acquiescent disposition that allowed for domination by a more forceful personality; from her mother, a tendency to be profligate, which reappeared as altruism as she squandered her possessions among beggars and the destitute.

Since the future St. Elisabeth descended from preeminent noble kin, we can deduce to some degree what type of family constellations might have formed her. They undoubtedly predisposed her to sainthood. Highly gifted personalities or those endowed with unusual character included her mother Gertrude von Andechs-Meran's kith and kin. There was her aunt Hedwig, the future landgravine of Silesia, a strong-willed woman with unusual inclinations who also became a saint. Hedwig divorced her husband after having given birth to six children and founded a monastery. She was quick-witted and politically savvy. Under the cover of religiosity, her personal proclivities found strange outlets: she kissed the choir seats on which nuns had sat and the towels with which they had dried themselves. She was radical in her care for lepers and in furthering their cultic veneration. It remains inconclusive whether the future St. Elisabeth modeled herself after her aunt or vice versa. Bishop Ekbert of Bamberg, as mentioned above, was a brother of Elisabeth's mother. Ekbert played a pivotal role in Elisabeth's future as a culturally prominent, but politically controversial church leader. Two other brothers of her mother had also taken religious vows, and another sister, Mechthild, served as abbess of a Benedictine monastery known for its

---

2   Translator's note: Pressburg is the former name of Bratislava, Slovakia. Hungarian sources recognize Sárospatak in northern Hungary as her birthplace.

educational achievements. These facts alone do not yield much information about Elisabeth's character. However, we stand on firmer ground when we consider the milieu of the German high nobility of the Hohenstaufen era. As we shall see, it robbed Elisabeth of her greatest strengths as she tried to prevail over it.

Human beings are formed by their family heritage and the influences of their environment. They can mature in harmony or in opposition to their psychological surroundings. They can circumvent adverse conditions with cunning or attempt to remove them through energetic action. Unconsciously, they may fight psychological traits of their ancestors or negate in protest an environment in which they cannot feel an affirmation of their individuality. The secret of personhood, its ethos and its impact, arises from this kind of protest in counterpoint with the simultaneous desire for self-assertion. Its traits and actions can thus be inferred from its origins and yet remain at the same time unique, independent, and stable.

The child became a member of one of the best families among the German high nobility. Landgrave Hermann of Thuringia ruled over a cultured and spirited court.[3] Every great figure of secular medieval literature received hospitality and appreciation at his palace. Heinrich von Veldeke was a protégé of the unusually erudite landgrave; it is at his court that Walther von der Vogelweide and Wolfram von Eschenbach met each other. Always welcome, artists and knights-errand were provided with courtly leisure and free lodging. It is no surprise that the century's poets praised this place of high aristocratic culture, and that the locale of the legendary minstrels' contest was moved to Wartburg castle. Its sophisticated flurry of activities likely offered a fitting background. A guest extolled Landgrave Hermann with the poetic phrase that "a Thuringian flower blazes through the snow." Such praise meant that he provided meals for all during the worst of economic times. In Walther von der Vogelweide's words, "The Landgrave is of such disposition that he consumes all his wealth with proud heroes. I know his lofty way of life: even if a cart load of wine would cost a thousand pounds, never would a knight's cup remain empty." Consequently, people of all ranks of life crowded the Landgrave's household. The castle must have resembled a county fair. There was continual coming and going, a succession of festivities without end despite precarious financial political circumstances. Walther von der Vogelweide comments, "My advice is that whoever suffers badly

3   Medieval Thuringia is not identical to either the contemporary ethnic definition of Thuringia or the new political concept of Great Thuringia. It constituted a large mid-German realm, which included Hesse and other tribal regions. It extended from the river Oder to the river Main.

from earaches should avoid the Thuringian court. If he stays there, he will go insane. One group arrives, another leaves whether it is day or night. It is a great miracle that anybody is being heard."

This affluent and magnificent life at the Thuringian court was to be dissolved by a child.[4] The fabulous aristocratic lifestyle ended when Elisabeth and her spouse, Landgrave Ludwig, Landgrave Hermann's successor, assumed their financial and household responsibilities. Elisabeth opened a soup kitchen and hospital for the poor and mendicant, where Wolfram von Eschenbach composed the sixth and seventh books of the Parsifal epos and where Walther von der Vogelweide experienced and performed his songs of courtly love, *Minne*. People watched as she used the prized headdress, the superb part of a noblewoman's outfit, to clean the wounds of impoverished men and women who suffered from skin diseases. Landgrave Ludwig, on the other hand, discarded the army of poets and minstrels, of male and female freeloaders. He lived so "virtuously" that his biographers could not marvel enough at his abstinence. Unlike their parents, neither spouse aspired to further refine the luxury and appearance of feudal cultural life. Indeed, the young Landgravine avoided or rebuffed the type of men and women, admired in the sculptures of the Naumburg Cathedral, who exemplify noble and chivalric culture.

What turned the descendant of a highly talented noble family and the wife of one of the finest representatives of the Hohenstaufen era toward contempt of her social environs and toward the rejection of her culture's lived beauty? To rephrase the question in the language of her era: how did she become a saint? When the four-year-old daughter of the Hungarian king arrived at the Thuringian court to become educated as the future wife of the landgrave's eldest son, she was deposited onto foreign soil. She grew up without parents. Although not mistreated in her childhood, she was constantly reminded of being a foreigner. Her parents provided her with the company of two Hungarian nobles named David and Farkasius, most likely clerics, to watch over her wellbeing. According to legend, she was also served by a Hungarian lady in waiting who could play the harp. She thus did not forget the language of her home country and remained aware that from earliest childhood, she belonged to two parental homes—or none.

---

4   Landgrave Hermann's famous "court of the muses" did not take place in the Wartburg castle proper as memorialized for all times by Schwind. The palatinate's headquarter was located in Eisenach at the foot of the castle, which at that time had an exclusively strategic function. Therefore, Elisabeth's childhood took place in Eisenach. It was her spouse who turned the castle into his living quarters proper. It is culturally and geographically exceptional that thirteenth-century Thuringia could take center stage for a court such as the landgrave's. Medieval chivalric culture was otherwise limited to the West and South of Germany.

A growing isolation, the cause of her asocial development, can be explained through such rootlessness. A lonely child observes her environment more keenly than she is expected to. Loneliness engenders precociousness. Her social destiny compelled Elisabeth to mature early. Her partially Southern constitution, as evident in the blend of her parental blood lines, would also lead us to expect an earlier onset of adulthood.[5] At an early age, Elisabeth was able to recognize the contradictions of the splendid and famous court and its dedicated celebration of the muses.

Elisabeth must have also realized soon enough that *Minne*, the pursuit of courtly love in the service of aristocratic women, defined as the purest expression of chivalry and promoted and welcomed by the head of the household, was embedded in quotidian jealousy, intrigue, and vanity. Courtly love in its manifold possibilities always depended on a code of secrecy for all its relationships, even those of a more intimate and tender nature. How much fearful caution, how many secret messages and nightly rendezvous did the child Elisabeth witness unwillingly, yet not without awareness? She was predisposed to notice the shadow side of aristocratic chivalric culture, its excesses of power and its hypocritical cult of femininity. Long after her death, Elisabeth's famous contemporary Mechthild of Magdeburg interpreted the whole of her earthly existence as the rejection of chivalric civilization, of the wives and daughters of the Hohenstaufen nobility. Mechthild hears the voice of God pronounce, "Elisabeth was my envoy whom I sent to the corrupt noble women in their proud castles, who, poisoned by their promiscuity, bloated by arrogance, and lost to vanity thus were lawfully doomed to the abyss."[6]

Social criticism does not need to result in isolation and separation. Through love, friendship, interests, and hope for the future, young and responsible human beings remain bonded to a society they will find fault with. However, in one key instance, Elisabeth lacked a connection with the feudal culture to which she belonged. Elisabeth was without close kin. For medieval people, especially women, this meant an enormous dearth of protection. Her birth family lived far away in foreign lands. A wide network

5   Translator's note: Elisabeth Busse-Wilson does not provide sources regarding regional differences in the onset of puberty. Current cross-cultural research suggests that the onset of puberty is determined by the impact of stressful environments. See N. Colich, M. Rosen, E. Williams, and K. McLaughlin, *Biological Aging in Childhood and Adolescence following Experiences of Threat and Deprivation: A Systematic Review and Meta-Analysis*, Psychological Bulletin 146, no. 9 (September 2020): 721–64. DOI: 10.1037/bul0000270.

6   Mechthild of Magdeburg, *Book of Visions*. Translator's note: See note 28 on Mechthild of Magdeburg.

of blood relations capable of providing her with stability and security was missing. She felt the impact of such absence not only in her youth, but also at decisive critical junctures later in life. In patriarchal societies, a woman without relatives to support her will be pushed aside.[7]

Once her adoptive father, Landgrave Hermann, who also served as the guardian of her engagement, had died, she immediately had to face her new status as a person without kin, that is, as someone who was not worthy of respect. Her birth father was an indistinct king without political clout, and her brothers lived far away in Hungary. Marrying into such a family did not seem to offer much anymore to the house of Thuringia. It was therefore only natural and even self-evident that efforts were made to annul the engagement and to search for a better match for the high-ranking heir.[8] Ludwig, however, did not want to break the contract.

There are numerous legendary stories about his faithfulness to the bride who was chosen for him from childhood. For example, while riding with him, a knight asked Ludwig about his future with Elisabeth. Ludwig answered that even if the highest mountain of Thuringia were made of gold and offered to him in exchange for Elisabeth, he would not separate from her. The mere existence of such stories proves that reasons for annulment must have existed. Since women and especially girls were purely pawns of family politics without a will of their own, this perfectly legal trafficking in women and female children caused the isolated foreigner to feel anxious and insecure. To be sent back home was not honorable. She also had no home left in her country of origin. Thus, she was doubly justified in fearing for her existence, even though she was raised in luxury.

Legendary tradition also claims an "evil mother-in-law" for Elisabeth. She is supposed to have worked on the annulment of the engagement by reasoning that "Elisabeth is more suited to be a maidservant than a land-gravine." Landgravine Sophie was a talented and exemplary representative of courtly culture. Historical scholarship could establish that she practiced

7   Today, a sense of the relational and ethical power of family bonds has receded to such a degree that the concept of "family" only denotes the narrow companionship of parents and children. It is assumed that this nuclear family unit is to be defended, while family in the true sense as kin or clan, has ceased to exist as a social force long ago.

8   The young Landgrave Ludwig, successor to his father, was beseeched to search for a more advantageous relationship. Dietrich von Apolda wrote about it extensively, and the monk Nikolaus, first editor of the *Libellus*, emphasized the hostility that Elisabeth received from the landgrave's family. There is no reason to assume that these stories belong to the realm of the imagination as proposed by historians. The *Libellus* likely does not mention this dark chapter of her past for good reason: the instigators of the canonization process were the landgrave's family.

extensive charity and that it is likely that St. Elisabeth apprenticed with her as far as aristocratic charity is concerned.[9] Yet this fact does not need to be understood as contradicting the legends. Landgravine Sophie remained a lady at court, yet her religious daughter-in-law Elisabeth was intent on begging in the streets. A tense relationship could not be avoided. In addition, the landgravine already had two daughters of her own. She would have been an exceptional woman if she had loved and understood her stepdaughter as much as she did her two birth daughters.

Elisabeth's marriage to Landgrave Ludwig was finally made official. The lonely girl could feel reasonably secure. In the first year of her marriage, Elisabeth and her spouse traveled to Hungary to meet her father and siblings. At the Hungarian royal court, she observed unrest, antagonism, weakness, and brutality. Her father had been pushed to the sidelines. Her mother was dead. These experiences confirmed that the world of her kin and of her own origins was a realm of instability, permanent mortal danger, and sorrow.

Yet such alarming and frightening knowledge had already assaulted Elisabeth at a much younger age. At the age of eleven, news traveled to Thuringia that her mother Gertrud, queen of Hungary, had been murdered in the presence of her own children. Gertrud had become the target of a conspiracy by Hungarian nobles in response to her imprudent German politics and her boundless greed. A child who barely knew her parents learns that her birth mother becomes the victim of a crime. Already lonely and isolated, she experiences the loss of a central component of what constituted her meaning of "home."

In support of the canonization process, her childhood companion Guda testified about the precocious piety of the saint. Guda reported that even as a little girl, Elisabeth was so "pious" that she preferred most of all to remain by herself in the castle chapel. She loved solitude. Frequently, she was found praying in front of the altar or pretending to read in the psalter. When playing with other children, she feigned involvement in a game and took every opportunity to retreat from the group. While playing tag, she habitually hid behind the chapel door to avoid participation in the pastime. Behind this door, she could be by herself and with herself. Outside, she had to play-act being a carefree child and pretend that all was well.

Sometimes she kissed the chapel's walls and doorstep or the ground before the altar when secretly escaping her entourage, whom she perhaps found wanting in acts of tenderness toward her. Growing up without parents and

---

9   Karl Wenck, "Papst Gregor IX und seine Beziehungen zur heiligen Elisabeth," *Hochland* 5 (1907).

dependent on her own inner resources, she attached herself to saints, the figures of her wished-for world whom she had chosen as her guardians. It is possible that she felt already then that her private piety and intense prayers were belittled and did not fit into the domestic milieu of her upbringing.

A resourceful child, Elisabeth found ways to perform a self-imposed prayer practice or a prostration with the unusual force of will that she applied to all of her religious decisions as an adult—especially when she felt hemmed in by those around her. If her self-imposed set of prayers were not completed by bedtime, she would continue to pray while in bed.[10] To be able to perform prostrations while at play, she would say to another girl, "Let's see which one of us is tallest." They would lie down on the ground next to each other, so that she could carry out prostrations that remained unnoticed by others. Prayer vows became her life's secretly chosen anchor. Already in childhood, play turned into a pretext to hide her inner life.

At the height of a game, she used to say, "When something is at its best, I will renounce it for the sake of God." If a dance began a second round, she would refuse to partake again. "Once shall be sufficient for me." Even as a child, she displayed the precocious caution of a human being who has experienced a great deal—a mistrust of the permanence of happiness and an existential mood, which quietly announces an adult renunciation of the world: now it is quite beautiful, but I do not want to take happiness for granted; instability is the only predictable fact we may expect from life.

It was unavoidable that the future Landgravine Elisabeth's ethical principles and worldviews did not match her early environment. She possessed no significant affective bonds with others during her childhood. Who loves, tends to the beloved with care. Thus, she was able and free to critique those around her without reservation. For this reason, all her future actions—from the smallest gesture to the most ingenious character trait—are infused with protest against her feudal milieu. Her unqualified devotion to the lost and poorest of the poor constitutes a rejection of courtly culture. Her contemplative, radically detached piety is the result of rejecting the official and very public religiosity that characterized her aristocratic milieu. A stance of protest against the daily life of her relatives and her caste turned into the fertile ground of her religious and intellectual individuality and her saintly virtues. At the beginning, they manifested as innocent rebellion against the feudal lifestyle practiced around her. She began with a boycott of the fashionable dress code and its luxuries.

10   All incidents are recorded in the *Libellus*.

Aristocratic material culture was highly developed at the time. The display of luxury relied on different objects than what is used to that purpose among the bourgeoisie of the twentieth century. There was little furniture, and the actual living space in late Romanesque castles was narrow and limited. Even the richest castles lacked glass windows. Wealth was displayed instead on one's own body, similar to traditional rural attire in the nineteenth century, which was designed to prove the wealth of their owners by including the literal display of coins. Both sexes went to great lengths to dress up in jewelry and precious fabrics. With ingenuous enjoyment, men, as much as women, desired and displayed gold and silver headbands, necklaces, bracelets, rings, and colorful fabrics from the East. For both sexes, the preeminent showpiece of a wardrobe was the coat, lined in silk, bordered with fur, and clasped at the breast with a precious brooch. The sources record that as a young landgravine, Elisabeth especially enjoyed distributing these sumptuous outfits among poor women. Such gifting appears to have always been a moral need. Even later, after she was placed under legal guardianship and lost free access to her wealth, and even though the luxurious outfits were highly impractical for impoverished peasants, giving away aristocratic clothing indicates how unconsciously symbolic the experience must have been for her.

Before she became landgravine and lady of the manor, Elisabeth strengthened her boycott of fashion with a vow. Once she became lady of the manor, she proceeded more systematically and recommended to the ladies at court that they refuse certain new fashions. She specifically targeted a new fashionable type of sleeve and headdress. The sleeves would fit snugly on the upper arm, and like a kind of arm train, trailed to the ground in an extremely wide bell-shaped swath of cloth. Silk ribbons were artfully wrapped around and woven into the hair. Other women would have hardly appreciated the puritanism of such a refusal. Women would rather forgive each other for an ostentatious outfit than for an intentionally simple set of clothes, which signified a break with their social group. Simplicity as a medieval aristocratic expression of "cancel culture" was therefore experienced as more antisocial than extravagance. One may indeed define all of Landgravine Elisabeth's lifestyle as a deliberate undercutting.

The young Elisabeth likely did not rally the male sex behind her cause either, even though the cultural atmosphere of her upbringing was saturated with the practice of courtly love. No documents exist that describe Elisabeth's behavior toward men at court who craved discrete glances, friendly gestures, and what poets repeatedly referred to as "Minne's greetings," where women would take the lead in greeting a knight. The hostility of nobles toward the widowed young landgravine corroborates that she knew from an early age how to boycott men—in this case, by ignoring them. Men, like women, experience no greater insult than being snubbed when expecting attention and regard by the other sex.

Over the years, Elisabeth's rejection of feudal customs escalated into provocative actions. As a result, her own need for social contact, now without an outlet among her social peers, had to be redirected to other domains: "upwards" toward transcendence, and in a radical social transfer, "downwards" toward the poor. It is said that already as a child, she would offer small gifts to playmates poorer than herself, and that she was incapable of rejecting a request. Her precociousness and her isolation and internal distance from her social world caused her to lavish her innate kindness and warmth on the underprivileged and lower caste. Events that occurred later in life prove that she extended sympathy and compassion only to those below. Charitable care, the most constructive aspect of her religious exploits, turned into the cause of her tragic struggle and her ultimate demise and failure among her feudal contemporaries. St. Elisabeth's biography thus becomes a paradigm of the inevitability of society's forceful impact on the course of a human life.

Lack of a homeland defined her childhood; transplanting the four-year-old Hungarian princess to a foreign country signifies an early and decisive uprooting. The resulting loneliness generated a growing intentional self-isolation and rebellious attitude against her social environment. It was fueled by the resistance of those around her and predictably resulted in the landgravine's catastrophic eviction from the Wartburg castle. Although historically undocumented and dismissed as legend, the expulsion seems plausible from a psychological point of view. In any case, her break with feudal society was absolute.

Her effort to begin life anew in Franciscan poverty ended in woeful failure and had to conclude with her "internment" in the Marburg hospital. At the same time, Elisabeth's double uprooting nurtured a growing religious depth. Individual creative success consists in the reformulation of societal pressures as a gateway to new personal freedom that overturns social coerciveness. Elisabeth's exemplary achievement is to have succeeded in the transformation of adversity into religious passion. Her sanctity thus can be meaningful and respected even in our contemporary era.

Landgrave Ludwig and St. Elisabeth's Marriage

Even if caution is exercised in assessing the praise showered upon St. Elisabeth's husband, Landgrave Ludwig IV, the image of an unusually sympathetic character persists. The last scion of his dynasty, all medieval chroniclers, especially religious authors such as his chaplain Berthold, sang his praises. His figure was unjustly pushed aside since his wife, Landgravine Elisabeth, received sainthood very soon after her death and thus became the public focus of a Thuringian ancestral cult. In truth, however, Ludwig was a *gentiluomo perfetto* of the Hohenstaufen era's nobility.

He spent his youth under the influence of his father Landgrave Hermann's volatile politics and carefree lifestyle. The court's economic foundation was in tatters. To finance the journey with Elisabeth to her home country of Hungary, undertaken in the first year of their marriage, Landgrave Ludwig had to pawn a country estate. He exemplifies the rule that children often choose interests and life goals opposite to those of their parents. He turned into a reverse image of his milieu. Despite his young age at the time of assuming political responsibilities, he grew into a fiscally responsible and prudent ruler. The army of poets and minstrels, whether talented or barely so, disappeared. Wartburg castle became quiet. The young landgrave matured in step with his bride Elisabeth. As a political leader, rejecting his milieu resulted in vigorous reforms; as a practitioner of spiritual poverty, Elisabeth chose to renounce society entirely.

The change from a life devoted to the hustle and bustle of festivities to that of a frugal household economics motivated especially the clerical authors of his era to characterize Ludwig as a representative of ascetical and ecclesiastical piety. This is incorrect. Neither his participation in the sixth crusade (as was true for all his social peers) nor his seemingly puritanical views (such as his strict rules about the use of profanities, obscenities, and blasphemies at court) ought to be interpreted as evidence of an especially religious or ascetical bent. On the contrary, Ludwig displayed plenty of savvy political instinct. In contrast to the capricious decisions of his paternal predecessor, he pursued a straight path. He was devoted to the emperor, yet also canny enough to not cross the papal curia.

With sociopolitical insight, he supported and legalized his wife Landgravine Elisabeth's unusual and generous charity. He understood that his father's politics caused the misery of pauperized peasants. The exorbitant financial and militaristic strain on the country had forced them into a life of begging and debt accumulation. Ludwig's *Vita* notes:

> He was afraid and shocked when the retainers who served him had to offer penance because of a transgression or wickedness, yet he did not like it when justice was not served. He wisely found a compromise in such conflicts so that secular ways were affirmed. He allowed for the imperial

laws to be enforced yet was wise in his own right and capable of making [independent] decisions. Ready to exercise compassion, he examined the case of impoverished criminals who had committed all types of crime. He felt greater love for those who were inwardly poor than for the powerful and noble. He aided and protected orphans. He offered fatherly comfort to those who suffered. His life is illuminated by the light of charity as he was gentle, humble, and strict with himself but genial with others. He taught and encouraged those who had stumbled. His life and conduct were adorned with the precious jewels of numerous virtues, especially compassion, to such a degree that he felt a special sympathy with the poor who were condemned in court proceedings. He disliked shedding blood except when justice had to be served.

This almost awestruck praise of the young landgrave's unusual administrative virtues was penned by his chaplain Berthold, who seems to have been very fond of him. In his *Vita St. Elisabeth*, Caesarius von Heisterbach, free of Berthold's court-related dependency on Ludwig, commended the landgrave, noting that, "He established such a long-lasting era of peace for his duchy that it appeared as if the age of Augustus had returned to Thuringian lands and those whose were under its rule."

Landgrave Ludwig's sense of justice, his social disposition, and his political steadfastness would have been sufficient to garner a reputation as the finest medieval ruler if his wife Elisabeth had not exceeded his renown. As a well-recognized model of aristocratic care for the community and country, Elisabeth's fame caused an accidental confluence of family politics and historical circumstance that eclipsed Ludwig's achievements. The truth is, however, that the landgravine's generous and uncommon charity, which is the cause of her fame, would not have been possible without her husband's benevolent assistance and sponsorship. The church valued his loyalty to his saintly wife's limitless charitable efforts only as ancillary; for this reason, Landgrave Ludwig IV of Thuringia was never officially canonized. Yet by spontaneous popular sentiment, he received the epithet "the saint." The young landgrave acquired his repute of extraordinary strength of character not only because of his administrative benevolence and intelligence but also because of his matchless personal attitude. Chaplain Berthold gushed over "the peculiar Joseph who was exclusively faithful to his spouse." While Ludwig's saintly virtues may seem to be matter of fact by today's bourgeois standards, he transgressed the moral standards of his peers and his age.

Ludwig was often forced to live for months separated from his wife. Finally, having observed him closely, noblemen in his company made a comment that was out of line with chivalric values: "Lord, why don't you act like other dukes and aristocrats? Since you are rarely spending time with our Lady, and since it must be difficult in your youth to live like that, why don't you get a few girls?" Ludwig remained silent. After some time, they asked him the same question. According to Caesarius von Heisterbach, he answered angrily, "My Lords, if you care for my patronage, be careful not to repeat such words. I have a wife and feel bound to her in faithfulness." A similar scene has been recorded by Chaplain Berthold. According to vulgar sexual views, which are still present among certain army officers and student circles today, a man is only a man if he has more than one "broad." Aristocratic Thuringian men were not too pleased with what they observed about their leader. What were they to do if the highest-ranking aristocrat, whose lifestyle set the social norm, was surpassing them in virtue?

There exist several even more telling anecdotes about the landgrave's chastity. They all follow the same plotline. Once, a nobleman who hosted Ludwig wished to be attentive to his guest's needs and offered his friend and peer a female companion for the night. However, the landgrave ordered her to be led away and remarked that, "truthfully, even if I didn't care about the sinfulness and depravity of adultery, I would not want to cause misery for my beloved spouse and sister Elisabeth." It should be noted, however, that the host's attentive nocturnal gift was not an expression of frivolity, but the gradually disappearing feudal expression of an original and conventional offer of promiscuity provided for guests.

Precisely because the landgrave was a happily married man, nothing was further from his mind than puritanical sexual conduct. The "peculiar chastity" noted with appreciation by his ecclesiastical biographers should rather be understood as an already strongly individualized sexuality, which aims at loyalty to a specific person. Oddly enough, for Ludwig this person was his wife. Throughout the Middle Ages, a demand of exclusive physical and sexual fidelity applied only to women but not to men. Besides, marriage as such was not the domain of individualized eroticism. As for Ludwig, the elevation of a Christian patriarchal peer marriage to loving personal companionship was an unusual anticipation of future norms. It even included male physical faithfulness.

Another rather unusual story told in praise of his virtue illustrates Ludwig's sense of humor, camaraderie, presence of mind, and upper hand in risky situations:

At that time in Thuringia, a knight lived in a castle at the forest's edge. He was married to a beautiful and noble wife, but they had no offspring. This was the fault of the husband and not the wife. The knight was saddened that his castle and extensive possessions should fall to heirs outside the family. One night he complained about this to his wife and let her know that he would rather have her produce an heir by a secret dalliance with another man than that he would have to bequest his property begrudgingly to other people. Modestly, his wife objected and said, "I would rather beg for bread as a widow." The knight countered that he would find a man who would protect her honor and mentioned the virtuous Landgrave Ludwig who was said to be so chivalrous, pious, and wise that the knight would approve of receiving an heir through Ludwig's assistance. He managed to have his wife agree to the plan. Then the knight rode to Wartburg castle, appeared before his Lord the Landgrave, lamented his dire straits and asked him for advice and assistance without being insulted by the request. The landgrave smiled at him and named a day for a visit. The wise and god-fearing landgrave then sent for his medical experts and ordered them to make a strong salve to help with the knight's predicament. When the agreed-upon day arrived, Landgrave Ludwig went hunting in the forest with his medicine box tucked away in his hunting satchel. During the hunt, he left his hunters, so they would not know his whereabouts and made for the knight's castle. He was received with joy and amity and provided with food and drink in abundance. When the host, hostess, and Landgrave Ludwig sat by themselves in a room, the Landgrave took his salve container and put some of it in the knight's wine. They continued to sit together in good spirits. After a little while, the knight could feel the power of the unguent and since the bedtime hour had arrived, the host asked his wife to leave and spoke to his lord, "Dear merciful Lord, please do not be cross with me if I have a matter to discuss with you. I thank your Highness for your visit, but I beg you to take gracious leave. The reason for your visit and my concern has vanished." The Landgrave laughed and said, "I did not visit to sin with a woman, but to relieve you of your infirmity." He gave him the container with the salve and left the castle that very same evening.

The well-intentioned childless knight's solution for resolving the question of heirs is congruent with ancient German customs and conventions yet appeared antiquarian to a "modern" person of the thirteenth century such as Landgrave Ludwig. The landgrave, amicable and superior, grasped the awkward request for what it was: the naïveté of a helpless, somewhat old-fashioned noble. Ludwig is "enlightened," consults scientific methods, and responds with a good-natured smile to the sorrows of his vassal. With poise, he directs matters in such a way that he does not insult the good knight with his assistance.

Courtly Love and Marriage

For medieval women as well, marriage did not constitute a matter of love. As the foundation of social and sexual order, marriage entailed nothing but duty and law. Marriages were a tool to consolidate dynastic aristocratic power and, as was true for other estates, the merger of fields and livestock. Since marriage was not the private affair of people in love, both partners could maintain a matter-of-fact approach. In its most finely tuned repercussions, the moral stance of patriarchal family arrangements that a marriage is not to be entered into as an individual expression of love, but as a self-evident social duty, remained in place until deep into the eighteenth century. Sexual morality changed decisively into its opposite only in the age of individualism, when personal inclination and freely chosen love became the chief characteristic of dignified sexual relationships. This ethical attitude has become so pervasive in contemporary society that relationships formed not by "love" but because of business interests are considered obscene. The latter, lesser motives, when existing, must be carefully kept a secret. By way of illustration, the very distinctive expression to refer to children born out of wedlock as "children of love" is obviously meant to imply that children born in a marital union are indeed not "children of love." As a socio-historical medieval survival, this expression is quite instructive. It has become nearly incomprehensible today given the obvious contemporary acceptance of love marriages.

For a medieval woman, a marriage of duty in an era of extreme patriarchy brought work and pregnancies, but no eroticism. This is precisely the reason for the phenomenon of courtly love. Inclinations of the heart and intensely personal feelings needed to be compensated outside of marriage, because marriages were not based on individual affective choices but on early parental decisions on behalf of their children. Landgrave Ludwig's marriage is therefore rather "abnormal." The object of courtly love was the wife of another man but never a young girl. Courtly love came into being as a rebellion against patriarchal marriage and an expression of a personal desire for freedom and love. Despite its emphasis on extramarital relations, courtly love was not frivolous. In the history of human psychology, it constitutes a giant step forward. For the first time, heterosexuality becomes individualized. Most importantly, women stop being merely an object of male sexuality. Women can freely choose to gift what was previously and still is defined as male prerogative in a patriarchal marriage. A sophisticated and soulful *ars amandi* flourished under these conditions; erotic tension and melancholic intimacy originated in the space between a simultaneous possession and non-possession of the other.

It is therefore not wrong to define aristocratic courtly love as practiced in the west and south of Germany and Austria as an era of women's freedom and women's rule. However, historians of culture in particular overlook the fact that the unescapable counterpoint to courtly love was the institution of unsentimental, androcentric, and caste-specific marriage. Landgrave Ludwig's marriage presents the unusual psychological situation, much admired by his contemporaries, in which he refused to act as the head of a patriarchal Christian marriage and did not take advantage of the male aristocratic right to extramarital relations. In his generation, his sexual lifestyle garnered a reputation of saintliness. Given the rare characteristics of St. Elisabeth's husband, the question arises how the wife of such a kind and enlightened man could turn to asceticism and world denial, even passionately fight against her own femininity. As a wife and high-ranking aristocrat, Landgravine Elisabeth could expect much from her society. Her short life was lived in the heyday of courtly love, which was cultivated extensively at the court where she grew up.

Much like her spouse, the young Elisabeth followed an unusual and extraordinary path. She loved her own husband. Landgravine Elisabeth chose neither of the two choices that constituted a medieval woman's preordained path: an austere and unsentimental arranged marriage or the daring eroticism of courtly love. Unconsciously, guileless folk historiography is on the mark when it glorifies the unusual faithfulness of the young aristocratic couple. Today, we would barely register that very young spouses are deeply in love and attached to each other. In contrast, the *Libellus* notes:

> There was such affectionate love between St. Elisabeth and her spouse Landgrave Ludwig that neither could bear being without the other for long. She had the habit of sitting next to her spouse at her Lordship's table, which was not the custom at other aristocratic houses, eating and conversing with him. St. Elisabeth followed her Lordship wherever he was, near or far, and shunned neither rain nor frost.

By rare coincidence and luck, two human beings agreed on this pivotal and extremely unconventional view of marriage even though it was politics and convention that had brought them together. Both had overcome the brutally antagonistic relationship between physical and psychological attraction and devotion, and even more fundamentally, between love and marriage. The young landgravine might almost be perceived as being heartbreakingly dependent on her spouse. Permanently threatened and uprooted during childhood, she focused all sense of home and belonging on a person assigned to her by convention. According to the *Libellus*,

> She already performed all works of compassion and good reputation during her husband's lifetime, and she lived with him in an admirable marriage. They loved each other with astounding affection and encouraged each other graciously to pious service in praise of the Divine.

It greatly astonished contemporaries that their marriage was not only a matter of fine companionship but also of great tenderness. Chaplain Berthold notes that when reunited, "she kissed him nearly a thousand times on the mouth." Yet not everybody was pleased with such harmony. The young landgravine's austere budget cuts, with which she thwarted the old regime's dashing and grand lifestyle, could not be blocked. Scheming against her was useless, since the young landgrave remained the closest friend and protector of the young woman. He guarded and promoted his wife's way of life and religious inclinations at all times. The oldest sources underscore that this was not an easy task. Unsurprisingly, complaints were brought before him that she wasted her own funds, and likely also those of the aristocratic household, on the poor instead of sharing them with her peers. Ludwig bestowed upon her unconditional financial authority without denying the validity of his vassals' point of view. When he was once again reminded of his wife's actions after having been away for quite some time, his only comment was, "As long as we can keep the Neuenburg and the Wartburg castles." Personal affection combined with political savvy propelled him to back his wife while keeping peace in the castle and his family.

It was the ideal of physical and psychological accord rather than saintly asceticism or harsh puritanical morals that formed the exceptional marriage of Landgravine Elisabeth and Landgrave Ludwig. The *Libellus* offers detailed accounts in those sections that—seemingly contradictorily—describe Elisabeth's marital abstinence and prayer regimen. Soon after her wedding, the young landgravine began a rigorous nocturnal penitential regimen—first independently, then under the guidance of her confessor. She left the marital bedstead and knelt to pray for long intervals. Young and exhausted, she fought drowsiness but remained prostrate on the carpet in front of the bed. The landgrave, unhappy and worried about her torturous sleep deprivations, only asks for her to return to him before too long. Although the nightly routine does not appeal to him, he gives her free rein with consideration for her wellbeing. He held her hand while she prayed. According to the *Libellus*:

St. Elisabeth often asked her maidservants to wake her up at night so that she could pray at special nocturnal hours, and only when her spouse slept or pretended to sleep. They were afraid to make their Lordship angry when waking her and asked for a signal. She ordered them to pull her foot. It once happened that Isentrud pulled her Lordship's foot when she meant to wake her Lady, because he had turned his leg toward his lady's side. He awoke, noticed what had happened, and endured it patiently.

This situation, transmitted by primary sources, would strike us as very funny if it did not testify to the landgrave's unusual tenderness and refusal to exercise his customary patriarchal marital prerogatives. When, after a joyful time together, his adolescent wife withdraws to reassert her sense of self, prayer is her chosen means. Caring deeply for her, he protects the need for independence and self-preservation of a young person who had just begun to come into her own through passionate religiosity. He is free of the erotic mistakes of uncouth men who interpret a woman's need for boundaries as feminine flirtation and a disguised invitation for further intimacy.

The marriage produced three children: Hermann, the oldest, was born in 1222, and two years later, Sophie. Another daughter, Gertrude, was born in 1227, soon after her father's death. It is probable that the landgravine was strongly attached to her biological children, since she was widely known to have dedicated herself to the care of destitute children even during the wretched years of her widowhood. While none of the historical and legendary sources narrate a specific situation that sheds light on the nature of her motherhood, we can guess the extent of the suffering caused by her initial fight for her children. Later in life, when confronted with the choice to either live in the unpretentious hospital that she founded or to live the life of an ordinary widow, she selected to relinquish her children. The subsequent character development of such a feminine and child-loving woman might have been prompted by the separation from her children.

Even though Elisabeth's marriage was an unusually happy one, her character's tragic disposition did not result in the exclusive faithfulness to one man only. After a few years of marriage, Konrad von Marburg made his appearance in the castle. With her husband's knowledge, the landgravine soon became dominated by her confessor in all aspects of her life. Due to this relationship, little of the marital bond remained intact for the landgrave, even though he endorsed Elisabeth's relationship with her confessor.

In the final analysis, the adolescent landgravine and her happy marriage fell victim to a man whose age and religious status were far in advance of both landgrave and landgravine. He inspired fear even among more experienced and powerful aristocratic contemporaries. Religious historians have applied their own value system to interpret the willingness with which the landgrave released his wife into the custody of a religious figure. In their view, accepting the authority of a religious guide and counsellor as superior to his own marital rights made Ludwig the perfect husband.

His sheer limitless patience raises the question whether the young landgrave's masculine identity was fully developed. However, his character, his substantial political savvy, presence of mind, good-natured superiority, and his allegedly ample physical qualities seem to preclude a role as an inexperienced and marginalized player in this *ménage à trois*. In any case, the landgrave seems to have felt the religious relationship's ambiguity more acutely than a spouse addicted to religious authoritarianism. Despite her unbridled servitude to a religious tyrant, Elisabeth's commitment to her husband never slackened. The end of their loving relationship is so romantic and touching that nobody today would dare to invent it. In this case, all details are authentic and "historically" accurate.

After six years of marriage, Ludwig joined the crusades. A few weeks after his departure and before he had set foot on the Holy Land, news arrived of his death. He was twenty-seven years of age. Precisely because it was so happy, Elisabeth's marriage turned into the cause of her demise. Without an extended family but with a strong inner sense of opposition against her milieu, she had focused her love and social needs on this one human being. Widowed at the age of twenty, her life turned toward an uncompromising asceticism. Without loyalties to her feudal social milieu, she refused to live through the life stages of an ordinary aristocratic woman. When she found herself in difficult circumstances vis-à-vis her husband's kin and vassals, she destroyed the last ties to home and country and threw herself into the arms of holy Lady Poverty. All her activities from this point on were repercussions of the one great calamity that befell her: the loss of the person who signified home and love to her.

Christian Asceticism and Its Modern Misinterpretation

St. Elisabeth's saintly virtues, her simple if not shabby dress code, her nightly prayer exercises and avoidance of sexual relations, and her gestures of self-humiliation and self-abasement are all behavioral expressions of asceticism. Sexual abstinence is one of its most noble challenges, yet not the only one. Elisabeth often rose at night to pray. Due to the long duration of the prayers, she frequently fell asleep on the carpet in front of the marital bed. According to the *Libellus*, her maidservants asked why she didn't prefer to sleep next to her husband. She answered, "Since I can't pray at all times, I thus force myself to be separated from my beloved spouse."

She asked to be awakened at night so as not to miss the hours of prayer. Apart from these common penitential practices, she also demanded that the maidservants flagellate her during fasts before major church holidays. A full-fledged portrait of "repression" seems to emerge if we add other types of the newlywed woman's self-punishment, her complaint to her confessor that she had lost her virginity, and her solemn vow to not remarry should she become widowed. These traits, characteristic for a common type of saint, will be used by an average cultural historian to build the cliché of a pitiful monk or nun: fraught with guilt, incapable of a natural balance between body and soul, and imbued with such inhibitions and repression that not even natural sexual relations in socially sanctioned circumstances are permitted. Even restorative and relaxing sleep, the innocent toll to be paid to nature, becomes frowned upon.

However, the young wife Elisabeth's nightly sleep interruptions, the fanatically adhered to prayer schedule, her worries about loving her spouse too much, the need to withdraw after joyful times spent with him—all these seemingly perverse self-tortures should merely be interpreted as "healthy" and natural reactions by an adolescent girl who became a mother for the first time at the age of fifteen. She withdraws from situations that she does not experience as unpleasant—she admits that she was happy. She justifiably feels that they have been psychologically overwhelming. Her ego, the center of her intellectual self, wants to protect itself from the premature onset of sexual experiences and maternity. She is not entirely a child anymore, yet neither is she of adult age.

The nocturnal penitential exercises and marital refusals can be interpreted as proof that, although still a child as defined by our contemporary standards, she was a human being with a desire for a life that transcended sexuality. Modern science would construe this type of "neurosis" as self-punishment for a sexuality experienced as sinful. However, these behaviors should be understood instead as an effort for female self-preservation and as a defense of the overwhelmed young ego encountering psychological pressure.

The precondition for medieval asceticism is not an a priori repressive and anti-sensual view of the world as such. Rather, it derives from its opposite. As a matter of course, medieval men and women were sexually active at a very early age. In the Middle Ages, young people entered the full status of adulthood with all its responsibilities and professional and marital duties at an age when their modern peers are still treated with gentleness and supervised to make sure they attend school.

Even Luther, who is not considered a denizen of the medieval world, and whose sexual ethics became formative for the bourgeois epoch of Protestantism, notes in his *Little Book of Marriage* (*Ehebüchlein*) that the best age to get married is between eighteen and twenty for males and between fifteen and eighteen years for females. In medieval legal texts, the age of female marital maturity was set between thirteen and fifteen—a rule abolished only now in the extremely conservative English legal system. This implies that the life stage we call adolescence is completely absent in the medieval period proper. With the onset of puberty, a person was considered to be fully adult. Nobody was surprised when Konradin, the last Hohenstaufen, began his political career at the age of sixteen.[11] Courtly society did not consider him a child. Landgrave Ludwig, St. Elisabeth's spouse, assumed his father's rule as a seventeen-year-old. His contemporaries considered him to be a young lord rather than a child. In this manner, medieval people could already enjoy rights and desires as youths for which today's twenty-five-year-olds still thirst.

For this reason, the sexual act was such a normal occurrence that being deprived of it was unheard of. Furthermore, not only did medieval men and women marry earlier, but they also married more frequently. On average, men married two to three times and women twice.[12] Mortality rates were extremely high due to the physical wear and tear of early marriage for women and the frequency of military duties for men. This is also true for Elisabeth of Thuringia. Married as an adolescent, she became a widow with three young children at the age of twenty. She was legally entitled to give orders to others at the age of fifteen. This life rhythm was entirely normal for a medieval woman specifically and a medieval person generally. It was especially true, commonplace, and internally consistent for the aristocracy. Men and women had to be married early without consideration of their love interests. Patrimony had to be upheld as an institution to preserve property holdings and to advance political connections. Love marriages would have eventually destroyed aristocratic privilege. Non-aristocratic men and women married a little later, and according to our own standards, yet still without being fully adult.

The increasingly frantic tempo of modern social life inversely decreased the developmental stages of contemporary adulthood. Our present era

---

11   He received the diminutive name "Little Konrad" (Konradin) from the Italians because he was even shorter than the already petite members of the Hohenstaufen dynasty generally.

12   One should note, however, that women were in the majority in Western Europe during the fourteenth and fifteenth centuries, accounting for an up to twenty percent higher population number due to early widowhood.

necessitates the longest possible protection of the human nervous system and therefore provides for a rather extensive adolescence. A dangerous development can already be detected at the end of the nineteenth century when the stage of non-adulthood becomes extremely prolonged. The already quite adult man or women must deal with a tragic delay of independent living. This negative development, however, also engendered a positive discovery. Adolescence yielded an entirely new life phase, puberty. Although puberty has become recognized as valuable and unique, and is admittedly an immensely important psychological gain, its recovery served at once to sanction a state of semi-adulthood that could seem interminable.

A contemporary delay of the onset of adulthood seems as unhealthy as its untimely early beginning in the Middle Ages. Nonetheless, scholars, pedagogues, and moralists alike have extolled both as proper and good. Every generation and gender experience their own burdens as fundamentally natural and healthy. We have legal proposals to extend guardianship for men and women until the age of twenty-five. The twenty-five to thirty-year-old "young girl" has evolved into a seemingly healthy and normal social phenomenon. A fifty-year-old male still waits for success because he cannot gain access to leading positions in politics, administration, or business before then, even though he has entered the final third of his life. The freedom of the individual, this gift of the Renaissance and modernity, turned out to be a Trojan horse because it contains a compensatory period of extended suspension that covers at least half of one's life span. It is highly instructive that the discovery of "repression" coincides with the peak of the economic crisis in the last third of the nineteenth century. Even in the first half of the nineteenth century, psychoanalysis would not have been relevant to the extent that it is today. At that time, a male could achieve rank and office at the age of twenty-five rather than being artificially delegated to a second puberty. Likewise, a young woman was considered fully adult at the age of sixteen.

The early customary enjoyment of all that life could offer a medieval person also encouraged a type of behavior abhorrent to a modern person, namely asceticism. An asceticism of power, defined by medieval moral psychology as humility, and sexual asceticism, defined as chastity, must be explained as acts of self-preservation by a human being of whom was asked too much too early. This is true for all social ranks. Everybody was satiated before even feeling hungry.

As members of this late bourgeois epoch, we are inclined to arrive at false conclusions when reflecting on the unique emotional disposition of medieval asceticism. They are based on our own compulsory deprivations, of our own belated entry into full adulthood, and of our youth's dangerous and destructive inability to move forward. We feel sorry for the medieval nun without comprehending that the secular asceticism of a modern bourgeois wife, who in the best-case scenario may experience sex and love at the very end of her youth, is far harsher and more severe than the spiritual life of nuns. Monastic enclosure did not so much signify a torturous denial of sexuality than self-protection from sex that was too early and too much. It constituted the only possibility for female emancipation. A woman could achieve intellectual self-actualization in at least some monastic orders. If talented and suitable for administrative tasks, she could rise to positions of leadership and power as an abbess. Asceticism in this sense signified freedom, not pressure.

One cannot overlook, however, the gloomier aspects of asceticism, which aim at a weakening of vitality and libido. Monks and nuns self-flagellated and invented scores of other penitential exercises to curtail their sex life. They did not always freely choose chastity. Parents with many children bought a monastic place for them early in life. From a demographic perspective, monasteries functioned as an asylum for a male and female population surplus. Those who were forced into it had to find their own psychological ways of coping. For these reasons, despair and torment did exist behind monastery walls, but the dangerous phenomenon of repression did not. Sexuality was freely visible to everybody; the enemy was in full view. Denial and rejection, which cause repression in the unconscious in the first place, were impossible. Rather, asceticism signifies more than anything the recognition of sexuality as a great and powerful force. Everybody was clear about what was at stake in this fight with "the devil." In contrast, our generation has "forgotten" this fact. In the Middle Ages, knowledge of the erotic existed undisguised and for everybody. The Saxon aristocratic canoness Hrotsvit of Gandersheim, esteemed today as the most learned woman of her century and the most learned person of the Ottonian Renaissance, composed plays for the use of her monastery to avoid use of offensive texts written by ancient Greek and Roman authors. Hrotsvit had lived in a monastery since the age of twelve and thus had no "past" of her own. Yet her works often display such juicy erotic vividness that the question arises, what must the erotic knowledge of illiterate nuns, lay women, or even men have been like?

The sexual practices of two different eras are ultimately beyond comparison. Identically occurring activities like infidelity must be judged on their own due to their specific historical conditions. However, we can generate an objective value standard if every era is analyzed on its own terms with self-critical contemporary judgment. In this manner, seemingly incomparable and absolute facts will become immediately relativized. An average and unremarkable member of today's bourgeoisie, especially in its late manifestation, would thus appear to be far more ascetical than a medieval person whose asceticism evoked immense admiration among her peers.

According to the documented moral standards of the medieval millennium, it took very little effort to gain a reputation for a "singular chastity," whether the judge was religious or a lay person. If a man or woman refused an unequivocal invitation to have sex, it was reported as a noteworthy deed. Spicy stories of attempted seduction are part and parcel of narrating a saint's youth, such as the adolescent years of the rightfully famous and distinguished St. Bernard of Clairvaux. In every case, a saint resists. Today, no man can claim saintly chastity if he refuses the solicitation of professional sex workers. Our contemporary standards of sexual morality appear to be far stricter and, in every way, more ascetical. What once counted as the ultimate challenge has turned into the barest of requirements. If fulfilled, it does not make an impression.

As for the lives of medieval lay people, the moral yardstick was set even lower. Both lay and religious literature attest to it. At the end of the fourteenth century, the Knight of Thurn composed a devotional book for his young daughters, or "teenage girls," as we would say today. His "exemplars of the fear of God and respectability" exclusively discuss infidelity and successful seductions. Women were considered "honorable" and "virtuous" if their sexual activities stopped short of actual intercourse. The practice of courtly love confirms this view. Whoever did not avail herself of these liberal conventions stood out.

The many anecdotes from the life of St. Elisabeth's spouse are equally instructive of the medieval scale of sexual morals. At the age of seventeen, Landgrave Ludwig assumed his father's reign. Five years later, he married his bride, the future St. Elisabeth. His entourage and court seemed to have taken note that he did not "enjoy" himself with other women in the meantime. One of the older aristocrats at court decided to test whether Ludwig was indeed "normal." The reason: "Rumors started that he was not able to consummate a marriage." As was to be expected, he splendidly resists the effort to seduce him. Even if monks invented this story to demonstrate Ludwig's unusual chastity, the implicit principles at work in the story are plain enough. If someone today would have to wait until the age of twenty-one to get married and refrain from sexual contact with women up until then, nobody would think him to be abnormal or a chaste saint, as was the case for medieval people.

These and other examples are not evidence of a sexual deviance typical of the aristocracy. Among the peasantry, these attitudes were, if anything, even more explicit and direct. Neidhart von Reuental composed a dialogue between a peasant mother and her daughter in which the mother opines that the daughter, barely sixteen years old, is too young for marriage. The daughter responds, "Oh mother, you had already lost your virginity as a twelve-year-old." Likewise, a secular cleric who kept to his celibacy almost amounted to a spectacle. Throughout the Middle Ages, sexual abstinence was never maintained as strictly as among today's Catholic priesthood, at least in German-speaking countries. The only reason the priest Konrad of Marburg could cohabit with the widowed landgravine in Marburg was that his strict adherence to monastic rule caused a sensation and generated widespread respect. This proves that to remain celibate was not a given.

Medieval moral standards in the realm of sexuality were far lower than the secular asceticism of modernity, but we also greatly overestimate the individual performance of physical penitence as an ascetical practice of medieval saints and monastics. There is no doubt that dreadful self-inflicted penitential tortures took place. Between the ages of eighteen and forty, Henry Suso, hardly a world-despiser, but rather someone with an affable temperament who appreciated women, carried a wooden plank studded with nails that bore into his naked flesh. The deeds of other saints are comparable to Suso's penitential activities. Nonetheless, holy men's efforts to curb their sexual drive by bathing in cold water, such as a mountain lake, were praised as "heroic deeds," whereas modern athletic men always practice this physical discipline consciously or unconsciously without making much of it. One might even state that if a medieval monk or a nun extolled for their severe mortifications of the flesh would be asked to engage in the physical efforts and performances that are entirely normal for a modern person when at work or playing sports, they would tightly grip a crucifix and appeal to the Virgin Mary and all saints to protect them from such appalling tortures. Yet in today's world, mountaineers who push themselves up a rocky chimney with bloodied hands, the pilot who is suspended between heaven and earth in fog and icy cold, and finally also the young hikers who "clock" their forty miles with only little food and who sleep on a cot—all perform a completely normalized secular asceticism whose severity would have made many a monastic ascetic professional declare defeat in the Middle Ages.

Elisabeth's Intentions

St. Elisabeth's ascetical self-inflicted torment during the first half of her life thus should not be judged as an expression of an unnatural lack of poise. The young Elisabeth had not the least aptitude for the life of a nun. Likewise, she never envisioned the Franciscan beggar's poverty as part and parcel of monastic life, a poverty ideal which she embraced both in religious and moral terms later in her life. Her nocturnal penitential exercises, undertaken despite a happy marriage, her austere dress code, and the renunciation of dance, play, and courtly love are, rather, productive expressions of an adolescent who fought for her self-preservation and sense of self. Similarly, in her view, the vow to remain a lifelong widow and her regret not to have kept her virginity constituted merely a desire for spiritual values. Early widowhood was extremely likely for a woman of her era, and another marriage customary and a matter of course.

Our saint can also not be suspected of one major reason for ascetical behaviors—neither the young landgravine nor her spouse belonged to those of few means. As is true for most great female and male ascetics of the Middle Ages, St. Elisabeth was not only intellectually, but also physically well-developed and therefore spared any potentially reactive hatred of life. Admittedly, the legendary tradition of noting her beauty is conventional. Some historical sources testify that her physical appearance showed her to be more the daughter of her Hungarian father than of her German mother. Her skin was brown, her hair black, and her eyes dark. She was small and delicately built. Short references such as these can be found in the late writings of Père Archange (1693) and Ursinus (1547), both of which depend on a French hagiographic tradition of Elisabeth legends. In any case, the physical representation of Elisabeth, who was frequently depicted in medieval art and whose image became typologically standardized in nineteenth-century art, did not exemplify the ideal of a tall and powerful Thusnelda appearance. A woman who gives birth to three children before the age of twenty and keeps severe fasting vows during her pregnancies could not have looked other than lean and slender. As concerns her external appearance, Elisabeth certainly must have looked "Gothic" in the popular sense: narrow shoulders and hips, a childlike body with an adult face.

Even though a slight and delicate little person, her brunette type stood out in a crowd of other women. She made an impression, as demonstrated by many legendary stories such as the following episode by Dietrich von Apolda. Dietrich transcribed it from an oral tradition, but it is remotely possible that the priest, who surely must have enjoyed sharing the anecdote, still knew Elisabeth personally:

> At a time when St. Elisabeth stood in attendance of Holy Mass, keeping her
> hands under her coat and praying fervently, she was surrounded by such an

abundance of heavenly clarity that one could barely look at her. This was observed by a pious priest whose eyes were opened by God so that he could see her face lit up by a brilliance like the sun's rays; for this reason, he had to avert his eyes. The good man was secretly in shock because of what he saw, but he praised the Lord God for it and revealed everything in his honor.

The good priest allowed himself to be impressed by the attractiveness of the young woman in prayer, and for a short time, lost his composure, became confused, and "had to avert his eyes." This story exemplifies the enchantment the young woman could exert over him and certainly not just over him.

In its second half, Saint Elisabeth's life displayed a very different type of nun's life. Following her failure to live independently in the small town of Eisenach, she turned her back to the secular world as a Franciscan penitent in exclusive service to the poorest and sickest men and women at Marburg's hospital. However, this renunciation, the separation from everything she loved, from her female companions and her children, did not occur entirely as an act of free will. Rather, Elisabeth was forced into this role by her disciplinarian master. As the wife of Landgrave Ludwig, she renounced dancing, participation in the fashion of the day, and the full exercise of her aristocratic privileges. Nonetheless, she was at that time without hatred for the secular world. The Marburg phase of her life, however, was entirely different. Personal destiny pulled the isolated woman into bitterness. She once cut a girl's beautiful braid without a semblance of legitimate reason, spitefully arguing, "Thus you'll at least stop attending dances!" (*Libellus*). The difference between voluntary austerities that strengthen, invigorate, and offer support, and a forced renunciation which results in another woman's humiliation is clearly visible in Elisabeth's two stages of asceticism.

When Landgrave Ludwig died, the young widow lost all will to live. In religious terms, she experienced her "awakening" at that point. She was only twenty years of age, but just like her, other, even exceptional, medieval personalities commenced their transition into the life of a hermit, or a monastic, and the renunciation of secular life as well. It would be wrong to define this sudden turn as merely a transient and curable secondary symptom of young adulthood. The psychological situation was the opposite. Elisabeth and her medieval peers chose to step into creative wretchedness from the starting point of a secure, stable, and abundant life. They were jaded. Those who find everything at their disposal at the age of fifteen are ready to forego all that the future might bring in their early twenties.

It is a common reaction among young people who encounter their first great sorrow to believe themselves incapable of continuing life. To them, the world has come to an end. When losing a beloved, they are certain that they will never love again; when experiencing failure, they are finished with trying—at least this is the conventional psychological viewpoint. Medieval people, however, remained in this frame of mind even if no other blow of fate assaulted them. Already at a young age, they refused to be healed. They clung to their intention to renounce and forego the world and life and continue to cultivate it. Such intentionality inevitably turns into the genesis of a new state. If persons under these conditions possess sufficient intellectual independence and psychological energy, they may begin a new life precisely in such a crisis. Yet this new life must be fundamentally different—supernaturally, spiritually—in short, it must be a saint's life. The frighteningly early wear and tear of vital energy, which, as has been argued above, fatefully affected both genders in the Middle Ages, also provided fertile soil for the transformation of an acute sense of disappointment in life into a permanent state of world-weariness and world-diffidence.

We have inherited a biological record in a work of high art which demonstrates with gruesome realism the premature and hopeless depletion of medieval human vigor. We are referring to the extraordinary portrait of his mother which Albrecht Dürer created in 1514. The chalk drawing is frightening. Drawn with medical precision, an owl-like aging head sits on a stick of bone and sinews rather than a neck. Even though this woman has long ago fulfilled her biological function, she continues to be alive, wizened, and bare like a tree that cannot yet topple. The frozen, vacant, and broken expression of the protuberant eyes can just barely communicate that the body continues to live against its own will, that life is a burden and a weight—a living corpse, the image of a hundred-year-old female. Yet in one corner of the drawing, we find the words, "This is Albrecht Dürer's mother, she was sixty-three years of age." Today, we are used to seeing women of this age being fully engaged in life. Dürer's mother, however, experienced a life cycle typical of a medieval woman. She married at the age of fifteen and gave birth to eighteen children. Her third was the painter Albrecht Dürer.[13] It was women's fate to give birth without pause.

---

13   Dürer and his parents lived in an age that we have labelled as medieval for quite some time because the attitude toward life in his century was still the same. We also know based on medieval art proper that the Gothic ideal of beauty was in no way healthy from a biological perspective. It is true that, especially in sculpture, stately female and tall male forms exist. Yet another type is very frequent: small heads sit on long necks, and overly long arms and hands, together with the accompanying facial expression, produce an impression of great helplessness. The shoulders are remarkably small, and even among men, the waists are unnaturally slender. Members of the German imperial dynasties, all of whom were born in adolescent marriages,

If she would not have had the good luck to die young, St. Elisabeth would have looked at us like the spent and hollow face of Dürer's mother. She fully experienced the precocious skepticism and nervous temperament of a medieval psyche but was spared the body's horrific physical destruction. Matured early and equally early exhausted, she retreated from the world much like many others of her kind. She awaited her death in conscious self-torment after much difficult psychological suffering. When death took her away at the age of twenty-four, she had become an old woman.

St. Elisabeth's creativity and religious impulse were shaped by a social order which threw a human being into the maelstrom of life prematurely and without consideration. Modern humanity is a prisoner of its own social order, much like a medieval religious person was hemmed in by hers. To justify their predicament, both have found a moral justification which enables them to endure their respective societies: a medieval religion of world denial and monastic life for one, secular asceticism for the other.

Both advocate for their ideals with a comparable idealism and passion. Both human types demonstrate their inner freedom and creative strength precisely in the ability to reinterpret, or rather, to reexperience the restrictions of disciplinary coercion which constrains them as a higher destiny. The monastic saint of the Middle Ages who ends up in retreat from the world, and the representatives of the late bourgeois era who live more ascetically than medieval monks and nuns because they are only permitted the legalized pleasures of life at a late age, they both become liberated through a creative affirmation of their distress. Both worldviews and emotional attitudes become the carriers of original and creative impulses through a social dialectic.

Patrimonial Charity and Christian Caritas

Even today, the region of Thuringia, with the Wartburg castle at its center, is one of the poorer German provinces. All its back country is covered by extensive forests. It was known as Germany's starvation zone in the nineteenth century. How miserable life must have been for people during the Hohenstaufen era. The landgrave ruled over this despondent populace of foresters, farmers, and charcoal burners, whose interest in his subjects only extended to whether they paid their taxes or not. His main concerns were

often tended to be intellectually gifted and above average. Yet none belonged to the type of the masculine Germanic warrior.

focused on the Italian imperial court. In 1226, a terrifying famine spread across all of Germany, caused by failed harvests and an increase in the cost of living.[14] Whereas the impoverished Thuringian population, surrounded by forests and paltry fields, could barely subsist in ordinary times, its situation turned disastrous during this nationwide state of emergency. Just one crop failure could cause despair and an utter loss of hope if no food could be imported from as yet unaffected regions. The pendulum swing between dull resignation and a deeply selfish greed for life, which is consistently reported to have occurred during times of plague, likely will have occurred during this famine as well.

Mass impoverishment even during normal times was an everyday social phenomenon in the early, high, and late Middle Ages. The proletarization of the peasant caste was rapid. A single failed harvest or the death of family members could ruin a peasant living in semi-bondage. Debt led to imprisonment and thus to absolute pauperization. In such manner, a medieval peasant's status declined to that of beggars, a caste of human beings who were formally recognized as a distinct social group. The beggar is the proletarian of the Middle Ages, but in distinction to the latter, they suffer from permanent unemployment. Once fallen into the caste of the vagrant homeless, they belong to it in perpetuity. The boundaries with the "traveling folk," the itinerant male and female musicians, jugglers, actors, and folk healers, remained fluid.

The gigantic army of beggars absorbed all the nearly destroyed human lives. It included those driven out of their huts onto country roads by the emperor's voyages to Rome, by the crusades, by aristocratic feuding, and by pauperization. Like flocks of birds, they descended upon towns, camped in front of castle gates and monastic doorways. The drifters and the homeless clung to the households of the wealthy, pleading for donations. These belonged predominantly to aristocrats and monastics.

An additional and separate category of the poor consisted of widows and orphans who joined the ranks of beggars either temporarily or in perpetuity. Medieval Christians considered the protection of widows and orphans as one of the main Christian virtues. This class of women was especially under duress because a widow enjoyed no legal social rights. In legal practice, she also had no inheritance rights. If it did not prove to be lucrative to remarry

---

14   The famine is widely assumed to have lasted from 1224 to 1226, yet some accounts limit it to the year 1226. It is likely that 1226, the last year of the reign of Landgrave Ludwig and Landgravine Elisabeth, was indeed the worst because of an epizootic outbreak. Once cattle and other domestic animals were annihilated, the destitute populace was condemned to mass death by famine.

her, she, too, suffered pauperization. The number of young widows exceeded that of other widowed age groups. Perpetual wars took their husbands. The custom of marrying girls at the onset of adolescence joined them frequently to significantly older men who died much earlier. Even without war, young wives thus quickly found themselves alone.

This caste of the disabled and the beggars, of widows and orphans, became the focus of Landgravine Elisabeth's charity. Material destitution went hand in hand with the terrifying public health of economically insecure social groups. Marriage at a young age, lifelong malnutrition, and alcohol use disorder produced an unknown number of infants with congenital disabilities. The beggars' caste absorbed these human beings as well, who were unfit for work and an unassisted life. With a lack of scientific insight into the cause of illness and complete helplessness when confronted with the spread of epidemics, paupers and beggars were always the first casualties of infectious diseases, and they, in turn, became carriers of contagion due to their vagrancy across regions and municipalities.

Between the turn of the first millennium and up until the eighteenth century, Western Europe was host to a steady succession of epidemics. Minor and major psychopathic illnesses, such as the St. Vitus Dance, occurred in tandem with the most terrifying menace, the plague and leprosy, neither of which disappeared during the medieval period. They made their appearance intermittently and effected mass death on a catastrophic scale. These commonplace illnesses fed on the Thuringian people's poverty, indigence, and unsanitary living conditions. They escalated the perils of famine.

All medieval human suffering was public. Modernity hides misery and keeps it locked up behind institutional walls. Those with mental health conditions, neurodiversity, and various disabilities; those with polio and microcephaly are today kept in institutions that remove them from the public eye. In the Middle Ages, however, they were always visible on public plazas or at fairs, and especially so in front of church portals and castles. They existed as living and grim ornaments of the most prestigious medieval architectural works because their numbers were by far greater than today relative to the size of the population overall.

The medieval solution of the "social question," a satisfactory care of these and other manifestations of human misery, was administered solely by recurrent solicitations for alms. The higher their social rank, the more "gentleness" was expected of the representatives of worldly power. Sometimes more, sometimes less so, the clergy continually pressured the high aristocracy to feed and clothe all those who hassled them—whether minstrels or the unwell. Besides such pleading, it always remained one of the main monastic duties to feed the hungry and provide shelter for the broken. The social-charitable innovations of the Catholic Church are immense, although they reached their full potential only as late as the Baroque era.[15]

The church was equipped for such tasks solely because of the material wealth ushered in by medieval donations and because of an army of supporters comprised of monks and nuns, those without property, and the spiritually destitute. Only they were furnished with the psychological preconditions necessary for service to the poor.

Charity as a self-evident moral obligation of secular and religious elites, however, conserved the class of beggars. Medieval society cultivated the custom and habit of begging. Once joining the caste of beggars, a poor person was not meant to regain the ability to work. The beggar's simple obligation was to pray for the donor's soul upon receiving alms. This form of charity, as much as it was embedded in the logic of a medieval religious worldview, carried the harmful social side effect of moral corruption. The habit of taking without an obligation to give something back in return will always be fatal. For this reason, as "secularized charity," contemporary secular social services on the federal and county level attempt as much as possible to empower indigent populations to become independent again, and to limit financial support without at least some contributions by its recipients. Even the 1922 disability laws aim to "turn every disabled person into a working member of society."[16]

In contrast, medieval charity lacked objective judgment of charity's harmful side effects, due to its religious foundation and aims. It was focused on the benefactor, not the recipient. The poor, the socially marginalized, and the unwell provided the welcome occasion for pious men and women, including Landgravine Elisabeth, to perform one of the three obligations necessary for a God-pleasing life, i.e., fasting, praying, and almsgiving. According to medieval sensibilities, worldly goods were sacrificed to receive a moral good. Charitable service functioned

---

15   So, for example, in the work of the Würzburg prince-bishop Julius Echter von Mespelbrunn (1545–1617), the extraordinarily successful founder of the most outstanding charitable institution, the Julius Hospital. It combined hospital, asylum, hostel, and nursing home for the elderly in one grand design.

16   Translator's note: The issue of how to care for those who were living with various disabilities, especially soldiers returning from theatres of war after World War I, was hotly debated in Weimar Germany and clearly influenced Busse-Wilson's historiographical reflections on the topic as this reference demonstrates. Disturbingly, euthanasia was suggested as a solution in some circles even then. See Carol Poore, *Disability in Twentieth-Century German Culture* (Ann Arbor: University of Michigan Press, 2007).

as a moral capital investment and as a security deposit in preparing for one's death. While "pious works" did not guarantee the right to a place in heaven, they offered an easier path to reach it. The understanding of charity as a moral capital investment well worth the effort is still reflected in the contemporary adage "Good deeds result in blessings." Pious medieval Christians gained high interest on their charitable works, their endowments, and their alms. At the moment of death, they withdraw the accumulated capital of good works. Well-endowed in this manner—and as the opposite of morally shabby have-nots—they enter eternity. This calculating character of religious sentiment is alien to us today, yet it extended even into mystical suffering. Christ gave so much in enduring his passion that human beings must rebalance the account through their own voluntary suffering. In this logic, poverty, misery, and illness are God's will and designed to punish original sin. They must not be abolished in order to offer opportunities for a more fortunate person to practice the Christian virtue of charity.

Such is the medieval gain of all acts of charity, even if they are as personal and kind as those of the landgravine of Thuringia. She humiliated herself and wore herself to the bone when nursing and caring for the old, those with physical disabilities, and the homeless. She pursued her duties with affection and compassion even during times of greatest sadness. In her own medieval worldview, not kindness but the asceticism embedded in this achievement was her true merit and work.

Charity thus formed an element of the far-reaching and all-pervasive willingness and aptitude for suffering that is emblematic of medieval religious men and women.[17] Whoever arranges for an exceedingly arduous life on earth might just be lucky in the next world, especially on the date which counted the most, Judgment Day. Christ himself kept the accounting record of all grievances and sorrows a human being freely chose when caring for each and all those who were unwell and in need. Thus disarmed, God would surely pronounce that neither toil not torment had been in vain—toil and torment would lead to eternal joy. For the poor, the hereafter was an equally fortifying concept. A materially concrete model of the afterlife was the only available possibility of democratizing and rebalancing the distance between rich and poor, contented and despondent. Death, the great equalizer, was the sole avenger of the destitute. The medieval depiction of the Dance of Death, which transports emperors, kings, and abbots to hell without distinction, is proof of the belief that all are equal before God.

17   See the section "The Art of Suffering" in Chapter 3.

The Transformation of Social Ethics

Today, nobody can stomach the kitsch of Renaissance ornaments—those spirals, pilaster strips, cupolas, and arches that even run of the mill artisans cram onto the most ordinary utilitarian buildings. There was a time, however, when the objects that today decorate every single wooden music pavilion once turned the world upside down. Today's ornamental kitsch was born in a storm of new ways of seeing and designing when their original creators Brunelleschi and Verrocchio dared to construct them in their hometown Florence.[18] Modernity's deluge of imitations and flattened reproductions compels us to see even the originals through such counterfeit filters.[19] The image of St. Elisabeth underwent similar changes. The standard for establishing the authenticity of her charity became rather blurred, because we unconsciously tend to bend our understanding of her original pursuits toward the activities that take place today under her name.

Viewed honestly, her type of medieval charitable works, propelled by a combination of aristocratic authoritarianism and wealth, is precisely what should not be practiced today. Landgravine Elisabeth's charity was originally a manorial custom whose favorite expression was almsgiving. Today, the social ethos has changed such that alms are experienced as an insult even to the poorest of the poor. Whoever among our contemporaries wishes to make a donation must be mindful to avoid the impression of almsgiving. Modern donors tend to be more impersonal when giving and receiving. They do not expect divine recognition or human gratitude. A woman dispensing charity today is therefore not any longer a benefactress but a bureaucrat who is fulfilling her duties in the service of a general improvement of the social order. Yet in the year 1225, a chatelaine's activities were quite different. Even in the year 1825, a version of the same attitudes was still rather common. The social distance between a female aristocrat and the impoverished life of her tenants and indentured peasants was experienced as divine law and unchangeable order. Both could thus rely on a transcendental foundation, the dependence on a divinely ordained fate. Loving care and consolation were dispensed and received without reserve, since neither party could imagine a radical change in the social order.

18   Filippo Brunelleschi (1377–1446), Renaissance polymath, is counted among the first modern architects and engineers. Andrea del Verrocchio (1435–1488) was an important Florentine sculptor, painter, and goldsmith.

19   Translator's note: As discussed in the introduction, Busse-Wilson wrote her dissertation on the history of ornaments; here is another example of how she used art history as a compelling analogue in support of her comparative cultural theses.

All of Landgravine Elisabeth of Thuringia's altruism constitutes mere moments of support with short-term impact, whether they concern cases of sickness, impoverishment, or debt. She cured symptoms. As the *Libellus* reports, "She once visited a destitute sick person. She overheard him lamenting his debts, which he was unable to pay. Therefore, she paid them for him." Yet the cause of debt and penury, that is, the medieval economic and legal system as such, did not interest her or any other representatives of medieval charity.

Despite the ideological conventionality of medieval almsgiving, Landgravine Elisabeth's charity demonstrates individual creativity. Compared to the static ethos of her social caste, her acts of kindness carried a vital and regenerative energy. Her personal attention to circumstances, which counted for even less in her aristocratic medieval milieu than today, testifies to the authenticity of her emotional engagement and ingenuity. She was truly fond of those who were disabled and infirm, the children and widows, who for other aristocrats presented merely a public social obligation to practice generosity. For this reason, she could put an individual face onto each member of this great mass of suffering humanity. Without vanity and a desire to be admired, she dedicated herself to her service.

All this proves that she drew from a novel attitude toward life. Those who lived with disability and destitution lined the roads and were barely ever noticed by her aristocratic peers. In contrast, she was able to perceive what others overlooked. Her moral gifts are based on such a psychologically sensitive acuity of perception. After a long day's ride, every traveler who arrived at the castles she called home received a warm bath with scented herbs. Yet attended by no one, the exiled and infirm, with their festering wounds and terrifying skin diseases, camped outside the gates. Elisabeth discovered that these unvalued creatures were human beings.

Conscience is the descendant of a moral vigilance that frequently leads to a rebellion against existing norms and traditions. Equipped with such a gift of discernment, human beings discover within and without social inconsistencies that become disturbing. The ensuing internal turmoil gives rise to nonconformist moral decisions. If active and creative, such human beings will create a new order, whether religious or social. Landgravine Elisabeth was not the founder of innovative social norms. Yet she is a consummate figure in Christian history. It is customary to contrast charitable Christian love with pre-Christian eros. Christian love itself does not recognize this distinction because it unites charity and eros. It perceives the same breath of eternity in all human creation, whether healthy and gifted or criminal and wretched.

Compassionate Christian love favors the unwell and weak, the insignificant and the less than beautiful. The Christian attitude toward life does not distinguish between up and down, high and low. For this reason, Christianity in the true sense is not hostile to life. It affirms life. According to Christianity, the divine exists no less in the breath of an infant than in the stammer of an old woman. This attitude requires a certain moral aptitude. Nobody can be taught to be a Christian. One must be born a Christian. In the Middle Ages, the landgravine of Thuringia was a person equipped with such Christian sensibilities.

In the present era of secular humanism, Christianity as the expression of an active love of neighbor is much more widely known and accepted than in the Christian Middle Ages. Protection and respect for every human life, including those without property and inheritance, has become an intellectual demand for self and society. The fundamental recognition of every person's individuality, even that of the socially underprivileged, was unknown during late antiquity, although it contained humanistic leanings.[20] The same is true for the Christian Middle Ages.

Only modern humanism turned almsgiving and charity into a major branch of a nation-state's mandate. The present-day cultural absence of devotees to an exclusively aristocratic benevolence demonstrates how much a Christian love of neighbor succeeded in becoming the norm. Generally speaking, nobody takes seriously the objection that a protective preservation of biologically "inferior" lives would lower the overall quality of society, and that the curbing of mass mortality with a concomitant improvement of public health would only intensify the collective fight for survival. The same is true for suggestions that rapidly expanding population growth should be controlled by "natural" selection.[21] These representatives of an aristocratic view of history are unsuccessful, because in the modern unconscious, Christian love has become the measure of all things. Nobody dares to declare in earnest that the origins of intellectual life and the flourishing of cultural life are dependent upon the existence of a wretched proletarian underclass. Likewise, war is judged to be a crime by all modern peoples, proven by the fanatical effort to assign guilt for the cause of war to other parties and

---

20   Translator's note: The cultural and art historical concept of *Spätantike*, literally "late antiquity," has been used by German-speaking historians since its popularization by Alois Riegl (1858–1905). See Alois Riegl, *Historische Grammatik der Bildenden Künste: Gesammelte Aufsätze* (1929).

21   Translator's note: Elisabeth Busse-Wilson did not anticipate the wide propagation of such views by National Socialism. Her reference to natural selection seems to evoke the German biologist and philosopher Ernst Haeckel (1834-1919) and his circle of German social reformers. Haeckel was a champion of scientific racism.

nations, while to medieval social sensibilities, feuding, violence, raiding, and strategic scheming in its service were legal and legitimate, even honorable.

In the Middle Ages, a social ethic as such can only be observed in its earliest, weakest beginnings. It is for this reason that Landgravine Elisabeth's charitable activities, her care for the poor, children, and prisoners conferred on her a reputation of singularity. Whatever would have been ordinary and quotidian would not have been observed as especially noteworthy. The fact that Catholic church history has elevated Landgravine Elisabeth to the status of charity's patron saint proves not how socially ethical the Christian Middle Ages were, but how rare it was to find novel types of Christian charity.

The Landgravine's Charitable Practices

The Landgravine visited the parents of poor children frequently and shared words of comfort with them. Any time their messengers or other sick people asked her for assistance, she visited their homes and cultivated her compassion and patience through what she witnessed. Even if their flimsy dwellings were far away, and even if the path was dirty and steep, she entered the hovels. She did not shy away from the squalor she found there. She provided ease and whatever else was needed most.

The image transmitted by the *Libellus* seems to fit well the conventional icon of a chatelaine who enters the shacks of the poor as a helping angel with consoling words and bags of gifts. Even the worst of contemporary novelists do not dare to use such kitsch. It is safe to state, however, that at the Landgravine's time, such kind of aid existed without a precedent. Her social peers likely had no inkling to bother with such efforts. The path leading down from the Wartburg castle was cumbersome and steep.[22] Aristocratic women only left a castle by horse on social occasions, such as hunting, and certainly not during inclement weather. To enter the wattle and daub homes of destitute Thuringian peasants was an inconceivable notion for them. It sufficed to reach into their alms purse, which was part

---

22   The final section of the ascent to the Warburg is rather steep even today despite excellent modern traffic and road construction. Seven hundred years ago, without existing routes in our contemporary sense, not to mention gravel access roads, ascent and descent must have been rather unpleasant and arduous. In medieval towns during the winter months, one would sink deeply into the mud. Elisabeth's spouse, Landgrave Ludwig IV, expanded Wartburg castle as a living space. Elisabeth began living there only in the second year of her marriage. Before that time, she frequently stayed at the Kreuzburg castle on the river Werra, where her first child was born. It is therefore accurate to state that the Landgravine's charitable work took place on the Wartburg castle near Eisenach.

of a manorial lady's outfit and attached by string to her girdle together with a small ivory mirror.

Besides the sick, the landgravine housed many poor children in a separate dwelling. She cared well for them. She treated them so kindly and affectionately that they called her "mother." When she entered the building, so the *Libellus*, they ran to her and gathered around her. At the time of the *Libellus*, composed in the year 1235, the landgravine's charitable care of children certainly had to be seen as an innovative and emotionally unprecedented accomplishment that surpassed existing moral conventions. Despite an over-abundance of Madonna representations, the Middle Ages were an era of general disregard for children. Medieval literature does not evidence esteem for children, even though descendants were valuable to such a degree that a childless woman would be considered most unfortunate. Yet under patriarchal rule, childhood as such is void of special regard or care.[23] Adulthood began at an early age because a human being was merely an individual who had left behind childhood.

As an independent initiative of a true friend of children, the landgravine's sewing of children's baptismal dresses and her role as godmother cannot be explained as a now faded patrimonial trait. Testimonies in the primary sources that she initiated the baptism of paupers' children should not merely be interpreted as an expression of feudal-manorial paternalism. Since the indigent could not afford the consecration of life's important benchmarks, baptism, marriage, and funerals, she transferred these privileges of the wealthy and the aristocrats to the common people. For her, the child of a logger or charcoal burner was not of lesser worth than a young heir to the throne. Even during her grief-stricken Marburg years, Elisabeth saw to it that children did not receive less during the distribution of alms and fought passionately for the child of an impoverished new mother. As the *Libellus* notes, "She was kindest to the children infected with scabies, the children who were sick and infirm, the most unwashed and those with the most disabilities. She touched their heads with her hands and placed them on her lap."

It seems to us today a mere charitable feudal convention and tradition when Elisabeth, while ruling as landgravine, founded a hospital and served in it. Yet in Elisabeth's time, these activities communicated an ethical boldness. Even though ruling families would make donations in the form of hospital foundations, nobody would have personally worked there like Landgravine Elisabeth, who regularly fed, bathed, and bandaged the occupants. This was

---

23   Despite an array of charitable services, orphanages did not come into being before the fifteenth century. Children joined adults in an asylum.

unparalleled and the reason why Thuringian history commemorates her as nurse and the mother of hospitals.

During the time when her crusading husband was on his way to the emperor in Apulia, all of Germany suffered from a steep price increase, which caused many to die of hunger. Already then, Saint Elisabeth was noted for her virtues. Known throughout her life as a comforter of the poor, she now became wholly and fully a mother to the famished. She ordered a hospital to be built next to her castle, where she placed those who were the most ailing and weakest. She provided works of charity for all who came and asked for alms.[24] According to an old tradition, the hospital was located halfway up the Wartburg mountain, where the commemorative Elisabeth Fountain is located today. It is assumed that its primary purpose, like that of all medieval infirmaries, was to serve as a home for invalids who could not attend general alms distributions at a specific location such as a castle.[25]

Only nineteen years old and harnessing all her slight physical strengths, she performed every necessary service for the bodies of the ill and weak.[26] Twice daily, in the morning and evening, she visited the hospital's occupants. She considered each need, including providing toys for the hospital's children. The hospital gathered ailing and repulsive members of a famished population unable to care for itself; Elisabeth suffered from the malodorous air caused by the concentration of the sick in small spaces under the worst hygienic conditions during the summer months. But she prevailed. Not so her companions and the aristocratic ladies in waiting who belonged to her retinue. They did not care for such ascetical welfare activities, even "suffered it with aversion and backtalk" (*Libellus*). How much must they have turned their noses up at the sight of the landgravine carrying patients on her back who were unable to walk on their own? Despite Elisabeth's efforts, the

---

24 This hospital, called *magna domus* in the *Libellus*, could have only been a provisional building. Soon after Elisabeth's departure for Marburg, it disintegrated and disappeared, perhaps not by accident, since her extended family rejected her charitable extremism for understandable reasons. According to tradition, she is said to have bathed lepers in what is known today as "Elisabeth's Fountain," a site that is encased in Romanesque architecture. It is quite possible that the hospital was located, there since it would have had to be built next to a well. The St. Anne's Hospital in Eisenach, however, still exists today. It was founded at the same time as the *magna domus* and serves the same purpose now as it did then. In 1906, the last late medieval structures made room for a modern hospital building.

25 See the section "The Marburg Hospital and Elisabeth's Charity" in Chapter 4.

26 According to Caesarius, she personally bathed the feet of twelve paupers. The act symbolized a ritual celebration of Christ washing the feet of his disciples. A conventional and widely observed ceremony during Holy Week, it is still frequently practiced today, so for example in Italy and at the Holy Cross monastery near Vienna.

mortality rate remained staggering. With her own hands, she sewed clothing for the funerals of the dead. She touched the corpses with her own hands and attended their burial. She cut a large piece of white linen into sections to be used for the interment. While it is one of the Seven Works of Mercy to bury the dead, generally, the corpses of paupers were treated brutally, even more so when infectious diseases were the cause of death. The cadavers were placed into the ground naked and without a protective coffin. If mortality rates increased, dead bodies were pulled out of houses by their feet, thrown into carts, and buried hastily in mass graves. With an attitude toward life that had moved beyond all conventional patrimonial beneficence, Landgravine Elisabeth carefully bedded and dressed the unsightly and cheerless final remains of even the most wretched creatures and buried them with all honors. Every dead person is a candidate for eternity.

Those in need assembled in great numbers at the castle gate. Together with her maidservants, Elisabeth organized daily copious distributions of food and drink. The image captured so often in artistic representation was historically true: a woman in noble attire holds a pitcher in one hand and bread in the other while the needy reach out to her with their empty bowls. She stockpiled income from her farmsteads and even from the full harvest of the preceding year to distribute as victuals during the year of famine. She arranged for large distributions of food and money not only at Wartburg castle but also in other parts of Thuringia. In this year of increased prices, she must have experienced near complete exhaustion when we add to such extraordinary activities the personal visits to the huts of the poor, the custody and care for the asylum's children, and acting as a godmother to many. She was driven by an immense tireless industriousness. It stands in stark contrast to the resigned passivity of her later Marburg years. The fundamental mistake of medieval charity and of Landgravine Elisabeth to only give but not to generate opportunities for value-creating work certainly existed already in her activities at this time. However, this early secular period is far different from her Marburg era, which is characterized by the indiscriminate distribution of gifts and the symbolic and unreserved gift-giving of herself. The *Libellus* records that,

> When she had sated the multitudes until the next harvest, she gave all who
> could work a shirt and shoes so that their feet would not ache, and sickles for
> their use so that they could use them and live from the work of their hands.

She thus regarded her generosity during the time of famine as distributing emergency provisions with the goal of supporting the indigent until the next harvest. She still possessed a notion that her gifts of precious clothing and silk fabrics to poor women were inappropriate. On such occasions, she admonished the recipients, "Do not adorn yourselves with such things but sell them so that you have the money you need. Beyond that, work hard" (*Libellus*).

In general, however, her unbridled charity must have already invited frequent abuse. Medieval impostors and intentionally maimed beggars belonged to the business of mendicancy then as much as today. The following episode from the *Libellus* proves how easily she could be swayed and how quickly she fell prey to deceit:

> Among the women was one whom she gave shoes, a shirt, and a tunic. This woman was so happy with the presents that she fell to the ground. It seemed that she had died for joy. She exclaimed that she never before had experienced such delight. When St. Elisabeth saw this, she became saddened thinking that she had given too many gifts at once and thus perhaps caused her death.

It appears more likely that the female recipient of her gifts only simulated fainting or dying for joy to cajole Elisabeth into donating even more. Or, perhaps, she considered the gift as lacking proportion but wished through play acting to encourage Elisabeth to continue her generous activities.

Either way, we can conclude with confidence that the landgravine immediately satisfied any need that was brought to her attention. She belonged to the compliant type of character who is unable to say no. Thus, everybody could get through to her. Through her abundant generosity, she desired to make everybody happy. The *Libellus* describes how "once, she wished to milk a cow to satisfy someone who wanted milk. The cow, however, resisted and did not allow the milking." Raised as an aristocrat, she never learned how to work on a farm and thus, somewhat touchingly, made a fool of herself.

Motivated by a certain zeal, even paranoia, and in line with romantic traditions, contemporary historians have purified the original sources of her life. This includes even authenticated records about the hostility the saint encountered during her lifetime. These incidents were excised without further comment and relegated to the realm of fables. It only requires a little common sense to recognize that clashes between the landgravine and her feudal peers were unavoidable given the extent and character of her charitable initiatives.

Even the earliest historical source hints at not only limitless and joyous but also utterly unsystematic generosity. She seems to have been open-handed to a fault in managing supplies of foodstuffs and clothing. It was a common experience that at every doorstep where she donated goods to a pauper, the following day she would find additional candidates. To what degree the demand must have increased in an era when begging was seen as a profession![27]

To successfully conduct mass feedings, she could not spare the pantries of the landgrave's court. As was true for both small and big farming operations during the Middle Ages, the household economy on the Wartburg castle was organized based on stockpiling supplies. These supplies were difficult to replenish. An aristocrat's wife would ensure that the harvest of one summer could cover the needs of the winter months: flour, legumes, wheat, honey, wool, and fuel. Chaos and confusion reigned when the supplies were withdrawn arbitrarily on the local level rather than in a well-coordinated large-scale distribution scheme, which was difficult to orchestrate given the rudimentary medieval transportation and distribution infrastructure. Landgravine Elisabeth used all goods produced on her personally owned Thuringian farms for the sole purpose of charitable donations and the care of the hospital's inhabitants. This negatively impacted her courtly retinue who were used to living well.[28]

Different comments indicate that a dearth of provisions was a frequent occurrence. A short miracle story tells of never-ending drink in the pitcher and of baskets that were never emptied of bread during meal distributions to the poor. The story is proof that the supply of natural victuals indeed did not suffice. Only a supernatural increase of bread could overcome the shortage. The fact that, in two early sources, Elisabeth is said to have sold jewelry and precious clothing items to procure money for almsgiving provides additional evidence not only of her self-abnegation but also of disarray and extravagance. The circumstance that Elisabeth selected large swaths of linen to wrap the dead must have appalled her peers as well. Linen was an aristocratic luxury good. The common people used wool instead. She had to stop using linen, possibly because she felt that such profligacy could not continue. She ordered that corpses should not be covered in new linens and new shirts but in used clothing. Good fabrics were from then on reserved for the living.

---

27   According to Dietrich of Apolda, she fed about 900 persons every day. This is the exaggeration of a legend. Yet, even if she only fed ninety, the number would have been impressive given the sparsely populated region. It is estimated that Germany at the time had about eight million inhabitants.
28   The retinue and the court itself would have received the wealth that Elisabeth guided toward the poor. A feudal lord's retinue included not only his kin but also squires, minor aristocrats, and ministerial nobles. Everybody who served administratively in his region, and not just those we consider servants today, was provided with clothing and alimentary provisions.

Given Elisabeth's standards of care and almsgiving, the Wartburg castle must have witnessed a very unusual mode of operation. It caused rightful consternation and unease among the castle's inhabitants. Even more upsetting than the wasteful almsgiving practices of the young landgravine was her upending of cultural traditions at the landgrave's Thuringian court. The new lifestyle must have alienated aristocrats used to the old regime under Landgrave Hermann. The beautiful Wartburg castle, just recently completed in the most modern, that is, high Romanesque style, was the center of noble courtly traditions.[29] It was turned into an asylum for paupers and the destitute. The growing crowd of itinerant beggars waiting for the distribution of meals or alms must have been experienced as an eyesore.

For these reasons, the legends surrounding Elisabeth's days on the Wartburg usually focus on the conflict between her limitless charity and the lifestyle of her peers. As such, they are correct and likely drawn from historical events, especially when justified through supernatural interventions and the causal logic of miracles. The most popular miracle of the saint's life is the miracle of roses, which has been depicted frequently in art.[30] Landgrave Ludwig encounters pious Elisabeth as she is walking downhill from the Wartburg castle carrying a basket filled with goods for the poor and unwell. He asks what she is carrying away. She tries to diffuse the situation with a small lie, answering, "Roses, my Lord." Without delay, Heaven assists its "chosen friend" against human ill will and transforms the bread. No reason exists to believe that the landgrave was critical of his wife's boundless charity. Records testify to the opposite. Nonetheless, the emergence of this trifling miracle proves that a sufficiently large number of people among Elisabeth's kin and around court watched Elisabeth closely and viewed her almsgiving with disapproval. The legend of the donated coat, which miraculously reappeared at its original location, underscores this view:

---

29 The Wartburg castle was upgraded to living quarters by Landgrave Herrmann, and its expansion was completed by Elisabeth's spouse. Even by the architectural standards of the highest-ranking aristocrats, the castle's improvements were unusually grand and spacious. Its splendid new design could compete with any emperor's palace.

30 The popular modern figure of St. Elisabeth is the Elisabeth of the Miracle of Roses. The motif of a transformation into roses is very old and can also be found as an attribute of other saints. However, Dietrich of Apolda does not report it, nor does Johannes Rothe. We conclude that it stems from a comparatively recent Elisabeth tradition.

Translator's note: For a contemporary scholarly study of the miracle, see Rainer Hohberg and Sylvia Weigelt, *Brot und Rosen: Das Leben der heiligen Elisabeth in Sagen und Legenden* (Wartburg: Wartburg Verlag, 2006).

When Landgrave Ludwig returned with St. Elisabeth from Hungary, he summoned his counts and dukes, knights and servants, ladies and young aristocratic women who travelled with him to Hungary, as well as several of his male retinue who had remained at home and held magnificent court at the Wartburg castle. As the time of supper arrived, the guests stood up and awaited the arrival of their Lady St. Elisabeth. She procrastinated and stayed hidden. The reason: as she descended to the hall, a poor man, naked and pitiful, lay under the staircase. He cried out and implored her to have pity on him. She looked at the wretched man and answered, "I do not have time nor gifts to give you right now, but I will send for food for you." The pauper did not acquiesce but continued to bewail his nakedness and infirmity. This moved her heart. She took the sumptuous coat that she wore and threw it over him. The pauper quickly took the coat and left. Many of the servants had watched this event. When the landgrave with his knights and other honorable lords and ladies continued to wait in vain for St. Elisabeth, the head cook addressed all guests and attendant knights, speaking, "My Lord shall judge for himself whether it is right and proper that our gracious Lady Elisabeth stays absent for such a long time, delays the refreshments for you and the pleasure of her company for so many noble ladies. Just at this very moment, she has clothed a naked pauper. She gifted him her most precious coat and thus is unable to appear before these honorable guests." It was the custom at this time that noble women would not appear among guests without a coat. The pious Duke Ludwig responded with a laugh, "So I will go myself and fetch her." He left and found her in her room. With great kindness, he said to her, "My dearest, wouldn't you like to join us for supper?" She answered, "I am ready if you would like for me to join you." Then he asked, "Sister, where is your coat?" She responded, "It hangs on the clothes rack." Her Lord spoke to one of her maidservants, "Go and fetch it for her." And when the maidservant went to fetch it, she found the coat hanging on the coat rack and brought it to her. Saint Elisabeth put it on and went to attend supper. This coat was sky blue with small golden images woven into it in places. Now it has become a chasuble for the Franciscan Brothers in the monastery at the foot of the Wartburg castle.[31]

---

31   This story is quoted from Lulu von Strauß und Torney, "The Legend of St. Elisabeth," in *Deutsche Volkheit*, ed. Lulu von Strauß und Torney (Jena: Eugen Diederichs Verlag, 1926). The same legend has also been told for a more important social and political event, the Nürnberg Princely Council in the fall of 1225, where the Thuringian ducal couple celebrated the wedding of the landgrave's youngest sister with an Austrian duke. The tale of the miraculous coat began to be circulated by the Reinhardtsbrunn monastery soon after the landgravine's canonization.

It is utterly possible that the landgravine engaged in such reckless and spontaneous gift-giving as described by the legend. Such ostentatious gestures of protest were not atypical for her. A coat constituted the magnificent showpiece of an aristocratic lady's wardrobe without which she would never make an appearance at a social event outside her living quarters. The quandary of appearing without her coat among such an illustrious gathering was of such weight that the theologian-scribe could only resolve it with a miracle by conjuring up a substitute coat on the spot. Of course, only after the fact. What remains authentic and truthful is the disconcerting reaction of her peers, even her servants, who were not willing to ascribe "saintly" motives to her actions, and the bewilderment expressed by male aristocrats. An analogous small anecdote, the story of the jewel-encrusted sleeve which the landgravine gifted to a beggar, and which a knight in turn bought from the beggar, seems to suggest a comparable gesture. Not all who witnessed the event felt joy. Otherwise, the legend would not need to invent an ending, which would resolve the problematic situation in miraculous fashion. Historiography has made every effort to shape the catastrophic events after Ludwig's death as Elisabeth's "banishment from the Wartburg castle." However, these two earlier miraculous episodes, the young woman's lack of any economic prudence and her oppositional stance on the cultural traditions at Landgrave Hermann's famous court, are already clearly evidenced by biographical facts. They render the eruption of hostilities among aristocratic circles against the young widow, now without any protection, very likely. All later developments support this interpretation. Despite her many harsh experiences, a personality trait which early on manifested as an addiction to profligacy reasserted itself as she grew increasingly despondent. The landgravine was unable to find a compromise with her aristocratic peers. She continued to pursue her works of charity, even for the price of her own exile.

The Franciscan Creed

The initial spirit of Franciscan idealism is evidenced by the landgravine of Thuringia's choice of activities, by the significant decisions of her life, and through her real-world religious impact. She is among the most interesting and earliest representatives of the immense religious movement, which

Translator's note: For more on Lulu von Strauß und Torney, a close friend of Elisabeth Busse-Wilson, see the introduction to the translation.

was launched in Italy and soon gripped all of Europe. As is true for all thirteenth-century heretical sects, such as the Waldensians, religious historians consider Franciscans as forerunners of the Reformation. No matter what their significance might have been, all these movements were latently anti-clerical lay religious formations in rebellion against Roman Catholicism. Yet as preached by St. Francis, holy poverty cannot be merely registered as a chapter of religious history. The phenomenon of Francis's extra-ecclesiastical experience of God and world had the character of a primal religious power which exists beyond all historical differentiation and distinctions among religions.

As was true for late antiquity, wealthy and well-established people were suddenly grasped by the desire to resign their government posts, to distribute their wealth among the poor, and to join the new religion of Christians. Spiritually awakened men and women of the thirteenth century married Holy Lady Poverty. Francis, the son of a rich merchant in Assisi, and Landgravine Elisabeth of Thuringia, one of his most radical disciples, were motivated by an identical elemental drive to oppose medieval high culture. As individuals, they stepped out of the circle of their peers. But to claim them as the first Protestants would diminish their personal uniqueness.

The social-revolutionary tendency, which is assumed to characterize early Franciscan thought, can be tracked to aphorisms by St. Francis such as "every rich person is a thief or the heir of a thief." This seems to anticipate the famous French Enlightenment maxim "property is theft."[32] The well-known renunciation of the world by the Poverello was built on the assertion that "love for God and neighbor are blocked by property over which human beings worry and fight. It is more difficult to enter heaven from a palace than from a shack." Francis himself never assumed that this ethical axiom would amount to an attack on the Catholic Church's secular might. With saintly innocence, he believed until the end that he was supporting the Church. Neither he—nor certainly his German disciple St. Elisabeth—ever criticized the Church.

In the view of contemporary ecclesiastical and cultural historians, the material wealth of the church and its institutions, including its monasteries and foundations, represent a desertion of original Christian ideals and a coarsening of original Christian principles. In truth, medieval ecclesiastical

---

32   Translator's note: This maxim has roots in early Christian writings but was made famous by anarchist Pierre-Joseph Proudhon in the mid-nineteenth century. In addition, Busse-Wilson might have had in mind Jean-Jacques Rousseau's arguments in *Discourse on the Origin and Basis of Inequality among Men* (*Discours sur l'origine et les fondements de l'inégalité parmi les hommes*), 1754. On Busse-Wilson's engagement with socialism and communism, see Großmann, op.cit., 100–104 and 213–21.

ethics in the thirteenth century did not exist in a state of degeneration or sin when permitting the accumulation of material riches. Rather, it expressed a stage preceding a more advanced ethics, where a knowledge of "good and evil" was not yet detached from an obligatory division between spiritual and material interests. For this reason, up until the early Franciscans, the mixing of religion and economic life could not be experienced as impurity.

In a similar vein, nobody had yet discovered the contradictions inherent in linking sexual love and economic advantage. A marriage would not necessarily be entered without love, yet the dowry or other binding contracts regarding the capital worth of a bride were considered the necessary foundation of any marriage. They were negotiated between parents on behalf of their children. In like fashion, no ethical outrage was caused for centuries by the fact that the foundation of the church rested on the materially tangible ownership of landed property and the exercise of political power.

It is a misunderstanding on the part of modern interpreters to endow the medieval psyche with a dualistic split between earthly and spiritual values. Rather, the average medieval Christian practiced a completely innocent fusion of both types of values. Only a small avant-garde of spiritually gifted Christians were able to grasp the contradiction. This insight, a rarified ethical sensibility, raised an ideological wall between both groups. Without question, most monks and clerics belonged to the former faction.

A modern person who declares having great respect for the transcendent philosophy of leading medieval figures and for whom religiosity and the Middle Ages are synonymous neglects to envision the mentality of an average medieval individual purely as that of a peasant. The true type of medieval person is not a monk lost in fervent visions and prayers, a crusader knight who sacrifices himself for the Holy Sepulcher, or a religious philosopher and mystic. To identify the spiritual characteristics of these groups as expressing medieval religiosity generally makes the same mistake as someone who labels all of humanity in the second half of the nineteenth century natural scientists because this epoch is distinguished by the accomplishments of Virchow, Helmholtz, Robert Meyer, and other great scientists, while the majority of the population fully subscribed to the worldview and emotional disposition of the Biedermeier era.

The medieval assessment of sexuality was materialistic. Accordingly, the standards for ethical challenges were extremely low. This down-to-earth materialism also held true for all other values. Even the medieval reasoning about Landgravine Elisabeth's saintliness proves medieval people's ingenuous and nonspiritual religiosity. In her name, a cult of holiness was reflexively mixed with an economically advantageous flourishing pilgrimage operation.

Before the Reformation era, accusations such as "you are members of the clergy and yet own private property" would not be experienced as finger-pointing. Self-doubt could only spread with the rise of a more austere Protestant sensibility, which vanquished medieval sentiment and retroactively reconfigured Catholicism from the bottom up. Contemporary Protestants who judge as apostasy, even as treason, the material wealth of medieval ecclesiastical institutions superimpose their modern dualistic sensibilities and nuanced ethics on an ethical era which was not yet adept at such distinctions. The same holds true for contemporary Catholics who are embarrassed about the Catholic Church's past claims to secular power.

For these reasons, Francis did not launch a reform movement when proclaiming the incompatibility of worldly wealth and gospel piety. His religious initiative did not understand itself as a restauration and corrective against widespread abuse and decline as has been posited by Protestant Church historians. The movement's significance was self-sufficient in and of itself, and something entirely new. Francis's singular achievement was precisely not a rebuttal of the clergy's materialism and spiritual weakening as has been true for Luther's later appeals. Francis's contemporaries were enthralled by a primal religious affect.

Francis did not turn against the church. Yet neither did his strongest energies develop within the church, not even in the form of a new order. At the beginning of his vocation, the Poverello imagined the estate of holy poverty as a nomadic communal and fraternal existence. His brethren, like Christ's disciples, were to journey across the land and preach. Without carrying provisions of money and food, they were to beg peasants for the bare minimum necessary to stay alive. He initially rejected a permanent monastic settlement. As a religious obligation to remain inwardly and outwardly free, he often recommended to his brethren to pick up and carry the beggar's staff as an objectively valuable life choice. One of his authenticated aphorisms, that "through begging, God has set the table for everybody," is a scandalous axiom not only for today's public but also for its private morals. In like manner, even Francis's contemporaries, such as Pope Gregory IX, immediately sensed the axiom's social destructiveness. Its echo proves a cultivated Hohenstaufen era's elemental desire for the archaic sources of religious life, even though Francis had to retract the demand for absolute mendicant poverty in favor of a rational formation of his order.[33]

---

33   Translator's note: Despite Busse-Wilson's consistent use of developmental stages as an analytical tool, she did not conceive these stages as static and irreversible. As this discussion of Franciscan spirituality demonstrates, older "archaic" stages and "primal" impulses could

The Thuringian landgravine must have obtained a rather accurate knowledge of her role model early on. Her works of charity imply that she must have known of her master teacher's activities in great detail and comprehensiveness, especially in regard to her hands-on practical aid for the sick and her service to lepers, but also in regard to numerous individual traits of her new existence, such as her sojourns in the most abject and crude dwellings—a barn in Eisenach and a derelict farmhouse near Marburg.[34] Her source of such familiarity was a handful of Franciscan brothers whom she settled at the foot of the Wartburg castle in Eisenach in 1223 after having heard their sermons. She became enraptured by their message.[35] Elisabeth remained in close connection with them and solidified a Franciscan influence in Thuringia as its sovereign protector. According to the *Libellus*, she even spun and sewed the Eisenach Franciscans' robes. The Franciscan Rodeger became her first confessor; in all likelihood, he was the decisive impulse for her Franciscan discipleship.[36] We know that Rodeger traveled from Erfurt to Eisenach in 1223 and captivated his audiences while preaching with other Franciscan missionaries. The landgravine must have belonged to his listeners. An Eisenach church was immediately made ready for him.[37] Much later, when Elisabeth would wander aimlessly through the miserable small town of Eisenach, driven by a mixture of ecstatic joy and despair, the small band of Franciscans failed to support her. Entirely left on her own, she had to defend her Franciscan loyalties against a world of enemies.

No trustworthy tradition confirms whether St. Francis knew of the landgravine. A legendary Franciscan tradition relates that he sent her his patched traveling coat as pledge of his approval. In 1226, the year of Francis's death and a year of famine in Germany, the charitable activities of the landgravine reached their zenith. It is possible that in his final years of life, Francis might have been made aware of the passionate female disciple in Germany, a country

upend linear progression at any time, and not for the worse of it. The eruptions of older forms into new cultural configurations signified cultural regeneration and rejuvenation.

34 Wegele notes already in 1861 that St. Elisabeth of Thuringia was a student of St. Francis (Wegele, *Historische Zeitschrift*, 1861). Translator's note: It is Lori Pieper's great accomplishment to have (re)discovered and edited a Franciscan vita of St. Elisabeth, which confirms Busse-Wilson's emphasis on Elisabeth's Franciscan sympathies. See Pieper, "A New Life of St. Elizabeth of Hungary: The Anonymous Franciscan." *Archivum Franciscanum Historicum* 93 (2000): 29–78.

35 These brethren belonged to the earliest Franciscan missionaries, who arrived in Germany in 1221. They were commanding personalities and persuasive representatives of the movement. A reference to the Franciscans is found in the *Epistola*.

36 See Karl Wenck on Elisabeth's relationship with Rodeger in *Historische Zeitschrift* 69 (1892).

37 It was situated at the market's southern slope, above the town church St. George. It would twice play a significant role in Elisabeth's future.

which only recently had been opened to Franciscan missions. How inspiring must have been knowledge of such notice for the radical young woman.

Landgravine Elisabeth's emotional life, even her religious program proper, ceased to be religious and ethical in a "normal" sense after contact with the early Franciscan messengers—not in the context of her era, and not according to today's ethical standards. She rejected the security of monastic contemplative life, which had been the conventional choice of her female aristocratic contemporaries. Nor did she aspire to become a "nurse deaconess," an ahistorical choice projected onto her by modern interpreters. The cause for such misinterpretation is intrinsically tied to a mistaken understanding of the early Franciscan movement's social ethics.

Elisabeth of Thuringia's unusual capacity for devotion to the plight of the downcast and St. Francis's itinerant life among peasants and paupers pose a temptation to assume a social ethics cause for their choices. The stance of "most holy poverty" did not aim at lifting the conditions of the economically impoverished or the socially destitute. How could have the mass of paupers become richer because of the heroic self-denial of a small band of ethical anarchists? The Franciscan movement did not come into being to improve the lot of the poor. Rather, all of humankind was intended to become radically dispossessed.

The unpropertied condition of those religious men and women did not merely extend to worldly goods, the relinquishing of home and hearth, but also to culture, education, and personal happiness found in love, marriage, and friendship. The voluntary pauper wants to be free of all these ties to society to be closer to God. "Naked you shall throw yourself into the arms of your Savior" (cf. Job 1:21). For this reason, the voluntary pauper joins a sympathy walk-out on behalf of the poor and in protest against society. The will to change the world is not part of a religious person's makeup. The Seven Works of Mercy as performed by Elisabeth and Francis often brought practical relief for the destitute. Yet the actual meaning of their descent to the caste of paupers did not concern the redemption of the world but the redemption of the self. This is true for Elisabeth's service in Eisenach and later at the Marburg hospital. In contrast to the logic of modern ethics, the landgravine did not embody the model of a compassionate nun and nurse even if theologians of both confessions assert this claim. Service to outcasts was intended first and foremost as self-depreciation, not as the elevation of others. The course of her religious development clarifies that her charity was conceptualized mystically and without any desire for social reforms.

While still living in aristocratic splendor, Elisabeth longed for abject poverty with all her heart. She often spoke with her ladies in waiting about holy poverty. When in their company in the castle's great hall, she dressed in a shabby coat, covered her head with a threadbare kerchief, and declared, according to the *Libellus*, "I shall walk like this everywhere when begging and enduring misery for God's sake." Her genuine religious goal was to abandon her aristocratic status and to pick up a beggar's staff. She always stayed true to it. Preferably, she would have liked to have entered the "holy state of poverty" with her husband the landgrave. Since she was of the highest social rank, she had to place herself among those of the lowest social rank to demonstrate her commitment to the Franciscan way of life. Moreover, she had despised Hohenstaufen aristocratic society since childhood.

Following her husband's death, the landgravine's Eisenach period demonstrates the total failure of her first attempt at achieving Franciscan poverty. She lacked the vigor and buoyancy of the prodigious religious genius who can tolerate stepping into the world of the exceptional and cutting all social ties. She was not a St. Hildegard of Bingen or a St. Teresa of Avila, who could break the double barrier of their gender and their monastic vows. Later, Konrad of Marburg blocked Elisabeth's renunciation of her wealth and her radical choice of poverty. He diverted her religious impulses toward legal activities and moved her into a Marburg hospital setting. Despite the tragic interior and forced exterior capitulations to reality, she clung with great tenacity to the Franciscan ideal. As we shall see, her biography confirms with how much blood and tears such faithfulness had to be purchased. Her path remained Franciscan and therefore a path of vicarious suffering from the days when she tried to join the rank of paupers until her wretched end in the Marburg hospital. During times of religious clarity, a new self-confidence emerged from a plethora of refractions, which she had to experience as a human being and as a woman. "Incipit vita nuova."[38]

Unlike anybody else, the hermit of Portiuncula and Elisabeth of Thuringia dared to step from a sound existence into poverty, annihilation, and lack of civilization's bounty without compromise or the choice of return. This did not always engender a breakthrough experience of vital creative forces. Among the crowds who joined Francis, certainly not a few chose to marry Lady Holy Poverty with the unconscious wish to coast more easily through life. Many who dared to take on the challenges of an unheard-of spiritual and physical asceticism did not advance beyond justification to enjoy life without work and professional responsibilities. Francis recognized the kind of offspring his movement gave birth to. It was only among the few

---

38 Translator's note: "A new life begins." The author quotes from Dante Alighieri's *La Vita Nuova* (1294).

truly poor that the full weight of the burden, restlessness, confusion, and excitement of the era was being felt. The movement of voluntary poverty, eventually resulting in the creation of a mendicant order with preaching responsibilities, was originally prompted by an immense fear of the world. In Germany, Elisabeth of Thuringia was the first who recognized the collapse of an old world and the beginning of a new emotional epoch as a lived, embodied experience. For this reason, it is entirely immaterial that all her charitable works, extending to the smallest details of her daily life, are mere imitation. Works are irrelevant in the context of authentic religious feeling. The landgravine's charity was designed as a religious experience. This is inconceivable for those who are not religious.

Elisabeth as a Franciscan

Even though refuted and surmounted by scholars, "public opinion" continues to propagate heroic tales in all types of high and low literature and across long stretches of time. The force of such folk mythologies is stronger than that of scholarly research. Historiography on the level of folk mythology absolutizes a heroine or hero's fate. Their lives are remembered as exceptional, unique, and unrepeatable. They do not seem to be ruled by the same social causality that governs ordinary mortals. The heroic protagonists seem to suspend it with incomparable achievements. This non-scientific attitude has not yet been fully overcome even among academic specialists. St. Elisabeth has been absolutized in this way as well: scholars have overestimated her heroism and self-discipline instead of relativizing her apparent uniqueness through a historically more accurate assessment of her Franciscan discipleship. The originality of her achievements, all conditioned by her social context, was thus misunderstood as well.

The famous scene of the *Nibelungenlied* where Brunhild and Kriemhild fight over who should enter the portal of the Worms Cathedral first exemplifies the type of religiosity practiced by medieval aristocrats: squabbles over rank trumped religious passion. Members of the highest noble ranks leveraged attendance at Mass as an opportunity for representation. For a feudal household's processions and attendance at church, no expense was spared. One woman lampooned another's dress. Furthermore, church attendance offered opportunities for men and women to meet and to arrange for a rendezvous through eye contact and secret notes. This is still the custom today in Romanic countries.

Landgravine Elisabeth thwarted her peers' customary religiosity. She took advantage of every major ecclesiastical holiday for a personal religious retreat much like St. Francis moved religious feast days to the straw-roofed shacks in the rural solitude of Portiuncula. According to the *Libellus*, her first church attendance as a new mother, which her aristocratic contemporaries usually staged with pomp and circumstance, was reframed as an unpretentious excursion. Developed as a habit during her adolescence, she insisted once again on boycotting noblewomen's fashion.

Elisabeth walked on foot even when outside the castle and stood among commoners when listening to a public sermon. It was meant as a gesture of humility in imitation of her role model.[39] An aristocratic lady would travel on horseback but never on foot. Elisabeth even tried her hand at spinning wool, the task of female servants during the Hohenstaufen era.[40] These and similar activities express the protest of a genuinely religious human being against a culture that she experienced as contrary to her own sense of being in the world.

Elisabeth's cult of the lepers, while patterned in accord with Francis's practices, signified more than such forthright protest.[41] Unlike the more widely shared Franciscan rejection of aristocratic culture, it flaunted extraordinary and radical action. To fully understand her interactions with lepers, we must first envision the climate of fear and contagion psychosis which defined Francis and Elisabeth's century.

The impact of the widespread and horrifying disease of leprosy crested during their lifetime. Nothing could stem the epidemic caused by crude living quarters and conditions. Since it was incurable, the only preventative measure at hand was the interment and segregation of these unhappy human beings in hospitals.[42] Social ostracism was the harshest social means of

39   Her preference resonates with the story of St. Francis mingling with beggars in an international crowd of pilgrims in Rome to ask for alms.

40   During Carolingian times, an aristocratic lifestyle resembled that of a wealthy farmer; even royal daughters spun wool. In the High Middle Ages, however, an aristocratic woman had become a "lady." She had ceased to contribute manually to home and agrarian productivity. The landgravine spinning wool with her female servants thus became a striking figure, which was even recorded in art as, for example, in a woodcut by Hans Baldung Grien.

41   Translator's note: For more on the social context, see Robert Ian Moore, *The Formation of a Persecuting Society: Power and Deviance in Western Europe, 950–1250* (Oxford, UK: B. Blackwell, 1987), esp. 26–42; Herbert Covey, "People with Leprosy (Hansen's Disease) during the Middle Ages," *Social Science Journal* 38, no. 2 (2001): 315–21.

42   Even today, this illness is incurable despite all modern medical innovations. Largely due to prophylactic means, however, the improvement of general hygiene helped extinguish it in Europe. It was not until 1850 that Iceland closed its last leprosaria. Extensive colonies of lepers exist today only in Greece, Dutch India, and China. Translator's note: Leprosy has been curable with multi-drug therapy since the mid-1960s, about thirty years after the publication of Busse-Wilson's study.

self-protection to keep a dangerous person at bay.[43] A special set of clothing, a clapper, which infected persons had to sound to announce their presence so the healthy could keep their distance, and even their physical appearance transformed people with leprosy into outcasts. They were socially dead before their final physical demise. Their physical appearance turned an ordinary corpse into an image of soothing consolation.

In the early stages of the disease, reddish and brown spots appear on the face and extremities. After that, repulsive excretions from nose, mouth, and throat set in. Eventually, the face begins to swell. Hair, eyelashes, and eyebrows begin to fall out. Blisters and tumors form. The face and extremities become sites of terrifying deformations. In the final stage, all those who were not relieved of their affliction endure the conversion of leprosy into *lepra mutilans*. Festering sores destroy the tissue of the lower extremities. The thinning bones of hand and foot joints and the nose cartilage disintegrate. A mask with lifeless eyes replaces what once was a face. A human body decomposes while still alive. The stench of the steadily flowing pus, but especially so the psychological changes to be expected during such suffering—a leper is consistently described as being spiteful, churlish, and malicious—generate an image of those suffering from leprosy as dreadful living decay.

The *Libellus* records that,

> On a Maundy Thursday, she [Elisabeth] gathered many lepers, washed their hands and feet, and kissed those areas which displayed the most boils and were the worst to look at. She threw herself at their feet with utmost humility. Wherever she encountered lepers, she sat next to them, comforted them, and admonished them to be patient. She did not fear the lepers more than those who were healthy, and offered them gifts in abundance.

The theological justification for Landgravine Elisabeth's Maundy Thursday gathering evoked the memory of Christ's passion with the intent to inspire acts of voluntary suffering and auto-humiliation during Holy Week. Christ washed the feet of his disciples. Following his example, Christians should equally humble themselves with service to those of low social status.[44]

---

43 This practice is already documented for the Carolingian era. According to some, perhaps exaggerated, sources, 20,000 leprosaria might have existed in medieval Europa as a whole.

44 Translator's note: The term "Maundy Thursday" refers to the ceremony of foot-washing as modeled by Jesus of Nazareth (John 13:14–17) as a *mandatum* for his disciples to love one another. A medieval audience would have understood St. Elisabeth's actions in this context.

Christ carried his cross. Elisabeth carried the unwell on her back. Yet even in this theological framework, the landgravine's service to lepers is hard to defend. It had nothing to do with helping and healing charity as proclaimed by ecclesiastical historiography.[45]

The scene as transmitted to us in the original sources lacks both eros and caritas. Kissing the suppurating ulcers of those evicted and abandoned by society remains a grotesque and ghoulish act, not to mention the public health irresponsibility of such theatric piety. The landgravine had small children; she was a spouse and hospital worker. Since the dangers of infection were known only too well, it does not make sense to evoke therapeutic intentions on her part. Nonetheless, we also do not want to diagnose a primary pathological disposition, such as a perverse coprophilia, as it is not our intention to explain away the core of her Franciscan ideals as an adolescent aberration, when Elisabeth roamed the world begging and property-less.

Simply put, we cannot measure the spectrum of religious sentiments according to standards of bourgeois "normality." The nucleus of any truly creative spirituality inclines toward the far-fetched. Further arguments against a reductionist diagnosis of pathology rest on the facts that St. Francis was a man of wide-ranging and extraordinary talents and endowed with a psyche free of resentments, and that the landgravine Elisabeth lived in an unusually happy marriage. St. Hedwig, landgravine of Silesia, according to her character and biography an equally gifted woman, was perhaps even more radical in the cult of repulsiveness.[46]

We should assume that the squalid figures with their terrifying looks were indeed repugnant to these saints. Yet precisely because they felt an entirely natural aversion, they approached them. Landgravine Elisabeth and her prodigious role model thus chose such disconcerting forms of service to lepers as a form of self-control. At the beginning, Francis was not able to personally present lepers with alms. His survival instinct revolted. Yet

---

45 Several remarkable saints practiced auto-humiliation during the Middle Ages and Baroque era whose primary concern was, however, Samaritan care for the very ill. Such heroes of a works-oriented Christian charity include the semi-mythological St. Rochus, the patron saint of the plague; and St. Aloysius of Gonzaga during the Baroque era, who courageously tended to the victims of a plague epidemic in Rome. The Order of St. Lazarus was founded specifically for the care of lepers.

46 As is true for other exceptional saints, it is written that she drank the water that was used to wash lepers. She served the poor, kneeling before them during her regularly scheduled meal distributions. She secretly kissed the footprints of paupers. To enjoy the happiness of having eaten bread that was donated to the poor, she bought the bread given to them and then ate it, thus communing in a Eucharistic meal with Lady Holy Poverty. Translator's note: St. Hedwig (1174–1243) was an aunt of St. Elisabeth.

the nagging self-criticism remained that he was not able to master himself. During the time of his most difficult crisis, the transition from secular life to that of a saint, he once encountered a leper while horseback riding. This was the moment where everything shifted. Francis dismounted the horse. After a brief, terrifying battle between the instinct to protect himself and the ecstasy of self-annihilation, he kissed the leper's decaying face. After this victory, he entered a state of elation not unlike that of an unexpected meeting between lovers.

Francis advanced gradually in this dreadful *ars amandi*. After a lonely hike in the mountains, he arrived in Gubbio. He was now able to squeeze and drain leprous sores and treat the wounds. A voice told him, "You must despise and hate all things that you loved and desired sensually. Once you begin practicing, all that seemed sweet and lovely now will turn bitter and unbearable, and all that you have previously loathed will change into great sweetness and exuberant joy." This incident proves that the purpose of a religiously sanctioned service to lepers was aimed at radical self-transformation and self-transcendence, rather than at an expression of Christian "love." Human nature is fought as an adversarial principle. It is meant to be thrown to the ground, so that the unnatural becomes natural. Elisabeth "did not fear the lepers more than those who were healthy." This statement reveals that she, too, surely experienced mortal fear of the maimed and battered figures, whose proximity awakened the primal instinct to escape their presence. Yet she overcame her reflex for self-preservation. Her sense of victory provided her with a new type of pride: being stronger in her fight against herself than those usually deemed the strongest.

The saints' performative disregard for medieval norms and common sense is mirrored in the behavioral response of the outcasts to the "homage" that was being directed at them. One may suspect that the poverty-stricken pariahs, thus kissed and seemingly made happy, must have looked rather embarrassed. St. Francis once bathed a leper who turned ever more vicious as the saint became increasingly more affectionate. The leper experienced kindness as mockery.

Once expelled from society, outcasts cease to expect respect from those considered normal and in good health, never mind those of high rank. If not turning suspicious of excessive tokens of friendship, their alternative emotional option is bitterness. The degree of their squalor does not permit the possibility of any true equality. In contrast, the saints relied precisely on such psychology. Elisabeth was only able to calmly kiss lepers because the distance in rank between her, the landgravine, and the people was enormous, even more so between a young healthy woman and a pariah. Mutuality was never envisioned. Since the possibility of a sympathetic exchange among equals was ruled out, the aristocrat could enter the awkward situation with equanimity. Over the years, it became the norm for her that the wretched, cared for people were perceived as impersonal objects. Especially during her final Marburg years, she increasingly turned acts of charity into a mystical marriage with Lady Poverty.[47]

No hagiographical accounts reveal how secular society during the High Middle Ages thought about the cult of lepers and the displays of charity directed at them. This omission in the written tradition is in and of itself a tradition as well. The episodes written in praise of saintly virtues and transmitted in the canonization protocols disclose more than intended about what has been silenced by other historiographers. According to the *Libellus*,

> When she still lived in worldly splendor and stateliness, she secretly took in a sick pauper of repulsive appearance. He suffered from scabies on his head. She cut his hideous hair with her own hands, placed his head on her lap, and washed his head in a corner of her little arbor, so that nobody would be able to watch. When she was discovered by the ladies in waiting, she laughed.

In this charitable rendezvous with the scabious pauper, a putrid and foul-looking representative of social misery's lowest rank, deprived of all individuality and only existing as member of an unruly crowd, the landgravine herself felt that such service did not signify honor in the eyes of the court. She kept her grooming efforts a secret. Walther von der Vogelweide and Wolfram von Eschenbach lived in Wartburg castle. It was here that they composed the most explicit, but also the most tender love poems. Instead of receiving knightly admirers in her castle's gardens, the young chatelaine reversed the courtly custom in a gruesome fashion. In protest, she privately staged the most degrading scenario—and this in the cultural era of courtly love, which worshipped women as goddesses.

According to the *Libellus*, she tried to keep such cultic acts hidden. She was found out, however. Gossip about her, already circulating widely, embellished the event even further. This explains the genesis of the miracle story about a leper Elisabeth placed into the shared marital bed.[48] Next to the miracle of the roses, it is among the most popular miracles related to her person:

---

47 See the section on "The Art of Suffering" in Chapter 3.
48 Due to its popularity, this scene has often been depicted in art, especially paintings: so, for example, on altars in Dinkelsbühl and Lübeck and in frescoes in Frankfurt-Sachsenhausen

At another time, Landgrave Ludwig stayed at Neuenburg castle with his mother Lady Sophie and his wife St. Elisabeth. A sick and leprous man named Elias was there as well. St. Elisabeth prepared him a good bath and secretly placed him in her husband's bed. When her mother-in-law noticed this, she approached her son, took him by the hand, guided him to the bed, and spoke: "Look how much your wife loves you—she lets the leprous and sick soil and poison your bed." When she pulled back the cover, Landgrave Ludwig's eyes were opened, and he saw the tortured figure of our Lord on the cross laying in his bed. Then the pious landgrave understood that the Lord God Himself was welcomed when the poor, forlorn, and wretched were taken in. He asked his wife St. Elisabeth to place the sick in his bed wherever they traveled.[49]

This miracle story proves a legend's penchant for begetting new variations. The scene with the scabrous pauper in Elisabeth's little arbor had metamorphosed into the abuse of the marital bed. Only a tendentious theological desire to justify the scandalous lepers' cult of the canonized landgravine could generate such narrative expansion. Nonetheless, nothing less than a miracle was needed to legitimize the fad. Elisabeth's violation of medieval custom was far greater than it seems to us today. The union of bed and table was protected by the strongest social and ritual taboos. It is precisely here that we can uncover the historically correct fact that the landgravine's extravagant care of lepers caused public condemnation for as long as she lived without papal approval and, after her death, had achieved the status of canonized saint.

It seems psychologically probable that, as told in this anecdote, the mother-in-law (another version references aristocratic men) complained to Landgrave Ludwig about his wife and her activities. It is also equally credible that he protected his wife and sought to explain her choices, even though he likely did not go so far as to state that "St. Elisabeth... placed the sick in his bed wherever they traveled." These and similar rumors corroborate indirectly once more that her aristocratic peers labelled Elisabeth's unrestrained behavior toward people with infectious diseases as disruptive and asocial, and thus as one of the causes of her formidable lack of popularity.

and other places. See Schmoll, *The Depiction of St. Elisabeth Between the 13th and 16th Century* (Marburg, 1916).

49   This miracle story stems from the Reinhardtsbrunn monastery's tradition and was added to Dietrich von Apolda's vita by an amanuensis. The excerpt follows Lulu von Strauß und Torney's popular book about St. Elisabeth (*Deutsche Volkheit*, op.cit.). The motif of using the marital bed for care of a leper has also been applied to other pious women's biographies, yet its origins as a miracle story begin with St. Elisabeth.

Her noble peers got even after her husband's death. They took their revenge once it became possible: the ladies whom she angered because she refused to follow their fashion and disturbed their festivities with her puritanical attitudes; the ladies in waiting and her female servants who were forced to care with her for the sick in the overcrowded and putrid hospital; the older aristocrats of her father-in-law's generation, whose literary and artistic inclinations she ignored; and the young noblemen to whom she refused all opportunities to serve her in the spirit of courtly love and approach her with amorous reverence.

Konrad of Marburg

World literature is filled with lovers, the fate of heroes, and heart-rending events. The actors are drawn from the fragments of legends and meager lore. If asking for the historical sources underlying these immortal stories, we find that their scarcity and leanness barely sustain the sublime or convoluted emotional catastrophes that literature created. For example, the biblical story describing the end of St. John the Baptist (Mark 6, 17–30) does not justify an interpretation of Salome as demonic. Yet it became the nearly inexhaustible topic of art and poetry for centuries.

If creative imagination can build an immense structure of human intrigue from a paltry tradition, the opposite is also true. A sometimes entirely clear-cut fact and its fully accessible interpretations will be completely overlooked. This is the case with the relationship between Konrad of Marburg and Landgravine Elisabeth of Thuringia. The pair belong to the immortal manifestations of the human soul, even though their relationship does not resemble that of Paolo and Francesca da Rimini and Abelard and Heloise. There are good reasons why the couple has not yet been discovered. Their destiny was not a love affair in the common sense, even though both partners were fatally addicted to each other. Compromising episodes were lacking. Whoever wants to surmise that theirs was the tragedy of a cuckooed husband is looking in the wrong direction and misses the gripping emotional core of the drama. A demonic, destructive tendency filled it from the beginning. It crushed all three actors: first Elisabeth's spouse, then Elisabeth after a dreadful time of suffering, and finally the cause of all that was destructive, Konrad himself. The tragic through line in all three lives is not only the damage done to one another but also the self-destruction involved. To recognize this, we must understand the psychological depth dynamics underneath the thinly woven layer of primary sources and the sacred pathos of the legends. Not poetic "intuition" but a commonsense knowledge of human nature is sufficient to this end.

The spiritual bonds between especially gifted monks and nuns are often far more revealing and interesting than "normal" love stories. They contain greater tension, because they are not geared toward a bourgeois aim in the sense of the erotic utilitarianism that is characteristic of secular life. It would be tasteless to point out that they were "only" friendships. It would be uncouth to label them unwholesome because they lacked a physical outlet as a philistine teleology would have it. Without a deep and unconscious erotic connection, the magnificent creative relationships of St. Francis and St. Clare, St. Jerome's friendship with St. Paula, and of the mystic Suso and the nun Elsbeth Stagel would have been impossible. It is the reason for their charm, their unusual emotional and mental productivity, and their relationship's life-long vigor. The more sexuality in the narrow sense was excluded, the stronger became the intensity of their emotional closeness.

A superlative professional rapport began like many secular love stories of young people. The agility with which Francis arranges with the sixteen-year-old Clare to escape her family's watch and meet him on Palm Sunday testifies to a strong personal interest in each other. It was more than joy and gratitude that a girl from a rich family professed her loyalty to Francis, who at that time was looked down upon as a misfit. He could not yet rely on the reputation of a religious order, nor on the security of a religious office. Their adventure was more than justified by their mental and characterological strengths. Both were canonized eventually. From the spiritual wedding at the night in the Portiuncula, where Franciscus clothed Clare in monastic garb, onward, both remained true to their spiritual convictions with verve and faithfulness.

In contrast, Church Father Jerome, not unlike St. Elisabeth's confessor, was animated by a naïve masculine selfishness in his relationship with St. Paula. In the name of Christ, he asked of her the most difficult sacrifice: to abandon her five children and her Roman homeland and to move with him far away to Palestine in the service of monastic piety. In both cases, we discern how personal desire becomes embedded in supra-personal demands. But precisely for those reasons, Jerome remained the chivalrous admirer of a woman he revered. Despite his vanity, he acknowledged her superior mastery of the Hebrew and Greek languages, which was considered at the time the apex of intellectual accomplishment. The cordial and productive association was the profit that justified his investment. Their friendship could be regarded as a milestone in psychological history especially because these two human beings belonged to a waning Roman civilization and yet saw themselves as the avant-garde of a new Christian outlook. They carried the full weight of the clash between these two mentalities.

The frequently praised and better-known spiritual couple, the Dominican monk Suso of Constance and the nun Elsbeth Stagel, lived in the fourteenth century. Suso's interest in his fellow monastic sister is the exact opposite of Konrad of Marburg's emotionally perverted guardianship. Suso described the story of his spiritual friendship with a sense of gratitude.[50]

Only the impoverished and diminutive Landgravine Elisabeth, helpless and weak, was nothing but a victim. She was unable to generate a productive dimension of her spiritual relationship. Whatever intensified as spiritual tension or tender eroticism between Suso and Elsbeth, and in many other spiritual relationships, turned into terrifying torment between Saint Elisabeth and her confessor.

Only the psychologically undeveloped standards of a century in which science existed not autonomously but as the handmaid of religion were the cause of not recognizing the relationship between St. Elisabeth and her confessor as a cruel tragedy of self-destruction.[51] And this despite a flood of literature about St. Elisabeth. A long-suffering Griseldis character was drawn into a gendered bondage to a sadistic man, who possessed fiendish powers of manipulation.[52] The former landgravine perished solely because

50 "At the time of the story about the servant [Suso], a spiritual daughter of the order of preachers lived in a cloistered monastery in Töβ. Her name was Elsbeth Staglin. Externally, her conduct was saintly; internally, her disposition was angelic. Her noble turning toward God with heart and soul was so strong that she renounced all those vain things that make many a person forego their eternal bliss. All her diligence was focused on spiritual teachings through which she hoped to be guided to a perfect way of life, and which she desired with all her might. She wrote down anything that would give her and others the pleasure to be guided to divine virtues. She was like the hard-working bees who harvest the sweet honey of many different flowers. The blessed daughter got to know the servant of eternal wisdom [Suso]. God directed her to his life and teachings with great devotion. Secretly, she teased out of him the manner of his break-through to God and wrote it down in the way it is written here and further on. The servant wrote to her in response, 'Recently, you showed me a few enthusiastic thoughts which you selected for me from the sweet teachings of the holy Meister Eckhart, and as is right, which you treated with such tenderness. I am marveling greatly that after such a noble draught from the high Meister you reveal yourself as thirsty for the low servant's (that is, Suso's) coarse beverage.'" Translator's note: While St. Jerome is generally regarded as an affectionate friend to St. Paula, his translations and other writings are filled with the misogynist stereotypes of his era. See Jane Barr, "The Vulgate Genesis and St. Jerome's Attitudes to Women," repr., http://The Vulgate Genesis and St. Jerome's Attitudes to Women – Medievalists. net, accessed December 2, 2023. For a more critical view of Suso's attitude toward Elsbeth Stagel, see Ulrike Wiethaus, "Love and Death in the Vernacular," in Ulrike Wiethaus, *German Mysticism and the Politics of Culture* (New York: Peter Lang, 2014), 111–12.

51 Translator's note: This statement is another example of Busse-Wilson's use of cultural evolution theory. It is not clear, however, to which century the author refers specifically.

52 The primary sources *Libellus* and *Epistola* offer sufficient evidence about St. Elisabeth's relationship with Konrad.

of this relationship. The humiliations and torments that targeted her as a woman constitute the core of her suffering. It is this biography's new truth. Her heroic squandering of her energies and resources were turned into Protestant-rational charity. Her gestures of ascetic self-abasement were reinterpreted as a type of sensual *Minne* and maternal instinct. In like fashion, her self-destruction under Konrad's guardianship, who demanded the sacrifice of her life, was recast as a normal, exemplary, factual, and harmless rapport between a penitent and her confessor, albeit with a few harsh undercurrents.[53] Modern hyperrational historians always only saw one alternative: either the couple shared a nonsexual life goal, or they engaged in an ordinary sexual relationship. Since the latter supposedly was nonexistent, it had to be the former. To their satisfaction, whippings and the moral and spiritual enslavement of Landgravine Elisabeth seemed to be fully explained by normal monastic discipline or, in other words, their historical context.

Yet one statement must not be doubted. We are looking at a "pure" bond in its common definition, even the prime example of such a bond, that is, an extended affiliation between a man and a woman without the presence of physical sex acts. This appealed to most Protestant and Catholic historians to such an extent that further reflection about the odd bond between the

---

53 Nonetheless, all biographers sensed that something was wrong with Saint Elisabeth's relationship to her confessor. Already the thirteenth-century monastic hagiographers Dietrich and Caesarius attempted to obfuscate or rationalize the original reports of the concerned parties. The modern historians of the nineteenth century noticed Konrad of Marburg's inhumane emotional severity and the tyranny with which he treated his penitent. Yet nobody attempted to interpret the relationship. Ranke (in *Allgemeine Deutsche Biographie*) hints very obscurely at seductive situations; Hausrath describes Konrad as a mad despot. Based on the primary sources, only Wegele and Justi must have recognized St. Elisabeth as the targeted victim of the diabolical inquisitor. However, they did not touch on the psychological contexts. "The most bitter accusations must be directed against the confessor of the saint. In this role, his spiritual tyranny directed one of the most noble and pious landgravines, endowed with a most splendid predisposition, away from her proper life's journey. He tormented her mentally and physically until she wasted away in her twenty-fourth year. When death took her away, Konrad sought eagerly to place her among the saints." As in this quotation by Justi, Wegele as well voiced concerns. The position of these older scholars of the nineteenth century was abandoned by younger interpretations (since 1880) in favor of bourgeois rationalizations of this dark relationship. In his treatise about Saint Elisabeth, the Protestant historian Karl Wenck explicitly rejects the "folkloric opinion" "which interprets Konrad of Marburg as the tormentor of the young unhappy woman" (published in his monumental study *Die Wartburg*, 1907). Such trivialization of Konrad of Marburg and the liaison with his penitent constitutes an erasure and dilution of his study of Saint Elisabeth published in 1892 (*Historische Zeitschrift*). It is Winkelmann, however, who dares to reverse the situation. He depicts Elisabeth as a floundering hysteric who caused trouble and misery for her confessor Konrad.

fanatical priest and the canonized landgravine seemed superfluous. It did not fit into either of the two categories of a common analysis: it was not a violation of a monastic oath, which lost its attractiveness to collectors of interesting literary plots, and it was not one of the intellectually creative friendships between religious men and women that church history feels entitled to. The prevailing, antiquated definition of sexuality as sexual intercourse barred the insight that the couple's relationship was sexual in its entirety. Given the characterological mix of the two partners, sexual tension turned into a gruesome battle. The obvious symptoms of a strong mutual obsession were always buttressed by a suprapersonal spiritual collaboration. Konrad's tyrannical ministry, his beatings of his penitent, the régime with which he controlled her personal life, and the immense personal sacrifices he demanded of her were never issued in his name but in the service of the ideals of a world-negating ascetical piety.

In truth, both strands are interwoven: the mutual obsession with each other and the supra-sexual goal of a spiritual life. Konrad's personal jealousy about anything other than himself that was important to Elisabeth was masked by moral or religiously framed disciplinary goals. One plays into the other. Justified by the pursuit of spiritual ideals, Konrad chased his companion from one torment to the next. In turn, she endured all his deeds as divinely ordained affliction. In this manner, both could act bona fide in a long and tormented liaison which degraded Elisabeth but which both believed served mutual sanctification. The philological naïveté of Konrad of Marburg's biographers is almost touching when they try to legitimize and render harmless his true motivations, which they can sense some of the time. One even writes that Konrad of Marburg never thought to alienate the landgravine from her spouse.[54] No doubt, this, or something similar, never occurred to him. Nor did the landgravine think along these lines. The martyrdom of her spiritual marriage was the natural expression of an irrefutable experience of authority, that is, of the primacy of spiritual over secular authority. Although she truly loved her spouse, in good faith, she could and she had to place her spiritual above her secular marriage. The true nature of her dependency was hidden from her own self-awareness as much as her disciplinarian was unaware of the reasons for his religious pedagogy. Their unconscious mutual entanglement never reached the threshold of their conscious mind. At least in the first half of their relationship, both believed strongly that they fought with might for supernatural perfection, rather than being enthralled in a terrifying battle of the sexes. The driving

54 Mielke, Dissertation.

forces of life cannot be parsed as neatly and cleanly as historiographical erudition and the work of philologists would like to. And in any case, if the perpetrators and those who suffer from their crimes, torments, and degradations were aware of the true motivations of only half of these atrocities, human suffering would be merely an experience of childhood but not the all-encompassing, bloody drama of the five-year-old spiritual marriage of Elisabeth of Thuringia and Konrad of Marburg.

Konrad of Marburg's Personality and Work

> In those times, one could still find abundantly just and holy men among the bishops and priests who would serve as a model for Christians. Among them was the honorable Lord Master Konrad of Marburg, whose virtuous life radiated across German lands like the light of stars. He was a deeply learned man. His life and conduct were beyond reproach. Devoted to holy Christian faith, he was an earnest persecutor of heresy and unbelief. He rejected wholeheartedly the possession of wealth, earthly goods, and ecclesiastical posts. He was satisfied with a simple and poorly made priestly garb. His manners were mature and sober, his mien and facial expressions grim. He was amicable and benignly inclined toward Christians, but harsh and unforgiving in revenge and judgment.

This prologue was composed by Dietrich of Apolda, an ecclesiastical chronicler who tried to present the Thuringian landgravine's confessor in a positive light.[55] Yet even Dietrich was forced to remark that Konrad's looks were sinister. They gave the impression of a conspicuously harsh person, who was unusually severe when pursuing his enemies. Earlier, Caesarius had described Konrad as a gloomy and exacting man who was feared by many. These are the main characteristics that were transmitted by trustworthy sources about Konrad of Marburg—with the one exception that some reframed his severity and harshness as "eagerness."

He entertained relationships with princes and high-ranking ecclesiastics. He was a friend and favorite of the pope himself. All career choices in the church were open to him. Nonetheless, he lived a miserly and paltry life as a mendicant and itinerant preacher. A characterological study of Konrad of Marburg is more intriguing than that of his pupil St. Elisabeth, who seems to float above the masses because of the force of her canonization. However,

---

55   Dietrich's account is confirmed in the vita of St. Ludwig, IV.

the scarcity of sources about Konrad causes difficulties in reconstructing his personality from a gestalt-psychological perspective with the same depth as our study of St. Elisabeth.[56] Born into humble circumstances, he abruptly entered the stage of German history as a man of advanced age. Known only to historical specialists today, his role was short but impressive. He lived on intimate terms with his spiritual daughter Elisabeth for six years and was murdered two years after her death. Only the final stage of his life is truly well known. Unsurprisingly, Protestant and Catholic historiographers describe Konrad of Marburg, Germany's most cruel inquisitor and persecutor of heretics, in a different tone. In any case, he was a man gifted with unusual talents and even more uncommon character traits. He demonstrated the ability to be a political leader in grand style, albeit only under the condition of an absolute position of masculine power.

His name, "Konrad of Marburg," is derived from a minor aristocratic lineage that likely provided custodial care for the Marburg castle in Hesse, or at least lived in the vicinity of this frontier castle of the Thuringian-Hessian realm near the city of Mainz. Konrad's rank was that of a secular ordained priest. Some scholars mistakenly assume that he was a Dominican or Franciscan friar, since by nature and personal lifestyle, he lived like a monk.[57] Dietrich of Apolda reports that he was exceptionally well educated—more so than an average cleric. He likely would have acquired the title of "Master," used in all primary sources and as a self-designation ("magister Conradus, predicator verbi Dei"), at a French or Italian university. German universities did not yet exist at the time. While living abroad, he established relationships with leading ecclesiastical figures, especially the future Pope Gregory IX.[58] The relationship facilitated Konrad's singular position as inquisitorial judge

56 Translator's note: This is the only place where the author identifies her approach as an example of *Gestaltpsychologie*, a theory that was developed in part by another forgotten pioneering woman scholar of her generation, Gabriele von Wartensleben (1870–1953). The psychological theory posits, as evidenced in Busse-Wilson's methodology, that individual aspects of a personality must be understood as part of a larger personal pattern that remains consistent across individual choices, emotions, and actions. See Gerhard Stemberger, "Gabriele von Wartensleben (1870-1953): Die Gestalt-Gräfin; Pionierleistungen in der Frühzeit der Gestalttheorie [Personenlexikon zur Gestalttheoretischen Psychotherapie," *Phänomenal – Zeitschrift Für Gestalttheoretische Psychotherapie* 2, no. 1 (2010): 42–45.

57 See Hausrath, Henkel, and Winkelmann. It has been assumed that he was a Dominican friar because he might have participated in the persecution of heretics in Strasbourg in 1212. Yet because Caesarius of Heisterbach, who knew him personally, called him a secular priest, the assumption that he belonged to a religious order must be incorrect.

58 Translator's note: Ugolino di Conti, the future Pope Gregory IX, studied in Bologna and Paris.

with special powers and his unusual mentorship of Landgravine Elisabeth in Germany. When Cardinal Ugolino di Conti assumed the pontificate in 1227, he provided Konrad with privileges that elevated the simple cleric above the authority of German bishoprics. As inquisitor, he turned into a veritable dictator of all of Germany. The fact that Konrad of Marburg, a man without a distinguished ecclesiastical rank, was close to one of the most important medieval popes (at one point, he received three personal briefs from him), and achieved such an exceptional posting suggests that he was not an ordinary person.

Three papal privileges were extended to him: preaching the crusade (i.e., officially promoting participation in a crusade); the office of papal inspector of German clergy and monasteries; and, most significantly, the persecution of heretics. As we shall see, he executed the latter with such terror and dictatorial force that he gained the reputation as an inquisitor of extreme inhumanity and cruelty. He caused his own demise for precisely this reason.

These three of Konrad's professional obligations are more telling of the nature of his character than a full biography, for a profession chooses a person and not the other way around. As his official title "Visitator Monasterium Germaniae" indicates, he was at liberty to disseminate his asceticism and abstemiousness to the fullest. His traits, coupled with his intellectual and analytical abilities, enabled him to become a major ecclesiastical player. He was an autocrat. Imposing his style of religious austerity on the ecclesiastical caste of his time, he turned into a scourge of the German church.

Rural clergy lived in an unconstrained culture of rustic simplicity. Celibacy only existed in theory. Higher ranking clerics and monastics also did not shun the earthly joys of life. An excerpt from a letter by Pope Gregory IX to Konrad dated June 12, 1227, sheds light on the daily life of priests.[59] In the same letter, Konrad receives authorization to force clerics to separate from their mistresses. He doubtlessly used the same ruthlessness and obduracy when cracking down on ecclesiastical immorality as when persecuting heretics.

Preaching the crusades was no easy task. The great era of crusading enthusiasm had passed. Furthermore, the pope's newly demanded crusade—the

---

59 "German clergy, which ought to spread the sweet scent of virtue, instead emits the odor of death. We were informed that priests and others who have received ordination forgot their own dignity and infected subordinates with their depravity whom they ought to lead by modelling an honorable life. As water pours out of a vessel without a lid, they recklessly succumb to every bawdiness, openly abide with their concubines, and live a life of luxury. 'Blush, Sidon, spoke the sea' could be applied to them, because they dare to do without hesitation what lay people abhor." Translator's note: The quotation cites Isaiah 23:4.

sixth—turned into an object of a political play of catch between the pope and Emperor Friedrich II.[60] Since the frenzy of crusader volunteerism had died down for both aristocrats and commoners, the church resorted to extreme means to fill the ranks of the crusader armies. All participants willing to wear the crusader cross were granted nearly all-inclusive indulgences. In a climate of dejection and religious indifference, Konrad of Marburg could rescue a church in distress. Through his charisma and powers of persuasion, he knew how to arouse a lukewarm public once more to participate and sacrifice in such an unusual manner. According to Caesarius of Heisterbach,

> Sitting on a pitiful little mule, he [Konrad] hurried through nearly all of Germany. An infinite number of people of both sexes from different parts of the country followed him, chained to him by his eloquent words and the significant indulgences which he granted at individual stops.

Considering the widespread lack of popularity of the crusade, the German resentment about the oppressive crusading tax, and the wholesale acceptance of meritless men as crusaders, Konrad's advertising activities and his success indicate an extraordinary talent for demagoguery.[61] Apart from two other high-ranking clerics, he remained the only one daring to advertise recruitment across Germany, while German bishops remained idle.

Originally, Konrad's uncompromising character might have had something of a Savonarola. When it came to the persecution of heretics, however, we can only perceive an unscrupulous despotism rooted in the will to power. His later life demonstrates how latent traits of cruelty and a need for destruction rose to dominance.[62] Under the protection of his office, he could condemn and punish his human prey without hindrance and supervision. His unrivalled powers must have been personally gratifying to him in his role as monastic inspector, and later as grand inquisitor.

60 Friedrich II had pledged this crusade as early as 1215, i.e., let himself be blackmailed into it, but did not embark on it in earnest until he commenced with preparations in 1220. Only seven years later did the armed forces, which included Elisabeth's spouse, begin to move. Yet even this effort failed. The crusader army collapsed in Italy due to an epidemic. Ludwig died during the epidemic in Otranto.

61 For example, prayers were asked for a male recruit who was an arsonist, a murderer of six people, and who had impregnated his sister. This case serves as an indication that everybody had to be accepted when volunteers were enlisted.

62 When he was first authorized to work as inquisitor in Germany in 1214, he did not pursue his responsibilities with quite the same temperament and decisions as later in life. Until after his appointment at the landgrave and landgravine's court in Thuringia in the year 1225, he usually avoided bloodshed.

At the end of his life, his extraordinary papal authorization and his victims' lack of social protection seduced him to abuse his inquisitorial authority. Konrad's secular contemporaries in Germany turned against him. An assassination finally got rid of the man even though inquisitorial courts were commonly regarded as legal and necessary. Pogroms generally tend to be popular only if conducted at the expense of powerless targets. For reason of his cruel and baseless inquisitions, void of all sense of justice, he grew into one of German history's most notorious figures.

Becoming the target of a doubtlessly sadistic character: in the public eye, this was the situation of his political victims when he performed his tasks as inquisitor. Privately, it was also that of his penitent, Landgravine Elisabeth. Caesarius of Heisterbach, always eager to praise the controversial man, notes that "Master Konrad's body turned haggard and wretched due to rigid fasting and much labor so that no fault could be found in him." In the eyes of the world, it was his asceticism, especially his sexual abstinence, which safeguarded his position as the guardian and companion of his female penitent. Konrad disarmed any objections through a praxis of genuine moral self-discipline. His somber face, his unaffected monastic charisma and masculine autocratic demeanor elicited submission even where he might have encountered hostility toward his personal plans and intentions.

His public image preempted criticism and serious introspection. His sexual and moral exceptionalism and his severity toward himself absolved him. It also gave him permission for the disgraceful psychological rape and gagging of his female student, the young landgravine, even when her spouse was still alive. Subconsciously, he could consider his pastoral transgressions as "prepaid" on a personal level. He raised the bond with his female penitent to an extreme level of objectification. The relationship's unexpressed eroticism was vented through a seemingly asexual yet equally charged sadism. His ascetic regimen provided him with a clean conscience and thus the freedom to remain indemnified.

His aptitude for austere self-discipline, combined with his character's erotic inexperience, endowed Konrad with something daemonic and irresistible. Indeed, he impressed all, including men, and it was only because of these traits that not only his female penitent but also her spouse and his noble kin granted him exceptional privileges that far exceeded courtly custom.

Yet he, who "neither feared kings nor bishops," was in his own way obsessed with ecclesiastical power and authority. The church defined and circumscribed the range of his imagination. In constant self-censorship, he adjusted and submitted his intellect to her. A psychologically independent inner life was stymied early and prematurely. He was only able to sustain pitiable remnants of a capacity for human relationships, and only when he finally met Landgravine Elisabeth. The intriguing, passionately religious young woman gripped his heart with force and might. Even here, however, his obsession turned into a perverse desire to torment. He seems to have been incapable of genuine warmth and affection and did not even care for himself. Otherwise, his harshness and anti-eroticism would not have grown into the cruelty and callousness which shaped his inquisitions and his relationship with Elisabeth.

His encounter with the royal Franciscan disciple was fateful for him as much as for her. Even though he trampled his victim into the dust, his attachment to the young, religiously gifted woman carried the seed of a factually true but tragic desire for redemption. But it was too late to be redeemed, or even just to soften and diminish his destructive and misanthropic tendencies. His inner life had atrophied.

No tradition exists to explain fully how Konrad arrived at the Thuringian court. The Franciscan Rodeger, Elisabeth's previous confessor, was called from Eisenach to Halberstadt. Landgrave Ludwig is assumed to have contacted Pope Innocent III, who recommended Konrad of Marburg to him. Yet it seems highly unlikely that a German vassal approached the pope himself to ask for a confessor for his wife. Historian Wenck offers a psychologically subtle observation in this regard.[63] He suggests that Landgrave Ludwig searched for a confessor who was not a Franciscan to reign in his wife's boundless self-denial. Inadvertently, he invited into his home instead a patron of Elisabeth's monasticism. The most innocent of the three actors thus appears to have initiated the drama which destroyed him and his entire kin.

It was not only a young landgravine hungry for guidance who came under Konrad's influence. At the very least, he also strongly influenced his employer, Landgrave Ludwig. Following Caesarius's *Vita*, one must assume that Konrad first established his influence over Ludwig so he would authorize all measures taken regarding his wife—a clever move in line with Konrad's behavior in other contexts. Insinuating himself to his young lord, he succeeded in advocating his church-political principles of harsh clerical reform. Ludwig's *Vita* records Konrad's directive to Ludwig that it would be "more permissible to slay sixty men by his own hand than to give a single parish or another ecclesiastical post to an unworthy or unlettered priest."[64] This meant, of course, that only a person chosen by Konrad could find

---

63 Wenck, *Hochland*, 1907.
64 *Vita*, IV, 3.

employment. Later, Konrad of Marburg allowed this key administrative duty to be officially transferred to him. This is proof that he managed in just a few years to impose his will at court. According to Caesarius, he was also entrusted with the education of the landgrave's younger brother, named Konrad, for the priesthood.

The landgravine must have made Konrad's personal acquaintance before she asked her husband for him to become her confessor. The psychologically most likely scenario is that he arrived in Thuringia as an itinerant crusader preacher, and that the landgravine was as fascinated by his charisma and unusual rhetorical gifts as anybody else. Elisabeth's contemporary Caesarius of Heisterbach confirms this view. He even claims that she followed him on his preaching tours much like other people. More than likely, she would have been entranced by Konrad's sermons.

She would have travelled through Thuringia to hear him speak as much as was possible. He in turn might have been delighted to encounter a noble listener, a woman who understood him like a disciple would. Most of his audiences in all the years of his itinerant preaching tours were merely afraid of him. It is possible that both parties carried a certain affinity for each other even before Konrad settled down at Wartburg castle.

"Quasi propheta reputabatur" ("He was regarded as a prophet"). It was thus entirely reasonable in everybody's view, including the landgrave's, that a man of such unusual reputation and talents would be invited to serve as the landgravine's confessor at the Thuringian court. He moved his place of residence to Wartburg castle in 1225. Soon a different religious climate began to prevail. The fourteenth-century Strasbourg Passional tells of St. Elisabeth's penitential exercises in preparation for the arrival of her spiritual director. When his appearance was announced, she rushed to him, fell to his feet, and said, "My Father, receive me as your daughter in God. I am not worthy of you but allow me to be recommended to you by my spouse." Even though not a contemporary eyewitness account, this emblematic story is correct in naming her craving for a father and guide. It attracted his instinctual penchant for power. The landgravine's character weaknesses quickly turned her relationship with Konrad into bondage and doom. Since she had lacked both a father and mother in her life, her desire for an authority figure had not been gratified until now. Her husband did not play the role of her master, which he should have assumed according to the patriarchal ethos of the Middle Ages. She found herself in the role of a ruling noble woman while still an adolescent. She craved authority because she could sample any type of freedom in her private life as much as in public. The sum of these conditions fostered a need for submission, and more intensely so for a woman with certain inherited characterological tendencies. As noted earlier, her father allowed himself to be dominated throughout his life.

Konrad found in her characterological disposition a perfect correlation to his own motivations and instincts. Both possessed traits that foreshadowed an unusual relational reciprocity. And whereas nature rarely produces "pure types," it was the case for this couple. A pure "sadist" met a pure "masochist," an extremely masculine man met an extremely feminine woman.[65] It appears to be the case that both became obsessed with each other the moment they met. It would be wrong to say that they loved each other. She immediately assumed the role of the devout daughter, and soon began to be afraid of him. A woman who had thrown herself at the feet of pauperized lepers with a need for self-abjection that she barely understood herself could easily become suitable prey for a tyrannical leader in priestly garb.

Another circumstance influenced the landgravine's growing self-enslavement. Konrad of Marburg was significantly older than his spiritual daughter, perhaps by as much as twenty years. She was about eighteen years old when he appeared at Wartburg castle.[66] All conditions for an absolute position of authority as a fatherly figure were in place. As the *Libellus* recorded,

> And she performed everything with devotion and joy that Master Konrad
> ordered her to do, so that she might receive the rewards of her obedience
> and follow her Lord Jesus Christ, who was obedient unto death.

Since obedience is one of the heroic virtues, all those scenes of St. Elisabeth's submission, which seem so offensive to us today, were included in the canonization dossier.[67] According to the *Libellus*, Elisabeth once said during her time in Marburg, as if to justify the association with Konrad to herself and her peers:

> I could have chosen as guardian a bishop or a wealthy abbot. Yet I thought
> it better to select a poor person to be without the comfort of worldly

65 The terms sadist and masochist are not used here in a sexual-pathological sense, but characterologically.

66 Konrad began his work as a confessor on the Wartburg in 1225. However, he did not always live there. His many professional responsibilities, crusader sermons, inquisitional tours, and his post as monastic visitator kept him frequently on the road.

67 Translator's note: Together with chastity and poverty, obedience is one of the three so-called evangelical counsels, which St. Francis used as foundation for his religious order.

relationships. Whatever else he might be, he is not a bejeweled ecclesiastical ruler but a poor mendicant monk. For this reason alone, I chose him,
and for this reason alone, I suffer him.

The tragic mistake of her choice was a misreading of the intellectual type
that Konrad embodied. He was the direct opposite of St. Francis, the pious
and humble disciple of evangelical simplicity, whom she had hoped to find
in Konrad. It is for this reason that Elisabeth's religious goals remained
incomprehensible to Konrad of Marburg. She mistook his ascetical severity
for Franciscan simplicity.

Although they seemed to have chosen the same path, Konrad and Elisabeth parted ways in their actual religious work. Despite serving the church
and living like a monk, Konrad of Marburg had not an ounce of religiosity in
him. By talent and inclination a proponent of power politics, he attempted
to reach his ambitious goals through skill, will power, and lack of scruples.
She, however, always remained one of the most genuine students of the
saint of Assisi. Elisabeth and Konrad's relationship thus approximates a
paradigmatic clash between religious and political principles.

Yet neither could live without the other. Their psychological needs complemented each other in an ideal fashion: one satisfied the unconscious
and instinctive desires of the other. The young woman's absolute and freely
given submission rendered him the sweetest pleasures; she took him on as
a father substitute.[68] For Elisabeth, the relationship turned destructive. It
threw a bleak shadow over the second half of her life, when she became a
widow and an undemanding object in the possession of her confessor. All of
Elisabeth's actions assured him that his position toward her was safe. This
is the tragic debt of her life: it was only possible to be freed of him with a
payment of her own death.

And as to Konrad: it would be psychologically inaccurate to only recognize
the repressed love of an aging monk at work in him. Love and passion aim
at reciprocity and equality— two ideals that were never pursued by the
harsh demagogue. His soul had turned into a burned-out and barren crater;
the pursuit of power had replaced a desire for love and expanded ever more
rapidly because of it. The experience of absolute power over Elisabeth

---

68   Translator's note: The author insists on Elisabeth's freedom of choice throughout her study,
even when the young woman's choices became increasingly limited. This includes Elisabeth's
decision not to resist Konrad's abuse but to choose her own death as an act of liberation from
Konrad's sadism. Both decisions safeguarded the saint's overarching priority, her religious
commitment to live as a Franciscan *soror in saeculo*, or lay sister, even when harmed by current
secular and religious norms and rules that tolerated abuse such as Konrad's.

constituted the spell that bound him to his penitent. Without any hope for a resolution, his hatred of the barriers that blocked ultimate possession of her generated the intensity of his fixation. These immutable barriers included his dignity as a priest, her marriage to another man, and the significant social distance between him, a man from a nearly peasant-like lower nobility and a landgravine of royal descent. Konrad's draconic educational measures were derived purely from his impotence to overcome these obstacles. They were only superficially congruent with the Franciscan goals of his pupil. St. Francis and Elisabeth's spouse were his two rivals. St. Francis retained first place. Elisabeth's husband could be easily thrust aside.

Konrad as Pedagogue

Konrad of Marburg begins the *Epistola*, the short biography of St. Elisabeth, which he added to his canonization request after her death, with the statement that, immediately upon his assumption of the role as her confessor, the landgravine told him that she regretted her status as a married woman and would have preferred to remain a virgin. Without a doubt, he would not have straightforwardly invented Elisabeth's statement. Yet he uses it with great skill to prevent a charge against his person. The reason: neither did Elisabeth's kin fully approve of Elisabeth's mentor, nor was the deceased herself ever truly happy while under his spiritual guidance. Konrad, however, was intent on depicting the painful school of defeminization which he forced upon his prey as entirely wished for by herself. From the landgravine's point of view, it would not have constituted a betrayal of her husband had she indeed placed the ideal of virginity and monastic life above marriage. All her contemporaries regarded monasticism as a higher way of life. For medieval women, it constituted the only choice of intellectual self-preservation and protection against biological exploitation.[69] Yet as voiced by her confessor, the "wish" that his penitent would prefer monastic life to marriage takes on a different meaning. Konrad barely manages to hide his personal interest, which for a monk had to shift from positive to negative meaning. He expressed it as an ideologically framed battle against her marriage. According to the *Libellus*,

> She [Isentrudis] testified that St. Elisabeth took a vow of obedience to Master Konrad of Marburg while her husband was still alive. He gave his

---

69   See the section "Christian Asceticism and its Modern Misunderstanding" in this chapter.

approval except for conjugal rights. She promised Konrad eternal chastity should she survive her husband.

This took place in Eisenach in the monastery of St. Catherine (i.e., in the monastery's church).[70] Konrad of Marburg is not content with a mere transfer of his penitent from her spouse—his lord—to him. He feels more secure by way of coercing her conscience, which is achieved through a promise given at the altar, that is, through a vow of obedience shrouded in an aura of sacredness. She was thus induced to undertake her transfer into his possession herself. Formally, such demonstration of obedience was borderline customary, even if not frequently practiced.

This half-way completed nun's vow was clearly a compromise. Conjugal rights were barely respected. The oath's internal logic points to eliminating these rights as well. The second part of her pledge, to not remarry in the case of widowhood, was an explicit agreement that secured in advance Elisabeth's life-long dependence on Konrad. In her guileless view, the vow carried ethical significance as an objective spousal commitment to chaste faithfulness. The demands on Ludwig concerned only the realm of spiritual leadership. Therefore, Ludwig could not object to Elisabeth's relationship with her spiritual teacher and mentor Konrad. The person to which Elisabeth bound herself was, after all, not a man but a monk.

In taking the vow, Elisabeth could move neither forward nor backward. She kept the vow of obedience until the end of her life with slavish faithfulness, sworn to her confessor while she was still a lay woman, a landgravine, and a wife. There was no demand that she did not fulfill. She allowed him to beat and bully her. After the death of her spouse, she relinquished even her personal honor in the service of obedience to him. Konrad of Marburg thus had built a solid foundation through Elisabeth's irrevocable self-enchainment in the Cistercian women's monastery in Eisenach. Once this unalterable bond was in place, an escalating educational program could proceed with ease. According to the *Libellus*:

After she had offered her [vow of] obedience to Master Konrad, she assumed the habit of frequently leaving the bed that she shared with her

70   It is in this monastery that the landgravine widow Sophie lived, who was Elisabeth's mother-in-law. For this reason, Wenck (1908) suggests that Elisabeth submitted to Konrad's unlimited spiritual authority not merely with the permission of her closest kin but on their explicit wishes. In any case, it attests to Konrad's circumspection and influence that he recruited both her mother-in-law and husband as his allies. The outcome of his spiritual guidance proves that he abused his legal power in the service of his own impulses.

spouse. Entering a secret chamber, she let herself be severely castigated by the hands of her female servants.

The nocturnal prayer sessions, which the landgravine had imposed on herself on her own initiative with the goal of interior recollection, were obviously not sufficient for her confessor.[71] They had to be intensified. It has not been recorded that Elisabeth regularly used the "discipline," that is, the training tool of physical self-mortification for a monastic lifestyle, before she met Konrad. Yet if Konrad prescribed self-castigation for his lay penitential daughter, his actual aim was to unravel marital union—or in any case, that it was to be consummated only with a bad conscience. The education in chastity must be understood, as is true for the mentoring relationship, as the consequence of personal and unconscious sexual desire on his part. His mentoring efforts expanded to include separating the landgravine from her social environment. The goal was to uproot her not only as a wife but also as the lady of the manor and landgravine. Nothing is more suitable to disrupt a sense of belonging among kith and kin than to impede commensality. According to the *Libellus*:

> After having made the vow of obedience, Master Konrad ordered her to not live on those of her husband's revenues about whose origin she could not be absolutely certain. She executed the order with great vigilance. Even when she sat next to her spouse at the table, she abstained from all fare which was derived from the levies and taxes of bondspeople.[72] She did not eat a dish if she could not be sure that it was made of her husband's lawful revenues. If something was served that stemmed from illicit income, she frequently pretended to eat with the others. Under the vassals' and servants' eyes, she distributed bread and other dishes, and passed them around so that nobody noticed when she herself did not eat.

Master Konrad thus began his pedagogical program by ordering his pupil to avoid food, a prohibition that she followed meticulously and with uncritical devotion to his spiritual paternalism. Despite its religious motivation, this rule of avoidance carried not so much an ascetical or even social affinity, but church political bias. According to the master's opinion, all foodstuffs were "impure" that were submitted by manors and farming villages which

---

71 See also the section "Landgrave Ludwig and St. Elisabeth's Marriage" in Chapter 2.
72 In the economic system of the time, taxes consisted of *naturalia*, mostly foodstuffs for the landgrave's kitchen.

originally belonged to the church but were confiscated by the landgrave's Thuringian house. This is the most likely possibility given the single-minded man's church political confluence of interests. Landgrave Hermann, Ludwig's predecessor, had been especially active in this regard and annexed manors belonging to the archbishopric of Mainz. Konrad, in turn, misused his pupil to introduce a permanent protest against these possessions—a clever intrigue indeed. In no way did he intend to draw attention to the burden of high levies for poor peasants. Nothing was further from his mind than sympathy for the plight of the people. Instead, he deftly turned the land-gravine's hypersensitive Franciscan conscience into a tool of ecclesiastical political protest through a tendentious mandatory food taboo.

Following the order, her "permitted" meal once consisted of only five small birds. Since her three closest maidservants had also pledged food abstinence and, like her, suffered the pangs of hunger, she left them most of this meal. As the *Libellus* notes, she suffered more on their behalf than from her own hardships. How much this went against a healthy instinct and her own will to live is demonstrated by the following reaction. In the rare case when she did not have to feel scruples while eating or drinking, and her tortured young body finally was given its due, she experienced explosive outbursts of joy. According to the *Libellus*, "She clapped her hands and exclaimed full of delight, 'All is well for us, now we may eat and drink together.'"

When all ways of getting permitted foodstuffs were blocked—when free game or products from manors in the landgravine's private possession were not available—then she sent her servants to strangers to plead for bare necessities. This caused Konrad to tighten the noose. He forbade her even this escape. According to the *Libellus*,

> It happened frequently that she endured great discomfort. Sometimes she only ate small cakes filled with honey. She and her revenue would have been content with plain bread if some had been available that she could have consumed without uncertainty about its provenance.

Crude priestly educational programs and efforts at reinforcing their ideologi-cal dominance have always leveraged rules of avoidance and separation. The essential psychological aim of self-castigation, which Konrad demanded from his penitent, was the continuous generation of scruples and moral self-doubt. Through this tactic, she found herself chained to him as the infallible provider of all "rightful" norms. Elisabeth's single-mindedness, blended with a mix of childlike innocence and submissiveness, endured her "practice" with heroic self-discipline. Most of the time, however, she lived with the anxiety that she might violate the male taskmaster's rules and commit a sin by eating forbidden food items. The horrifying prospect arose as doubly sinful every time she desired a morsel of food. And this was precisely how it should have been. The rules were intended to cause torment. Soon, the master teacher had reached his desired goal: by force of her conscience, voluntarily and even in his absence, his daughter proceeded in her assigned self-abasement.

At this stage, Konrad was not as much interested in the execution of his tendentious boycott as in confusing and breaking Elisabeth's self-confidence. Indeed, the young woman found herself in one plight after the other. At a richly decked table, she had to remain hungry and pretend, with a growling stomach, that she partook of the food like others. Above and beyond such perfidious psychological torment, enduring a starvation diet had to undermine her physical and emotional stamina. During this time, she also gave birth to three children in quick succession. And all these ordeals took place while she was not even twenty years of age.

Once, Master Konrad's spiritual daughter went on a horseback ride of eighty German miles in the company of her spouse. During the length of this exhausting journey, she ate nothing but a large piece of black bread. It was so dry that it first had to be soaked in warm water. According to the *Libellus*, she did not dare eat other food items. Thus was the extent of perfecting self-enslavement under her confessor's guidance. While on this starvation ride, she lost so much of her strength that she fell from her horse. One of the accompanying vassals caught her while falling. The hagiographic tradition, intent on amplifying the situation's heroic asceticism, fused another incident with her fainting spell. While intercepting her fall, the vassal noted that she wore a ragged, coarse penitential undergarment under her robe.[73] Elisabeth was embarrassed about this discovery and asked him to keep it a secret given the excessive scrutiny and gossip that she was exposed to already.

The landgrave suffered the most because of the perplexing relationship. Yet he practiced extreme patience. He balanced the young landgravine's abstemious and conspicuous activities and her devout obedience toward her confessor with superb confidence. As was true for his wife's charitable activities, he defended her alimentary boycott and was willing to bear certain social annoyances in return. However, it was also prudent to support her and the author of these divisions in the justification of the new abstinence

---

73 This incident is recorded in a Franciscan vita of Elisabeth that dates from the fourteenth century, located at the Koblenz State Archives (Staatsarchiv). The vassal was rewarded for his assistance by a miracle that took place after Elisabeth's death.

rules. He even helped her by discreetly assisting her in choosing food items. According to the *Libellus*, if he noticed while seated at the table that she was hungry, he secretly gave her a sign to indicate which dishes she could eat without scruples. When she asked him whether he was upset that she and her ladies disturbed table rules in plain sight, he responded diplomatically that he would prefer to join their fasts if consideration for his peers and kin would not prevent him from doing so.

The landgravine's provocative boycott vexed her social peers to the highest degree, despite her ostensible efforts not to act conspicuously at official events. Her peers felt their own good conscience become unsettled by the public rejection of income, which they had all reason to accept as legitimate. They believed themselves to be accused, albeit indirectly. Elisabeth's apparently merely personal asceticism was understood precisely as what was intended by its spiritual creator, a public protest. Feudal society must have felt already challenged and its status questioned by her earlier activities, including the unusual care for indigents, which she executed with intense determination. By generating ever new apprehension, the young landgravine became unpopular. Life in her social circle grew increasingly impossible. We arrive at this conclusion not only through a combination of her new contexts but also through proof from the primary sources. The following text from the *Libellus*, casually overlooked until now, reveals a great deal in this regard:

> She as well as her spouse endured much vilification by their kin, some of which was expressed straight to their face. It was caused by her strange, unusual, and conspicuous lifestyle. They endured it all with great patience.

A source geared toward endowing the saint with every right of exceptionalism vis-à-vis her society cites social hostility only as a proof of the "patience" and saintliness of Elisabeth and her husband. How untenably bad must have been the young woman's real situation. Elisabeth scholars have denied this fact, but when viewed through the lens of her society, one cannot doubt the truth of the antagonism that was directed at the disconcerting female nonconformist when she lost all her protection. Endowed with the peculiar recklessness of a zealot, she provoked people without an instinct for the precariousness of her own existence. Had she possessed a gift for compromise and courtesy, she could have advanced numerous changes in the aristocratic way of life. Yet the opposite happened: the grim demagogue's belligerent drive to divide not only engendered inevitable isolation, but soon enough created his pupil's active need for setting boundaries. From this point of view, her food boycott turned into one of many different and obvious causes for the catastrophe of Elisabeth's isolation after the landgrave's death.

Her spiritual guide Konrad, the author of all these conflicts, did not shield her from the dangers of social isolation. Rather, he aimed at undermining her position as landgravine and lady of the manor with the pretense and assistance of his educational demands. The more she inevitably made enemies because of her new spiritual exercises, the deeper she became dependent on her confessor – and this was the purpose of the drill. Konrad irrevocably locked her mind into an attitude of protest, which, as discussed above, was already present in her childhood.

The worst result of this process of self-generated social alienation became the transformation of her personality into the character role of a nun. Rather than emulating the Franciscan monastic identity grounded in world transcendence, her new monastic persona was defined by hostility toward the world. The landgravine began recruitment for her lifestyle and attempted to impose it on others. If a person who is isolated by her own sectarian way of life becomes aware of her loneliness, she endeavors to overcome her seclusion not by concessions but by the increasing need to proselytize. According to the *Libellus*, Elisabeth, "as it were," preached to visiting female aristocrats by giving moralizing speeches and urging the women to join her in her way of life. She pressured them to make a vow, if not of spiritual widowhood, so at least of a boycott of modern fashion or dance. She could not have gained much popularity through her exhortations to lead an austere life, nor did she achieve personal moral success. She lacked all support as the crisis of her public life befell her. Her disciplinarian's mentoring broke and abused the spirituality she had developed according to Franciscan ideals. It violated the nonpartisan asceticism which she had applied only to charitable service to the indigent. The *Libellus* notes that:

When her spouse was absent, she spent many nights with vigils, prostrations, flagellations, and prayers. She put her beautiful clothes away, changed her veil, and dressed like a widow and nun. She frequently wore wool or a hair shirt on her bare skin, even under outfits encrusted with jewels or of crimson coloration. But when she heard that her spouse was on his way home, she carefully adorned herself. On these occasions, she would say, "I do not beautify myself because of vanity, but because of God. I only adorn myself to not give my spouse a reason for infidelity in case he does not like something about my appearance. He ought to love me alone in marital love and fidelity so that we both will receive the crown of eternal life from the one who sanctified marriage."

Besides the flagellum, which Elisabeth generally only used after she had come under Konrad's influence, all characteristics of monastic life make an appearance in this text segment, likely all allotted by her confessor: the nocturnal penitential exercises, the nun's habit, the hair shirt used for bodily mortification.[74] The increasing "nunnification" seems to have turned into a source of distress for her spouse. He felt that Elisabeth began to withdraw from him, slipping away into another world. This might be the meaning behind the landgravine's change of clothing upon her husband's return home. Especially true for the year of famine in 1226, when he was gone for most of the year, the landgrave frequently spent time away from home.

During his absences, she lived as if she were indeed already a widow. Medieval and Renaissance dress codes distinguished garments for girls, adult women, and widows by types of head dress, color, and style. Seeing his spouse wear a widow's garments must have struck the landgrave as disconcerting symbolism. And not for her own sake, and not because she still was in love, did she put the neutering monastic garments aside upon his return home. It was only for Ludwig's sake. She intended the change of clothing as a didactic moral tool for herself and her ladies to exhort marital fidelity. Such displacement of justifications and her need to rationalize her actions are in and of themselves already quite telling.

Konrad had succeeded in shattering—or rather, in rendering super-fluous—the marriage even before the landgrave's departure. We cannot interpret his hostile attitudes toward marriage and secular society only as sexual envy or the resentment of a man who was condemned to live in involuntary chastity. To the contrary, his success must be approached as sexual desire that turned into a craving for power. It becomes obvious in specific actions and reactions, which drop the mask of originally vague vows and seemingly objective measures. Konrad's demands for the exclusive possession of Elisabeth reach the point where he throws fits of anger and enacts appalling scenes of revenge when she withdraws from him even just once—and not for reasons of indifference toward him but out of necessity. The *Libellus* reports:

> Even when her husband was still alive, she was obedient to Konrad to such a degree that once, when he asked her to attend his sermon, she was unable to be present because of the sudden arrival of the landgravine of

---

74 Wearing a rough hair shirt, at times derived from goat hair, was a widely used means of monastic training. The landgravine wore it under civilian clothing as a form of imitation and impersonation.

Meissen. Konrad was so offended that he sent a messenger to her with a notification that he would cease his care for her due to her disobedience. The next day, she rushed to him and asked humbly if he might forgive the offense. Yet he did not wish to do so. She then fell to his feet. She and her maidservants, whom Konrad held accountable in this matter, were undressed down to their undershirts and he beat them severely.

Her nonappearance at the announced sermon was such a slight to him because, in a sense, he preached it for her. He did not make the effort solely for a few peasants of that poor region and the squires and knights of the castle. His impotent rage was triggered by the objective justification of her absence. This small incident obviously taught him in a very tangible manner about the social distance between him and his royal penitent. It continued to exist despite all ceremonial and sacramental acts of obedience. He thought her to be his wholly undivided and subservient possession, yet she remained landgravine, ruler, and chatelaine in a social circle that was closed to him. She still was able to withdraw from him and to keep other friends beside him. It is for these reasons that he believed he could only counter her evenhanded cancellation with the alternative of demanding "all or nothing." It was not the emotional blackmailing of a snubbed lover when he informed her that she was no longer of concern to him. It was a final and extreme attempt at controlling the situation.

The master's threat did not fail in its intended effect. On the following day, a trembling landgravine rushes to him and begs for his forgiveness. He lets himself be courted and pretends to be unmoved. Then she throws herself at his feet. And this was precisely the situation that he craved and needed as much as other people need kisses and tenderness. It cooled his rage. He got even for the affront. He batters the undressed woman in her undergarment and her maidservants. This was his *unio mystica*. The beatings became the spice of their spiritual marriage while St. Elisabeth lived in Marburg.[75]

75 All hagiographers up until the historians of the nineteenth century were notably uncomfortable with the fact that Konrad of Marburg beat his spiritual daughter while she was still landgravine and chatelaine. Indeed, already Dietrich of Apolda, the Dominican who wrote her biography sixty years after Elisabeth's death, shifted the original text at precisely this point. He notes, "ad pedes eius humiliter se prosternens filia regis veniam prosteret. Ancillas vero eius durius verberibus castigavit" ("The daughter of the king, humbly prostrating herself at his feet, begged for forgiveness. But he punished her handmaids with severe blows."); however, the original text reads, "ipsa ad pedes eius procidens et ancille eius, quibus magister Cunradus culpam imposuit usque ad camisiam exapoliate bene sunt ab eo verberate" ("Falling at his feet, she and her maidservant, on whom Master Konrad laid the blame, were beaten hard by him, even to the extent of [first] removing the shirt"). This minor falsification underscores the personal

The long chain of Elisabeth's acts of self-annihilation and self-denial, which she mustered in the service of her vow of obedience during the second half of her life, is purely an internally consistent progression of her earlier self-discipline. It was introduced by the owner of her soul with the seemingly negligible rules related to her food intake, and grew into a renunciation of her secure and satisfactory life, her high social status, and everything that made her life joyful and interesting up to the heaviest personal sacrifices: the separation from her children, from her spouse, and from all those whom she loved; and finally, the renunciation of life itself.

The Turning Point

Meanwhile, Konrad's educational efforts needed further stabilization. He had to confront the fact that despite spiritual exercises, penances, and the steady enforcement of obedience, he did not possess sole ownership of his spiritual ward. Furthermore, the landgravine expected yet another child. And this despite two-and-a-half years of instructions for a monastic lifestyle. He therefore decreed that Landgrave Ludwig was to leave for battle when after much delay, Emperor Friedrich II finally called for a crusade in 1227. Participation in a crusade would keep the landgrave away from home for many years—if he ever returned. We can be certain that he did not wish for the death of his lord. His imminent departure was likely most inconvenient for Konrad since he would lose an influential position at the court of a powerful feudal lord. Moreover, Konrad's assignment was to serve as a preacher for the crusades, that is, as a recruiter for the military campaign that Friedrich II had promised long ago and yet deferred repeatedly. He could not afford to waste this opportunity to win a leading German aristocrat for the pope's cause. One Landgrave Ludwig weighed much more than hundreds of landless peasants, which he could win over in his sermons to the masses. Ludwig was doubly enticing given this ecclesiastical enterprise's lack of popularity.

Considering her moral dependence on Konrad, it was easy for him to cause Elisabeth to feel guilty when she refused to sacrifice her spouse on the altar of the church. Ludwig as well was manipulated into accepting the

decency of Elisabeth's hagiographers (Caesarius of Heisterbach as well tries to superimpose a semblance of legal punitive action on this incident), but it does not free modern historiographers of a commitment to truth. What was exceptional during Elisabeth's reign as landgravine became the rule for the relationship in Marburg after the landgrave's death.

crusade as a religiously meritorious deed. Securing this onerous sacrifice, which Elisabeth made *nolens volens*, Konrad succeeded in delivering the first significant destructive blow to his victim. The mixture of his motivations—those that were ecclesiastical, objective, and visible in plain daylight and those that were personal and hidden in the shadows—was at play here and became increasingly more obvious in his subsequent actions.

The crusade for which Ludwig was recruited signified an excessively nonreligious affair to members of every social status, including the enlightened Friedrich II, who participated only reluctantly.[76] Medieval crusades are comparable to the dynamics of the national wars of modernity. At first, there was the momentum of immense heroism, a frenzy of self-sacrifice and mass altruism, which certainly contained authentic religious roots. Such idealism, then and now, could only be sustained under one condition: that the war does not last too long and is not repeated too frequently. A world war every twenty-five years is unbearable.[77]

The crusade which was proclaimed in 1227 was the sixth European military campaign in 130 years. Consequently, aristocrats and commoners alike contemplated the new crusaders' military invasion of Palestine with great sobriety: it would bring terrifying travail, grueling and unfamiliar military strategies in a murderous climate, and in the best-case scenario, a return home after many years, one's body spent and maimed. These were the political opportunities which everyone gauged without illusions.

The Thuringian landgrave thus had no intention of participating in the crusade. Apart from him, only two other German feudal lords followed the emperor's solicitation. At the time, Ludwig had just consolidated the Thuringian principality through several lucky wars. The country needed his presence. Pressured by Konrad, Ludwig's sole reason for participating was the prospect of ample political compensation, that is, an entitlement to Lusatia and significant sums of money.[78] For his part, Konrad did not forget to ensure the continuation of his influence in Thuringia during Ludwig's long absence. He secured Ludwig's authorization to exercise the right of ecclesiastical patronage for all of Thuringia before Ludwig's departure. This significant office authorized him to fill all ecclesiastical posts in Thuringia and to participate in the country's internal politics.

76　See the previous section for further discussion of the crusade.
77　Translator's note: The author published her study in 1931, halfway between the end of World War I and the beginning of World War II.
78　Wenck, op.cit.

Landgrave Ludwig's departure from Thuringia and his early death have been described in detail by thirteenth century sources.[79] He intended to keep his undertaking hidden from the landgravine. When she discovered the sign of the cross on his garment, she fainted in distress. In the attempt to escape fate, they promised their unborn child to the church. Elisabeth followed the Thuringian army for several days without finding the courage to bid farewell. After the separation, she collapsed exclaiming, "Woe to me, most unfortunate woman!"

These scenes of separation and sorrow strike us today as sentimental and worthy of dime store novels, thus entirely unhistorical. Yet the same rules apply as for all of Elisabeth's medieval sources: the chroniclers would not have mentioned these features if they had been considered self-evident. Furthermore, they prove the opposite of the hagiographical insinuation that Elisabeth was single-minded in her determination to send her husband off on the crusade out of a sense of religious duty. The wives of medieval feudal lords would commonly not have fainted in agony if their spouse fulfilled his military obligations. The main male occupation was war. It was as much a matter of course to marry one or more times as it was that war loomed large as a central aspect of a marriage. A lengthy absence of a husband and his male retinue spelled welcome domestic relief and respite for his wife. She was also freed of annually occurring pregnancies.

Yet in Elisabeth's case, the psychological situation was more complicated. She loved her spouse. When he left, she could foresee her coming collapse. With the departure of her only friend, she suddenly became aware of the dual worlds and of the contradictions in which she lived. She secretly began to fear absolute dependency on her confessor, to whom she had dedicated herself and whom she could not leave. Only her happy marriage made this constellation somewhat tolerable. Now she had to face him all by herself. Moreover, she had plenty of enemies among her husband's kin and the aristocracy. This tangle of vague fears and premonitions and her genuine sorrow over the separation from her beloved overwhelmed her at the moment of taking leave. "Woe to me, most unfortunate woman!" The legend has intuited her psychological dilemma.

Landgrave Ludwig never reached the promised land. In the middle of June 1227, he and his military retinue left the Thuringian homeland. The crusading army could not even board the ships in southern Italy because

---

79   Several episodes from the Reinhardtbrunn monastery found their way into Dietrich of Apolda's 1293 *Vita S. Elisabeth*. Dietrich retrieved other segments from oral traditions. For a discussion of their reliability, see Chapter 1. Another extensive source is the *Vita S. Ludwig*.

an epidemic, most likely typhoid, raged among the troops and decimated their numbers.[80] The landgravine had just given birth to her third child at the end of September when news of his death reached the Wartburg castle. She raised herself from her childbed with great anguish and paced aimlessly, crying and wailing like a person who had lost her senses. All who were present could barely contain her. "Dead, my whole world is dead!"

The madness of the young woman's anguish resembles only superficially the words that any human heart tortured by grief may utter. In the life of St. Elisabeth, it is the thin thread on which hung her excruciating existence as a homeless ascetic and her incipient life as a saint. The young widow's actions in the following months and years must be understood as a psychological reaction to fate's heavy blow. They inexorably shifted the course of her life and turned her previous existence in all its details alien and distant. Her saintly deeds, her abandonment of Wartburg castle, her aimless wandering under the most wretched conditions, and her radical contempt for the world and renunciation of it were cultivated during her life at Marburg. They must be understood as the pendulum swings of her singular grief. A year later, she is ready to pronounce,

> I call on God as my witness that my own children are not nearer to me than those of strangers. I have handed them over to God. He may do with them as He wishes. All that was my earlier life is now nothing but straw and dirt.

The sweeping de-feminization contained in these words, which marked the second half of her life, does not constitute a betrayal of her former existence as wife and mother but is an expression of her terrifying loss of it in every way. The descent had been too steep and too deep. Her only option of fighting her sorrow over the landgrave's death was to deny everything that had preceded her choice of a monastic life.

Our modern way of thinking expects a young person suffering through their first bout of love's disappointments—the landgravine was twenty years of age when her spouse died—to open a new chapter of her life with courage or to seek a new love. This is especially true if her life's significance is affirmed by the existence of three small children. St. Elisabeth did not choose this common ethical and rational path. Her decision makes her

---

80   The emperor halted the enterprise. The renewed delay caused the pope to begin a long multi-year war with the emperor. It was not until 1229 that the ill-fated crusade was finally launched.

existence and her activities interesting. It jarringly reveals the difference between the medieval and our own attitude toward life. It is impossible to measure the first half of her life with the contemporary standards of rationalist ethics. The attempt to paint her in the second half of her life as the carrier and exemplar of evangelical charity is to commit a historical lie. She could only endure the dreadful abnormalities which filled the remaining four years of her life because they were embedded in a chiliastic, otherworldly religiosity. It had nothing in common with a human hope for a better life or with the universal characteristics of youth.

Elisabeth had to live through fearsome experiences to reach the status of such sanctity, that is, she had to become desensitized to suffering and thus dead to the world. Her first station of the cross was the days of misery known in history and legend as her expulsion from the Wartburg castle.

3   On the Road to Sainthood

The Art of Suffering

Why does sorrow follow the human soul? Since Job, the interrogator from a lost people, every religion and every philosophical era has attempted to resolve this problem, according to its own fashion. A guileless human being howls once and then, without transition, forgets. A more complicated person retains the traces of the axe's blows raining down on her.

Those who are the heirs of ancient cultures and ancient races, however, have a third experiential option. The psychological disposition of those who suffer, and who have overcome the first terrifying shock of pain, may surrender to a feeling of liberation as lesser pain surges forth. They consciously experience sorrow ebbing away, and almost regret its complete disappearance. The wistful-conscious endurance of pain, or what we may call world-weariness, always indicates stages of emotional development that are more or less mature. It requires the ability to turn one's self into an object of reflection. This is not difficult if a person is not directly involved in the situation, and whose reflections can therefore remain on the purely philosophical and epistemological level. However, if someone is directly affected and fully immersed in the experience, this ability represents a tremendous achievement. It is only then that any insight, any world-weariness metamorphoses into true freedom and turns into a victory of spirit over mere existence.

The tactic of fighting pain through eradicating as many causes of suffering as possible is typical of our present era. However, it is not as one-dimensional as it might seem to us, oversaturated by Enlightenment thought as we are. This approach requires intrepid objectivity and a consistently critical analysis of reality. It demands a disposition of selfless social ethics and not merely a presumably happiness-seeking attitude. The former aims at the salvation of all humanity; world-weariness as such merely aims at salvation of self. An immature discontent with civilization has the tendency to underestimate the rational fight against suffering; it reasons that if one source of suffering is eliminated, another will immediately take its place.

Busse-Wilson, E., *St. Elisabeth of Thuringia: A Psychological Study* (1931). Amsterdam: Amsterdam University Press, 2025

DOI 10.5117/9789463725804_CH03

Such discontent pronounces it foolish to expect too much relief from an improved social order, from a more just distribution of wealth, from the fight against illness and epidemics, or from new marital laws. This philosophical stance is characteristic of those who are mere spectators; for them, no intellectual game can be staked too high. Those who are actors rather than spectators, however, thirst for any kind of alleviation of their suffering, even if it may be small.

Nonetheless, realizing the unpredictable and irrational character of human life, an objective observer would be correct in doubting that an authentic fight against suffering may bring redemption. Fate assigns life's disappointments and love's woes to every human being. Heartache is the fundamental threat par excellence since it cannot be avoided by either rational attempts at prevention or philosophical reflection. Religions have wisely generated diverse rules of conduct to counteract the fatal, raw, and elemental impact of emotional pain. Hinduism teaches the techniques of psychological desensitization; Islam schools human beings in fatalistic acceptance.[1] Christianity is the only religion that sanctifies suffering without the relief of anaesthetizing the psyche. Christianity neither repressed nor set it aside. It did not intellectualize suffering but acknowledged it. "Become like Jesus, your king, who since the beginning of time and in eternity wills that nothing great can take place without suffering." This manifesto of suffering was composed by St. Catherine of Siena in one of her letters to Pope Urban VIII. It is accepted by each one of us moderns. Great deeds and great insights are indeed often the progeny of tough battles and personal hardships. Yet we are also recognizing the statement's moral and goal-oriented rationalizations. Greatness can only be born through suffering, but suffering does not always generate wisdom and maturity or heroic and redemptive doom. Frequently, suffering merely produces a passive descent into darkness without escape, carrying the cross to Golgotha without a promise of resurrection.

Christianity has sanctified even unproductive suffering. Since it has deified life, even when impoverished and insignificant, unheroic anguish is as revered as the prodigious travail that elicits great deeds and insights.

---

1   Translator's note: The concept of Islamic fatalism is now understood to be a stereotype rather than an authentic Islamic value. See Gabriel A. Acevedo, "Islamic Fatalism and the Clash of Civilizations: An Appraisal of a Contentious and Dubious Theory," *Social Forces* 86, no. 4 (June 2008): 1711–52. The author's claim that Christianity is the only religion that sanctifies suffering without psychological numbing would be challenged by contemporary scholars of religion. See John Bowker, *Problems of Suffering in Religions of the World* (Cambridge: Cambridge University Press, 1970).

Suffering conveys life itself. In contrast to the ancient world and its elitist views, the Christian art of suffering has bestowed dignity and consecration to the dismal, involuntary, and passive anguish of humankind, and to the fruitless sadness of life's disappointments. Yet the sanctuaries and sacraments of Christianized grief cannot liberate from suffering as such. The promised and often also experienced religious consolations only apply to a much later stage of suffering than to its first dreadful onslaught. Religious solace presumes that a capacity for reflection has come into effect. Up until that moment, however, human hearts and souls are floundering in the fangs of pain, bent and fighting against the disappointments of life or the loss of self-esteem.

For these reasons, medieval Christianity teaches the voluntary search for suffering. The goal is not to endure pain with humility or to transform it into work and achievement, as is true for the later Puritan-Protestant ethic, but to embrace it with a voluntary intentionality. The authentic disciples of suffering do not repress the torment of doubt about their choice but work through it again and again. The disciples of suffering will actively seek out situations that are beyond their capacity to withstand, that will dent their self-esteem and humiliate their sense of honor.

From this perspective, the symbolism of flagellation cannot be fully understood when merely defined as a mortification of the flesh. Rather, with the aid of penitential scourging, the ascetic intends to become well practiced in the endurance of pain, since pain constitutes the only absolute certainty that can be expected from life. Bodily discomfort is the mild precursor to the utmost psychological anguish. Widely respected Protestant psychologists are wrong to approach flagellation as a desperate repressive fight against sensuality. Abstinence from sleep and meals, a Spartan narrowness of one's cell, and sexual self-denial are only the inferior consecrations of asceticism. Whether self-imposed by pious individuals or as periodic public mass events of self- lashing during flagellant pilgrimages,[2] flagellations are always teleological; they display elements of apotropaic magic.[3] Part and parcel of all self-humiliations, including a rejection of social status and self-castigation,

[2]   The fourteenth century fraternity of flagellants travelled through German and Dutch towns, villages, and crowded cemeteries and marketplaces while performing a litany of prayers and scourging themselves. Pilgrimages peaked around the 1350s, the years with the highest mortality rate of Europe's plague epidemics. As the worst times of the plague gradually receded, so too did the flagellant movement.

[3]   Translator's note: Elisabeth Busse-Wilson might have followed Bronislaw Malinowski's theory of the social and psychological functions of magic in this instance. Malinowski studied with Wilhelm Wundt at the University of Leipzig around 1910. See Gerald Gaillard, "Bronislaw

is the effort to undercut fate. A secret fear of life may lead to the reasoning that if I voluntarily act malevolently toward myself, God will not trouble me as well. We thus preempt the sender of all things good and bad. We practice diminishing ourselves in a kind of preventative war whose battle front is turned against ourselves, but not against suffering and its causes. The deeper we stoop, the less cause is given for an attack—just as we crawl on the ground with a bent back in order to not be swept away by a storm. If someone is rich, healthy, and happy, fate can wreak havoc. But nothing much can happen to a person who takes a stance of existential minimalism to all of life's aspirations to happiness, intelligence, and physical comfort. Medieval asceticism functioned as an existential safety guard, a means to make life bearable and free of suffering. In the final analysis, medieval asceticism thus turns on its head as an anti-asceticism. The art of suffering is an art of living practiced by those who know that they cannot confront the disappointments, blows, and vicissitudes in any other way.

Medieval people had good reasons to be perpetually fearful for their lives. Deteriorating, life-threatening, and insecure living conditions were to be found everywhere. The Horsemen of the Apocalypse, Death, Famine, and Pestilence harassed an impotent humanity with abandon. Today's common epidemics, such as tuberculosis and sexually transmitted infections, are minor complaints when compared to the medieval horrors of leprosy and the raging of the plague. On average, a medieval woman gave birth to fifteen children. Only four or five of them reached the age of thirty. Such perpetual birthing and dying could generate only one attitude about life's value: that it was nothing.

The mysterious medieval psyche's disposition with its precocious disdain of life, its desire for death, and its depressive moods, arose from very concrete existential experiences and impressions. We easily forget that only the contemporary measures of battling epidemics through hygienic and rational public health education stomped out the most inordinate causes of misery. At the same time, they eradicated the main source of medieval world denial in Christian garb. A certain contemporary view of history has promulgated a snobbish contempt for the Enlightenment and for the achievements of modern civilization.[4] It artificially separates culture and

Malinowski," in *The Routledge Dictionary of Anthropologists* (London: Taylor & Francis, 2004), 137–39.

4   Translator's note: The author returns once more to her discussion of cultural evolution, this time making a case for the advances and benefits of modern science, public health initiatives, and medicine as prime examples of the evolutionary stage of civilization. At other times, however, Busse-Wilson critiques modern civilization as overly rational and philistine. For example, the section "Konrad of Marburg" sharply rebukes the bourgeois sexual norms of her era.

civilization and pronounces that a preference for culture over civilization is what truly defines higher education. Yet it is civilization that has succeeded at improving life for contemporary humanity, which is not as threatened, helpless, and perpetually insecure over basic living conditions as were medieval people.

In the Middle Ages, freely chosen suffering offered optimal psychological protection, especially for those who were spiritually inclined. The proactive and sensual apotropaic symbolic value of a strictly physical asceticism became transformed into psychological asceticism by more sophisticated representatives of monastic life. Religious content, such as the experience of Christ's passion and the many facets of monastic renunciation, was elevated to a generalized knowledge of life and loss. Suso, the great medieval savant of the art of suffering, asked, "What does a human know who has not suffered?" At their core, his mystical writings are the purified literary condensation of the type of attitude toward suffering which characterizes a religious person in the Middle Ages.

A veritable typological hierarchy of anguish and distress led to voluntary and welcomed misery as its end goal. The truly wise trained for ever greater challenges. They provoked the "devil's" temptations to win more concessions from him, the mortal enemy of life. Initially, human vitality bristles at the continuous breakdown, yet gradually everything becomes easier. Suso observes in one of his writings,

> At the beginning, he thought that when suffering came his way, O no, if only such suffering would end. Then the little child Jesus appeared to him in a vision, punished him, and said, you are not yet able to suffer. I will teach you. Note that when you are in the midst of suffering, don't focus on the end of this particular anguish. While it lasts, and this belongs to it, prepare yourself to receive patiently yet another tribulation. Proceed like a young woman who picks roses. When she breaks off one stem, it is not enough for her. She thinks about how to get more. Imitate her. Prepare yourself that when this anguish comes to an end, another will quickly take its place.[5]

In this passage, Suso describes the stance of an active endurance of pain and exemplifies the most developed type of fortitude in facing suffering. Spiritual

---

5   *Life of a Servant*, chapter 20, "Von wehtuendem Untergehn." Translator's note: Translated into modern German by Walter Lehman, *Heinrich Seuse: Deutsche Schriften* (Jena: Eugen Diederichs Verlag, 1922).

rules such as these represent its most condensed teachings, which we encounter repeatedly in the lives of extraordinary religious men and women.
One may react to pain in many ways: fighting and mastering it through work,
refining the discipline of averting one's thoughts, or surrendering to despair
until pain has exhausted itself; imploring, threatening, or beseeching the
Godhead to deter the unbearable; mind-numbing resignation. In contrast,
the creation of conscious suffering as found in medieval passion mysticism
offers a certain meta-historical wisdom. An animal's muted experience of
pain metamorphoses into a metaphysical embrace of suffering. An external
imposition is replaced by the wounded self's intentionally willed surrender
to suffering.[6] It pronounces, "I wish to be sorrowful" and thus renders null
and void destiny's assaults.

From conscious awareness of suffering, the path continues to the active
embrace of pain. Anguish is not a state of being, it is a task. Personal life,
whether monastic or secular, turns into a Via Dolorosa. As the body's internal
voices and desires become weaker, one enters the battlefield of social life.
The friends of God rejoice at having enemies, at being treated badly and
maligned by others. They pursue humiliations and a good kick in the back.
They do not "repress" these experiences. Mechthild of Magdeburg, Elisabeth's
contemporary, writes in her spiritual autobiography that she "gladly wishes
to be without honor, disrespected, gladly to be alone, silent, unsightly, a mere
creature." When Suso once visited a women's monastery, and its inhabitants
inquired about his well-being, he answered, "I am afraid that things fare badly
for me, and this for the following reason: it has been now about four weeks that
nobody attacked my body or my honor. I am afraid that God has forgotten me."[7]

The landgravine Elisabeth of Thuringia had to withstand catastrophic
damages to her self-esteem: disregard by her social peers and her people,
incomprehension of her ideas, even active perfidy. She did not have to endure
it passively but could encounter suffering and disdain actively. *Spernere
te sperni*—to despise the fact that we are despised. The motto urges us to
become fundamentally invulnerable because the anguish that is imposed
on us cannot be escaped.

Bending oneself preempts being bent. This is the reason "she congratulated herself for her vilification and calumny by others," as was said about

---

6   In his treatise *Über die tragische Kunst* (1792), Friedrich Schiller (1759–1805), the greatest
and least-known psychologist of the nineteenth century, presents a secular description of how
to win inner freedom when confronting external pressures by making the aggressor's will one's
own, thus outwitting the enemy in a way.

7   Suso, *Vom unermesslichen Adel zeitlichen Leidens.*

her time in Marburg. It does not mean she did not feel her denigration; rather, she reinterpreted it by affirmation. The destruction of one's personal honor, the most radical and deepest extinction of individual self-esteem, is a strangulation of self that physical pain alone cannot accomplish. St. Elisabeth experienced such a profound deprecation on at least one occasion. Once, when an indigent woman pushed her into the gutter, "she happily and with laughter thanked the Lord that he deemed her worthy of being despised by all the world for his sake." This is the freedom of a self-aware creator of the art of suffering: to embrace suffering actively and intentionally. According to Suso,

> All saints are the cupbearers for human beings in pain since they tasted it before them. They pronounce in unison that it is a beneficial drink without poison. To be patient in pain is greater than being able to raise the dead and to perform other miracles. Pain is the narrow path that leads to heaven's gate. Suffering makes you a companion of martyrs; it leads to praise; it leads to victory over all enemies. Suffering clothes the soul in a dress of purple roses. The soul is adorned with a wreath of red roses and carries a scepter of green palm fronds. Suffering is a shining ruby in a virgin's chest clasp. It sings with a sweet voice for all eternity. With untamed courage, it intones a new round dance that no angels' choir can perform, since angels never feel pain. To state it succinctly: the world calls those in anguish poor; I call them blessed, since they are my chosen ones.[8]

Unity with the divine is the reward for believers who accept pain and suffer freely. This is the deepest reason for all self-humiliation and bodily asceticism. The deadly flower of divine union was able to grow in the field of self-destruction. In rare hours of ecstasy, whoever graduated from this advanced school of dehumanization with the victory prize in hand could achieve fusion with the highest being. For those who fought and suffered, the vision appeared. All humiliations and disappointments were nullified through touching the supreme being. Defeats turned into triumphs only known to those who courted God. This authentic and entirely sui generis saint's life expresses the central psychological productivity of religiosity. Its manifestation depends on strongly formed character traits or creative mental powers and is developed fully only by the most gifted men and women. St. Elisabeth had this ability.

8   Suso, ibid.

The school of sanctification through self-annihilation is not the sole property of Christianity. It belongs to the esotericism of nearly all *Hochreligionen*.[9] The passion of Christ, however, provided motivation, example, and reward for the agonistic battles of God's children. The painful defeat of the founder of the Christian doctrine, the contradiction of his ignominious and terrifying death, his execution, his original life's intentions and demands, the bitterness of the lonely end—all these came to symbolize the inescapable pain at the core of all human experience. The passion of Christ simultaneously signifies suffering's meaning and suffering's meaninglessness. Christ's agony, distress, and abandonment served nobody. The proposition that he redeemed others through his anguish is merely a rationalization for those in need of logic. Pain cannot be turned into logic. Suffering, however, carries meaning, especially when it is endured innocently and thus cannot be explained by rational reasoning. Yet such suffering carries redemptive powers only for a Christian who is also a mystic. For the mystic, suffering reveals itself as a divine force that enfolds the secrets of life and death. Mysticism is not bound to a specific century. It can be found in the early Middle Ages as well as during the Baroque. It reached its most sophisticated literary height during the thirteenth and fourteenth centuries. Every religion contains mysticism; Christianity's mysticism is passion mysticism. The cross conveys salvation. The anguished symbol of one human being became transformed into a symbol of religious vision itself. Pain carries its own rewards and values. "Suffering redeems": the possibility of moving closer to the divine grows with the greatest possible increase in empathy for the Savior's copious suffering. The experience and reimagining of his stations of the cross and of the anguish of Mary, mother of God, thus belong to the core of a mystical knowledge of God and movement toward him.

Such painful commonality of a shared experience of anguish guides a disheartened human being, filled with self-doubt and timidity, into a harbor. Nonetheless, the vast status difference between the Savior and his

9   Translator's note: In the early twentieth century, the German technical term *Hochreligion* (high religion) was widely used to distinguish "organized" religion from "folk" religion; its usage relied on unilineal developmentalist criteria, for example, a movement from "simple" to "complex," from "local" to "universal," from "oral" to "written," and from "magical" to "rational" religious expression. Developmental models of religion have fallen out of use in religious studies due to their inherent racism. To an extent, Elisabeth Busse-Wilson subverts the Western-centric unilineal developmentalism that dominated the religious scholarship of her time. She characterizes modern Elisabeth scholars as engaged in mythical thinking, and the much-touted achievements of the Christian Middle Ages as exemplifying the apotropaic magic of earlier religious "developmental stages."

sacrificial death and a human being always remains intact, even in the best effort of mimetically experiencing the passion of Christ. The practitioners of the art of suffering thus can never be at rest. Their psychic torture, even when freely chosen and administered, will always remain imperfect when compared to the unattainable ideal.

The experience of involuntary, deep, personal sorrow is frequently the reason for a person's intentional crossover into the world of cognizant self-torment, monastic poverty, and the imitation of Christ. A pious lifestyle has not infrequently become camouflage for hysterics and neuropaths, that is, those too fragile to face life. Religious personalities of high caliber, however, choose it as a deliberate result of life's vagaries. The external symbols of flight from the world, abandonment of home and hearth, the renunciation of wealth and social status, a stone for a pillow, and homeless migration were chosen by poverty's apostles, including St. Elisabeth. The insignia of beggars and monks were always already pointing to an immense personal knowledge of suffering.

Without the motivation of a terrifying turn of fate, neither Francis nor Elisabeth would have grown into sainthood. These two humans, prodigiously and authentically poor, took the decisive one-way path into poverty and deprivation only after difficult defeats and bitter experiences. Belonging to the rank of burghers, young Francis endured his life's great disappointment and setback when attempting to join the knightly class. A study of his biography before and shortly after his religious transformation reveals that courtly society thwarted his ambitious goal. After he allowed himself to be taken advantage of by everybody, he must have tasted countless humiliations. It hit twice as hard, since he was not good looking. Short, unprepossessing, and with protruding ears, he tried everything to overcome these physical "inferiorities" through social success, yet his efforts failed throughout his secular years. In like fashion, the landgravine Elisabeth of Thuringia experienced a collapse caused by her husband's death and subsequent events that drove her to the life of a recluse for the remainder of her life. Francis and Elisabeth must be counted among those great personalities who can neither be halfway happy nor halfway sad. Neither wanted to continue living and be restored to health. It would have been sensible for Francis to return to a more modest career after the defeat of so many of his masculine ambitions. Yet he was psychologically unable to take over his father's cloth business and become a well-adjusted citizen of his hometown Assisi. After her husband's death, Landgravine Elisabeth could have created a meaningful life in the service of her children. But following her role model, she desired to plunge into her anguish and face her abandonment without any hope of recovery. The damage done, neither of them took refuge in common sense, reflection, and a sober effort to make do under new circumstances. This is how they arrived at the mystical wedding ceremony with Lady Poverty and at a commitment to voluntary suffering.

Intellectually schooled men and women who live a life of self-awareness well beyond instinct may suddenly and with full intention create extraordinarily undignified situations for themselves. They may engage in the most sordid of sexual relationships. Their transformation may mystify pedagogues, psychologists, and criminologists. Yet unbeknownst to anybody, they have experienced such powerful psychological collapse and long-lasting, if not chronic, existential disappointments that their resistance to immediate threats and humiliations has become nil. Anguish and misery may thus lead to an incremental decline of ambition. The steady drip of disappointment may destroy any desire for a better life. When a return to the world of pain-free everyday life appears impossible, such agony may pull a person as if into an abyss. As a rare and radical outcome, the only option left may seem to sink into the void ever more deeply and willingly. A law of relativity takes effect at this point. The deeper a person plummets, the less power pain appears to wield. Anguish turns into an irresistible poison for someone deeply infected with suffering. In due course, she becomes numb to it.

This was St. Elisabeth's lot following the death of her spouse. Constitutional psychological anomalies cannot explain Elisabeth's humiliating and undignified Marburg role as a subjugated woman. Not a predisposition to sexual pathology, but merely the force of earlier calamities cut to her core and splintered it. The failure of her intellectual-religious goal of a life lived in the spirit of the original Franciscan movement, the hostility she encountered everywhere as a helpless widow, the death of her spouse and sole friend, and finally, the confiscation of her children—considering such overwhelming circumstances, any resistance on her part had become futile.

The Landgravine of Thuringia's path led to destitution and despair without the possibility of psychological recovery. The genuinely creative and spiritual dimension of this historical personality emerges in the conscious affirmation of her anguish. Only a rare religious ability and disposition, which is lost to modern men and women, even modern Christians, could turn Elisabeth's actions in the second half of her life into positive ethical choices. A down-to-earth charity took a back seat. She never thought of it as her true core anyway. Her true accomplishment and purest passion were her ability to suffer, to embrace her demise and even her death. Despite her spiritual simplicity and embarrassing Griselda traits, Elisabeth thus became a genuine protagonist of the Christian era:

Look, God has received my prayer. I do not love my own children more than I love the children of strangers. Everything I owned before is now mere dust to me.

This reported statement by Elisabeth, seemingly a mere declaration of having overcome human nature, in truth expresses her willingness to be broken. Her reason: "No human being enjoys observing a successful knight during a tournament as much as the heavenly host looks upon a human being who suffers well."

Descent into Destitution

Popular historiography and Christian tradition propose that soon after the death of her spouse, her brother-in-law Heinrich Raspe banished Landgravine Elisabeth from the Wartburg castle, the residence of the Thuringian landgrave. Scholarly critics, however, declared the banishment story a "legend" and quickly rejected it as unproven. To a typical Enlightenment historian, the story's circumstances seemed adventurous and unrealistic; they could only make sense as a martyr's legend in the making. A protagonist endowed with all Christian virtues, she can be showered with praise as she patiently endures persecution. Literature and art thus most frequently depict the episode of a young widow leaving her husband's castle. Under the cover of night, accompanied by her enemies' foul words and abandoned by all, she searches for shelter in the little town of Eisenach at the foot of the Wartburg castle.[10] Only one reliable primary source, the *Libellus*, offers a remarkably brief note about this pivotal event.[11] All other sources remain silent. Other female eyewitness reports in the *Libellus* contain detailed descriptions of the young landgravine's adversities after the landgrave's death. Because of the statement's unusual brevity, historians have assumed that the departure from the castle signified Elisabeth's voluntary choice in the pursuit of Franciscan poverty. This interpretation is currently the canonical academic position on the topic. The truth of the unhappy woman's forced expulsion has ceased to exist.

---

10   Modern visual arts privilege this scene. Moritz von Schwind's famous frescoes at the Wartburg castle include it as well.

11   "Post-mortem vero mariti eiecta fuit de castro et omnibus possessionibus sui dotalici a quibusdam vasallis mariti sui" (After her husband's death, she was expelled from the castle and dispossessed of all of her dowry by certain vassals of her husband).

The short sentence in the *Libellus* leaves no doubt that a group of noblemen dispossessed the landgravine of Thuringia of her property and legal rights. They terminated her residency at Wartburg castle or, at the very least, made her life there impossible. From a psychological point of view, the continuation of the *Libellus* narrative presents no contradiction. The *Libellus* states that upon leaving the castle, the unhappy woman experienced a jolt of rapturous joy:

> She, however, walked into the town situated below the castle and entered a pitiful room in the courtyard of a tavern that housed the innkeeper's barrels, tools, and pigs. She remained there for the night in great happiness. Yet around the middle of the night, she attended Matins at the town's Franciscan order and asked them to sing a Te Deum. She was filled with joy and thanked God for her trial.

Once again, the legend asserts its rights vis-à-vis critical historiography. Our depiction reinstates the legend of the young landgravine's expulsion to its erstwhile truthfulness. Although contradicting critical historiography in this case, we can still leverage and respect its version as complementary to historical research.

The coexistence of multiple causes and motivations precondition a person's decisions that may lead her into unusual territory. This is also true for the religiously effusive type. The indirect catalytic assistance of secondary circumstances, such as material causes or bitter hardship, are necessary for even the greatest and most heroic deed. Having smoldered unseen in plain daylight for a long time, unpleasant and acute causations often aid a secret intention to break through and break free. No "pure" deed exists separately from mental or material self-preservation. Every action is also a reaction. Courage thus may be a form of self-punishment to combat one's weakness, to challenge oneself or the world. Deceptive actions may cover up personal defeat yet look heroic from the outside. Reversely, outwardly inconspicuous, and even ridiculous acts may constitute a hidden personal triumph. In this case, Elisabeth's essential religious achievement was the emotional reinterpretation of misfortune as a divinely ordained challenge.

Even if we assumed a voluntary departure from Wartburg castle, we would have to reach identical conclusions. We cannot interpret such a drastic decision without assuming deeper personal causes. Every historical controversy overlooks the actual core of a dramatic turn of events if no attention is being paid to deeper personal causes. It remains certain, even after a critical assessment of the earliest sources, that the landgravine was forced to leave home and hearth after the death of the landgrave. Her relatives hunted her like a wild animal without refuge. Yet this is not as important as the way she descended from the feudal castle on a hill to a fleapit in the wretched town below. Elated and in ecstasy as she dared herself to suffer—this is her voluntary and spiritual achievement. The first night in the former pigsty, under empty barrels and in wintry weather, became the night of being born into spiritual independence and superior psychological power. It is for this reason that on this night of flight, the Franciscan brothers sang a Te Deum for her and celebrated with her. It is true that Elisabeth was cast out, but her misery became her triumph.

What is true for the first part of her passion—the endurance of her peers' hostility— remains true for all subsequent blows of fate. She never asked for them, but affirmed them in a religious sense as an experiment and a test. She transformed involuntary adversity into a voluntary readiness to suffer. Such "activism in passivity" gradually grew to breathtaking dimensions.

Aristocratic and familial hostility against the young woman have been interpreted as an expression of her contemporaries' limited understanding of the pious ruler's charity. Not only the legends but also modern interpreters agree on this point. In truth, however, this view is merely a testimony to the inadequate disposition of modernity to enter another era from a sociological point of view. Modern men and women refuse to acknowledge that in a patriarchal and status-conscious society, a passionately religious type such as Landgravine Elisabeth was doomed to fail. The hero-producing tendency of legends (and any heroic fable) to blame secular society and to excuse the saint by painting her as a victim can only lead to misinterpretation. It loses sight of the historical Elisabeth's genuine tragedy. Her own culpability in generating the hostility toward her engenders the beginning of her stations of the cross. Her agency and choice rather than a presumed victimhood turn her life toward a future of metahistorical consequences.

The research for our biographical study leaves no doubt that beginning in childhood, the landgravine increasingly distanced herself from the social milieu into which she was placed. She created the intensely religious person's illusory self-justification that her isolation was an expression of society's alienation. She justified her loneliness through incessant social critique to be able to endure it. She eventually learned to maintain this state of affair as a form of self-affirmation.

If, like the landgravine, religious zealots opt out of creating a political party or a monastic order, social pressure will eventually crush them. The more sectarians drift away from socially acceptable frameworks, the more they will attract followers who are also socially marginal or disaffected. In need of illusions, they will grasp fanatically at any protest ideology and will eventually become dependent on it. The religious zealot is not capable of gaining influential and socially well-adjusted friends who would love them without criticism. Thus, their life becomes mired in tragic self-isolation and a feeling of being misunderstood. The scenario is typical of many political and religious personalities.

This is Elisabeth's characterological onus. It caused the prodigious sin of omission to not become the founder of a community of peers. Besides her spouse, the pious Franciscan appears to have had no friends unless we count her faithful companions Isentrud and Guda.[12] The young women, especially Isentrud, seem to have been attached to Elisabeth with devotion and loyalty. They imitated Elisabeth's actions in detail. They participated in the food boycotts and took a vow of chastity. They permitted themselves to be beaten on her behalf and were her shadow in all ways. In short, their lady served as their model. Yet the women appear to have been nothing but social and material dependents and, as such, dedicated and uncritical devotees. This type of servile attachment could not serve as a monastic starting point for the landgravine Elisabeth's provocative public life; provocative because she was a woman who never smiled at men but kissed mangy beggars. A backlash was unavoidable.

As long as Landgrave Ludwig, the male head of the household, protected all of his wife's interests—from her bailiwick support of the indigent to her confessor cult—the hostile faction among the Thuringian aristocracy and her husband's kin did not dare to make a move. After his death, however, as is true for any régime change, the party could easily leverage the new circumstances to block the widow's "new policy." Under the threat of her success in stabilizing her religious agenda, they attempted to restore the old traditions of Landgrave Hermann's grand era. The shared goal that brought everybody under its banner during a time of changing rulership was to protect the magnificent Wartburg castle, an equal to all the emperor's palaces, from being ruled by a patroness of beggars and her sinister spiritual guide.

The young landgravine and her confessor caused a stir in other ways as well. In the eyes of her enemies, the landgravine's unrestrained charity constituted a challenge beyond an inexpedient wastefulness. The boycott of certain foodstuffs was a provocation and cause for resentment among

---

12   These are the women that the sources named "ancillae" or "pedisequi." They were female feudal gentry who constituted the retinue of an aristocratic lady. Isentrud provided most statements in the first part of the *Libellus*. Guda lived with the landgravine from the age of five. Isentrud, a widow from Hörselgau, lived with her from the age of eighteen.

the nobles at court, who preferred to live life unperturbed. Again and again, the medieval aristocratic caste had plenty of reasons to be affronted by an insider critic of their own infallibility, given how used they were to their own status, power, and self-assuredness. Already during the landgrave's lifetime, they opposed her. Although she "was attacked and reprehended to her face" (*Libellus*), she did not heed the warning.

By settling into a fantasy world which cohered increasingly less with reality, she contributed to her own demise. A narrow perspective, typical of men and women captivated by ideological and religious enchantment, added further destabilization. Her status as a foreigner without kinship ties that could provide her with robust support weakened her situation as well. Finally, Thuringia was in a state of near anarchy because the legal heir to the throne was underage. As a result, a revolution shook the palace in the winter after the landgrave's death. The historical core of the controversial story of expulsion is comprised of all these factors.

According to popular legend, her brother-in-law Heinrich Raspe, who had become regent, banished Elisabeth from Wartburg castle. As noted at the beginning of our study, historically impeccable proofs for the "evil brother-in-law" are as nonexistent as those for an "evil mother-in-law."[3] Since Heinrich Raspe was still underage when the Thuringian landgrave died, he would not have been able to expel his brother's wife. On the other hand, he did not in any way support her nor did he advocate on her behalf. Caesarius found it necessary to apologize for him by stating that Heinrich and his brother were under the influence of the ministeriales and the nobility. This apology admits much. We can conclude that a faction had formed in support of the future leader, which hoped to advance its own interests by becoming his followers.

It is certain, however, that Heinrich Raspe welcomed his sister-in-law's lack of popularity, whom he never seems to have respected much.[14] Even if he himself did not chase her away from her home and rights, he clearly did not prevent his associates from doing so. Elisabeth's son Hermann, the inheritor of the throne, was only five years of age at the time; the young

---

13   According to the late-medieval poem of the "auctor rhythmicus" about Elisabeth's life, Elisabeth and Sophie were dismissed from the Wartburg in tandem. The likely truth at the core of this narrative tradition is that after the landgrave's death, his closest female relatives, his wife, and his mother were left without influence and authority.

14   In a letter to the Teutonic Knights at Wiesenfeld about inheritance disputes related to the Marburg hospital that ensued after her death, Raspe refers to her as not quite of age and as a simple woman. His interest in her only piques later when his dynasty could reap a significant increase in reputation and prestige through the possibility of her canonization.

widow was a disliked foreigner. The idea of usurping the throne was so tempting and the opportunity so favorable that only an unusually strong personality would not have exploited the situation. However, as is evidenced by future developments including his short-lived role as German anti-emperor, Heinrich Raspe was politically ambitious. In addition, Irmingard's testimony about the Marburg era in the *Libellus* unequivocally certifies Heinrich Raspe's hostile attitude toward his sister-in-law.[15]

For these reasons, the story of the callous and evil brother-in-law who ousts the young widow exists not without cause. It is fed by invisible subterranean springs that turn the legends into a frequently valuable source for us. Without offering direct proof of historical occurrences, they offer indirect evidence of Heinrich Raspe's share of moral culpability. The legend extends a folk tradition into the present moment that "vetted" sources have driven to the margins. In this case, the folk tradition proves to be more reliable than the "neutrality" of official historiography, which propelled modern historians to proclaim the expulsion story as utter nonsense.

The one sentence in the primary sources that reports the landgravine's removal contains two clear-cut legal points: her disinheritance and the refusal of her right to residence.[16] The revolting aristocratic party's denial of her right to dwell on the Wartburg castle amounts to a public breaking of the law. It was customary that a widow of high aristocratic status would move to a smaller and less significant castle after the death of her spouse. However, she would not retire to her new location until her oldest son had come of age and the household could be transferred to him. Elisabeth was expelled illegally and against custom.[17] Yet even without the eviction,

---

15   The statement can be found in a hidden segment of the *Libellus* in an entirely different context. It slipped below the scribes' attention threshold and proved only that the main statements about the expulsion have been cut in deference to the landgravine's family: "Mortuo marito ipsius non fuit beate Eizabet permissa ad tempus uti bonis mariti sui prepedita a fratre mariti sui" (After the death of her husband, Elizabeth was not allowed to use her husband's goods for a time, being prevented from doing so by her husband's brother).

16   The role that Heinrich Raspe plays in later versions of St. Ludwig's biography is shaped by the biased Reinhardsbrunn tradition. He is presented as intentionally violating the law and acting malevolently toward Elisabeth. This characterization could not have been without a basis.

17   It is characteristic of nineteenth-century rationalists and their enlightenment "persecution" of all traditions that seem to smack of romanticism or pure literature that some modern scholars insist at all costs on the normalcy of the landgravine's departure from the Wartburg castle. Following A. Huyskens and others, her move to the widow's residence in Marburg is described as fully legal. However, she is subsequently expelled from the Marburg castle (why?), then led back by Konrad, and so forth. Huyskens dropped the hypothesis of an eviction from Marburg. See Huyskens, *Korrespondenzblatt der deutschen Geschichts-und Altertumsvereine* no. 10/12 (1929): 231.

Elisabeth would have been rendered powerless simply because of a second legal violation.

Her husband's rebellious vassals and some members of her extended family withheld and embezzled her widow's pension. As a committed Franciscan, Elisabeth could not care less about her widow's pension, that is, the revenue and taxes from her widow's landholdings. Yet the withdrawal of her pension placed her in an uncomfortable private and public situation in a more utilitarian way. She had lost access to funds for her charitable institutions and, for the first time, was forced to experience the cruelty of personal limitations and quotidian constraints. Even if morally fortified by voluntary self-negation, expropriation by others was and remains today a predictable humiliation. The reinstatement of her widow's pension took place eventually, but only against the obstinate resistance of the hostile party and with the assistance of Konrad of Marburg's agile diplomatic skills. These circumstances allow us to infer the opposition's previous acrimony and determination.[18]

In early and high medieval society, a woman was legally without power and had not even been granted legal adult status. Before her marriage, she was an uncared-for member of her own kin. After marriage, she remained as such in her husband's kin. This is the reason why it was considered a special virtue and magnanimity when men distinguished themselves as the protector of widows and orphans. Since a widow was not entitled to an inheritance, the institution of widow's pensions was even more important and their withholding all the more dire. But might precedes right. On one hand, a woman was the object of courtly love, or *Minne*, and of amorous admiration. Yet as was true for the landgravine, the courtly principles of female protection ceased to apply to a foreigner without kin and thus without power. She did not count for much more than a landless peasant without any recourse, who could be subjected to mistreatment. This sociological and psychological correlation is more persuasive than an emphasis on merely pragmatic issues implicit in Elisabeth's banishment. The latter must repudiate the deed along with its motives. Such an emphasis has not only to deny the expulsion, but it must also erase the history that caused it. For Elisabeth, a loss of power did not happen abruptly, and it did not begin with the new ruling faction in place.

---

18   Elisabeth's pension was eventually "invested" in her Marburg hospital. It must have been of considerable value. Otherwise, the Teutonic Order, the Franciscans, and Elisabeth's brother-in-law would not have fought over it after Elisabeth's death. Neither would her relatives have tried to embezzle her pension right from the start of her widowhood.

What is missing in the written tradition is the genesis of the hostile atmosphere in all its aspects: the insulting harassments, the locking of larders, and the many petty acts of spite in daily life. Certainly, the removal of foodstuff from her widow's landholdings must have caused Konrad's penitent the gravest moral affliction and suffering.[19] All this was done to a very young and dejected widow. For a woman of her era, Elisabeth found herself in dire straits: at war with her husband's kin, separated at a great distance from her own relatives, with no friend at her side except for a confessor whose goal it was to alienate her from her surroundings and whose ethical-religious principles constituted a challenge to the feudal caste as well. It cannot be doubted that even someone with a personality stronger than Elisabeth's would have sunk into despair. She felt evicted even without the use of brute force. Thus, she left, but not, as would have been reasonable, to join a monastery or to live at a remote and minor castle. In a complete break with her past and her social status, she opted to join the ranks of the common people and chose a life of destitution in the barn of a dilapidated house. Who would elect such conditions without deeper motives? In any case, whether forced directly or indirectly, her departure was not chosen freely.

Historians of the nineteenth and twentieth centuries have rejected the possibility and reality of her banishment because they doubted what seemed to have been exceptional and daringly malevolent acts. They did not sense it was precisely a breach of law and custom that had to be expected in an era such as hers. Medieval political history is exclusively a chronicle of betrayal and crude selfishness. A lack of responsibility characterized the course of feudal relationships—from the lives of mid-level and low-status lords to that of even an emperor. For us today, this can only be comprehended as an exception to the rule. Modern democratic and lawful states have turned an unabashed and matter-of-course identification of politics with personal advantage into a moral proscription. Assured of their power and unbound

19   At least among the landgravine's own social class, the upper nobility, a legally sanctioned custom had evolved that guaranteed a widow a standard of living among her in-laws that was commensurate with her social status. Besides her dowry, it included objects and persons for personal use (jewelry, clothes, riding horses, and female servants) and agreed-upon regular income through specially designated real estate property called *Wittum*, which was guaranteed for life. Elisabeth's Wittum property was already mentioned in the *Libellus* in the context of her food boycott. She preferred their alimentary yields to avoid eating unjustly gained foodstuffs ("quiusdam bonis specialiter in dotem sibi assignatis" [certain goods specially assigned to her as a dowry]). Regarding her Wittum's legal issues, see Heymann, "Zum Ehegüterrecht der Heiligen Elisabeth," *Zeitschrift für thüringische Geschichte und Altertumskunde* 19 (1909).

by checks and balances, a medieval cast of rulers could indulge in what must at the very least be denied pointblank today. All events that took place after Landgrave Ludwig's death, such as the immediate formation of an oppositional clique striving for power and supporting the governing administrator's efforts at usurping the throne and the ruthless harshness against a person who could disrupt its new sphere of influence—these were not singular events in medieval Thuringian history but standard political and moral practice. Disloyalty and the despicable greed of vassals and noble kin against a feudal lord who had perished in war and legal breaches against his defenseless widow were merely the natural manifestation of a boorish lack of polish. We will only perceive it as inconsistent with a highly refined culture among the leading social classes of the high Middle Ages if we project our own overall more disciplined moral and emotional style onto the era.

Where was Master Konrad of Marburg during these critical days of a catastrophic time for Elisabeth? It is rather peculiar that the landgravine's mentor, who otherwise controlled her behavior day and night, cannot be found by her side. It is at this juncture that one should expect his guardianship and protection in the first place. In the *Epistola*, Konrad keeps silent about the departure from the Wartburg castle and the days of misery in Eisenach, even though this period should have been a cause for praise of his penitent's Christian patience. He remains reticent about the entire period between the landgrave's death and their joint move to Marburg.

He likely does not mention the events that are to be counted as the most pivotal in his protégée's life because during this time, Elisabeth apparently became independent and thus terminated her allegiance to him in some way. In any case, he is forced to admit disputes with the landgravine after her husband's death. And this in his biography, which is a masterpiece of diplomatic shrewdness, containing no lies but skillfully avoiding anything that could discredit him. He notes sanctimoniously and cleverly that he counseled her how she should direct her new life, whether in a monastery, in a hermitage, or in any other way that would please God. She, on the other hand, always insisted tearfully on her determination to live a life begging in the streets. Even though he resolutely rejected her intention, she maintained her claim with the words "I will do that which you cannot forbid me to do."[20]

Perhaps the thought of going begging from village to village and from town to town could have made an impact on him as the irrational wishful

---

20   "Hoc faciam, quod me non potestis prohibere" (*Epistola*). Wenck (1892) perceives Elisabeth's statement to be the key to all aspects of the catastrophe. In protest of the tyrant, she left the castle. Wenck later abandoned this view in favor of a more legalistic interpretation.

product of a religious mood. Yet translated into social reality by Elisabeth, a
princess and woman, it was utopian. As was so often the case, the confessor
was at least formally on the mark when he forbade this plan. A young widow
such as the landgravine would have made the normal and obvious life choice
to remarry. Since she refused this common path both in terms of action and
intent, the alternative option of withdrawal to a monastery was still open.
Yet living in a rapture of suffering and loneliness, the abandoned young
woman had no conventional solutions left. Only one possibility remained:
to truly wed Lady Poverty. After the loss of her husband and friend, her
world had turned to ashes. It is at this juncture that the true goal of her
religious desires came into view. Only an absolute way forward remained
to be considered, a way without concessions and compromises: the step
into the sphere of an authentic saint's life. Everything or nothing. Radical
devotion to St. Francis by holding the begging staff in her hand offered a
new kind of support. "Nakedly you should seek your Savior's arms."

Nothing was further on Konrad of Marburg's mind than religious passion. He did not become the teacher and counsellor of a landgravine with
royal blood to live in want and beg on country roads in her company. The
relational dynamic between the two, the radically religious type and
the politically driven authoritarian type, now burst forth in full force. It
must have been fought out in personal battles. How much fiercer must
their fights have been if the pastoral mentor can write in a letter to the
pope, whom he personally wishes to impress, that his confrontations with
Elisabeth in the Wartburg were obstinate ("proterve"), and that she had
cried bitterly.

Now that Elisabeth was neither landgravine nor wife, Konrad planned
to pursue her binding commitment to him, pledged at the Katharine
monastery in Eisenach, in all its consequences. Only through the death
of the landgrave could both become equal in power. And since both were
without wealth and marriage obligations, Konrad believed that he could
catch up on everything he did not dare or was not able to carry out earlier.
Yet the landgravine's guardian was forced to make a most unpleasant
discovery, which nearly cost him the fruits of several years of educating
her. His penitent developed sainthood much faster than he would have
liked. She gained a moral leading edge that disarmed him precisely at
that moment when he believed her to be the most vulnerable and most
dependent on him. Caused by great suffering, she grew exponentially both
spiritually and psychologically. The brunt of social isolation awakened her
religious independence so radically that she was able to sever the ties to her
spiritual advocate and guardian, by whom she was enthralled until very

recently. With courage born of despair, she turned away and absconded from the castle toward an existence where old bonds did not matter and where social and moral customs could not reach. She broke the vow of obedience to her disciplinarian.

As she withdrew from his diabolic constraint, however, quotidian reality broke her even more cruelly. Landgravine Elisabeth could only reach the gate to a desired new life and collapsed exhaustedly at its threshold. All the while, her soul's owner waited patiently. He anticipated her inability to endure the heroic emulation of St. Francis, an effort which could only end unheroically. When his runaway pupil was forced to return, she would become ever more securely his prey—and never able to leave him again. Elisabeth's significance as a religious personality is not diminished by having failed miserably at living an uncompromised Franciscan existence.[21] When she left the castle and hid herself in a dilapidated shack in Eisenach, she matured into the state of joyful certainty and calm which all major religious figures describe as a coveted spiritual experience. This ecstatic state, which Elisabeth experienced even if only for a short time and in a cold hovel, did not generate any rational and sensible decisions. For this reason, it is nearly incomprehensible to us today, for whom religiosity in its essence signifies an altruistic motivation to act morally and lawfully. Yet Elisabeth's ecstatic state constitutes the authentic religious ur-experience.

A Wedding with Lady Poverty

The Brothers should be happy if they spend time among low and despised human beings, among the poor and the weak, among the sick, the lepers, and those who beg on the side of the road. And if necessary, they must go and beg for alms. And they are not allowed to be ashamed of it, but must remember that our Lord Jesus Christ, the Son of the living almighty God, hardened his face like a rock and was not ashamed of it. He as well was as poor as a foreigner and lived on alms, much like the Blessed Virgin and His disciples. And if people wish to disgrace the Brothers and not give alms to them, then the Brothers should thank God for that as well... And they should know that such disgrace is not made the responsibility of those who suffer it, but of those who dispense it.

---

21   Translator's note: St. Clare of Assisi and her female disciples were also blocked from a mendicant life and forcefully constrained by enclosure. See Emily Northcutt, "The Battle for Poverty: Pope Gregory IX Against St. Clare of Assisi," *Magistra* 24, no. 2 (Winter 2018): 4–21.

When St. Francis, who authored these words, chose his descent to the poor, he encountered the mistrust of peasants and townspeople. He and his companions, named *pazzi*, that is, crazy men, were not allowed to be seen in his hometown Assisi. Yet his life of begging and praying under the mild Umbrian sun was almost an idyll when compared with Landgravine Elisabeth's martyrdom, which began in the instant that she intended to begin a new life in the town below her castle. In a drab quotidian context, marriage with Lady Poverty turned for her, a royal aristocrat and a woman, into a terrifying and disastrous event.

While sheltered as a lady of the manor and wife, she entertained a naïve notion of life in poverty. She is said to have once remarked to her husband that she imagined a simple and divinely pleasing life together co-owning a small farm only big enough so he could plough it by himself, while she would tend to the sheep and milk them.[22] Her new experiences thus must have been exponentially more devastating. Just as was true for Francis, Elisabeth encountered nothing but mistrust and both open and hidden hostility in her hometown. She learned to taste the bitterness of a proletarian existence, of scarcity and disrespect. In the usually arid records of the *Libellus*, the accounts of Isengard, who shared these days of misery, are filled with descriptions of an extremely harsh life.

Eisenach, the early location of Elisabeth's passion, was a wretched hamlet. Like other towns during the Hohenstaufen era, it was a mere village surrounded by fortifications. All its inhabitants practiced agriculture. There were no stone buildings apart from churches and monasteries. Surrounded by Thuringian forests, Eisenach cannot be imagined paltry enough. The landgravine found shelter in the storage room of an inn during the first ecstatic night after her departure from the castle. In another section of the *Libellus*, it is called a "filthy abode." It had served as a pigsty in the past and now housed any kind of empty barrels and tools. In that first night, it turned into a numinous space. As the Virgin gave birth to the Messiah in a stable, Elisabeth endowed this nook with the rank of the birthplace of her intellectual freedom and independence. The tight grip of other human beings, especially that of her authoritarian confessor, was shattered, the path opened to a new life. This was enough of a reason to ask the Brothers, her Franciscan friends, to sing a Te deum laudamus for her.

---

22   One is tempted to interpret Landgravine Elisabeth's remarks as so modern and "Tolstoy-an" that it comes across as a textual fraud. However, this conversation can be traced back to Caesarius of Heisterbach, who was a direct contemporary and who references Bishop Dietrich of Trier as his informant. Bishop Dietrich later became Konrad's collaborator during the Inquisition. Konrad might have continued telling this story to present his pupil's goals as utopian and thus himself as indispensable. The textual tradition thus seems to be trustworthy.

The ecstatic joy of her victory could not last long. When Elisabeth awakened the next morning in her hideout, the temperature had dropped to a bitter cold. Perhaps it was only now that Elisabeth became aware of the consequences of her decision. The morning arrived with the important town news that the landgravine had left the castle during the night and was lodging at the inn, that she came on foot and without a retinue, and that, as became obvious very quickly, she did not carry enough ready money. All the details seemed to indicate she had obviously run away. No woman of rank would behave in this manner in public; it was a scandal. It quickly became clear that a rift existed between her and the castle's other inhabitants, who were now in a position of power. The townspeople treated her accordingly. The landgravine of Thuringia and Hesse, who chose evangelical poverty as her bride, discovered the bitter truth that a queen without a throne counted for nothing. Having once poured a cornucopia of gifts on the poor and caring for lepers and orphans, she herself had now become disrespected, abandoned, and in need of shelter and protection.

On the morning after her first night at the inn, she walked from house to house to ask for lodging. She had become a beggar. A return to her old life was impossible. The situation turned untenable when her three children, accompanied by the loyal Guda and Isentrud, arrived from the castle to join their mother. The children were five and three years old, with the youngest barely a few months of age. It was cruelly cold. Yet the well-to-do burghers, who would have been able to offer her shelter and who would have generally been hospitable according to the custom of the time, pleaded an atypical excuse. On this matter, the *Libellus* account is very explicit. The burghers were afraid. The town was founded as a colony of knights, and the semi-free townspeople lived in absolute dependence on the landgrave.[23] Furthermore, caused perhaps by their bad conscience, Wartburg's ruling family tried to bring Elisabeth into disrepute. On one hand, the hostile party of nobles had reached its goal of the landgravine's departure. On the other hand, the victors could find themselves the cause of an embarrassing scandal given the unexpected sensation of her exodus. Perhaps they even ordered to keep Elisabeth in the town to lessen the indignity. This seems to be the only reason why the group of outcasts stayed in Eisenach despite the all-around shabby treatment.

It is in this manner that the disciple of St. Francis went begging from house to house with female companions and three children in tow, followed

---

23   The town did not even have an independent mayor, but a prefect who was chosen by the landgrave.

by the townspeople's gossip and malevolent stares; this is how she physically experienced the fearsome misery of true poverty, homelessness, and itinerancy. If she sat in church for long periods, as noted in the *Libellus*, then surely because she did not know where else to go.[24] She finally approached a priest as a representative of Christian compassion to find shelter for her children during the coldness of a winter's night. She could not even stay in the church. According to the *Libellus*, she was driven into the house of a personal enemy. Desperate to care for three small children, she had to accept whatever was offered to her. To let her know how unwelcome she was, her "hosts" moved her to a very small room without any furniture. They behaved with such heartlessness that despite rain and frigid temperatures, Elisabeth preferred to leave the next morning:

> And she bid goodbye to the walls because they sheltered her from rain and coldness, and said to them, "I would rather express thanks to human beings, but I don't know of any reasons." She had no choice but to return to the dirty shed where she had spent the first night. At this point, she parted company with her children so they would not starve.[25]

The otherwise plausible fear of subjugated vassals cannot fully explain the malice that sent her hither and tither. Their malevolence must have also been an expression of intentional humiliation and personal animosity. The pious benefactor and mother to the poor must have been disliked not only by her peers but also by other social circles. It remains suspicious that she did not search for shelter in monasteries, all of which kept a guesthouse beyond the boundaries of the cloister. It is in those places that the medieval homeless generally found asylum and which functioned much like the inns of today. During Elisabeth's lifetime, even a small village like Eisenach hosted seven monasteries, including female ones. The Cistercian nuns lived outside and the St. Nikolai Benedictine nuns within the city gates. It is likely that her fervent discipleship of St. Francis was at odds with the Benedictine spirit, which embodied the feudal counterpoint to the Franciscan ethos. Access to the Benedictine house was thus out of the question.

---

24 Her children are mentioned only in the Eisenach episode. This is proof that the Wartburg nobles nurtured feelings of aggression and hostility toward her. If she asks a priest to have pity on her and her exiled children ("those in her charge," *Libellus*), it becomes obvious that the castle's inhabitants desired to cut all ties with her.

25 "She sent her little ones to different faraway locations so that they would receive sustenance," *Libellus*.

The greatest cruelty of her fate, however, was that even her closest friends and companions, the Franciscans, would not grant her support and assistance, even though she had previously provided them with protection and upkeep in Eisenach. The gap in the *Libellus* account indicates they, in particular, who were the cause for the unhappy woman's choice of a Franciscan path of voluntary poverty, were either too cowardly or too helpless and insignificant to guide her with prudent advice or active sustenance through the extremes of her destitute situation.[26]

Yet there ought to have been at least one class of people who secretly must have loved and sided with the exiled noblewoman, even if they perhaps could not have offered anything in terms of assistance and shelter. The class of the indigent, the invalids, the beggars, the orphans, the uncared-for sick, and the widows, who received the excessively rich gifts of their female ruler, ought to have formed her secret entourage during these days of distress. The dependent and fearful petty bourgeois could not understand the heroic and desperate aristocrat. The small number of Franciscan brothers failed her through their passivity and incompetence. The *Libellus* recounts the following incident of her Eisenach period:

> An ailing widow who had frequently received alms and kind gifts from her that improved her plight met St. Elisabeth when the saint was on her way to church. The encounter took place at a narrow, deep, and muddy pass where steppingstones served as a bridge. The widow did not want to step aside. She pushed St Elisabeth into the muck with such force that she fell and could not avoid covering all her clothing in dirt. The saint endured the episode with patience. Laughing aloud, she got back up and joyfully washed her clothes.

In its gruff triviality, this encounter with the female beggar points to a more valuable tradition than many monumental and immortalized situations recorded about secular and religious leaders of the Middle Ages. The vignette reveals the medieval character of an average woman of the people without the heroic patina of Gothic spirituality and interiorized piety. Without a doubt, the old beggar would have devoutly kissed the landgravine's feet and merely touched her purse of alms had she met her

26   Translator's note: Lori Pieper has embarked on rehabilitating the Franciscans' support of the saint based on new manuscript evidence. See Pieper, *The Voice of a Medieval Woman: St. Elizabeth of Hungary as a Franciscan Penitent in the Early Sources for Her Life*, 2nd ed. (New York: Tau Cross Books and Media, 2016).

riding a horse in the company of several female servants. Yet Elisabeth strove for something greater than her status as a ruler and intentionally chose to look unprepossessing. For precisely this reason, she did not impress the indigent woman, who therefore did not step aside for the landgravine in the narrow passageway. Instead, she pushed her with a motion that could be interpreted as accidental, yet which lands Elisabeth headlong into the filthy street.[27]

Oppressed people carry a dormant yet enduring need for revenge. Elisabeth, despite all a child of the ruling caste, did not suspect the need for revenge among the powerless as a response to her wealth and status. In inverted proportion to the degree of personal cowardice and impotence, their need may grow into individual acts of revenge that occur independently from any personal animosity whenever a previously intimidating and powerful person encounters misfortune. Schadenfreude is the purest of joys. Especially when the fall of the mighty seems without cause and reason, less powerful bystanders might experience their calamity as a case of preordained higher justice. Those in the Middle Ages who were condemned to perpetual poverty did not dare believe in a just recompense for either justice or injustice in this life. They took refuge in trusting blind chance as an avenging force. Even though their religion taught a belief in justice for the life to come, the bitter reality of daily life remained.

Schadenfreude explains why the oppressed not only rejoice when their tormentor suffers, but also when their fellow enslaved encounter misfortune. A beggar could not but foster a sentiment that the disenfranchised landgravine's experiences were quite just. Precisely because of feeling subjugated, an oppressed person assumes that those far above their station, the powerful and the wealthy, must therefore be doing well. For a person with a great deal of naïveté, the difference between those of high and those of low social status consists of affluence and glamor. If someone travels as non-aristocratically as the landgravine Elisabeth, who seemed to have lost all access to power, she will be treated insultingly even if she has a proven record of acts of highest virtue to her name. For these reasons, Elisabeth experienced ridicule instead of admiration when she became a Franciscan. In a status-conscious world of an inflexible patriarchal social order such

27 Caesarius attempts clumsily to portray the event as an old woman's unintentional mistake that nonetheless signifies an injury to Elisabeth by exchanging "nolens" for "volens": "vetula vero venienti cedere volens, trusit eam in lutum… quam iniuriam famula dei ridens sustinens" (But the old woman, wanting to give way, pushed her into the mud… laughing at how the servant of God came to harm).

as the high Middle Ages, social status rather than individuality generate respect and caring attention. Personal virtues did not elicit reverence, especially among the oppressed.

We cannot imagine the destitute as subdued enough or as enchained enough, who were the object of a social sense of duty among women of the medieval nobility. Only the "industrial enslaved" of our modern era can conceive of something like proletarian pride because they do not anymore (or at least only minimally so) adhere to an estate-defined social order and "bourgeois" or "feudal" ideals. They struggle to define post-estate values, and thus to fashion virtue from lack. For this group, strong individual self-confidence, however, is still impossible even today. In its stead, social-ist teachings offer a sense of collective confidence. In the past, neither existed. Precisely for this reason, a member of the medieval ruling class represented a particularly inflated representation of power rather than a genuine personality as such. Having lost her power, such an exemplar loses all respect as well. She devolved into a mere trigger to cool previously displayed sentiments of extreme devotion and fear by equally extreme brutality. It is thus that the face of a thrall grimaced in all its subaltern vindictiveness as the old widow encountered the saint. Yet the old woman's perfidy also reveals the fundamental wrongness of medieval charity, especially in the version embodied by the landgravine. In matters of soul and spirit as much as in matters of economic transactions, an underprivileged person reasons according to the principle that whatever is given freely cannot be worth much. Only that deserves respect which is bought dearly or taken forcefully. For this group, it is an all-defining experiential fact that in the world of labor, nothing is given freely. Whoever gives freely, whether in the context of political power dynamics, economic life, charity, or erotic relationships, is usually the one being duped. A government that offers concessions to another state without compensatory conditions will soon encounter unfriendly acts. Contemporary men expect nowadays that they will not get a woman "for free." Unconditional kindness and love without an expectation of reciprocity cause only confusion for the recipient and disappointment for the giver of such gifts.

According to this logic, poor people and, similarly, the ill who are neither capable nor required to provide compensation cannot bear boundless gifts provided by the healthy or wealthy. They are obliged to give the voluntary dispenser of gifts nothing but their own selves. And if they are nothing, they cannot but experience the freely given love as shame and humiliation. This is the psychological reason for the old saying that no good deed goes unpunished.

The blindness toward the common people's true attitude concerning Elisabeth speaks to the tragic isolation and narrow-mindedness of Landgravine Elisabeth's caste. At the very moment of their fall from power, all kings and landgraves who lost their crown discovered with astonishment and consternation that they were unpopular. Yet someone like Elisabeth, amid an internal as much as an external life crisis, was crushed by the discovery that, despite all her acts of charity, nobody cherished her. This she did not expect.

The united front of hostility directed against the pious landgravine, joining high and low society in a rare show of solidarity, was not simply a reaction to Elisabeth's personal traits. Rather, it reveals the typical social fate of saints in medieval society. The seeker of God, possessed by devotion, intent to live with the destitute, and faithful to her Franciscan ideals, is being stepped upon and persecuted. Medieval moral attitudes did not perceive a radically committed religious person as a model worth emulating. Nonetheless, modern literature and philosophies of culture have never openly acknowledged this to be true.

The biographies of saints as well as the annals of church history do not hide the fact that great religious personalities encountered rejection in the beginning. Secular and religious contemporaries labelled them as asocial, which would also be the case had they lived today. To serve God and "not humanity," they must leave their customary social circles. Through its elemental force, the experience of the divine changes "healthy" persons from the ground up.[28] They begin to isolate themselves from their usual surroundings. Uncannily, every a religiously productive person thus gives the impression of being stigmatized in some way. Feeling motivated by a moral impulse that differs from that of their social group, they inadvertently appear to be disruptive. They become shunned. As is true for any other age, medieval society feared religious zealots because underdeveloped group instincts always turn against outsiders. The church either removed the great anarchists of thought and emotion to special institutions and thus made them once again palatable or, in an act of reinterpretation, she pronounced them to be saints. As for their social milieu and era generally, religious radicals have always been unbearable.

Yet the ability to endure a lack of respect, which saints experience solely because of their deviation from the norm, turns into the main moral

---

28   Translator's note: This reference to a "healthy" mindset is likely meant to remind readers of William James' concept of "healthy" religious types. See James, *The Varieties of Religious Experiences,* chs. 4 and 5.

challenge. To be despised is a saint's causal and final corollary. A holy man or woman has no choice but to patiently accept a loss of honor. To loathe the world and to be loathed oneself necessitate each other as correlation. St. Filippo Neri's famous motto "spernere mundum, spernere te ipsum, spernere te sperni" (to despise the world, to despise yourself, and to despise the fact that you are despised) counted as a saint's highest penitence and yet also as the highest dignity. It does not signify fundamental arrogance but a defense on behalf of the endangered saint, spiritual self-preservation. To despise the scorn of others, even to affirm it, turns into a virtue out of necessity if Christian heroes do not want to relinquish themselves. "To despise the fact that you are despised" therefore means to make yourself invulnerable when your honor is harmed; you have greater allies than humans ever can be.

Still, saints retain the full capacity of feeling the hurt of insults hurled at them. Their superior moral achievement is to endure such suffering patiently. The episode of the indigent woman who pushed her erstwhile benefactress the landgravine into the street's sewage made its way into the *Libellus* as proof of precisely this intangibility in the midst of self-aware hurt and of Elisabeth's saintly humility:

> St. Elisabeth got up and walked to wash her clothes once more in the creek, and she thanked the Lord with joy and laughter that He deemed her worthy of being despised by all for His sake.

It does not prove that Elisabeth did not experience the full force of the old woman's cruelty if she responds, as a last defense, with embarrassed and uncomfortable laughter.

The rule of *spernere te sperni* appeared in ever new constellations as St. Elisabeth refined her art of suffering. Since the Eisenach days of misery, disregard by others became her constant companion. Her Franciscan lifestyle, the unusual living arrangements with her confessor, and the conflicts with her kin and caste could not but remove her from the social orbit of her status-bound fellow humans. She accepted it with heroic anguish and defiance. And when she later "congratulated herself for having received people's insults and slander," as is reported for her Marburg period, we encounter the character traits of a saint.

It is a matter of heroic legend when saints' lives pronounce people's spontaneous admiration and allegiance to a saint. Only a select few character types enjoy respect and influence during their lifetime; for example, we like to glorify personalities with unusual political instincts and exceptional calm during times of imminent danger. A similar effect occurs when saintly men and women perform miracles. Yet these tangible miracles are relatively superficial events. They include the resolution of seemingly irresolvable human conflicts and healings, which merely rely on solid scientific observation of the natural world or a knowledge of human nature. The magic power of a few words that brought to some a reputation of sainthood is rooted in their unconsciously applied psychotherapeutic talents. Indeed, leaders of a community, whether a city's bishop or an abbot, who helped a monastery or city achieve enduring peace and therefore wealth, received their saintly halo thanks to such exceptional success. Whether demonic, healing, or service oriented, these personality types enjoy popular devotion. Even though he was at his core nonreligious, the popular preacher and Elisabeth's confessor, Konrad of Marburg gained a spiritual reputation due to his unusual powers of suggestion and demagogy.

Generally, medieval people considered intellectuals to be extraordinary. All scholarly work made such a strong impression that people—most of whom lived illiterate and agrarian lives—suspected secret and magical forces at work. Even to this day, farmers tend to consider books as something uncanny. Medieval saints were considered philosophers and people who could manipulate reality. If these unusual qualities were complemented by a relatively chaste sexual lifestyle, we have the comprehensive image of a perfect saint before us. Hermits and professed ascetics enjoyed recognition only insofar as they bought their one-sided freedom with the public religious renunciation of all other types of freedom and earthly delights. Although living *extra legem* (outside the law), their unconventional lives were still tightly circumscribed and publicly acknowledged as such.

Francis of Assisi offers an example of what happens to saints before they achieve public recognition. At the time when he was a nobody and afraid to preach publicly, walking across the marketplace of his hometown with his begging stick and a bowl to receive food scraps, street urchins took their liberties with him. Francis gained respect and spontaneous devotion only after years of passionate and impressive preaching and the success of his religious brothers' charitable work. The Thuringian landgravine had nothing to present but her private piety and her zealous acts of charity. Her rejection was cold and sarcastic when she arrived in her town of Eisenach. Isolated and intrepid, she was treated like an outlaw. Nobody saw a reason to celebrate with her. She had made the obvious mistake that by rejecting her own caste, she elevated all other social groups as more worthy of her esteem. To be emotionally able to sever all ties to her own class, she overestimated the people she desired to join. This is an ever-recurring life experience of all those who shift from one social status to another. The tragedy of her situation is heightened by the fact that she was not significant or strong enough to force the approval of a class of people who were not at all interested in integrating her. Excluded from all parts of society, she became a leper herself.

Her heroic decision to choose holy poverty turned into a miserable lack of freedom as she became the target of disrespect and abuse. She desired to serve the poorest with humility and instead became their object of humiliation. She desired to live without property and wealth, since it was sinful, yet her relatives confiscated her assets and turned her religious desire to sacrifice all material wealth into a banal matter of disinheritance. She was determined to live among commoners because common folk please the divine.[29] Yet she felt herself to be shoved into their midst. She renounced an entire world, her home, and her children when she entered the grimy Eisenach tavern and was forced to notice that nobody was there to appreciate her heroism, not to mention honoring it. Up until this moment, she tormented herself with her penitential practices, but now she was made to suffer by the hands of others.

Life preempted her intentions in appalling ways; it devalued the moral and idealistic meaning of all her battles. It was distressing to experience her life's work and her own person in this way. The misery that she unintentionally brought upon herself not only overpowered her, but also made her three young children suffer deprivation. All that she had accomplished in pursuit of Christian humility and self-abandonment had sprung from an abundant source of psychological energy. It paled against the fear and psychological isolation that took hold of her in the hostile town. Elisabeth adjusted her emotional responses by renaming her experiences as acts of divine grace. She lived in the spirit of her teacher Francis, who once was asked by one of his disciples where one could find perfect joy. He answered,

> If we arrive at Portiuncula drenched by rain, frozen by cold, soiled by the muddy roads, and weak with hunger, and if we then knock at the monastery's gate, and the gatekeeper arrives angrily and asks, "who are you?", and we answer, "we are two of your brothers!", and he replies, "you are not speaking the truth, but you are two vagrant bandits who lie to people and steal alms from the poor; go away!"; and if he speaks in such a way and keeps the gate locked, leaving us hungry and standing in the snow and the water and the cold as the night falls, and if we endure such insults and treachery and behavior without becoming angry and without complaining to him, but instead think humbly and lovingly that

29   Translator's note: See, e.g., Matthew 22:1–10.

this gatekeeper knows us well, and that it is God who makes him talk so condescendingly – oh Brother Leone, remember that this is perfect joy! And when we continue to knock, and he steps outside angrily and continues to treat us like a pair of obtrusive scoundrels by hitting us; when he chases us away with angry words, yelling, "Go away, you brazen rascals, go join the lepers, you won't get either food or shelter here," and if we endure even this with patience and joy and love – oh Brother Leone, remember that this is perfect joy! And if we knock one more time driven by hunger and cold and the dark of the night, and ask him with hot tears to let us in for God's sake, just to be under a roof, and he becomes even angrier and shouts, "This is a pair of brazen rascals, they shall be treated according to their merit," and jumps out with a thick staff, grabs us by the hood, throws us on the ground, rolls us around in the snow, and beats us thoroughly with his staff; and if we endure all of this patiently and with joy and think of the sufferings of the most praiseworthy Christ and how much it is proper for us to suffer with him out of love – oh Brother Leone, remember that this is perfect joy!

The Vision

At least once during the "perfect joy" of the misery days in Eisenach, the disciple of Francis had an experience that caused pious medieval people to consider suffering as grace. As reported in the *Libellus*, she experienced a vision of the unmediated presence of God:

Once, on a day during the forty days before Easter, she leaned with bent knees against the wall and kept her eyes directed toward the altar for a long time. After that, once she had arrived back at her impoverished quarters and had taken a little food because she was feeling very weak, she began to sweat and, again stumbling against a wall, Isentrud had her lie down in her lap. After all others except for the previously mentioned young woman were sent out of the room, she looked toward the window and soon began to laugh softly. Her face lit up with joy. After about an hour and with her eyes closed, she shed innumerable tears, but soon she opened her eyes again, smiling cheerfully. She remained in such rapture until compline,[30] sometimes crying with closed eyes, and soon after laughing with her eyes open; her happy intervals lasted longer.

30   Until six o'clock in the evening.

After a long period of silence, she suddenly began to speak as follows. "Since you, Lord, wish to be with me, I wish to be with you, and never desire to be separated from you." Lady Isentrud, who was closer to her than all other servants, begged her to reveal with whom she had spoken. Overcome by her pleas, St. Elisabeth finally responded after she had come to her senses, "I saw heaven open and my dear Lord Jesus inclining toward me, consoling me in my plight and many afflictions. When I looked at him, I was happy and laughed. But when he turned his face away as if he wished to leave, I cried. When he took pity on me, he turned his joyful face once again toward me and said, 'if you wish to be with me, then I will be with you.'" Then she answered him as above. But Isentrud urged her to also speak about the Eucharistic vision she saw while in church. St. Elisabeth answered her, "It is not proper to reveal to you what I saw there. But know that I was extremely happy and that I saw the most miraculous Divine secrets."

This vision, combined with audition, i.e., seeing and hearing without any input by the senses, caused some modern scholars to interpret Elisabeth as a critically ill hysteric.[31] This view would have entered the mainstream by now if the barriers of a reputation of charitable maternity would not have deflected it. The view is typical of a contemporary scholarly interpretation, labelling all visions and revelations of medieval monastics and saints as psycho-pathological phenomena. Especially in the case of women, a suspicion of hysteria tends to arise quickly. Granted, a certain percentage of all religious enthusiasts belong in this category. Yet a medical explanation does not suffice to evaluate the religious and intellectual dimensions of their extraordinary abilities. Men and women with a fundamentally healthy constitution and disciplined character have been as capable of visions as despondent, psychopathic women.

In addition, the quality and degree of visionary states may differ to an extreme. Already in the late Middle Ages, Catholicism distinguished between legitimate visions, which transfer religious insights usually inaccessible to ordinary consciousness, and dreamlike states of limited awareness that frequently contained only wishful fantasies of forbidden desire.[32] The extensive account of the vision in the *Libellus*, which otherwise only offers succinct

31 Wenck and Kühn. Translator's note: The labelling of medieval women visionaries as hysterics has become largely outdated. See, inter alia, Jerome Kroll, Bernard Bachrach, and Kathleen Carey, "A Reappraisal of Medieval Mysticism & Hysteria," *Mental Health, Religion & Culture* 5, no. 1 (2002): 83–98.
32 The highly educated St. Theresa, who testified to her own supernatural revelations, applied critical standards when committing her precisely observed altered states to paper.

descriptions of Elisabeth's life and virtues, reveals what type of qualities formed the medieval foundation for defining religious exceptionality.[33]

Happy men and women do not have visions. The lives of the saints teach that hunger and sorrow, physical exhaustion and psychological pain are their prerequisites. To prepare for such experiences, the authentically called ascetic seeks out the most difficult corporeal deprivations. Most frequently, visions occur in times of grave internal crises. Elisabeth's vision proves to be an ecstasy born of despair and precipitated by a nervous breakdown. The stages of her rapture are recognizable as the symptoms of extreme physical exhaustion.[34] A lack of food, warmth, and rest during her days of misery undermined her. She had given birth to her third child just a few months before the Eisenach catastrophe. Such strain could not but burden a woman who was twenty-one years of age.

As she kneels for her prayer in the church, she becomes dizzy and leans against the wall. Her gaze immobilizes. Upon the return to her paltry lodgings, she enjoys a bit of food but faints once more. Breaking out in a sweat, as noted in the report, indicates great physical feebleness. Yet even a psychological collapse is more than justified by the young woman's turn of fate. It would be out of the ordinary had she not suffered an incident of severe depression. Her previous battles and psychological exertions overtaxed her psychological strengths. The trauma of the break with her social milieu added to the greatest of her burdens, the death of the landgrave. Uprooted and exposed to hostility everywhere, she focused her remaining strength on the fearless act of daring to choose poverty and freedom. It proved to be the wrong decision and led to a ghastly psychological crisis. Failing in the realm of her ideals, wounded to the death in her personal affairs, banned from society, she fell to the ground, trodden underfoot.

Her vision's alternating laughter and tears suggest that she relived the entire spectrum of her failed life in a short span of time. At its peak, pain transforms into a feeling of happiness. Teetering between health and illness,

---

33   Popular scholarship counts the ability to experience visions and to perform miracles as one of sainthood's main characteristics. In the official examination of a candidate for canonization, however, ownership of supernatural powers ranks only fourth. The main requirements are religious and human virtues. In the Middle Ages, uneducated Catholic laypeople and the average clergy preferred those who were graced with supernatural and magical abilities. Elisabeth's medieval reputation is proof of this stance, since it rests only on the miracles that occurred at her grave.

34   Elisabeth's Eisenach vision appears to be documented by a different ecclesiastical official. It is rendered in an extremely detailed and precise manner; furthermore, Isentrud is introduced as if an entirely new person, yet her testimony constitutes the basis for all of Part 1 of the *Libellus*. This shift is proof for the importance of the episode.

Elisabeth experiences a few hours of hyper-wakefulness in a betwixt and between state of consciousness. Her feelings oscillate between deepest despair and the arousal of a renewed will to live.

The apparition itself is comparable to a wish-fulfilling dream and must be interpreted as such. Not the Madonna but Christ appears to the despairing young woman. Like her deceased husband, he addresses her amicably and well-intentioned. Yet like him, he also turns away. Ludwig left her to join the crusades and never returned. The motion of turning toward and away from her repeats itself several times during the vision. It is countered by Elisabeth's outbursts of happiness and sadness, by her laughter and tears. Her life's greatest sorrow at the time was the loss of her beloved, her only one protection from an increasingly hostile court. In the vision, her recent loss is reexperienced in all its force and because of it, simultaneously overcome. In her vision, Elisabeth is joined with her spouse more permanently and perfectly than in her actual life, because he appears in the figure of an all-powerful helper. "I want to be with you and will never be separated from you." These words end all the suffering she experienced after his departure. Life in the brightness of day is never as frightening and terrifying as a dream, but likewise, it cannot ever convey a dream's pure sense of happiness. All human beings may perceive "heaven to be opened." We need to understand St. Elisabeth's comforting waking dream in like manner. The critical question about the value of each religious revelation, either in hours of greatest productivity or despair, is whether the divine speaks to a human being or whether a human creates the divine to their own end. In the case of the ill-fated Elisabeth's Eisenach vision, we must choose the second possibility. As all people of her age, she however believed that she spoke with Christ himself. With the assistance of this deception, many religious personalities, including those of great religious fame, fashioned the images of their own heart's desire into a visionary experience and gave it supernatural form.

Nonetheless, the apparition generated by the exhausted brain of a worn-out and powerless woman in miserable living quarters also contained experiences of a transpersonal character. In response to her friend's urging, Elisabeth said, "I have seen God's secrets and was filled with happiness." All great religious figures report this unutterable feeling of bliss and the certainty, which remained even after regaining intelligibility, to have received knowledge beyond the reach of ordinary life experiences. Elisabeth was capable of a grand experience: she transformed the suffering of perpetual threats to her bodily existence and self into the flawless joy of divine presence. Because of this, she offers proof of genuine mysticism not just according to the standards of her time, but of all time.

Her path to the religious certainty of being a child of God, however, strikes us today as odd and outdated. A vision, even Elisabeth's vision, cannot merely be approached as a symbol of an intense inner spiritual or psychological experience. Visionary sights of the divine must be taken literally. They were fully embodied. Elisabeth says, as do all visionaries, the same thing: she has seen Christ with her own eyes; she spoke with him, and he spoke with her. The perception of objects, colors, and sounds, which do not exist, constitute the core element of an apparition, even if this seems an illusion to modern people. Clairvoyance is perhaps a lost human capacity, which our species might have possessed in other epochs, and which was already in the process of extinction during the Middle Ages.[35] It might have served as a segue to visionary experiences for those who possessed genuine psychological creativity.

Constitutionally, St. Elisabeth was not a gifted visionary and certainly not generally given to ecstasy. We possess only the report of this one exalted hour. During her sorrowful time at Marburg, she sometimes gave the impression of experiencing ecstatic states when becoming entirely unresponsive. She could have created an enormous reputation for herself or used it as a weapon against her abuser, if she had tried to cultivate these mystical tendencies. Yet she remained objective and factual in her self-assessment. She did not exaggerate aspects of her inner life and abilities that could have gained her the admiration of her contemporaries. She endured all stages of her life's ruin with full awareness and without any kind of self-induced sedation. "Patience in times of distress is greater than performing miracles and raising the dead." The Eisenach vision was bought with anguish and destitution. Neither her youth nor her fragile health could endure what was extraordinary. After her days in Eisenach, she had lost her will to live, returned to the guidance of her mentor Konrad, and died a few years later. Only twenty-four years of age, depleted and worn out by sorrow, she had become a living corpse.

Capitulation

Elisabeth's time of affliction in Eisenach did not last long. Her fundamentally impossible Franciscan experiment concluded in a lesson of defeat and

---

35   Recent psychological research in eidetics may be able to explain optical perceptions during visionary states. A certain percentage of children and most artists are assumed to possess eidetic ability, i.e., they are capable of visual perception without external object stimuli.

exhaustion. Her aunt Mechthild of Andechs, likely alarmed by Wartburg castle relatives, traveled to Eisenach to return the impoverished young woman to a safe and sound life. This sister of Elisabeth's mother was abbess of the Benedictine monastery of Kitzingen at the Main river, famous for its scholarship and feudal tradition. We should imagine a woman of such high religious rank to be sophisticated and capable of sensible and judicious personal and political leadership. She immediately grasped the dynamics of the situation. Since a reconciliation with the Thuringian kin was apparently impossible, she brought Elisabeth, enfeebled by her sorrow and toil, to her uncle, Bishop Ekbert of Bamberg.[36] The downtrodden young woman found asylum in the Bamberg palatinate. The bishop cared courteously for her well-being and ensured that she was attended to according to her noble rank. Yet the relationship deteriorated quickly because the host intended to resolve the desperate situation of his protégée once and for all. The only solution was to remarry her as soon as possible. On one hand, this was the custom for a young widow of high status, on the other hand, he likely thought that any woman's anguish could be cured with such a type of remedy. Elisabeth resisted his efforts with determination.

Her residence at the Bamberg palatinate must have appeared to her as a betrayal of her Franciscan ideals. It was her life's goal to overcome precisely this kind of milieu. A bishop's residence, especially one that belonged to a sophisticated and powerful lord such as Bishop Ekbert, did not differ from that of a secular monarch. Her host's marriage project could only strengthen her resolve to flee the world. Yet she remained at her asylum, unsuitable as it was, because she was physically and mentally exhausted. At the very least, the palace offered her care, warmth, and quiet. She did not choose the natural and obvious path of a second marriage, but she did not opt for taking the veil either. Her new guardian faced a difficult situation, but so did she.

Today, the terms "uncle" and "aunt" are only relevant in the lives of children. They seem almost humorous when used among adults. In contrast, the family roles of an aunt or uncle signified power and highest authority among young men and women living in a pre-nation-state patriarchal era. As the landgravine of Thuringia's closest male relative in Germany, Bishop Ekbert had the right and responsibility to determine her life's choices. Marriage was not a private affair between two people, but the object of family politics and economics. A young woman was barely allowed to voice her opinion and objections. The *Libellus* proves at an extensive length to

36 Bishop Ekbert of Bamberg had arranged Elisabeth's betrothal. An influential religious figure, he initiated the construction of the Bamberg Cathedral as we know it today.

what degree Elisabeth felt cornered by the bishop's pressure to remarry. It notes her and her female companions' distress and the eventual miraculous providence of divine intervention, which seemed to be perceptible in an unexpected turn of events.

It was a given that as her uncle, the bishop was not impressed by the religious vow of perpetual widowhood that Elisabeth held in highest esteem. He might have also feared a quandary and appears to have already made certain binding promises to the Thuringian house. Elisabeth, however, threatened self-injury: "I will cut off my nose to maim myself so that nobody will take me." As a first step, the bishop ordered his stubborn guest to be removed from the Bamberg palace and locked up in a remote castle. While there, Elisabeth was to come to her senses and eventually give her consent.

An external event ended this mutually uneasy situation. The crusading vassals of the deceased Landgrave Ludwig arrived in Bamberg as they retreated from southern Italy. They carried the skeletal remains of their lord, which were intended to be interred at the family crypt in Reinhardtsbrunn. Straight away, Bishop Ekbert recalled Elisabeth to Bamberg and greeted the arrival of the procession with high ceremony and celebrations. He left town to meet the new arrival and brought the convoy into his city accompanied by the festive ringing of church bells. The coffer with the remains was placed in the cathedral. A mass for the dead was conducted, and Elisabeth received the remains of her husband's corpse.[37] She was shaken by an assault of intense grief. Even though it is colored by theological bias, the *Libellus* reports her words at that moment, which strike us as genuine. Elisabeth laments, "My God, you know how much I loved him." The *Libellus* continues:

> I do not regret that I offered my most beloved to you for the protection of the Holy Land. Could I get him back, I would pay with anything of this world. I would go begging with him forever. Yet you are my witness, God, that I do not wish to even receive one hair of his life against your will. I recommend him and myself to your mercy. Your will be done unto us.

Theological bias aside, these words express her all-consuming wish that divine dictate would not have caused her such great harm. Facing the casket with her husband's remains and meeting his vassals, whom she last saw

---

37   In *Life of St. Ludwig*, Chaplain Berthold describes in detail the transfer of Landgrave Ludwig's earthly remains from Italy to Germany. They consisted only of Ludwig's skeleton, his *Gebeine* (disassembled bones). The corpses of high-standing secular persons were treated post-mortem in such a way that only bones remained. Chaplain Berthold writes extensively about the process.

when she looked at her spouse for the final time, she felt the full weight of her loss and the dismal turn her life had taken. Her statement that she would have gladly become an itinerant beggar with her husband if only he would still be alive gained singular fame. Her wish does not express an ascetical rejection of the world and marriage but exposes a vital desire for love and companionship. "I would give the whole world for regaining him, because we only need each other and Holy Poverty." This episode lacks the fatalism that would dominate her during her Marburg years. In Marburg, resistance against her fate came to a standstill because grief had lodged itself deep in her psyche. The Bamberg episode constitutes the only reported evidence that affords us a glimpse of the former Landgravine Elisabeth's emotions. We can only speculate about all other and later battles, especially the appalling final separation from her children.

Her time in the shadow of the Bamberg cathedral signify the last days that she lived a secular life as a woman of high noble status.[38] Today, we regard the cathedral with reverence as a classical expression of high medieval creativity. Yet its marvelous architecture and artistically enormously valuable sculptures, which were fashioned around that time and still jolt us today, such as the figures of Synagogue and Ecclesia, likely barely impressed her. She did not focus on them. At most, the will to power that always serves as the impetus for great art repulsed her. As a religiously oriented person, she perhaps also lacked the ability to recognize the intellectual caliber of these creations. While in Bamberg, she must have once again and decisively experienced the dissonance between the aristocratic culture from which she came and her own vocation.

Yet to her misfortune, she proved incapable of creating a life beyond society's constraints. Filled with indecision, the next months of her life make this point. The arc of her life bent into a steep decline and led her back to the tyrannical protection of the barbaric monk. Elisabeth followed the Thuringian vassals from Bamberg to Thuringia. Their first stop was Reinhardsbrunn to bury the landgrave's remains. Bishop Ekbert abandoned his plans for Elisabeth. He let her depart with misgivings and only after the Thuringian nobles promised to do everything in their power to regain

38   The details of our knowledge about St. Elisabeth's days at Bamberg stem from the *Life of St. Ludwig*. The sections up until the burial in Reinhardsbrunn were likely composed by the eyewitness Chaplain Berthold. They therefore must be recognized as a primary source. Börner considers all sections until the landgrave's burial as the core of St. Ludwig's biography. Up-to-date archeological research has concluded that the bishop's palace, built by King Henry II, stood next to the Bamberg cathedral at today's location of the "Old Residenz," and not on the site of the Altenburg castle.

the widow's rights and inheritance. It seems that she returned to her home country without any firm plan. What could she have wanted there? The shared table with kin and community was broken. She did not choose life as a nun. The experiment with Franciscan mendicancy ended in disillusion. Sustained only by the restiveness of her grief, she followed the casket with the remains of the only human being she had loved and who had provided her with a home country. Still, her three little children lived in Thuringia, and she yearned for them.

As required by the status of the landgrave's noble lineage, the burial of Elisabeth's spouse at the Reinhardsbrunn monastery turned into a large public funeral. In addition to the Thuringian nobility, many commoners were present as well. Chaplain Berthold described the formidable extent of the festivity's effort and expense. Elisabeth attended the funeral, which also reunited the family, including the mother and brothers-in-law. A grand reconciliation at the grave would have been in order, but nothing of the kind occurred. Even the Thuringian vassals who promised Bishop Ekbert to take care of the widow's well-being were unsuccessful. According to the Reinhardsbrunn sources, one of them, Rudolf of Vargula, admonished Ludwig's young successor, Heinrich Raspe, of his duties.[39] Heinrich promised to provide the best possible guardianship for his sister-in-law and her children. While the *Libellus* confirms the Reinhardsbrunn source, it records the event in more objective terms. The brother-in-law offered her upkeep among her husband's kin in accordance with her rank (legally speaking, the *sustentatio*). At this point, however, it was psychologically impossible for Elisabeth to return to a life among the aristocracy after she had dared to transgress into the world of misery and poverty that existed beyond the boundaries of her class and caste. The *Libellus* notes that the landgravine experienced a grave conflict of conscience when faced with the option to live a life of affluence wrung from the poor: "Once again, she faced poverty and infirmity. Yet she suffered it gladly for God."[40] Even now, however, and despite a spokesperson of Bishop Ekbert's rank, her widow's fund was not released. Supported by the aristocratic faction, the young Raspe insisted

---

39 These comprise the added sections about St. Ludwig's life, which Chaplain Berthold did not author. Rudolf of Vargula's accusation mentions for the first time that Elisabeth was expelled from "house and home." The report is biased but not without merit, as is generally argued. The situation itself reveals that new negotiations, tensions, and efforts at mediation took place among the different parties, kin members, and the current regent Heinrich Raspe. There can be no doubt that Heinrich Raspe's attitude toward Elisabeth was fundamentally one of hostility.
40 This has been reported by Irmingard. She was not an eyewitness but lived on intimate terms with Elisabeth in Marburg.

emphatically on withholding it. His reasons were justified in that she would have simply bequeathed it all to the ill and destitute. It contradicted his noble kin's long-standing traditions.

As a result, in part freely, in part by force, Elisabeth once again took herself to a place of abject poverty. She remained in Thuringia, but the *Libellus* offers no further details. Her hopeless situation predisposed her to succumb to Master Konrad's rule once again, whom she had refused her obedience during the Eisenach catastrophe in an act of daring and despair. Konrad had observed the faltering path of his pupil from a distance. His patient strategy brought success. Elisabeth had proven that she was incapable of living a life of self-determination. Her guileless and brave effort to live in the spirit of St. Francis had failed. With her choices shipwrecked, Konrad gained easy victory. He had been correct all along. In compensation for the humiliation that she caused him by running away from him, he chose out-and-out revenge.

There are no eyewitness accounts of the reunion between the former landgravine of Thuringia and her confessor. No historical sources tell us about their battles. Yet we do not need them. In historical analysis, the shared life in Marburg that followed their reunion, Elisabeth's near incapacitation, and the character of this barbaric spiritual marriage leave no doubt as to the tragedy of the reunion.

Konrad of Marburg's Victory

Once he assumed her guardianship, Konrad of Marburg's unusual political and organizational talents surfaced first in the success with which he guided the worldly affairs of his pupil, the former landgravine of Thuringia. He accomplished what no one else before him achieved, not even an authority like Ekbert, the bishop of Bamberg, and the well-intentioned Thuringian noble lords: the release of the widowed landgravine's pension.[41] Her husband's kin, represented by her brother-in-law and current regent Heinrich Raspe, resisted the effort up to the end. Providing the widow's pension would have diminished the family's wealth, and to resolve financial and business matters in an already difficult relationship tends to be thorny. Konrad succeeded in receiving not only a payment of 2,000 silver marks, but also the income of

---

41 Konrad exercised his diplomatic skill more than once as the pope's arbiter. Already in 1219, his name is mentioned in relation to similar conflicts. In later years, he conducted crucial political negotiations between the landgrave Konrad of Thuringia and the archbishop of Mainz.

economically productive farming property near Marburg in Hesse.[42] This outcome was a skillfully negotiated transfer, since the landgravine's widow estates were originally located in Thuringia.[43] The successful negotiator, however, did not transfer the litigated inheritance to his female ward. She did not care for her property one way or the other and would have distributed the hard-won prize among the destitute. As we shall see, Konrad pursued other quite tangible ecclesiastical and economic goals. Elisabeth's inheritance was to be used for founding a new hospital in Marburg.

Despite Konrad's manipulative skills in dealing with people of high and low rank, and despite his demonic influence on his spiritual daughter, he was forced to call upon the strongest allies to be successful, whether personally or in business transactions. He enjoyed access to one of them, a man before whom not only a woman like Elisabeth but the whole world bent their knee: Pope Gregory IX. The *Libellus* notes that by sending paternal and benevolent missives, the pope encouraged Elisabeth to remain steadfast in her calling. Even if we ignore the theological and literary conventions in these papal letters, we still note that the pope clearly intended to inspire and almost flatter a hesitant Elisabeth to reach a difficult goal with all her might.[44] How could it be that an over seventy-year-old personality of Pope Gregory IX's stature takes pains to care for an insignificant former landgravine from Thuringia? Although Elisabeth possessed an intense interior life, she had no extraordinary achievements to her name. It was solely because of Konrad of Marburg's close professional relationship with him that the pope knew of her fate. Yet Konrad only informed Gregory IX about Elisabeth to the degree useful to him. Receiving a papal letter exhorting her that "from the small seed of tears, infinite days of joy in eternity might be gained," she was given no choice but to remain in her martyrdom.

The key purpose of this intervention was to place the former landgravine of Thuringia and her controversial property under papal protection. As was to be expected, the pope chose none other than Konrad of Marburg as the official guardian in both spiritual and secular matters. The encouraging and comforting letters were intended to serve Konrad's goal, and they did.

---

42   2,000 silver marks are worth about 80,000 Reichsmark today, yet were even more valued and valuable in a barter economy.

43   Otherwise, she would not have been able to keep Konrad's alimentary rule and receive her victuals from her own farms.

44   Wenck discovered a page of vellum in private ownership. Part of the Arensberg Psalter, it is a copy of a papal letter to Elisabeth of Thuringia. See Wenck, "Die Heilige Elisabeth und Papst Gregor IX," *Hochland* (1907).

Modern scholars (with unintended naïveté) present the naming of Konrad as Elisabeth's protector as the pope's independent initiative, but it only occurred as the result of Konrad's adept maneuvering.[45] Through the brilliant diplomatic move of papal authorization, Konrad's position as Elisabeth's guardian guaranteed his legally and morally unassailable power over her in full public view. Any external resistance against his mentorship was nipped in the bud because of his highest possible endorsement. Despite his reputation as a genuine ascetic, it violated custom that the cleric left for Marburg with the widow of a highly regarded German feudal lord. It could not but cause rumors and indignation among the former landgravine's family and the Thuringian nobility.

At first glance, Konrad's idea to build a hospital as her widow's seat should be credited as virtuous and constructive even from Elisabeth's perspective. She would thus become captivated by a task that fit the range of her previous activities. Yet the move to the desolate and distant location of Marburg and thus away from all of Elisabeth's connections, her children, and the memories of her past signified deracination on a large scale. Since she lacked realistic plans of her own, and since Konrad's influence reasserted itself at a moment when she was exhausted and without remaining options, she acquiesced and followed him. The relocation, endorsed by the highest religious authority, turned the former wife of the landgrave of Thuringia into Konrad's hostage once and for all. Elisabeth's last years in Marburg's hospital are proof.

In his ward's biography, Konrad reports precisely the opposite about this decisive step. According to the *Epistola*, she followed him against his will to this remote region "at the furthermost boundary of the Thuringian realm," led by the fear of succumbing to the temptations of the world. The opposite of a lighthearted and sensual worldly woman, this certainly was one of the least of Elisabeth's fears.

Konrad failed at least in this instance in obfuscating facts, even if the *Epistola* is otherwise cunning when presenting his role in the life of his ward in the best possible light. The unfolding of events counts as proof that in the wake of the fiasco of her attempt to escape, the helpless woman was incapable of resisting his will. Furthermore, the *Libellus* contains an eyewitness report by Isentrud, Elisabeth's closest confidante. She declared unequivocally that Konrad ordered Elisabeth to move to Marburg.[46]

---

45   In the *Epistola,* Konrad mentions twice that the pope himself named him as the landgravine's guardian.

46   Other scholars have reconciled the two starkly contradictory statements by assuming that given his status as a well-established man of high reputation and rank, the version of Elisabeth's

Bitter emotional struggles must have preceded the shared living arrangements in Marburg because Elisabeth was forced to purchase them with the surrender of her children. The landgravine's kin were doubly angered by her departure to Hesse: they had to release her widow's endowment and were obliged to provide funds for her children, with the eldest also being heir to the throne. This familial obligation generally applied only when children grew up with their relatives rather than with their birth parents. Nothing could have been more welcome for Konrad than for his penitent to be fully separated from her young children.

The disappearance of these tokens of life and love removed the last barriers to a "spiritualized" guardianship and sexless living arrangement. Thanks to a lucky coincidence, the spouse was eliminated; the feudal environment had moved into the background. Indeed, the children were the last of her bonds to society and because of the strength of maternal love, the most powerful connection to life as such. Obviously, Konrad did not demand these sacrifices for himself but in the name of a transpersonal religious goal. He could reference the deeds of saints, who frequently neglected their children and spouses in preference of their religious calling.

In Konrad's religious extortion and the displacement of his true motives, we find once again the fiendish method of his pedagogy at work, as evidenced in all his past and future wounding of Elisabeth. His success was total. He achieved her freely enacted renunciation of self—a kind of suicide, which he himself in some sense observed with pleasure. Elisabeth forced herself to experience the pain of separation at a time when her children became especially precious to her, because she had just lost her spouse. The children were about five, three, and one years old—that is, they were at an age at which no woman leaves her children. She abandoned children who had already lost one parent to the care of strangers.

It was only in one instance that she asserted her maternal rights. She took the youngest of the three children, the approximately one-year-old

---

confessor had more authority than its rejection in the *Libellus*. A very simplistic proof. Huyskens tries to paint the former landgravine's move to Marburg as the normal passage to her long-established choice of a widow's seat. According to a comment in the *Libellus*, the city and castle of Marburg belonged to Elisabeth's marital endowments. Yet this makes Konrad's statement in the *Epistola* even more suspicious and a rather incriminating qui s'excuse, s'accuse. Finally, even if it would be reasonable to assume that Elisabeth moved to Marburg out of her free will after the death of her spouse, it remains suspicious that Konrad transferred to Marburg at the same time as the landgravine and that he began living with her in Marburg. If no certifiable testimonies existed, future events in Elisabeth's life prove ex post facto Elisabeth's forced incarceration at Marburg.

Gertrude, born after Ludwig's death, with her to Marburg's desolation as the only memory of her earlier life. Impoverished in a much more humiliating fashion than through voluntary Franciscan poverty and self-effacement, she resigned herself to her new life. It broke the strength of her resistance to any new assault and degradation caused by her spiritual marriage to her mentor.

Despite everything, she was forced to seal her depersonalization and suicidal self-negation with a religious ritual of obedience more binding than her oath at the church of St. Katherine when her spouse was still alive. In the Eisenach chapel of the Franciscans, on Good Friday, Elisabeth placed her hands on the altar and renounced her family, her children, and her own free will. According to the *Epistola*, Konrad and a few Franciscan brothers served as witnesses. This second but much more radical pledge to abandon the world did not usher in a monastic life as the vow might have suggested. It signified only a deeper dependence on her confessor.

The contradiction that Elisabeth remained in the world yet was bound by monastic rules without enjoying their protection—monastic peace—signaled the final stage of submission to him.[47] As a representative of the divine, only he remained in her life. Children and relatives ceased to exist. The grand ritual abandonment of her will and the renunciation of her freedom were not her own decision. The subsequent implementation of the oath demonstrates the truth behind the vow. As Elisabeth dares once more to resolutely apply her Franciscan principles in this moment of surrendering earthly happiness, children, and family by also relinquishing her property and wealth, Konrad quickly intervenes.

According to the *Epistola*, he quickly prevents the much too consistent pupil from abandoning her assets. He had just negotiated the release of her widow's pension with substantial effort and diplomacy. It could not be squandered now. It was to provide a religious foundation in Marburg, which would also enhance his own reputation. He practiced the time-honored politics of ecclesiastical men to redirect noble women's wealth to monasteries, religious orders, or spiritual charities. As was true for all his medieval contemporaries, the material wealth of the church signified to him proof of her moral and intellectual authority. Church politics were economic politics. Yet he realized the religious incongruity of denying

---

47   Even Wenck, usually only noting legal transaction and intent on saving Konrad of Marburg from the suspicion of cruel disciplinary domination, notes that "in a little more than two years the third ceremonial act (that is, taking on the habit of a tertiary religious) took place, with which she tied herself to her foster father. With the renunciation of her own will on Good Friday, she acknowledged once more his dominion over her." Wenck, "St. Elisabeth" in *Die Wartburg*, 1907.

his daughter to relinquish her wealth when she was letting go of all other worldly ties. He therefore added in his report of Elisabeth's partial vow that she still had to pay her husband's debts and should have access to material means to dispense charities with her customary generosity.[48] Formally, as always, this is a persuasive rationalization of his far-reaching intents. As before, however, Konrad had no interest in the religious radicalism of Franciscan values.

The Good Friday vow in the Franciscan chapel in Eisenach highlights the collision between the church's material power as represented by Konrad and the evangelical poverty movement perhaps as clearly as the first encounter between St. Francis and the pope. Elisabeth, a compliant woman in all other ways, proved to be equal to her illustrious role model in terms of the acumen of her spiritual instincts. She could feel that her disciplinarian Konrad embodied the principle of her spiritual opposite. Even on her deathbed, only three years later, the opposing religious principles of these two characterological types clashed one last time, when Konrad suggested matter-of-factly that she compose a testament.

It is quite possible that Konrad sensed this deep contrast, even if only dimly so. Considering his pupil's futile previous attempt to escape, her renewed unconditional surrender through the ritual renunciation of a secular existence was therefore an even sweeter triumph for him. The now complete personal and material submission of the previously all too independent object of his domination must have felt more satisfying than the death of hundreds of heretics whom he condemned to death in the years to come.

48   The Good Friday vow is recorded in Konrad's *Epistola*, but not in the *Libellus*.

4 The Poverella of Marburg

Elisabeth in Marburg: Relocation and New Status

Every city has its own founding myth, ideally intended to trace its origin to the acts of heroes. It therefore makes sense that later local historiographies hesitate to destroy such founding or genealogical myths; it would violate deeply rooted interests and reputation. More objective historiographies with no local stakes are not sufficiently invested to dissolve or at the very least to examine these legends more deeply. For this reason, the fable that the landgravine founded a hospital in the city at the river Lahn, and thus became its patron saint, has endured through the centuries. In truth, the founder, director, and protector of this project was Elisabeth's spiritual teacher and mentor, Konrad of Marburg. In addition, not Elisabeth's three years of pious labor at the hospital but three centuries of pilgrimage to her miracle-working grave turned Marburg into Elisabeth's settlement. While living in Marburg, she received hardly any attention and died with little regard by others. The city's true historiography only begins after her death and once her name was leveraged to attract the formidable and lucrative tourism of pilgrimages and hospitality services.

When he earmarked the widow's pension of his foster child for the creation of a hospital, Konrad deliberately chose his own region as its location. He was motivated by far-reaching goals. Already in the year 1227, while still confessor on the Wartburg, he petitioned Mainz to provide Marburg with an independent parish. At that point, Marburg did not even have its own church but only the St. Kilian Chapel, which belonged to the parish of a neighboring village. To secure ecclesiastical support for his removed home village, nothing was more suitable than the semimonastic foundation of a hospital. In the thirteenth century, Hesse, including Marburg, was possibly the German center of Waldensian heresy. It is also possible that the agrarian region was still predominantly pagan or had relapsed into paganism, because Christianization in rural areas, even in the thirteenth century, was frequently quite superficial.

Soon, Magister Konrad's calculations proved to be successful and became even more so in the city's future. As always, whether planning monastic

Busse-Wilson, E., *St. Elisabeth of Thuringia: A Psychological Study* (1931). Amsterdam: Amsterdam University Press, 2025

DOI 10.5117/9789463725804_CH04

purges, a religious foundation, or the execution of heretics, he implemented his plans with rigor and careful attention to detail. Marburg's medieval significance and future development derives from Konrad's decision to establish the hospital in the town. Before the hospital, Marburg was not much more than a village with a few noble landholdings.[1] As a settlement with a border castle located between Mainz and the Hesse-Thuringian realm, its function was purely military and far removed from the splendor and representational heft of the Wartburg castle. Wartburg castle was a magnificent feudal court, the Marburg castle a small vassal's seat like many others. Even the great road to Frankfurt, which passed near the remote Frauenberg, ignored the village of Marburg. It was therefore not much more than a desolate settlement when the former landgravine moved to the location. The foundation provided Konrad not only with the means to develop his place of birth but also protected his own existential needs beyond material considerations. After many decades of rootless wandering from place to place, preaching, supervising, and inciting unrest, the aging man's need to settle down drove him into a haven that also offered a respectable background for his religious activities. Another motive was more hidden: to secure without any interference the total possession of a woman whom he had bound to himself with several vows of obedience.

Nobody but her spiritual teacher Konrad welcomed the former landgravine of Thuringia when she arrived in her new home with her companions Guda and Isentrud and her small child. Hesse's nobility—her social peers—boycotted her in the most offensive fashion. Nobody greeted or visited her. According to the *Libellus*, she was studiously avoided as an unstable woman of suspect manners. The hatred of unindividuated and rigid groups toward exceptional individuals constricted her here as much as in Thuringia.

A damaging reputation preceded her arrival. Her adventure among the townspeople of Eisenach, her quarrels with her kin, and her unusual religious lifestyle sufficed to isolate her. The scandalous symbiosis with her new life partner, who presented himself openly and publicly in Marburg as her lord and master, was more offensive than anything else that had occurred. Gossip spread that she obviously had quickly found comfort after her husband's death.

In any patriarchal era, a woman's family constitutes her sole socially acceptable circle of relationships. A single woman belongs to her family. A married woman has her place in her husband's kin. A widow remarries

---

1   Marburg is said to have already enjoyed the rights of a city at the time of St. Elisabeth's spouse Ludwig IV. However, it received city walls much later, under Henry of Brabant, landgrave of Hesse and the grandson of Elisabeth.

if young or accepts the tutelage of her oldest son if elderly. If she did not choose any of these options, the protection of a monastery, and later a Beguinage, was available.

The young, widowed landgravine of Thuringia lived in Marburg under exceptional circumstances. She was neither a nun nor part of a family. Her closest companionship was with a man who was not a blood relative. And this man was a cleric! In the thirteenth century, a critical period for the church's moral reputation, the dress of a secular cleric merely signified a carte blanche for licentiousness. At the very least, if a noblewoman had a love affair with a cleric, something not at all rare, then she should conduct the affair secretly. Landgravine Elisabeth settled in Marburg with her alleged lover in full public view. The actual tragedy of such slander, however, lies in the fact that the unhappy woman's relationship to her foster father was instead gruesomely "pure."

Thrashings took the place of kisses, orders that of troubadour courtship, psychological enslavement that of freely shared eroticism. Beyond her asexual bondage, she had to accept the public disgrace of being suspected of a banal love affair.[2] Having emerged from the psychological challenges of the painful separation from her children and her continuous struggles, she now found her new home an icy desert of slander. Her reputation only barely improved by the foundation of her hospital. The young woman's most personal accomplishment, the hospital's care for the sick, did not move her Hessian peers to the same level of admiration as was the case for nineteenth-century writers. It would have been Landgravine Elisabeth's socially appropriate task to launch a widow's residence that could offer the sons and daughters of the landed gentry a minor court appointment, or at least, to try to advance herself socially.

The last shred of her reputation was destroyed when she became a public witness to the world of Franciscan ideas by joining the Franciscan Third Order, or Tertiaries. Unlike nuns or monks, tertiaries form a spiritual order in the secular world by remaining immersed in their professional lives and maintaining their married status. They committed themselves to a

---

2   This is according to the *Libellus*. Drawing from the Marburg tradition, Caesarius of Heis-terbach is even more explicit in naming the character of these speculations: "dirty words" were being circulated. A popular ballad from a later source reiterated St. Elisabeth's reputation from this time: "Now the coarse and malicious people wished to interpret all things in a meanspirited fashion. They spoke, it's Master Konrad who abducted Lady Elisabeth; since her Lord had died, he got her wealth for her. This they wanted to consume together—and who could stop them?" The text is from the auctor rhythmicus (ca. 1460) and quoted in Adolf Hausrath's study, *The Heretics' Master of Marburg*.

life in evangelical poverty, that is, shunning personal possessions and at the beginning at least, the ownership and use of weapons, as well as a life of mutual service. Even today, membership in the Tertiary Order remains substantial.

Whether Elisabeth herself found a way forward by professing her adherence to Francis without joining a monastery, or whether her guardian Konrad recommended this compromise to legalize her presence in the hospital, in either case, her hybrid position between a secular and religious life became ever more obvious. Elisabeth was neither regarded as a nun, who could feel assured of non-sexualized respect and distance, nor was she conducting herself as a typical secular widow. It is said that Konrad himself vested her, yet not without demanding a vow of obedience (for the third time?).[3] The garment which Elisabeth received at the ceremony was a type of peasant smock to symbolize her identification with the status of the poor and dispossessed. In contrast to the long drapes of noblewomen's dress, it was short like her coat; the color was gray instead of the vibrant joyfulness of secular fashion choices.[4] Following the Franciscan order's custom, she usually went barefoot with a rope around her hips. In the Franciscan tradition, the coat came to be of great significance. It was her talisman and prayer covering and preserved as a precious relic after her death.[5]

With the defiance of a misunderstood person, she continued to stir the virulent disdain around her. The *Libellus* reports that "she lengthened her gray coat with a piece of cloth of another color because it was too short. Likewise, she mended the torn sleeves of her shirt with another color as well." It was not dire circumstances or a temporary quandary that forced her to add patches of another fabric. Stitching together unsuitable materials, Elisabeth intended to provoke. She walked around in public puritanically, austerely, and at the same time, eye-catching. *Spernere te sperni*: to despise the fact that we are despised.

---

3   Formally, Konrad had no right bestowing her habit upon her. He was not a Franciscan. According to a Franciscan tradition, however, she was vested by Burckhardt, a guardian of the Franciscan order, which might have eventually become confused with Elisabeth's second vow to Konrad. Tertiaries received their rule in 1226. Elisabeth joined the order in 1228. She became the first tertiary in Germany.

4   Dietrich of Apolda wrote, "She received from Master Konrad's hand the threadbare and short garment, dark in color and of little value... Her garment was ugly and dreary, the coat was of a gray color and short." Caesarius of Heisterbach notes a direct connection between the Hessian nobility's irritation and unfriendliness toward Elisabeth and her unusual dresscode once she had moved to Marburg. Nobody knew what to make of her lifestyle.

5   The Franciscan fragment of a Vita Elisabeth describes the provenance and fate of this relic in detail (Koblenz State Archive [Staatsarchiv], unedited manuscript).

The constant pressure of asserting herself against a world of resentment and lack of understanding had demoralized her as landgravine in Thuringia. Once again, it threatened to break her and turned her into an involuntary recluse. Soon after her arrival in Marburg, she chose to retreat. She left the castle and pursued a change of living quarters, which left no doubt in the minds of her contemporaries that she had completely lost her mind.[6] According to an early folk tradition, she searched for a hiding place in Wehrda, a village located about three quarters of an hour from Marburg, and found an abandoned farmhouse. The house was a ruin. The *Libellus* copyist Nikolaus described that an exterior staircase, which originally led to the upper rooms, served as a kind of roof for her primitive quarters. Tree branches were arranged to lean against it from the outside.

Together with a one-year-old child and her two female friends, she dwelled for a summer in this narrow hovel under a staircase. They cooked only the most essential foodstuffs on a fire outdoors. She became sick from the smoke, which hurt her eyes. Harsh weather pounded her haphazard cave. The report notes that she "endured all troubles with joy and gratitude" because it was here that she could find rest. Her hiding place kept her safe, and like an animal that was hunted and injured, she could now yield to a sense of being sheltered and soothed. For one year, she had barely had time to comprehend and process the near constant loss of loved ones. The best protection of her privacy then was that people thought her to be mentally unstable. Finally, she was alone; nobody could find the way to her ramshackle shelter, including the mentor who was preoccupied with the construction and organization of the Marburg hospital and a cause for never-ending anxiety. Most importantly, however, her shelter allowed her to reconstruct a sense of self according to her guiding star and role model. St. Francis lived as she lived now.

Early on in his work, the Poverello had emphatically rejected a monastic lifestyle for himself and his brethren. They built a hut next to the Portiuncula, a small rural chapel, made of woven branches, its roof covered with leaves and twigs. It was intended as a model for all other fraternal communities. After the radical break with her past, Elisabeth wished to feel like an authentic Franciscan. She braved primitive living quarters, wind, weather, and rain with contentment. At least this once, she had achieved the realization of her religious ideals. Even a notable intellectual cannot

6   Since the hospital had only just begun to be built and the town of Marburg consisted of only a few farmhouses, the landgravine could not have lived anywhere else but in the Marburg castle itself.

attain a higher degree of self-affirmation than what Elisabeth received in those summer months: the awareness that she remained true to herself despite all defeats. Far from those who vexed her and whom she feared, she was as happy as she could have been for the few months before the onset of her torments in the hospital. She was "in possession of the most perfect riches of the most holy poverty."

The Marburg Hospital and Elisabeth's Charity

Half a year after Elisabeth's move from Thuringia to Hesse, the hospital, her new home, was completed. The settlement was plain and unassuming. Elisabeth moved into a small private house on the hospital grounds. Both buildings, the hospital and her cottage, were constructed from wattle and daub as was common for the non-plastered half-timbered farmhouses in the region. They were situated outside the village near a creek on the southern side of today's St. Elisabeth Church.[7] The settlement must have incorporated a farmstead, since as a rule, even in cities a large communal household depended on agricultural self-sufficiency. The hospital grounds also included a half-timbered chapel.[8] In a few years hence, Elisabeth would be buried there. A fence surrounded the hospital, chapel, Elisabeth's cottage, and the agricultural buildings. The property and its improvements were part of Elisabeth's landholdings dower.

Medieval public health in both its physical and social aspects was significantly lower than among modern peoples with their emphasis on social hygiene. Despite its remote location, the Marburg hospital thus became a popular destination point. The country road functioned as the social space that defines today's urban centers: it was here that the majority of the unemployed, of the impoverished peasants, of the manumitted but propertyless indentured servants mingled. It soon became a well-known fact among them that something was to be gotten in Marburg. The unconditional charity of the former landgravine drew them in. The Marburg hospital must have generated great popularity in a short time; otherwise, no miracles could have happened at the location immediately after Elisabeth's death

---

7   Hospitals were frequently built next to a flowing water source. Their location outside of a town or village followed medieval trade regulations to avoid competition with guilds if free labor was performed at the hospital sites. The creek's name today is Ketzerbach.

8   The chapel was situated at the location of today's northern transverse of the St. Elisabeth Church.

and only three years after the hospital opened its doors. The miraculous healings that took place then resulted from the simple economic fact that many poor approached the charitable religious foundation as a much-needed service they wished to see continued.

The hospital was not a clinic in the modern sense. The caritative purpose of a medieval hospital such as Marburg's hospice was to congregate those who were unable to participate in the general distribution of alms due to old age, fragility, illness, and disability. It also served as a retirement home for people who were unable to work, and widows and widowers without relatives, the so-called prebends. It cared for the acute or chronically ill, and at times took in children who were orphans or who had been abandoned by their parents. Elisabeth's preferred task was the distribution of meals and alms to the region's migrant beggars. The Marburg institution was as much a home for the disabled as a home for the homeless. Everybody who had experienced ruin or needed aid found support and lodging free of charge. For all these reasons, the hospital resembled an asylum more than a clinic. As sole compensation for such assistance, those who received aid were obligated to pray daily for the founder of the religious institution, to go to confession, and to receive Holy Communion.

The half-timbered building did not encompass high ceilinged airy hospital rooms with snow white beds and translucent windowpanes. Compared to the scrupulous cleanliness common in the twentieth century, the hospital's hygienic practices were hair-raisingly crude. It is true that every resident was bathed as was the custom for all social groups. Even the smallest medieval town could boast a bathhouse. It is frequently mentioned that Elisabeth bathed those under her care. But no individual patient enjoyed a single bed just for their own use. The hospital founded by Elisabeth below the Wartburg castle was so crowded that as soon as someone died, their bed would be filled by their successor without changing sheets or airing the room.[9] The air was at least "purified" through the burning of juniper twigs.

Although expected to be prominently present in all modern hospitals, a doctor could not be found in any of the medieval hospitals, including the Marburg institution. Perhaps some had access to a monastic medicus, a professional common among religious orders who would also offer advice to lay people. It is possible that it was such a monastic specialist whom Elisabeth consulted in Marburg to receive advice about a fasting regimen that would not lead to life endangering starvation. Other than that, the treasure

9   The Wartburg hospital had room and board for twenty-eight residents, which was considered large at the time.

of folk medicine had to suffice for the daily hospital routines. Women were well-versed in its practice, and Elisabeth seems to have had knowledge of such traditional healing arts, as Konrad testified with some astonishment.

Despite its many uses, the hospital was small and likely offered room for no more than twenty-five residents. This makes it more remarkable that a large retinue of employees managed the daily operations. Konrad served as prefect and director. Other staff included a married overseer, a cleric, religious sisters and brothers, the household assistants Irmingard, Elisabeth, and later Hildegund (known for her beautiful hair), all of whom were most likely tertiaries. Konrad assigned two female guards to Elisabeth after he had removed her trusted companions Guda and Isentrud and installed a lay brother (a *Konverse*) as a financial manager of her wealth and income. In short, one could ask the same question of this medieval charitable creation as of many of today's nonprofit organizations, whether they were formed on behalf of those in need or on behalf of functionaries who merely wished to generate commissions and posts for themselves. Considering the many appointments to her small hospital, the former landgravine retained merely the role of nursing assistant, and even in this role she was constricted by Master Konrad's continuous guardianship and control.

At the very least, however, Konrad had successfully executed his responsibilities as guardian of the royal princess and former landgravine. Her widow's endowment was well invested, and his ward had been provided with an appropriate vocational task. Konrad, who could benefit from his knowledge of the region, had admirably demonstrated his clearheaded practical skills. The fact that Elisabeth went into hiding in a village in the summer that the Marburg hospital was built suggests that she left all construction tasks to her spiritual mentor. This includes choice of location, architectural design, and economic arrangements. Upon completion of the project, she consented to receive her guardian's hospital assignments.[10] The managerial presence of a lay brother ensured that the former landgravine did not harm herself or the project because of her lack of business acumen. Since everything was organized with such efficiency, Konrad could have left Marburg. However, he remained in place.

The saint who is celebrated today as the second founder of Marburg and the hospital's mother was deprived of all authority at the new site of her

---

10   Konrad was the official prefect, that is, director of all public and internal affairs. He lived either on the hospital grounds or nearby. The hospital's fate after Elisabeth's death proves that he understood himself as the Marburg hospital's founder and leader, or at least, co-owner. He negotiated the inheritance claims of her descendants and appeared everywhere as the patron of his foundation.

vocational pursuits. If she violated hospital rules, her disciplinarian slapped and beat her. As noted above, he also had two chaperones installed to keep her from acting irresponsibly. Nonetheless, Elisabeth contributed to the hospital by serving the sick with abandon. She rediscovered the passionately pursued charitable vocation of her time as royal landgravine. Representing one aspect of the Franciscan mission, she had the hospital named after him. The adjacent chapel, which served as her grave a few years later, was also named after St. Francis.

By coincidence, the otherwise sparse source materials about her spiritual life contain a description of one day in service of Marburg's poor. When she had received a very large sum of dowry money after a long period of great impoverishment, she invited all the poor and sick in Marburg's vicinity of about twelve miles circumference to convene at a special location on a certain day and ordered that 500 mark should be distributed all at once. And so that everything should proceed in orderly fashion, St. Elisabeth girded her skirt, walked around, and asked the people to sit down so she could serve them in likeness of the Lord's service.

This is how she liked to see herself: a splendid donor surrounded by a sizeable audience. One can sense how the need to experience herself as a generous benefactor had never left her, even when she had lost all legal independence. The 500 mark were a quarter of her 2,000 mark dowry, which her brother-in-law had to pay her. She could barely wait to distribute it among the people. As a Franciscan, it was sinful for her to hoard money and foodstuff. Nonetheless, her choice to distribute this (at the time) enormous sum of money was irrational and impulsive. Special measures had to be taken at this exhilarating mass event to ensure that nobody would receive a gift twice. Nobody examined in any depth whether everybody in the crowd was really in need of assistance. The alms distribution seems to have taken on the character of a folk festival. Dietrich of Apolda recounts that stout handlers were needed to keep the gathering under control. It is likely that people who faked lameness and imbecility mingled in the crowd to present themselves as deserving recipients.

Elisabeth's habit of unreserved almsgiving caused harm and mischief in Marburg as it did in Thuringia. Numerous vignettes are proof. As landgravine of Thuringia, she was hit with her fortune's hardest blows because of her extravagant charity. In the final analysis, her expulsion from court after the landgrave's death and her unanimous rejection by kin and nobles can be traced to their growing unwillingness to tolerate her squandering of money and other wealth. Legally disempowered and robbed of her reputation, she consequently suffered harsh deprivations for months. As soon as she regained access to regular income, she resumed her previous reckless charitable extravagance.

It would be tempting to diagnose feeble-mindedness if it were not the case that Elisabeth's motivations during the Marburg era lay elsewhere. She had to give and give because everything had been taken from her. Especially now, having lost her aristocratic status and finding herself instead in bondage to an unloved man, she desperately needed the gratitude of the poorest of the poor. For the last three years of her life in Marburg, her only motivation to live was to squander all of herself to as many people around her as was possible. Symbolically, the giving of gifts signified the giving of self. She amplified the depersonalization that fate forced upon her by reneging on her selfhood and choosing unconditional devotion to the poor. Whatever vitality remained was devoured by fear of her confessor. The *Vita* narrates,

> On the same day that the 500 mark were distributed as alms, a night followed with an altogether clear and bright moon. When the stronger among the poor had left, the sick and weak remained stretched out in the hospital corners and along the fence. When St. Elisabeth entered the courtyard, she remarked to her retinue, "Look, those who are tired remained behind. Let us gift them again." And she ordered that everybody should be given six Cologne denars and did not want that the children should be given less than that. After that, she asked for bread to be brought and distributed it among them. When this took place, she said, "We wish to give them complete happiness and also provide them with a fire." Then she let a fire be prepared and had the feet of many washed and anointed. Then the poor began to sing and feel comfortable. When the saint heard it, she said, "I have always told you that we must make others happy," and was joyful with the joyous.

This is the only amiable incident recounted from Elisabeth's life during the Marburg era. The day's evening, with Master Konrad having been absent— otherwise, he never would have permitted wasting the 500 mark—was filled with peaceful happiness for the downtrodden woman. She revives, cannot offer enough relief work, and as a friend of children, watches over the rights of the little ones as always. If Caesarius' *Vita* had not recorded the scene in the hospital court in all its details, with the cared-for migrants stretched out around the fire, singing their songs, and the brilliant moon shining over them all, it would have been declared apocryphal and interpreted with a "modern" point of view. "I always told you that we must make others happy." Elisabeth's statement on one of her very few contented days reveals her female heart's innate kindness and good humor. It also exposes the program of perverted self-destruction that her master designed for her as even more chilling.

Another miracle story from the *Libellus* resembles the night under the moonlight when unhurried alms recipients were glad to stay at the hospital and to receive a footbath and an additional ration of money and bread even though they already had received gifts before. It is the story of "a deceitful married couple, who were pulled back to their point of departure because of Elisabeth's prayer." The incident offers a vivid image of the boundless warmth of her care for the poor, but also of her equally bottomless partiality.

Once, while visiting the Benedictine convent at Wetter, she discovered a poor, pregnant woman in the town who was close to her time of delivery. She focused on her care for the soon-to-be mother with a diligence and concern that seemed to border on obsession, especially considering her previous preference for children and mothers. She transferred the soon-to-be-mother to be closer to her, arranged for a comfortable delivery room, and provided for the needs of the pregnant guest with a woman's knowledge and flair. She expertly nursed mother and child for another four weeks after the delivery, and when she discharged the woman, she showered her with gracious blessings. It included a coat, shoes that she had removed from her own feet, money, bacon, and flour. She let fur be removed from one of her sleeves to keep the baby wrapped and warm and added a pair of shoes for the father. Shortly before morning Mass, Elisabeth remembered that she still had a few coins in her purse and sent her maidservant to the family to give the coins to the mother. At this point, it was discovered that the parents had run away and left their child behind.

The destitute mother, like the female beggar in Eisenach but without her malice, reacted with obstruse ingratitude to such benevolence. But as a simple-minded soul, she could not act otherwise. She felt smothered, even assaulted by the abundance of benefactions. Unconsciously, she sensed that her child had already been adopted by Elisabeth, since the saint had the child baptized in her own name, not in the name of the mother. Despite or perhaps because of the blessing of gifts, the mother secretly absconded with her spouse. She abandoned her child with the naïve logic that someone who rushes to care for an unknown infant could also keep it and thus would not deserve any further consideration. Once again, while the episode reveals Elisabeth's lack of deeper insights into human nature, especially about the psychology of the poor, it also reveals her unshakable willingness to help and to nurture.

Once it was discovered that the mother had secretly left, Elisabeth's first thought was concern for the abandoned infant. She finds a wetnurse and orders a wide search for the irresponsible parents. The women in her retinue become fearful that Master Konrad could find out about the incident. The maidservant begs Elisabeth to pray with all her might for the return of the unnatural mother so that the stern master would not conduct a punitive interrogation. Of course, Konrad had observed more than once how Elisabeth's extravagant benefactions fell victim to fraud.

The two delinquents eventually reappear, motivated by a bad conscience and the futility of their escape. The hospital community agrees that the ungrateful mother ought to be punished by returning the donated coat and shoes. At first, Elisabeth consents, but then cannot bear the woman to resume her life impoverished and without clothing. Despite her bad experiences, Elisabeth gifts her shoes and fur once again. It seems that Elisabeth was attached to the woman with a secret force. Her almost meddlesome care, which was only strengthened by ingratitude, must seem to us today excessive if we do not understand it as a kind of substitute for her own lost motherhood. Since Elisabeth had to forsake her own small children, she attached herself to the destitute pregnant woman with the unconscious motivation of someone who had to even out a great loss. Other vignettes also tell of an almost fanatical care for new mothers.

With draconian strictness, Master Konrad impeded and limited the kind of charity evidenced in this story. His success was almost nil. Elisabeth always found a way to circumvent his rules of charitable giving and hospital service. Konrad forbade her to distribute any gifts whatsoever. Elisabeth let them be dispersed by others. Then Konrad rationed alms so that no beggar would receive more than one denar. Elisabeth arranged that any beggar could receive one denar more than once and expanded rations of bread. In response, Konrad ruled that only very small portions were to be given out. Her two chaperones were instructed to keep a close watch and ensure Elisabeth's compliance. Yet nothing could stop her drive to give alms. She secretly sought to sell whatever earthly goods such as gold rings and precious coats she still possessed so that she had money at hand when beggars approached her in public spaces. Even Konrad's humiliating punishments and slaps in her face were useless. The obsession to give was instinctual; yet lavishing all of herself onto others was only one part of her soul's will to self-destruction.

Spiritual Marriage

Since Master Konrad ordered her to disregard all worldly matters, she asked God ardently to teach her heart contempt for all that is transient, to remove her love for her children, and to give her the courage to disdain all defamations. (Caesarius of Heisterbach, *Vita S. Elisabeth*)

Elisabeth did not hold this terrifying program of breaking the self as her own moral property. Like an animal trainer, Konrad placed the religious task before his ward. One may feel repugnance when observing how Elisabeth's forced re-education resulted in the gradual victory of artifice over nature. It is the same unease we may feel at a circus performance where domesticated animals are coerced to behave like humans. The animal trainer offers the animal a treat or a loving gesture as a reward for a successfully completed performance. However, Master Konrad's moral drill lacked a conciliatory finishing point. The only outcome Elisabeth could expect was additional beatings and new assaults.

The *Libellus* reports:

And she said to her servant, the Lord has answered my prayer. All worldly things which I once loved are now like dirt to me. I also invoke God as my witness that I do not love my own children more than any other child. I delivered them to God. May He do with them as He pleases.

This statement, the only documentary witness of her relationship to her children, does not constitute proof of Elisabeth's unfeminine and unmaternal disposition. On the contrary. It testifies to the full extent of the self-destructive fight which she had to mount against her deepest impulse to love. These words are the fanfares that celebrate successful self-annihilation, if one can speak of victory when a human being self-destructs. Distressing conflicts must have preceded the desired quiet of the emotional graveyard, which the saint considered her most genuine achievement. Piece by piece, her soul was pressed into a shape and stance, which she initially resisted with the full force of her love of life and femininity. To overcome human nature, however, is the maxim of every saintly character. Separation from loved ones and the disregard for defamation constitute the canon of the spiritual art of suffering. Some pursued this path who were better known and more active than St. Elisabeth. In Elisabeth's century, Mechthild of Magdeburg wrote,

You shall stand alone. You shall nurture the sick. But you yourself shall own nothing.
You shall drink the water of pain and light the fire of love in a heart of virtue.

Mechthild and many others had the freedom and the right to extreme psychological asceticism because they could transform their inner torment into tangible achievements.

In contrast to Mechthild, Elisabeth was not a religious virtuoso. She lacked intellectual creativity. Unlike earlier years, she did not choose the suffering of her Marburg era. When she lived through a cold winter's night in the hostile town below the Wartburg castle, filled with despair and yet asking the Franciscans to sing a Te Deum, when she lived in the dilapidated farmhouse near Marburg, sick and without any resources, she still possessed an independent ascetic's pride in suffering. Her suffering was her own victory, her personal property, her own asset. Yet in the hospital, she had become nothing but a victim of rape. On her deathbed, she dared to confront her abuser by declaring that all self-annihilation and all renunciation of her human, feminine needs only took place because he commanded it.[11]

When she began her living arrangements with her confessor in Marburg, her scandalous reputation and the social ostracism prompted by her relationship with Konrad were difficult to face. Her statement as recorded in the *Libellus*, "I enjoy the vilification, the defamation, and the contempt that I encounter. I love nothing other than God" is an example of her self-deception. She deluded herself that her oppression and unhappiness were the result of her own choices and intentions. Apathy and disaffection soon began to take root in her, yet only her confessor had a need for them. Because he lived a monkish and asocial life, she had to become like him. Their asexual yet exclusive monogamy was only possible on this basis. Historians and, following suit, poets and writers preferred to depict the peculiar, almost obsessive interest of the high-handed man in the delicate young woman as the tactical result of Konrad's ecclesiastical politics. In this view, Konrad of Marburg, indefatigable in his work as preacher for the crusade, inquisitor and monastic visitor, passionate and successful in strengthening the threatened reputation of the Roman Church in Germany, systematically planned to turn his ward, the landgravine Elisabeth, into a saint. His unforgiving pedagogy was already part of his church political and entrepreneurial toolkit. The supposition that his strictness and harshness were employed on behalf of an impassive training for Elisabeth's sainthood is a *logificatio ex eventu* (justification after the event). It is deduced from the circumstance that Landgravine Elisabeth of Thuringia was declared a saint soon after her death and that Konrad of Marburg initiated and pursued her canonization

---

11   Letter about Elisabeth's death, possibly composed by Abbess Lutrudis of Wetter (published in Huyskens).

with utmost zeal. His interest in the unhappy woman, however, was only motivated by his personal, unconscious, and unacknowledged desire and by the bleak nether regions of his monastic sexuality.

Konrad had power over his spiritual daughter through a means that trumped even male rights in a patrilineal and patriarchal marriage. Elisabeth was Konrad's penitent. Sanctioned by pastoral privilege, he knew her desires, her wishes, her secret yearnings. As an absolute ruler over her thoughts and feelings, he enjoyed a gendered privilege that no secular male was granted.

He became privy to her "sins of thought." Perhaps he witnessed the woman whom he alone believed to possess, as she thought of all that she had lost, including her spouse and her children. Leveraging his power could be considered legitimate penitential practice and appropriate for his spiritual role. Konrad came close to being aware that the fraught disguise of his psychological abuse was a smokescreen for deep-rooted personal cruelty. His account in the *Epistola* offers a clever, skillful, formally correct, and precisely for these reasons more revealing picture. The *Libellus* notes:

> To sadden and pain her even more, he banished friends especially dear to her. And thus, he expelled me, Isentrud, who was so close to her. She discharged me with boundless tears and sorrow. Finally, he removed my companion Guda, who had been by her side since childhood and who was exceptionally dear to Elisabeth. St. Elisabeth let her go with tears and sighs.

Konrad's "educational" measure bespeaks first-rate perfidy. Guda and Isentrud were Elisabeth's dearest friends. Originally ladies-in-waiting, they grew closer to their mistress over time. They accompanied her on her unusual and difficult path with unconditional faithfulness. Isentrud, one of Konrad's targets, recounts in her own words how the separation broke her mistress's heart. Her report lacks the usual trope that Elisabeth rejoiced over her new torment.

Hypocritically, Master Konrad justified the affront to his victim as a necessary means to a spiritual way of life, writing, "Since I saw that she desired perfection, I removed all superfluous relations, and ordered that she had to content herself with three persons." He labelled her dearest companions, the only friends of the forsaken woman, "superfluous relations." He surely noticed the mendacity necessary to legitimize his cruelty. He resented the women's attachment to each other as a provocation to his claims of sole proprietorship of Elisabeth. The friends had to disappear much as the children had vanished earlier. Furthermore, the two young women reminded his spiritual daughter of everything from her past as landgravine. Posing a challenge to the confessor's claim to sole rule, the friendships had to end. The more he doubted his régime, the more her tears of losing her favorites comforted him. Her extorted tears and sorrows gave him a pleasure that was greater than the common joys of love and the wailing of heretics, whom he would soon be burning at the stake:

> Master Konrad proceeded with the best of intentions and full of holy zeal because he was afraid that any of the previous worldly glamour could transfer from us to her, tempting her or causing internal conflict. Most of all, he wished that she should be attached to God alone by removing all human comfort that we could provide for her.

Even the *Libellus* scribe senses that such a type of pastoral care demands a bit of sprucing up. He somewhat clumsily makes Isentrud add a theological justification to the forced separation, which had caused Elisabeth such anguish. Yet the unhappy woman was not permitted to grieve her abandonment in privacy, because true solitude would have meant freedom. Konrad writes:

> I ordered that she should content herself with three persons, that is, a lay brother who would manage her finances, a young religious woman of low reputation, and an aristocratic widow who was deaf and very austere. Her humility would be increased through the young woman's company, and her patience practiced in the presence of the exacting widow.[12]

According to his own words, Konrad replaced Elisabeth's friends with two official tormentors. He admitted that they were detestable. He covered his new cruelty with the shameless lie that it was dictated by Elisabeth's need to practice patience and humility. Yet her entire life had been a school of patient and freely chosen suffering. As a more transparent counter witness, the *Libellus* reveals the true reason for the women's hire. The newly hired women were to act as spies. The maidservants' contrasting version in the *Libellus* reads as follows:

> Master Konrad surrounded her with two stern women who oppressed her greatly. They acted with malice toward her as instructed by Konrad

---

12   Adolf Hausrath is one of the few scholars who did not ignore the nature of the relationship between St. Elisabeth and her confessor. He comments sarcastically about the hire of the new female servants to develop her patience, "it seems to us that Konrad's own behavior toward her would have been sufficient in this regard".

himself. Frequently, they informed on her by telling Master Konrad when she had been disobedient, when she distributed alms or ordered others to do so. Because of these accusations, she endured many beatings and slaps in the face.

During the jailer's frequent work-related absences from Marburg, Elisabeth had to be monitored like any other ward. What a pleasure for the lower ranking hired women to betray their mistress and deliver her to beatings and blows, and what pleasure especially for Konrad to cement his authority.

Since her move to Marburg, Elisabeth had lost her chances for an escape. She was forced to capitulate on every count. Her past as a free human being and woman was over. Her only remaining protection, that of kith and kin, had been taken away. Nothing blocked Konrad's unrestrained exercise of authoritarian power and violence. While Elisabeth was still a wife and landgravine, he did not dare to remove his mask. It came off now. His spiritual daughter had become enslaved, an abject beaten woman living in a dependence that was worse than any patriarchal marriage in which a wife was mere property.

In the end, the frightened woman did not need an external voice commanding her. She constructed a superego within, above, and against herself to abuse and press her own will into service to the will of another, her freedom into a tool of unfreedom, her own person into the jailer of all that she was. To overcome the unbearable feeling of bondage, some enslaved are tempted to outdo their abusers. Their voluntary excess of obedience reaffirms a sense of agency. All that is needed is to maintain the fiction that forced deprivations are not imposed, but freely chosen goals. By necessity, the strategy of outdoing the oppressor demands ever stronger dosages of self-denial, which turn into a never-ending progression of ascetic self-deprivation. This was St. Elisabeth's fate in her spiritual marriage to Konrad. Her self-enslavement increased with every surge in Konrad's attempts to break her will. Her fatalism and the blind obedience with which she responded to every harassment are hard to outdo:

> Once Master Konrad sent after her and asked that she return when she was on her way to visit a hermit. She answered the messenger, "We are like snails who retreat into their shell when it begins to rain. To be obedient, we will return from the journey we have begun."

Having given up on expecting logical explanations of her master's orders, she complied with his demands as with the laws of nature, indicated by her use of the image of snails retreating into their shells during rain. Elisabeth interrupts any activity if her master demands it, whether on short outings or across long distances, as when Konrad asked her at one point to follow him from Marburg to Eisenach. She had to be at his service in every way. At one time, Konrad's biological brother, who lived like the rest of Konrad's kin near Marburg, suffered a serious headwound. Because of her vow of obedience to him, Konrad ordered Elisabeth to immediately restore his relative to health. Elisabeth healed the substantial wound with prayers and the laying on of hands, "so that only a scratch remained." Konrad must have been satisfied with such a miraculous success.

The statement "she was obedient and willing in all things" implies that she did not engage in any activity or thought without being patronized by her disciplinarian. Elisabeth's depersonalization and self-destruction extend to freely renounce her heart's desire. The *Libellus* records that "she was so obedient to him that when we, Isentrud and Guda, the dearest of her friends which Konrad sent away, visited her, she dared not to offer us any food or drink nor speak with us without asking for his permission." As was Konrad's pedagogical goal, Elisabeth had succeeded in enslaving herself to the extreme. He had put her in chains without locking her up in a proper dungeon. Elisabeth's own acceptance of her role as slave is still the most mortifying and terrifying aspect of her bondage. At the end of her re-education, she desired to be nothing but a creature fearful of her master. The *Libellus* notes, "Irmingard also shared that Elisabeth feared Konrad greatly, but as one fears God. Elisabeth used to say, 'If I fear a mere mortal to such extent, how much more should God, the Lord and Judge of all things, be feared.'"

For her, Konrad operated as God's surrogate. He was father, godfather, lord, and judge in one person, the terrifying figure of the Hebrew Bible before whom human beings lower themselves to the ground. Even more: Konrad is a kind of über-God, since the almighty judge of the world cannot be more frightening and dreadful than her disciplinarian. Yet it is precisely this role, as her greatly revealing confession brings to light, that Konrad desired. Relishing his father-God position was the perfect consummation of his desire. A religious writer thought it appropriate to embark on a few theological rescue attempts of Elisabeth's bondage. Caesarius thus writes in the *Vita S. Elisabeth*, "Konrad's harshness turned without doubt into great merit for Elisabeth, since fear is the greatest of all penitence." Encountering such material, modern historians did not take notice even once.

Konrad never seemed truly elated about his out-and-out victory. The stronger the graveyard silence with which he surrounded his ward, and the more he felt her lack of love for him, the more he searched for formulaic pretexts to hurt her. Feeling cheated of her love, he was now motivated by a fear of loss. According to the *Libellus*, "Master Konrad frequently tested her fortitude, broke her will in all matters, and prescribed her tasks that she found loathsome." He escalated these demands until they culminated in a final act of cruelty as described by the *Libellus*. "He also commanded that St. Elisabeth separate herself entirely from her one-and-a half-year-old child so that she would not love her excessively and so that the child could not impede her service to God." This short sentence is all that is recorded of this harshest of all punishments. Nothing is mentioned about Elisabeth's tears or her gratitude for a divinely ordained hardship. Nonetheless, a world of sorrow and despair hides behind the short sentence, all legitimized by sacerdotal spiritual guidance. After being forced to abandon her two other small children when leaving Thuringia, this was the final blow against her womanhood.

Konrad, who likely had not taken notice of the small child at the beginning, probably began to increasingly observe with how much love Elisabeth showered her daughter. It was the only living tie to her life as wife and mother and as such, it substituted for all that she had given up. Konrad determined that the child's existence hampered his perverse pedagogy, or rather, that Elisabeth was impeded in her "service to God." The separation seals the diabolic bondage, since even this last breaking of her will is interpreted as an exalted divine and moral demand. Elisabeth had sacrificed the last token of her femininity. According to tradition, she carried her daughter in her arms, barefoot, on the long journey from Marburg to the female Premonstratensian monastery in Altenberg near Wetzlar. Hessian nobles, who took every opportunity to malign Master Konrad's strange companion, insulted the dejected mother by placing her child in the at that time paltry and impoverished establishment of only a few nuns.[13] There are no other sources about her sacrificial pilgrimage. They are not needed.

---

13   Blessed Gertrude O. Praem, Elisabeth's youngest daughter, eventually became abbess of Altenberg. It is possible that as recorded in the Reinhardsbrunn tradition, she was consecrated as an oblate before Landgrave Ludwig went on the crusade. In this case, she would have been dedicated by both parents to ensure the father's safe return. Generally, however, child oblates were not handed over to a monastic institution before the age of five or older.

  Translator's note: On the complexity of medieval motherhood as a mediating presence in their children's lives, see Tracy Adams, "Medieval Mothers and Their Children: The Case of Isabeau of Bavaria in Light of Medieval Conduct Books," in *Childhood in the Middle Ages and the Renaissance* (Berlin: De Gruyter, 2011), 265–90. Abbess Gertrude, who received financial support through her inheritance, celebrated and commemorated her mother as an equal to her father in a linen cloth embroidered with pivotal biographical scenes related to her parents. The pictorial tribute was created at the Altenberg Monastery, likely under her supervision.

Elisabeth died at the hour when she released her youngest child, believing it to be a lofty religious obligation. In truth, she yielded to the fiendish force of a stronger will. Pain, which had haunted her in ever new forms, had become her daily companion.

Perfect Obedience

> Take a dead body and place it wherever you wish: it will not resist. Does it remain at the same location, it will not complain; will you move it elsewhere, it will not protest. Place it on a chair, it will look down and not up; dress it in crimson and it will appear all the paler.

To praise "perfect obedience," St. Francis created the proverbial image of "corpse-like obedience" (*Kadavergehorsam*).[14] Elisabeth had become the flawlessly obedient cadaver in her spiritual marriage that her illustrious role model had wished for. Yet her unconditional submissiveness and eagerness to suffer provoked Konrad to escalate the expansion of his rights as her guardian. A despot's increase in power is dependent upon opportunities to play his role. Elisabeth believed that her compliance pleased him, but it only increased her tormentor's appetite. Since his worst attempts at breaking her bounced off her as it were, Konrad was progressively "forced" to increase his measures. He relied on the most banal and the most horrifying assaults. He removed her closest female friends and her child; she submits. If she leaves for an outing, he orders her to return; if he travels, she must follow him; if she neglects to ask for a permission that is unessential, he decrees that she must be beaten until bloody.

Later, as Germany's most fanatical and cruel inquisitor, Konrad of Marburg displayed a pitiless callousness and lack of compassion that was unusual even for his era. Yet he was encouraged and cheered on even here. He was allowed to kick and beat the wife of a highly ranked German landgrave with silent approval. The brutality of his future public activities proves that he had finally lost all inhibitions.[15]

See Stefanie Seeberg, "Leinenstickerei mit Szenen aus dem Leben der Heiligen Elisabeth," In *Elisabeth von Thüringen – Eine Europäische Heilige. Katalog*, ed. Dieter Blume and Matthias Werner (Petersberg: Michael Imhoff, 2007), 269–72.

14   *The Mirror of Perfection: Being a Record of St. Francis of Assisi Ascribed to His Companion, Brother Leo of Assisi.*

15   Among the few historians who attempted to problematize the relationship between the most notorious German inquisitor and St. Elisabeth, only Leopold von Ranke suggested links

The psychological dimension of the spiritual marriage turned diabolic because of Elisabeth and Konrad's characterological constellation. Elisabeth's character traits contributed to the terrifying dimensions of the relationship because she was responsible for allowing herself to be abused. Master Konrad beat his ward constantly, but modern and medieval authors who propagated Elisabeth's idealized maternal image minimized the scourging of the easily led woman, even though they apparently felt the degradation that it implied. Already Dietrich of Apolda, Elisabeth's first popular biographer, committed small forgeries of the original source materials about this bleak chapter of his heroine's life. While Dietrich usually copied the *Libellus* and the *Epistola* sentence for sentence, he notably summarizes now.[16] Shocking episodes such as the beatings at the Altenberg monastery disappear in their entirety. In the final analysis, all modern authors derived their stance from Dietrich of Apolda. To protect the idealized trope of maternal hospital founder and deaconess, the factual degradation of Elisabeth's person was either ignored or identified as the collective guilt of an era and its social conditions. Among academic historians, only Adolf Hausrath noted the truth succinctly and dryly, writing, "Konrad experienced the regular need to chastise the young woman with a switch, and thus created a cause with all [the] formality [of his position]." This statement is congruent with the testimony of trustworthy primary sources. Other scholars such as Balthasar Kaltner sensed that something in their relationship was wide off the mark, but engaged in a coverup with phrases such as "he, Konrad, always honored the woman and the landgravine in her."

between the origins of Konrad's inquisitorial unscrupulousness and the cruelty that defined their relationship. "We must add to the known number of incidents that mark his decline (that is, the illegality and extremism with which he conducted inquisitions) the irresponsible severity against the patient and always yielding Elisabeth. He misjudged the dignity of human nature and thus accrued guilt that no canonization can extinguish. After he made Elisabeth the victim of his crude ruthlessness, the laws of human ethical inclination dictated that when at the height of his powers, he feared nobody, and a king or bishop counted for as little as a poor lay person." Ranke, "Konrad von Marburg," *Allgemeine deutsche Biographie.*

16   Completed in about 1286, his biography of St. Elisabeth is confined to general statements such as "She maintained voluntary and absolute obedience on the most fierce and difficult occasions. If Master Konrad commanded her to appear even at distant locations, she arrived quickly and without delay; frequently, she endured the master's many castigations such as strikes across her face." See the section "Konrad as Pedagogue" for the misrepresentation of a violent incident during her time as landgravine. Translator's note: Dietrich's popular biography was composed in the 1280s. Caesarius of Heisterbach compiled her first biography between ca. 1236 and 1240, and Konrad of Marburg's very succinct *Summa vitae* was written in 1232. By Dietrich's time, willful amnesia in the service of her cult was already in full swing. See Kenneth Baxter Wolf, *The Life and Afterlife of St. Elizabeth of Hungary* (Oxford: Oxford University Press, 2011).

The monastic writers and the authors of the canonization files were more adroit by admitting the beatings that Elisabeth received from her disciplinarian, yet labelled them mystical experiences of suffering and exercises in obedience. The *Libellus* reports:

> All tribulations, all disdain, and the many beatings which Master Konrad inflicted upon her with best effort so that she would not waver in her resolution, she endured with great patience and joy...She withstood Master Konrad's many beatings and slaps across the face. She had formerly asked for them in remembrance of the blows that Christ endured.

Konrad was fully aware that the lashings with which he "educated" his penitent were abusive. Elisabeth was not beholden to a monastic rule. There was no transgression of serious misdemeanors such as proven heresy, which a monastic institution could legitimately punish with public lashings. Her guardian felt the need to defend his actions. To preempt rumors and accusations, he shrewdly noted and rationalized these violations of his authority in the otherwise concise *Epistola*, addressed to the pope:

> When I learned [that Elisabeth had housed a female leper in her private quarters], I gave her the strap with utmost force, because I was afraid that she would infect herself. May God forgive me.

With proactive insight, he presents the sinister aspect of his guardianship as if he had only once, impulsively, and with excessive care for her health, forgotten himself. In truth, he brutalized her regularly. The *Libellus* documents a scene from the Marburg era, which reveals both the unmitigated drive underlying Konrad's violence and the deep attachments implicit in his sadism. Irmingard stated that Master Konrad ordered Elisabeth to travel to Altenberg so that he could confer with her whether he should move her to a monastery. The nuns asked Master Konrad for permission that upon her arrival, Elisabeth could enter the cloister to visit with them. Master Konrad answered, "she may enter if she so desires," because he firmly believed that she would not do so. Nonetheless, she entered the cloister in the belief that she had permission, and because she trusted Konrad's earlier authorization in this matter. When Master Konrad became aware of it, he asked her to meet him, pulled out the book which he had kept at the ready, and threatened her with the reminder that she had sworn upon it to respect his orders by punishment of excommunication.

According to his logic, she had affected her punishment by entering the cloister. Together with Sister Irmingard, who remained outside because she had only opened the entry to the cloister after receiving the key, Elisabeth had to prostrate herself on the ground. Brother Gerhard was ordered to beat both with a rather thick and long switch.[17] During this event, Master Konrad chanted the Miserere Mei Deus. Irmingard stated that she received marks from the beatings that were still visible after three weeks. Elisabeth's marks lasted even longer because she was attacked more severely.

As was his custom when traveling, Konrad ordered Elisabeth to join him at the Altenberg monastery, where he stayed at the time. The nuns asked Konrad's permission to welcome Elisabeth inside the cloister, that is, without Konrad, since men were forbidden from entering a female monastery's inner precinct. Konrad answered with neither "yes" nor "no": "She may enter if she so desires." Sister Irmingard, Elisabeth's lady-in-waiting, who appears to have known him quite well, explained that "he firmly believed that she would not do so." Immediately after their arrival, Elisabeth and her companion enter the monastery to greet the nuns, yet without first announcing their presence to Konrad. This choice was already a mistake, since he wished to be greeted first and consulted on matters big and small. However, it was not the small lapse as such that annoyed him, but his spiritual daughter's deeper symbolic transgression. By entering the cloisters, generally a symbol of life-long commitment, before meeting him, she indicated her partiality for women's cloistered life when compared to her life with him. A female monastery could have offered enduring safety from her disciplinarian. The Altenberg monastery must have seemed like a harbor and a paradise. At that time, Altenberg had become the home of her youngest daughter, and its nuns were bonded with her in friendship.[18] When Konrad called her to him to consult with her about her admittance to a female monastery, she might have felt a flicker of hope to find the freedom of a separation from him.

In contrast, Konrad's unspoken expectation seems to have been that the assurance of his lifelong guardianship would circumvent her leaving him. Were she to reject his suggestion to become a nun, she would satisfy his hidden wish for affirmation of his interminable possession of her. She committed a small faux pas. Instead of first meeting Konrad to receive an

17   Brother Gerhard was Konrad's closest friend and assistant. He accompanied him on his journeys and as indicated by the report of Konrad's assassination, he was passionately devoted to his master.

18   At the time, the female monastery at Altenberg was a poorly funded convent of only a few Premonstratensians, whose meager existence must have pleased Elisabeth. She was in regular contact with the nuns and received raw wool from them to spin. Translator's note: Spinning wool for the nuns was a welcome source of income for Elisabeth's community.

entirely unnecessary permission, she proceeded immediately to meet the nuns. Her artless and self-explanatory entry into the cloister reveals hidden feelings and desires. In response, the hysterical, domineering man, deeply unsure of himself, turned wildly angry and agitated. First, he cornered his victim morally by threatening excommunication. This was the worst psychological intimidation possible for a medieval Christian and especially for a pious child of the church like Elisabeth. As the *Libellus* makes clear, Konrad was unable to accuse Elisabeth of entering the cloister against his will because he had not explicitly forbidden it.[19] Since Elisabeth herself, however, had not asked him personally for permission upon her arrival in Altenberg, he fabricated a breach of her lifelong religious vow of obedience to him. To make his point, Konrad pulled out the book by which she had sworn lasting obedience and the abdication of her own will. On its authority, and as if to make her offer a vow again, he can allow his unacknowledged emotions and his frightful disappointment in her unconscious infidelity to surface. Elisabeth and her complicit lady-in-waiting Irmingard, who only had fetched the key, are then forced to prostrate themselves on the ground. Brother Gerhard must beat both until blood flows. If Irmingard's body still exhibits signs of the beatings after three weeks, and Elisabeth's body for an even longer period, both women must have been undressed while being punished. And Konrad, maddened with agitation and pain, accompanied the incident with a religious chant. The perversity of the situation is hard to trump.

Not only modern scholars were puzzled (and made uncomfortable) by the Altenberg events. Dietrich of Apolda repressed the episode completely. Caesarius of Heisterbach, Elisabeth's first biographer, was so embarrassed that he attempted to prove Konrad's demeanor as a justified act of punishment which Elisabeth had previously acknowledged as deserved penance.[20] If this proof could be provided at all, Konrad's action could only be substantiated as even more perfidious cruelty, camouflaged by formalities. The perversity of the events could only intensify if Elisabeth had actively agreed with her treatment. Sometime after the Altenberg incident, the *Libellus* notes that Elisabeth said to Irmingard, who was beaten with her,

---

19   Legally speaking, only the female leader of a monastery could grant permission to enter the cloister. In this case, it had already been given.

20   It is indeed grotesque if historians (Huyskens) take seriously Caesarius of Heisterbach's effort to minimize the coarse act of despotism. Caesarius was a notorious supporter of Konrad and advocate of Elisabeth's canonization. These historians suggest preferring Caesarius' retrofitted version to the *Libellus* account, which was put together without Konrad's influence. Konrad had died before its creation.

It is proper for us that we endure such matters willingly because we are like the reeds in a river. If the river rises, the reeds will be bent and compressed. The overflowing waters soak them without injury. Once the flooding recedes, the reeds straighten up again and grow with vigor and joy. It is always befitting for us when bent and humiliated to get up and stand tall with joy and delight afterwards.

After the preceding humiliating beatings, the parable of the bent reeds can only cause discomfort and distress. The unprecedented masochism with which Elisabeth approves of the demeaning abuse exceeds the abuser's keen malice. After a degrading beating, so the meaning of her words, she feels better than before, "to get up and stand tall with joy and delight." Such a degree of consent could strengthen the suspicion, already raised elsewhere, that Elisabeth was a masochist in a sexual-pathological sense.[21] This interpretation raises the possibility of another, later tradition as authentic, which states "Konrad once beat his confessant until she fainted. When she regained her senses, he asked her how she felt. She answered, 'I feel as if I were in the third heaven.' He responded, 'Therefore I am sorry that I did not beat you into the ninth choir.'"[22]

Other events recorded in the *Libellus* sound as if the beatings of the saint were a pleasure. We encountered these passages earlier in our study. The *Libellus* notes in reference to the nocturnal penitential acts which Elisabeth imposed upon herself, "She left her husband's side, and in a secluded chamber, she let herself be castigated heavily by her maidservants' hands. After prayer, she returned joyfully to her husband's bed." Her childlike and naïve nature might have been the reason for her post-flagellation contentedness. Konrad had commanded her interruption of sleep. She obliged obediently and as content as a schoolgirl after a completed assignment, she returned to the marital bedchamber. Even an ecstatic sense of happiness after one of Konrad's beatings—"I feel like I am in the third heaven"—did not need to signify sexual rapture. Spiritual fatalism and a consent to be broken and

---

21   In his study *Sadismus und Masochismus*, (1911, originally published 1902), Eulenburg places St. Elisabeth and other medieval female saints in the category of sexual pathology. Translator's note: Importantly, Albert Eulenburg also acknowledged the toxic role of patriarchy and masculine power in his wide-ranging study.

22   The provenance of this episode has not yet been studied. It is part of a fourteenth-century passional, a collection of saints' legends. It cannot be found in the primary sources, but this does not necessarily challenge its authenticity. Perhaps it was repressed by the scribes. Even if the episode is not "historical," it could have been invented to explain St. Elisabeth's circumstances. It was a common spiritual figure of speech to evoke the third heaven and ninth choir in a prologue.

humiliated are much more disturbing than a sexual-pathological predisposition; the parable of the reed seems to precisely suggest that.

Konrad's psychological stance in his spiritual marriage is more complicated. Even if we assume that his sadism and Elisabeth's compulsive acceptance of her bondage are rooted in the two partners' sexual constitution, Konrad's pedagogy of the whip is not a "natural" consequence of the "purity" of their relationship. All of Konrad's actions give the impression of an overcompensated sex drive. The harsh abuse of his female partner, whom he never touches otherwise, and her submissive endurance do not add up to evidence of sexual pathology. They testify, however, to the barbaric lack of ethics in this spiritual marriage.

Even if it were correct to discern in Konrad of Marburg a monk who vents the inner turmoil triggered by a forbidden woman, the deepest reasons for the flagellations and cruel features of his guardianship lie elsewhere. Konrad did not so much fear breaking his priestly vow of chastity. Rather, he feared what precedes the onset of sexual attraction—an acknowledgment of love. A crass sexual affair was out of the question because of the spiritual and moral values of both partners. Given Konrad of Marburg's psychological makeup, a romantic liaison was even more unfeasible. If he had permitted himself to fall in love in whatever way, he would have been truly lost in the relationship with his partner. Had he replaced the switch with courtship, open respect, or loving authority, his warped masculinity would have generated feelings of disgrace and degradation. Furthermore, the "danger" of romantic attachment would have jeopardized his life's work. A professional executioner cannot allow himself to feel love. Konrad was forced to harden himself to protect his internal boundaries. His method of distancing himself became inhumane. In the end, however, Elisabeth conquered him in a roundabout way. She gained her freedom by risking her life. Already three years after the Marburg cohabitation was established, death liberated her.

Honor

> Once several unscrupulous and worldly people saw how St. Elisabeth obeyed Master Konrad and kept his company, they began to spread scandalous rumors about the two holy persons and sullied their reputations. When Lord Rudolf of Vargula, the ministerial cupbearer, heard this news, he visited St. Elisabeth and said, 'My dear Lady, please be careful and protect your good name. Caused by your frequent contact with Master

Konrad, vulgar and foolish people think the worst and gossip about you with indecency.'

The holy woman raised her eyes to heaven, joined her hands in prayer and said,' Blessed be my Lord and God who inflicts even this on me. I have renounced the noble status of my lineage for his sake to become a maidservant. I have spurned wealth and worldly honor. I became impoverished. I have destroyed the beauty of my youth and became unsightly, yet I have intended to keep the adornment of my female honor. Now I thank God that I may sacrifice it for him. So that you, Lord Cupbearer, will not think anything untoward about me, look here.' With these words, the holy woman withdrew her dress from her shoulders and showed the pious and honorable Lord that she was wounded with blows by a switch and covered in blood. And she said, 'Behold, this is the love the holy priest shows me to draw me to God. It is the love that I bear for God."

This episode is not documented in the original primary sources.[23] Yet even if it had been invented to free Konrad of Marburg and his royal ward from the suspicion of an affair, its mere existence proves that Elisabeth's relationship with her confessor was considered improper even while she was still alive. Most of all, the episode reveals the moral standards of her century, if not the Middle Ages as a whole. For these reasons, as is often the case, a legendary story such as this is more valuable for a modern biography than an authentic source which only conveys unrelated facts.

People suspect Elisabeth of a prosaic affair with her confessor. For Christ's sake, she is willing to hazard the consequences. In her view, her beaten and abused body is proof of her honor, because she is not ashamed to reveal the extent of her humiliation to the nobleman: she "showed the pious and honorable lord that she was wounded with blows by a switch and covered in blood." Rudolf of Vargula did not become agitated upon hearing of Master Konrad's abuses. The story does not note that he planned to avenge the degradation of his feudal lord's widow. Told to exalt Elisabeth, the incident in its totality today would be unbearable in terms of our own understanding of human dignity.

Since reliable reports of Konrad's "slaps and beatings"—as censored as they might be— can be found in the document that was to serve as the foundation for her canonization, it follows that the candidate's shameful

---

23   A monk at the Reinhardsbrunn monastery added the episode, among others, to Dietrich of Apolda's 1291 biography. The quotation follows Lulu of Strauss and Torney's *Volksbuch: Die heilige Elisabeth*, op.cit.

experiences brought her renown rather than dishonor. To have been beaten
was unfortunate, but not dishonorable. For this reason, the Altenberg nuns
did not expel Konrad when he ordered their patroness and friend to be
crudely abused on their grounds.

Modern people consider a medieval sense of honor to be incomprehensible. Put differently, medieval individuals did not possess our sense of
honor because they did not yet experience their psyche as identical with
their bodies. From a medieval point of view, it was only the body that was
kicked. Even symbolic acts of freely chosen self-abasement such as walking
barefoot, wearing rags, self-flagellation, and prostrations did not usually
affect medieval people's innermost core. When King Henry IV stayed in the
courtyard of the papal residence for three days in snow and rain and begged
to be absolved from his excommunication, it seems to us today to have been
a dubious matter and personal humiliation. At the time, however, it did not
constitute a degradation that diminished his honor as a man and as a king.
Otto von Bismarck's famous dictum "we are not going to Canossa" contains
the now customary misunderstanding of medieval honor.

There is, however, a difference between self-humiliation and humiliation by others. Self-humiliation in the service of a religious stance could
display pathos and a certain spiritual dignity because it was freely chosen
by those who were powerful, cognizant of their dominant status, and used
to humiliating others. They could certainly afford such gestures. In contrast,
to be the involuntary target of beatings and humiliations never increased
self-respect and personal dignity. It warped one's sense of self. This second
type of humiliation is rarely recorded in historical documents. Being weaker
than their abuser, the victims were condemned to silence. The weak are
always history's absent voices.

As is true for all patriarchal eras, medieval society with its institutionalized violence and power-sanctioned corporal punishment was kept in place
by the religious and moral privileges of the ruling class. This meant that the
strong were given free rein to beat the weak, the powerful the powerless.
Lasting long into the nineteenth century, the switch has remained the
symbol of parental force and pedagogy. Following a traditional German sense
of customary justice, beatings especially were considered the natural right
of a husband to such a degree that in fourteenth-century Breslau, a husband
accused of physical abuse was merely reprimanded to "only beat his wife
with switches when chastising and punishing her as this was customary
and proper for an honest man." Today's marital laws demonstrate how
deeply rooted this right of the powerful is even now. It is only considered
degrading for members of the upper classes if a husband uses physical

force as punishment. In principle, only gross "abuse" is allowed as a cause for dissolving a marriage.[24] The right to castigate one's male and female servants was a matter of course in the Middle Ages. While it had become culturally obsolete in the west of Germany, it was formally abolished across all of Germany as late as 1918 with the repeal of the rural labor laws.

St. Elisabeth lived under the pressures of a rigid patriarchy. Her guardian flagellated her, a significantly younger woman, according to the rights of men generally and fathers and husbands specifically. It endowed him in all circumstances with an unalienable position of power over women and children. Even though she was of royal status, St. Elisabeth was powerless, especially so when she lived in Marburg under Konrad's sole guardianship and stripped of the control over her wealth and legal rights. Patriarchal pressure was the reason she had to succumb to Konrad in all ways. With this choice of angle, Konrad's violent pedagogy could be explained in its entirety by the social conditions of his era. Indeed, in a certain type of historiography, nothing could be more welcome than an excuse of this repugnant relationship as an example of medieval custom and morality. At this juncture, historiographical method confronts a difficult philosophical question. If "everything real is rational," then it follows that it was rational when Konrad thrashed his penitent. Accepting this causal chain invites the danger that every phenomenon of human life is interpreted as legal and sound if it harmonizes with "historical necessity." If a medieval servant, a woman, or a child had to remain silent and acquiesce according to divine decree, they nonetheless suffered because of such "historically rational" customs. They felt the pain of humiliation as much as an individualistic modern person.

The reason: our century as well is filled with hardships. These hardships are experienced as unavoidable and frequently as "normal." Even so, we face our suffering as a source of sorrow, despair, and resignation. From a non-relativist ethical point of view, its oppressive effects and humiliation remain as degrading today as for any other epoch. Despite a view that justifies it as the expression of a specific time, society, and psychological disposition, St. Elisabeth's bondage was degrading in all its aspects. She experienced the humiliation of receiving a secular cleric's flagellations in its full force. She suffered with the helpless passivity of an animal unable to defend itself. The medieval chronicler wrote that she endured with a

---

24   § 1568 states, "Gross abuse is considered a serious violation of [marital] duty." In principle, this is not different from medieval marital law, which limits a husband's right to beat his wife only to the extent that he is not allowed to break her limbs.

"happy countenance" and in memory of Christ's beatings all violations and degradations that she received as a woman. She was not able, however, to spiritualize every incident as a self-chosen female imitation of the Passion. Some of her conduct during her Marburg years of misery offers evidence.

Resentment

It is impossible to fully reconstruct the inner world of human beings who lived 700 years ago, especially so when our knowledge of their psyches is dependent on a handful of Latin sentences. Despite unequivocal historical sources, one may doubt our interpretation of the royal patroness of Catholic charity and the Protestant deaconess on a throne as a destitute, legally incapacitated woman who lived in shamefully gendered bondage. Even so, the slim volume of source materials offers incidents that can test the correctness of our biographical analysis. For example, we read in the canonization files, compiled to praise Elisabeth, about the episode of Hildegunde, a young woman with beautiful hair. Abruptly and right before our eyes, the story opens a window into the saint's inner life.

On the day of the great alms' distribution, Elisabeth took specific measures so people would not be gifted twice. Everybody was asked to sit down and forbidden to leave so that changing seats could not lead to a second donation. The *Libellus* recorded that as punishment for ignoring the order, a shock of hair would be shorn off. Greed was to be stigmatized, even though only mildly and within conventional rules. At the beginning, everything proceeded according to directions. Controlled by a supervisor, the large crowd kept order. When the pious woman who gave alms "like the Savior" walked among the seated assembly and distributed money from her girdled apron, she was struck with an overwhelming awareness of her wretchedness as a young woman. The insight led to a terrible error. In the words of the *Libellus*,

> Suddenly, a young woman with beautifully adorned hair by the name of Hildegunde appeared in the crowd. She was not aware of the rules and did not wish to receive alms. Her goal was to look for her infirm sister. She was led to Blessed Elisabeth, who asked what she had done. When she saw the beauty of her hair, she ordered that her hair should be cut immediately even though the young woman had not violated her instructions. When she lost her hair, she [Hildegunde] immediately began to cry out. Even people who came to look and did not know that the young woman was

innocent, said to Blessed Elisabeth that she should have been punished with less severity. And she answered them, "At the very least, she will stop attending dances with her hair cut short."

From our vantage point, we ask what is more injurious: the self-importance and arbitrariness with which Elisabeth acted against law and right or the feminine envy with which she reacted against a member of her own gender, who was happier and more beautiful than she. Even though the newly arrived Hildegunde did not transgress any of her guidelines, the pious benefactress was provoked on a much deeper level than that of the immediate cause. Long and beautifully adorned hair is the most obvious symbol of feminine attractiveness.

Following her era's custom, the unmarried youth braided her hair without covering it. Her fresh and youthful appearance made Elisabeth aware of her own wretched diminishment in feminine attractiveness. She was not so strong or mature enough that she could not be provoked by looking at a living image of unselfconscious youthfulness. The young woman's ease, self-confidence, and attractiveness, who happened to be at the public almsgiving by accident without asking for alms, who was neither poor nor physically incapacitated in any way, pierced her heart. She was reminded of her own despised and broken femininity, which had been repressed and smoldered like embers in a dying fire. Without thinking, she ordered Hildegunde's hair to be cut, fully knowing that she was unjust. "I was made ugly and unfeminine—so you should be like me. I lost my freedom—you shall suffer for it." And she ordered to have the splendor of the magnificent braids cut off. The act destroyed the young woman's honor, since it was generally performed only to punish delinquents condemned to be pilloried, beaten, or executed. "At the very least, she will stop attending dances": Elisabeth's satisfaction with having slighted the young woman is filled with envy of her ample liveliness.

In an era of patriarchal power, a female ruler has no accountability. Yet the contemporaries in Elisabeth's environs feel the all too obvious injustice of the "punishment" and dare to argue that it missed the mark in a case without a guilty perpetrator. Driven by an impulsive desire for revenge, Elisabeth does not budge. She is not aware that she violated her own standards. When the young woman bewails her humiliation, Elisabeth exerts moral pressure and asks her whether she would not rather wish to lead a "better life." When the young woman indicates that no one with such beautiful hair desires to become a nun, Elisabeth comments, "The fact that you lost your hair pleases me more than if my son would become emperor."

No volcano could erupt more spontaneously than the malicious glee of Marburg's female hospital founder.

The maimed and dishonored young woman had no choice left but to join the Marburg hospital as a lay sister and servant. As an unmarried woman without a full head of hair, she was ostracized. Her prospects of a conventional life had dimmed. Turned into Elisabeth's victory trophy, the beautiful braids were displayed as votives in the hospital chapel. It seems that they were kept there for several years. The vibrant youth turned into Elisabeth's double: a nun, dejected, and unfree.

What Elisabeth encountered in this episode was not Hildegunde with her attractive hair, but her own self, her memory of her past, when she was a free-spirited youth who had not yet experienced the gradual destruction of her femininity. Only this once, her younger and now lost self resurges. She feels forced to violently reassert her current position, whose foundation has become fractured. In her youth, Elisabeth avoided the dances of her female companions without rancor and envy. Like an aging spinster, she now resented youthful enjoyment. In Marburg's cloistered confines, a nun's life turned poisonous. Despite her valiant capacity to suffer and endure and her great authentic and sincere religiosity, she could not entirely come to terms with the destruction of her femininity and the daily humiliations of her spiritual marriage. If her choice of a nun's life and her status as a penitent tertiary had been wholly in harmony with her true self, she could have easily tolerated the presence of an adolescent denizen of the secular world. Yet the resentment built up subconsciously and secretly, only to erupt with revenge into public view, fed by memories of her earlier life, of her husband and children, and of her once vibrant femininity. In that past, renunciation was an act of magnanimity, and asceticism signified exquisite self-enhancement. Elisabeth was unable to remain impartial and indifferent when representatives of her "other," earlier world such as lovely Hildegunde crossed her path.

This stance also seems evident in the episode of a youth named Berthold. The *Libellus* narrates how Elisabeth's prayer turned him away from a secular to a religious life. Berthold accompanied a noblewoman who went to visit Elisabeth. Perhaps he was a squire. He might have been dressed a bit too foppishly. In any case, he seems to have provoked Elisabeth. Since she could not cut his hair, she immediately assumed an aggressive didactic stance and admonished him to live a religious life. Since her reputation as an extraordinarily pious woman preceded the visit, the youth could not but bend to the force of her public persona. He asked for her intercessory prayer. In an instant, she obliges him and kneels to pray. He must do the same but feels extremely unsettled. Becoming nauseous, he fearfully asks her to pause her prayers, yet Elisabeth continues with even greater intensity. Berthold's nausea turns into heavy convulsions. He thrashes and flails wildly. His body writhes and shakes with the sudden tremors of a fever. Not coincidentally, the attack occurs precisely at the onset of Elisabeth's prayer. The whole situation becomes so uncanny that Berthold "escapes" into physical illness to avoid the strange religious figure. Perhaps because he experiences her as a witch rather than a source of support, he cries out "in the name of God, stop praying." Perhaps he believes that she caused his sudden illness through magic. Elisabeth, however, the gentle mother of the sick and downtrodden, does not cave in. The poor convulsing youth continues to flounder and fidget.

Elisabeth only stopped her prayers when the young man's lady and two other women approach and contain him. He immediately felt better. We are tempted to think that Elisabeth wished to crush the "worldly," that is, courtly looking adolescent much as she wished to belittle Hildegunde. Rather than arousing her sympathy, Berthold's seizures give her satisfaction. He reminds her too much of her life as a princess when she ignored the young men at her court who craved to serve her. To preserve her self-confidence, she is forced to grapple with the type of person she discounted in her past, or, since it is too late for confrontation, she must rather pull him down to her level of existence.

A year later, the young man joined the Franciscan order. As an epileptic, the military career of a knight was already out of the question for him. Elisabeth's prayer, however, becomes the outward reason for his decision. The grotesque incident thus finds its way into the *Libellus*.

Berthold's story reveals once more St. Elisabeth's somewhat embittered mood at Marburg. It demonstrates, much like the episode with the attractive Hildegunde, the battle between her ego, which pursued only love and appreciation and desired to live an active life, and her superego, which aspired to ideals that broke her abused psyche. Elisabeth could not tell the young adults Hildegunde and Berthold "Go away! Do not remind me of my past." She required a religious rationalization to justify her tormented and deadlocked life. Accusing others instead of herself, she covered her tracks with the widely accepted reasoning that she cared for the spiritual welfare of young people by removing them from dances and courtly service. This is a case of hypocrisy typical of those who are unhappy with their lives and therefore take revenge on others.

Even Elisabeth's charitable works are colored by this subconscious poisoning of her character. Although conducting herself usually with boundless caring and kindness, she once succumbed to beating a female hospital prebend with switches because the woman did not complete her daily religious obligations. Hospital occupants were required to pray and attend Mass daily. Even if we ignore the bizarre contradiction of trying to lead someone to a religious life with a whipping and acknowledge the aristocratic privilege of meting out punishments, Elisabeth still presents herself in these instances as the opposite of her usual self. She models the eager self-righteousness of a zealot, but not of the woman who usually practiced charity for charity's sake and who was not deterred by revolting ingratitude. The innocent and generous young princess changed in just a few short years of servitude to a man who did not love her, who beat her, and whom she was unable to leave. At twenty-three years of age, she had become an embittered zealot. Even an untainted psyche is poisoned and deformed by enduring the violence of someone more powerful. Asceticism generates creativity and greatness when derived from a sense of inner abundance and freedom. Yet it is humiliating when it arises from a lack of love or a diminished quality of life. In the past, Elisabeth's harsh self-discipline, her rejection of courtly love, beautiful clothes, dances, and sexuality were examples of admirable self-control. What once was voluntary renunciation now had turned into the female saint's victimization by her confessor. Defenseless and vulnerable, even the originally most openly feminine psyche had to become hardened and embittered.

Christian Humility as an Asceticism of Power

Initially, the gospel of neighborly love was preached to only a small group. Early Christians lived according to its principles among themselves but did not extend them to other non-Christians. In the first centuries, despite its spiritual achievements, this religion's literature is filled with an invidious and arrogant antagonism against the world of antiquity and a bias against pagan religiosity. Early Christian ethics stand as a classic example of navel-gazing morality and intolerant thinking without the intent to reconcile differences in a dialogue among equals. Nothing existed further from this religion than to love one's enemy or at least fairness in the assessment of those with different beliefs. This is understandable. In the first centuries of practicing evangelical love as a sect that was not fully accepted, at times even pursued with hostility, the Christian community was forced to remain largely insular.

Many generations in different epochs have tried to understand and interpret the Christian dogma of loving one's enemy. For entirely natural reasons, it was misunderstood. Leveraged as passive resistance, the dogma of radical nonviolence disarms and embarrasses more powerful opponents. At the same time, it frequently is also experienced as covert impudence. Indeed, no posture is more insulting than to not even acknowledge a fellow human with enmity. This antisocial, even socially corrosive character of early Christians was always fully understood as such among people of antiquity, even the best. The strange phenomenon that the early followers of Christianity were neither honored nor loved, and even experienced pogroms that were at times unleashed against them, can be traced back to the peculiar consequences of this "negative" love of enemies. The world at large justifiably experienced such nonviolent aloofness as antisocial.

Once the Christian church proved victorious, the ideal of a selfless love of neighbor had not yet become morally prevalent, even though the Middle Ages are perceived as an era of a fully developed Christian religiosity. In its stead, an inflexible patriarchy dominated the medieval world and affected every social relationship. The roles of lord and servant, king and people, man and woman, father and child were defined according to a religiously sanctioned patriarchy. All relationships were marked by violence. As was true for religious dogma, hardly anybody doubted the divinely ordained nature of patriarchy's distribution of rank and power. Only on rare occasions did a few emotionally revolutionary personalities break through the rigid coordination of power that characterized medieval society. They challenged the principle of authoritarianism with that of evangelical love. Through the force of their personality, they slashed a knot that future generations untied only bit by bit.

St. Francis was one of these rare forerunners. His cosmic love for all of life has secured the interest of modern humanity. For us, Francis has become nature's discoverer and the creator of a new sense of being. The core of his creative and ingenious talent for love, however, was his ability to love and respect everybody without generating new forms of authoritarianism. He approached society's poorest and most destitute. Unlike most other religious converts, he did not despise the social milieu that he had left behind. He never belittled the rich and powerful. He practiced kindness toward the pope, who represented the antipode of his principles; toward women, which he renounced as a monk; toward monasticism, which he knew to be corrupt; toward the aristocracy, which he got to know all too well during his own years of a lay existence. His love was not the reverse pleasure in power to which most self-abasing Christian ascetics aspired. He called himself *idiotus*, but was free from the egotistical smugness of the poor and the resentment against high culture and intellectual life that circulated among those without education and intellectual interests.[25] His authentic and strong capacity for love generated a democratic and non-discriminatory ethos that was missing among early Christians.

This genuine democracy, which instills great kindness, can only emanate from those of high social rank, but not from those who labor to become upwardly mobile. Only the rich have the desire to elevate the disadvantaged and to bestow upon them the same kind of well-being that they enjoy.[26] If this is not possible, the rich attempt to conceal their material wealth and social distance. They make themselves appear small so anybody who is truly small can keep in step with them. This stratagem is not in any way offensively charitable and caring but awakens a sense of self-worth in those of lesser social status. The inconspicuous are made to feel valued and valuable. The democrats of love make the small and the disfigured self-confident. Precisely because their social superiority is so easy to assert, they never use the weakness and lesser gifts of others as an occasion for testing their power and reveling in their authority.

Having become democrats out of love, not necessity, they fear only one thing: that others bare their vulnerabilities. They are ashamed of the wretchedness of others because they do not want to see anybody be less than what they themselves are. They avoid acknowledging their own sense of superiority even when it is in plain sight. They are love's equalizers and

25   Translator's note: Even though the medieval poor had every reason to be enraged about their social status, Busse-Wilson is stereotyping economically insecure populations negatively as selfish, jealous, full of bitterness, and resentful of bourgeois culture and education. For a deeper historical analysis of medieval poverty in the thirteenth century, especially with an emphasis on gender, see Sharon A. Farmer, *Surviving Poverty in Medieval Paris: Gender, Ideology, and the Daily Lives of the Poor* (Ithaca, NY: Cornell University Press, 2005).

In contrast to Busse-Wilson's psychological view, contemporary research uses the concept of strengths-based and deficit-based traits in a more nuanced and sympathetic approach to the psychology of people living in economically insecure conditions. See Willem E. Frankenhuis and Daniel Nettle, "The Strengths of People in Poverty," *Current Directions in Psychological Science* 29, no. 1 (2020): 16–21. https://doi.org/10.1177/0963721419881154.

26   Translator's note: Busse-Wilson's somewhat cynical theory of aristocratic benevolence is not considering the threat and impact of poor-led movements of social change. For the late medieval period in German-speaking countries, the German Peasants' War (1524–1525) and the preceding Bundschuh rebellions (1493–1517) are stark examples of poor-led social movements. Rather than being "democrats of love," late medieval aristocrats brutally extinguished the rebellions. While extrapolating on Franciscan-inspired economic elites, Busse-Wilson perhaps references the German religious socialism movement of her era, with which she was familiar. See Großmann, op.cit., 275–78. For a theory of poor-led movements, see M. Monique Deveaux, "Poor-Led Social Movements and Global Justice," *Political Theory* 46, no. 5 (2018): 698–725. https://doi.org/10.1177/0090591718776938.

the advocates of the marginalized, those in need and without advantages, be they among the proletariat, women, Jews, Blacks, or oppressed, small nations. Yet, as noted before, they are not aggrieved persecutors and despisers of their mighty and stronger opponents such as large imperialistic nations, the property-owning Christian bourgeoisie, and Christian men. Frequently, they must act as traitors to their own caste and nation. They do not hate the powerful as their enemy, since they are not interested in gaining their power. Their humility is authentic.

Rather than passive weakness, the doctrine of Christian humility can thus signify profound spiritual wisdom and true virtue when aimed at the strong and powerful, the superior in rank and the rich, the talented and those blessed by good fortune. In early Christianity and the Middle Ages, the doctrine was addressed only to them, and only for them is humility a virtue. The doctrine challenges and educates wherever we find power and happiness, the courtesy of the strong extended to the weak, and a sense of its independent integration in the world in its totality. But for the great masses, for the socially subordinate and the indentured, for the unsuccessful, the talentless, the weak, and the downtrodden, the same call for humility is nothing but mockery. However, the Christian doctrine was never so ignorant of human psychology as to recommend the virtue of humility without reservation. There is no need for humility where there is no excess of power. This was not stated explicitly anywhere, because the truth was so obvious.

Only later, caused by a grotesque but not entirely accidental misunderstanding, were Christian humility and the denial of self understood as a command for all Christians, even though it had been a plea to the moral conscience of the strong and powerful. Caused by this misunderstanding, Nietzsche's attack on Christianity is nothing but a punch into thin air. The medieval type of humility as an expression of personal self-negation, from caring for lepers and washing the feet of others to providing for beggars, falls prey to the same modern misunderstanding as the fabled medieval sexual asceticism.

The asceticism of monks and nuns could only make sense in societies where an early onset of sexual activities was widespread and considered natural. Likewise, the phenomenon of a saint's humility and self-negation depends on a social structure with unchallenged practices of domination and its many gratifications. The noble feudal lord relating to his peasants, the father of the house interacting with his servants, the husband with his wife, the wife with her maidservants, the abbot with his spiritual flock, the father with his son: in her or his domain, everybody held unquestioned and unchallenged authority, be it small or big. The exercise of power belonged to those aspects of medieval life which could be taken for granted, even among medieval people of low status. Practicing humility as self-abasement, those who were religiously inclined desired to experience an asceticism of power.

A position of social domination and an early embrace of life's sensual pleasures characterize the lives of saints, including Elisabeth's. They were the condition for an ever-new search for self-negation. Sympathy for outcasts, beggars, and those living in bondage was not motivated primarily by the urge to help and heal, but rather by calming one's social conscience if one felt burdened by an abundance of wealth and power. Such motivations are far removed from a sense of fundamental human equality and worth. They do not aim at the social elevation of those considered to be lesser even when washing their feet in a ritual saturated with symbolic meaning. It has been frequently observed that medieval charity always assumed that harsh social conditions could not be changed. Whether spiritually impoverished or of low social standing, whether physically ill or without legal rights: all those who were disadvantaged were expected to remain in their caste. It provided the raison d'être for charitable exercises in humility. As evidenced by Elisabeth, this does not exclude the fact that an authentic and warm love of humanity is frequently mixed into this cult of the poor.

St. Elisabeth's "humility" ought to be approached as the opposite of an impostor's boastfulness. If impostors attempt to appear as more than they are, practitioners of an asceticism of power wish to be seen as less than they are. Ascetics of power can never look too shabby; their lifestyle is never paltry and impoverished enough. For this reason, Elisabeth not only wears a coarse smock, but must add patches of a different fabric. An impostor reveals through inadvertent missteps that he is not truly a general or a prince. Likewise, an ascetic of power cannot but reveal her true high status despite her beggar's clothing and begging bowl, despite her preference for unpalatable food and her companionship with the downtrodden. The moral canon of her era labelled the desire to descend the social ladder as humility. Frequently, however, we recognize a personal pleasure in assuming this moral stance.

Saints' lives teach us that living in an immovable medieval social context, human beings endowed with a social conscience and willing to reject the use of their power for ethical reasons could not easily become democratic. By necessity, they had first to turn into the reverse, autocrats. Under the pressure of a fixed social ranking system, they were only able to choose either power or poverty, everything or nothing. This was also true for Elisabeth. Ideals could only be pursued and sustained through a total break with society. One was forced to become radical. Given the unbreakable social barriers, the only promising path to burst through them was that of spiritual opposition as practiced by the virtuosos of self-humiliation. They were not wretched, pathological, or infatuated with subservience. They did not act out of weakness. They were genuine activists seeking out those of lower social status in the only way possible. A medieval ideology of humility is the product of a social and moral order as constructed by power and authoritarian relationships. If we today judge the medieval humility ethos as antiquated, it is not because this virtue has become less esteemed. Rather, as is true for sexual asceticism, the reason is to be found in the fact that it has become an unconscious and commonly shared value. The vastly expanded rationality of post-medieval thought has made us more modest because it promotes an awareness of the interdependence and relativity of all insights and knowledge. Medieval humanity lacked this type of intellectual humility. Likewise, modern people are generally also more self-effacing in fulfilling the demands of daily life than their medieval predecessors. Today, thousands of people diligently perform their daily duties in the domains of medicine and social work without any special recognition. In the Middle Ages, these activities were considered a religious virtue and a model of Christian charity. Nietzsche and other enemies of Christianity misjudged this transfer of moral values from the religious to the secular realm, which in turn contributed to their rejection of the Christian ethos. Since Christian virtue became "secularized" during the Enlightenment, nobody took notice that a loving protection of the weak and Christian humility had succeeded so well. It is common to complain that we have "only" humanism but have lost Christianity on the way. To the contrary.

Christianity has fewer followers today precisely not because western societies lost their moral convictions, but because unnoticed and irreversibly, the demands of Christin ethics have become universally accepted. What once counted as a cardinal virtue and singular ethical victory has become today's minimal requirements. It was newsworthy in the Middle Ages when the beneficiaries of authoritarian social structures expressed any kind of social instinct. Today, when young people are educated in everything except in how to give orders, appeals to exercise humility are superfluous. As civic asceticism has become the norm in our bourgeois era, at least regarding work and lifestyle, the asceticism of saints has become outdated. This holds equally true for the unbridled enjoyment and exercise of power, which has been dammed in and controlled by democracy. Consequently, its moral and psychological shadow, Christian self-abnegation, has turned unintelligible and hollow. If a contemporary person gains power and high social standing late, or incompletely, there is no ethical need for wishing to experience oneself as abject. One might want to be a child again, but not diminished in any other way. From a psycho-historical point of view, it is of great significance that post-medieval humanity lost a familiarity with "humility fakes." The public performance of humility among devout Christians in the Middle Ages makes sense only because of their reverse social circumstances.

An Exercise in Humility or Mere Performance?

St. Elisabeth's individual development needs to be understood against the background of medieval social factors. Her demonstrations of humility can thus be interpreted as a psychological reversal of a grasp for power. Since she was used to giving orders since her teenage years, it should count as a conventional act of self-awareness when she became self-effacing. In this type of religious transformation, she retained the character of a true autocrat, a radical of "the below" who aims at total self-negation without however sharing her power. Even her charity is rich in traits that prove her sense of her objects' subordinate position in relation to her own.

According to Konrad,

> She placed those who were the most miserable and the most disfigured at her table. When I reprimanded her, she answered that she received especially from these kinds of people the exceptional grace of humility. Being a very thoughtful woman, she reminded me of her past and said that it was necessary for her to cure one extreme through its opposite.

With her answer, the saint reveals clearly enough which well feeds the humility that drives her to share her table with the indigent. It is the need to over-, or rather, undercompensate a past profusion of power through acts of self-abasement ("contraria contrariis curare" [to cure one extreme through its opposite], *Epistola*). The compulsion to counterbalance past abundance with poverty and the joy of life with listlessness explains not only her stages of social descent, but also to a large degree her submissive and self-effacing regime at Marburg. Even her extreme passivity and servility toward the flinty Master Konrad signified to some extent a guilt-ridden rebalancing of high with low status and penance for her happy marriage with Landgrave Ludwig.

All primary sources testify that this saintly humility focused exclusively on the objects of her care: the poor, the sick, the beggars, penniless women in childbed, maidservants, and children. It is no accident that no tradition mentions her accomplishments in her daily exchanges with religious and secular people of her own rank or with those who were neither beggars nor injured in any way. Only a few such references exist, and these are unintentionally damning.

She once visited a Franciscan monastery, where she was shown with pride richly ornamented golden statues. All twenty-four monks stood next to the interesting and high-ranking visitor and expected a small word of appreciation for their ecclesiastical treasures, which was the only shared possession they dared to own. According to the *Libellus*, the otherwise gentle woman dressed them down with vigor. Without mincing her words, she scolded them that they should have invested their savings into foodstuff and clothing rather than into church ornaments. Religious representations belonged inside a human heart, not on church walls. On another occasion, someone praised a beautiful image in a church. She gave the same unambiguous answer. Her religiosity was of an interior nature and did not need such sensual foundations.[27]

Elisabeth's aphorisms became famous because of their iconoclastic stance. It is self-evident that as a radical Franciscan, she was an opponent of the sensual glitter that embellished medieval Christian art. Yet the carefree attitude with which she countered well-intentioned proponents of Christian art who challenged her views reveals something of her social interactions. As is true for political and religious radicals generally, her ideological adversaries were not treated kindly and considerately. She did not possess the magnanimity and empathy to speak her truth without offending others. Her acrimonious experiences with her aristocratic peers after her husband's death offer the most obvious evidence. As tragic as the young, pious, and passionate woman's banishment from Wartburg castle was, it also reveals that she knew how to offend her peers. Among her fellow tenants in Marburg, Elisabeth insisted to not be addressed as "my Lady," because "we all partake equally in our poverty and ignorance." Her maidservants were asked to address her informally and by her first name. They had to sit at the table with her and share food from the same plate. According to the *Libellus*,

The maid Irmingard once said, "You are caring for your soul's salvation through us and overlook our low rank. We lose as many merits when not

27 Martin Luther, a deadly enemy of the veneration of saints, sincerely praised St. Elisabeth for her iconoclasm, which he liked. He noted in his *Epistle on Stephen's Day*, "Look, how simple, divine, and forceful her judgment is about things that everybody regards as valuable."

being able to serve you respectfully as you win merits by your humility."
Elisabeth answered, "It would be right for you to sit on my lap" and made
the young woman sit on her knees.[28]

For Elisabeth, sharing a table with maidservants constituted an act of
humility much like walking barefoot, wearing a beggar's frock, and washing
the feet of the destitute and homeless. It was not geared, however, toward
genuine equality or the abolition of social distance. The maidservant felt
clearly that her mistress's goal was religious self-improvement rather than
a friendly attempt at personal closeness. Without compromise, Elisabeth
remained her servants' superior. The maidservant knew herself to be used
as a means to an end. Signifying total depersonalization, it is the greatest
human insult possible. As Elisabeth becomes aware of it, she draws her
interlocutor on her lap, thus completely disarming her, since she can hardly
resist such friendly invitation.

Even more eye-opening is a small episode which belongs to the involuntary revelations of the *Libellus* we have encountered so frequently. Driven by
her zealous generosity, Elisabeth cut a piece of linen that might have served
as a tablecloth or wall hanging into bath towels for the sick, commenting,
"how good it is for us to thus bathe and care for our Lord." The maidservant
answered, "It might be good for you to do so, but we do not know whether it
is good for others." This voice from among the common people openly calls
attention to the fact that mystical charity does not always garner immediate
approval. The young woman wants to say, "You achieved something on
behalf of the poor and sick. But there are people in this house who would
have liked to keep the beautiful cloth to decorate our home." She feels the
unconventional exclusivity of her lady's love of Christ and the poor.

Dietrich of Apolda reports another incident when the maidservants
complained of the measly burnt meals that Elisabeth favored as a form of
ascetic practice. She merely smiled "humbly" when hearing of her maidservants' anger. The only too natural desires of the young women, who
were neither professional ascetics like herself nor belonged to the sick and
crippled, had absolutely no appeal for the friend of lepers and the destitute.
The episode reminds of Elisabeth's palpable injustice in her dealings with
the beautiful Hildegunde.

The nature of Elisabeth's charity suggests a selective and highly subjective
passion for altruism, in which the poor and sick figure as almost impersonal

28 In this vignette, Irmingard demonstrates her biblical knowledge. She likely referenced Rom.
13 and Heb. 13:17, which exhort Christians to submit to authorities.

targets. The disdainful ingratitude for her charity, which Elisabeth experienced repeatedly, was tragic. On the other hand, it uncovers to what degree she was unwilling to let go of her aristocratic rights and social distance and consider the feelings and psychology of those whom she served. She should have sensed that the woman in the village of Wetter, whom she pampered and showered with gifts, did not love her in turn, even was unworthy of her love.

Despite her caring kindness, the former landgravine remained an aristocrat in a patriarchal era even while wearing Franciscan garb. She retained an attitude toward those below her rank which until a generation ago, we generally reserved in our dealings with children. The child was not considered bad, but as a rule, rather something akin to a thing. We did not assume that a child possessed the full range of an adult's emotions. Children who were showered with gifts and cared for, who were given beds and kissed, always remained passive objects. Their task was to remain still and receive. There was no space provided for a child's active rejection, even active acceptance, love, or antipathy, indeed any kind of independent capacity for making decisions.

The wider the distance between the donor and her recipients, the stronger her search for social tension and release. The gap was stretched to the limits of human relationships when a princess chose the lowest of the low, the most wretched individuals, such as those suffering from skin diseases, as the preferred occasion for her aristocratic exercises in humility. This fact is the reason for Elisabeth's unconscious yet personally intensely meaningful choice to kiss open wounds and other "abnormal" behaviors. It was impossible for those who were honored in this manner to grasp its spiritual meaning. Often enough, they responded with a muffled sense of hatred, which always arises in people who feel themselves being used as an impersonal means to an end. It becomes palpable in the Eisenach scene where an old female beggar pushes her former benefactress into the muddy street's filth.[29] Most of those under her care were likely either too unsophisticated to explain in any depth their contradictory feelings to the high-born woman or were conniving enough to play act their gratitude so as not to lose the flow of alms.

If we want to understand her life's work accurately, we need to approach it as sketched above. Elisabeth accepted the toughest work assignments at the

29   Among the rare poetic works about Elisabeth that did not get stuck in a cloying romantic stance, Charles Kingsley endowed the female beggar's hatred with an insightful motive: "You do not need us as a Jacob's ladder of your fame/and step on our backs to heaven." Kingsley, *A Saint's Tragedy*, German translation Marburg, 1855.

Marburg hospital; she did not evade any nursing tasks; she labored in areas
that drew the lowest wages. Yet all these acts of humility did not only aim
at other human beings. On a more fundamental level, they were motivated
by a radical determination to live a religious life guided by Franciscan
ideals. Having never touched a sooty cookpot before, the manual labor of
the former aristocrat was entirely Franciscan in character.

When analyzed as a religious task, Elisabeth's self-negating efforts reveal
a fearless logic. Broken and involuntarily humiliated in her most personal
feminine aspects, unfree in her public activities, maligned or at the very
least regarded with disdain by others, she did not abandon her transpersonal
religious principles. Her role model remained Francis even when she had
begun to live in bondage to a nonreligious tyrant in religious garb. Despite
the few remaining options to lead her life as a disciple of Francis, she made
her meagre choices in his spirit. She continued to consider the ownership
of money and valuables a mortal sin. Although her guardian had legally
secured her widow's inheritance with such proficiency, she refused to
spend anything on her personal needs that she could not pay for with her
hands' labor. While she could not subsist as a beggar, the supreme goal of
humility, at least she was able to work like female commoners. A poorly
paid domestic source of income, she regularly spun the unprocessed wool
that she received from the Altenburg nuns. At one time, Konrad ordered
Elisabeth to travel to Eisenach. She would not leave on horseback until she
had returned an advance payment with the remainder of the raw wool to
her female employers. According to the *Libellus*, she only allowed herself to
travel with the money she had earned, but not with the advance payment.
Besides the appeal of low wage labor, spinning provided the satisfaction
of having earned the pennies that she could donate at church. She always
kept a spindle, a symbol of work, by her side. Once, when she was bedridden
and kept spinning without a break, a nurse on duty took her spindle so that
she could find some rest. Instead, Elisabeth sorted and pulled her wool into
strings to prepare for spinning.

People who fail at reaching their highest goals insist with even greater
resolve to fulfill them at least partially. According to credible sources, the
Libellus reports that a Hungarian count exclaimed, "Nobody has seen a
king's daughter spin before." The count belonged to a delegation, which was
ordered by the king of Hungary, Elisabeth's father, to investigate Elisabeth's
situation in Marburg. When he entered her hovel and saw her sitting on
the floor spinning wool, he was so shocked that he crossed himself and
cried out as quoted above. With this story, Elisabeth's drudgery had been
acknowledged as radically beyond the norm even from a neutral secular

point of view. In the tiered system of medieval society, manual labor such as the maidservants' spinning of wool was the destiny of the lower classes. Medieval aristocratic wives were primarily responsible for supervising their servants. Free males had access to only two respectable professions: hunting and war. Among the nobility, these occupations retained their reputation into modern times. Given that manual labor was held in such low regard, St. Elisabeth's canonization process included her kitchen toil in a list of her religious "works." In the *Epistola*, even Konrad noted it as extraordinary that Elisabeth prepared vegetables and washed dishes with a servant. Dietrich of Apolda recounted in detail that she cooked "even though she lacked the ability of preparing meals":

> Caused by the extreme inadequacy of the meals, and because she also burned these miserable collations due to her negligence, the maidservants were in a bad mood. Elisabeth, however, suffered it joyfully.

This description appears so true to life that it allows us to recognize clearly how her kitchen tasks had no home economical purpose. Instead, it signified freely chosen penitence, a relay on her path to perfect humility. She was as unsuccessful in her cooking as once in milking a cow, because as an aristocrat, she was not trained in manual domestic skills. One of the maidservants said with a degree of innocence that "she was also unable to weave linen." It did not matter to Elisabeth whether she could be of help in domestic matters. Here as well, she was attracted by the lowliness of the task. With a singular tenacity, she insisted on undertaking the unpleasant task of washing dishes. She even sent the maidservants away on an errand so that she could remain with her dirty chores.

The canonization documents highlight that she bathed the hospital's wards. She made their beds and covered them with a blanket. They also noted that "with her own hands," she distributed food items among the poor and inspected their shacks to ascertain that they owned sufficient bedding and clothing. Today, these activities are taken for granted by social workers and community nurses. Modern nurses work fourteen to fifteen hours daily amidst the beds of their patients and in surgery rooms. Protestant deaconesses and Catholic nuns obey an even harsher law of unreserved dedication. Day after day, female social workers visit the tenements in working-class neighborhoods. Medical history is a heroic chronicle of female doctors and nurses who remained at their posts during the worst of epidemics. Nobody admires these representatives of contemporary charity. Their service remains anonymous. As is true for the domain of self-control, the ethical standard for selfless professional activities is far higher today than was the case for medieval people. For Elisabeth, nursing and charitable work were not a vocation in the sense of a self-explanatory and freely provided service to a cause, even though she became its misunderstood symbol when nursing and caring for those in need was redefined as "labor." Her moral motto was not "work ennobles," but "work humbles." It is solely for this reason that she pursued her chores. Only in a democracy could the notion rise to the level of a widely recognized ethos that work of whatever kind ennobles and that it is a social requirement and necessity. The social ethos of modern followers of Leo Tolstoy, who wish to relieve others of their demeaning work so as not to be served by them was not Elisabeth's. She did not doubt that some human beings existed only to be of service.

Viewed objectively, St. Elisabeth's charitable activities in Marburg were those of an amateur. They become exceptional, however, when placed in the context of the thirteenth century. It was unprecedented that a woman dedicated herself to hospital care as a public activity outside the home. Today, we consider nursing the most feminine of all professions. As an outsider, Elisabeth's situation in Marburg was neither comfortable nor prestigious. Yet even she did not consider her care for the poor and the sick as her final ethical calling and challenge. Her hospital work was not so much redeeming the world but redeeming the self. The soul's welfare after death determined the charitable works of a subject and their object. Elisabeth beats with a switch every female hospital beneficiary who refused to attend mass. Today, the recipients of charitable support are considered unworthy if they refuse to accept work; in the Middle Ages if they refused to pray and confess. If an ascetic of power such as Elisabeth cleansed herself of all self-assertion through hospital and servant labor, a dazzling hope begins to come within her grasp. Her continued existence after death in the form of a beatific life became more probable.

Mysticism of the Cross

Medieval sculptures and paintings preferred to present Elisabeth as the patron saint of charity, yet until the sixteenth century, she was never depicted in the clothing of a Franciscan penitent. As the most broadly accessible historiography, sculptural depictions in particular immortalized Elisabeth as a noble lady with an emphasis on a certain feminine grace and sumptuous clothing. As symbolic attributes, her hands hold a plate with bread and a pitcher. Frequently, a beggar or leper are placed at her feet, intentionally depicted with gruesome realism to generate a visual contrast to the female benefactor's royal dignity and glowing health.

Her cult did not want to face who she really was—a tearful and long-suffering young woman. The cult desired the standardized image of a princess who could draw from never-ending supplies; who provided alms gracefully and humbly; and to whom one could look up to. Turning into a stereotype, she was to be simultaneously a rich princess and a caretaker of the poor, in other words, a royal friend of the people.

This rigid ideal represents a popular notion of how to solve social ills. Elisabeth herself, however, provides the correct answer to questions about the true religious core of her charitable efforts. When preparing linen towels for bathing her patients, she once said according to the *Libellus*, "How good it is for us to bathe and wrap our Lord in this manner." She did not nurse the sick, but Christ. Devotion to Christ's body, however, is an authentic mystical concept. Elisabeth's great contemporary Mechthild of Magdeburg repeatedly described personal Christocentric devotions and a personal love of Christ in her formidable poetic expressions of a transcendent eroticism. All those who are religious are also mystical lovers. As ascetics, they empathically reimagine the physical and emotional tortures of Christ's passion and frequently replace Christ's tortured and suffering body with that of a dead or living physical substitute as their object of devotion. It is this desire for devotional simulation that led to the creation of the Pietà.[30] Grasped by the force of the encounter, a medieval Christian experienced a *unio mystica* with the divine when viewing art that depicted Christ's passion. Elisabeth, a child of her century's mystical piety, approaches the sick patients of her hospital as the sacred body of Christ.

In yet another of Elisabeth's bitter disappointments, a poor woman whom she had caringly offered her own room as an abode ran away one night and took all of Elisabeth's clothing with her. Elisabeth faces the repellent ingratitude with satisfaction. The *Libellus* records her response as, "I thank you, my God, that you made me resemble you. Not only did you enter the world naked, but you were robbed of all clothing and hung on the cross without garments."

It is reported that as a child, she removed her golden tiara when visiting a church so as not to look at Christ with his crown of thorns in her worldly

---

30 Mary holding Christ's dead body in her lap was already a fully developed literary and conceptual theme during Elisabeth's era. The Pietà sculptures begin to appear in the fourteenth century.

splendor. Already then, she displayed a yearning to attune herself to Christ's suffering. It continued to grow steadily and demanded that her religious outlook and endeavors were defined as service to Christ on an intimate, personal level. When she was thinking about her ideal of Franciscan poverty on a rather theoretical level while still at the Wartburg castle, and as if in a rehearsal dressed herself rather poorly and beggarly in the company of her ladies in waiting, she said according to the *Libellus*, "This is how I will walk around when I beg for the Lord and suffer hardship for Him."

Elisabeth justified her grave psychological injuries and humiliations while at Marburg as mystical experiences of suffering. The *Libellus* notes, "She endured Master Konrad's many punishments and slaps across the face, which she desired with the wish to endure them in the memory of the beatings that Christ received." Christ's crown of thorns became the crown of her ill-treated womanhood. The cross of her confessor's destructiveness became Christ's cross. The foul gossip and slander of her reputation became the crowd's vilification of the man from Nazareth. Although appealing to modern people and modern values, her hospital service and charity were at its core mystical esotericism.

> Once, she accepted a badly disfigured woman with leprosy to her hospital. The woman was covered with wounds and pus. It was horrifying to look at her even from a distance. Elisabeth carried her and placed her in a bed. She dressed her wounds with cloth and cared for her with medicine. She flung herself at her feet, untied her shoes and even wished to wear them, but the young woman did not allow it. She drained the ulcers on her hands and feet and touched her face, which was covered with sores. After some time had passed, the young woman began to heal. She housed her in a remote corner of the infirmary, visited her frequently, and whenever she called her to her own living quarter, she cheered her up, made a bed for her, and comforted her.

She does not offer charitable nursing to the female leper. She is not merely a deaconess who feeds and bandages the rotting, stinking, and wretched creature. She is a religious ecstatic. She knew with religious certainty that someone would love her for her cultic behavior. According to an apocryphal tradition, Christ himself lived among humans as a leper. A leper's extreme isolation and lowliness exceeds the abundance of suffering that Christ shouldered on behalf of humanity. For this reason, Elisabeth does not recoil from "the wounds oozing pus as an act of love for Him who became a leper for our sake," as a biographer of St. Hedwig, another friend of lepers, noted. An exiled Elisabeth was happy when mystically venerating the nauseating signs of the young woman's disease. Through close communion with the repulsive figure, she succeeded in getting nearer to the divine itself, the redeemer. It was characteristic for her time at Marburg that ecstasy interlaced with the urge to humiliate herself. To not appear to have been passively humiliated in personal circumstances, she actively participates in her destruction. Despite its significance as a religious initiation, Elisabeth's relationship to the young leper remains embarrassing and repulsive when viewed from a rational point of view. Even as a miserable human wreck, the leprous young woman retained more common sense than Elisabeth. She does not want to allow Elisabeth to untie her shoelaces and put on her shoes.

Elisabeth knew that she committed a wrong by inviting the female leper to the hospital because it violated hospital rules. She asks her companions to not be angered by her decision, since medieval society generally suffered from a kind of leprosy infection phobia. Yet like someone who cannot refrain from pursuing a pleasing experience even if it is forbidden, she cannot stop herself. Eventually, she even hides the disfigured young woman in her own quarters. The secret idyll between the two women did not last long. Her two female chaperones betrayed her to Konrad. According to his own testimony in the *Epistola*, her beat he especially hard and threw the female leper off the premises.

The female object of this gruesome fetishism had a predecessor and was followed by a successor. Early on, Elisabeth grew fond of a boy who seems to have displayed all marks of physical unsightliness. Abandoned by his parents, the boy was one-eyed, paralyzed, covered with eczema, and suffered from bloody diarrhea. She cared for the squalid little bundle of misery day and night. With her own hands, she washed his soiled bed linens. She kept watch over him, and more than six times every night, she carried him outdoors, so he could relieve himself. At night, she put him into her own bed. He died despite her devoted care. The gap he left was filled by the young woman with leprosy. When she as well was removed from her and Konrad had left on an official journey, Elisabeth chose a new favorite, another sick and unsightly boy, who, according to the *Epistola*, was "so mangy that he had no hair left on his head." She cared for him so well that he stayed alive. She appears to have always kept him by her side. At the time of her final illness, he sat by her bedside.

The three stars that illuminated the last years of her life—the young woman with leprosy, the one-eyed boy with dysentery, and the boy with scabies—fulfilled a pivotal function in the emotional economy of Elisabeth's self-inflicted suffering. They replaced the missing objects of her love and soothed her tragic loneliness. Her husband and three children—the family she once loved—had been taken from her. Like an animal that instinctively looks for her lost young with quiet despair, she grasps for substitutions that cannot be taken from her. The three destitute creatures absorbed her maternal sorrows, but they had to be ill and maimed to minimize any memories of her own children. They came close to remind her that in the final analysis, she did not desire Christ, but human beings of flesh and blood. The ghastly self-deception succeeded because she took a living child's corpse to her bed at night. Yet the choice of her three foster children could be rationalized as a mystical service to Christ. The pitiful youngsters represented the infant Jesus, lying in a stable without a cradle. She took them in as a pledge that all personal suffering signified the passion of Christ and the grief of Mary, who was the unhappiest of all mothers.

Even her tormentor, entirely lacking in religiosity and mystical sensitivity, felt and respected her ability to experience spirituality in the narrow sense, that is, to experience the prodigious happiness that separates a mystic from the ordinary world. In the *Epistola*, Konrad reported that when she was in a state of rapture after having been in prayer for a substantial amount of time, she was as if transfigured. "The face radiated, the eyes lit up, and she could not find her way back to herself for hours on end." Even to Konrad, she was then sacrosanct. As has been true for many others, it was said of Elisabeth that after such hours of rapture, she remained without food for a long time. Like the great vision of the unhappy woman during her days in Eisenach, these were a reward for the hours of desolation and despair.

Elisabeth was given other moments of oblivion. She possessed the "gift of tears." Modern scholars regard the disposition to cry frequently, which recommended many candidates for canonization with skepticism and caution. Today, it is considered valid proof of a disordered mind, of dissimulation, or of trickery. However, medieval people possessed a much more embodied emotional and affective nature and cried far more frequently. They kissed and took a swipe at others more spontaneously than is permitted for more disciplined moderns. They drifted into outbursts of despair more frequently. In medieval society, tears were not seen as, feminine. During public appearances, men of lay or religious rank could make quite an impression if they began to cry in tense situations. It garnered approval. Physiologically speaking, the frequent crying that has been reported for all of Elisabeth's life is hardly surprising for a person who was already overburdened and exhausted at a young age. In contrast to false saints, it mattered to her that nobody would notice. She also never bragged about her state of deep prayer. The *Libellus* recorded about her time at the Wartburg castle that "she conducted herself always with a cheery and relaxed countenance; secretly, however, her tears flowed copiously."

Her tears were the authentic trait of a saint. Precise information about the kind and frequency of Elisabeth's tearfulness is not accidental.

When she was happiest, she cried the most. While crying, she never distorted or twisted her face, but the tears flowed as if from a spring, and her face remained joyful and bright at the same time.

It would be wrong to interpret the simultaneous presence of weeping and happiness as symptoms of hysterical instability. On the contrary, Elisabeth achieved full control over her will: she was able to transform a sudden burst of sorrow into joy, its emotional opposite. She turned the physiological manifestations of affect and the muscular facial tensions caused by weeping into joy and laughter. She allowed herself the release that nature grants a worn-out heart only as a mystical rite and religious service. According to the *Libellus*, "She said about those whose face was disfigured by weeping, 'It almost looks as if they want to scare God. Instead, they should give God everything that they have with joy.'" Tears were a libation that, as Elisabeth demanded, should be offered to God with a happy countenance. St. Bernard said of tears, "They are the wine of angels," since God receives them as the most precious substance. They are the physical materialization of a human heart's battles. For those who love and long mystically, Mary's and Christ's tears are the eternal symbols of human sorrow.

Elisabeth also shed Christ's tears on his way to Calvary. It enabled her to reinterpret the personal anguish, which she was forced to endure as a choice, that is, as Christ's suffering. She ceased to lament her imprisonment and the loss of her spouse, children, and honor. Life crucified her, but like all great religious figures of her century, she regained her sense of self in Christ's suffering. She was a stigmatic without physically visible stigmata. It is said that often, while enraptured, she did not notice that her garments were caught on fire and smoldered. She fell asleep at the open fireplace, either exhausted by tears, sorrow, and longing or by a state of deep prayer. The frequently attested joyfulness that she retained in the most wretched situations and her contentment in all calamities appear to be authentic. She lived in chiliastic expectation. The great change brought by physical death and with that her happiness in the hereafter were surely on the way.

Her Marburg passion lasted only three years. The *Libellus* recounts that once, while lying on the bare floor in the winter as a penitence, she said, "I am lying here as in a sarcophagus." The *Libellus* adds that "she was happy in her tribulation." Ever since the early days that she tried and failed to be at one with the poor until her squalid end in Marburg's infirmary, Elisabeth's path was that of a genuinely religious mind and her accomplishments those of a spiritually mediated misfortune. During times of visionary clarity, transpersonal consciousness surged from an abundance of humiliations and injuries. Once, her mother appeared to her in a dream, a woman who died a shockingly violent death as queen of Hungary. Her mother said, "My beloved daughter, pray for my delivery of the immense pain I am suffering until this day, because I have lived in sin. You are capable to do so." Elisabeth awakened from the dream image, wept, and prayed. When she fell asleep again, her mother appeared a second time and assured her that she now felt liberated because of her daughter's action. Dietrich of Apolda's story of her dream vision is not part of the *Libellus*, but because it is consistent with Elisabeth's psychological make-up, it might indeed have been true.[31] The dream provided a compelling form of wish fulfillment for a misunderstood and isolated human being. Always without a country, Elisabeth barely knew her royal mother. Now she yearned for her. Yet the mother's soul, suffering in purgatory, asks her, a mere child, for intercession. The child had outgrown the mother. Elisabeth once longed for her mother, but the dream vision signals that she does not need her anymore. Elisabeth's prodigious suffering had transformed her into the redeemer and savior of souls.

The dream vision of her supplicant mother marks the birth of a profound new self-confidence. The vision declares, "You can redeem me," meaning, "You are semi-divine." Christ accomplished his greatest work in vicarious suffering. In like manner, a faultless human being, a saint, can purify or redeem those who died in sin and adversity through their own pain and grief. As a medieval Christian, self-awareness of this new ability was the highest grace she could be granted. In her dream vision, Elisabeth experienced a remarkable justification of herself: the satisfaction that her suffering had not been in vain.

Elisabeth's Death

"I always told you that we must make others happy." The bon mot, uttered by Elisabeth on that joyous moonlit night, reveals one more time her cheerful

---

31   We know that at the time, Elisabeth's father was still alive. According to the *Libellus*, he sent Hungarian aristocrats to visit her and propose that she return to live with him in the knowledge that her circumstances were not especially honorable. This greeting from the land of her birth could have triggered the dream of her mother.

and amicable temperament. Yet mental and moral demands strangled her life-affirming attitude. The battle with herself required a degree of strength that her youthful feminine constitution could not maintain for long. It consumed her vitality too excessively and too fast. Only psychological suicide could succeed in "training" herself to extinguish her own nature and give victory to its opposite.

When the former landgravine of Thuringia began the life of a recluse in Marburg, she had just turned twenty years of age. Chances were that she could have lived for another fifty years. A singular grace of destiny spared her these decades. Had she remained only a few more years in a state of religiously sanctioned self-destruction, she would have become ever more hardened and embittered. Even then, the first signs of intolerance and misanthropy began to influence her activities. Her early death not only signified deliverance from an unbearable existence, but also prevented the increasing corruption of her magnanimous and innocent nature. At the age of twenty-four, she was old and worn-out. Her dying proper had begun after her husband's death and the frightful moral defeat of her Eisenach days. Her wish for self-annihilation and deadly exhaustion in the service of an irreversible oath of obedience commenced then and there.

Her premature death gifted her the final victory over her confessor. She paid for a lasting escape from him with the price of her own life. St. Elisabeth died of a broken heart, even if such a cause of death is not strictly accurate in a medical-scientific sense. A common illness as the objective cause of death does not contradict our statement. Frequently, physical illness is the last step that helps to extinguish a waning will to live. Elisabeth awaited her end as the consummation of her existence. She not only died gladly because her life had nothing left to offer her. Her thoughts had already taken root in the afterlife.

It is one of the most distinguished medieval Christian virtues to not fear death but to desire it joyfully as a union with the divine. As stipulated by the probatio virtutum, it is one of the most important proofs for canonization. For this reason, three of the primary sources, the *Epistola*, the *Libellus*, which otherwise skim over crucial changes in the saint's life, and a letter by Elisabeth's friend, Abbess Lutrudis of Wetter, describe her illness and dying with a host of minor related circumstances. We therefore know precisely how Elisabeth's final illness unfolded physiologically, including the cause of her infection, the fifteen days of confinement to her infirmary, her collapse three days before her death, and her peaceful departure.

This seemingly natural death signifies not only an accidental and premature liberation from an unbearable existence, but also a transpersonal achievement. It is the victory she won over her own nature. To attain an "easy" death demanded fighting the soul as much as the body over the span of many years. Its requirements were insufficient sleep, scanty food of a poor quality, and heavy physical exertion. Subconsciously, these ascetical practices were already factored into planning her self-annihilation. In the medieval context of aggressive disciplining of the body, Elisabeth's achievements were not unique. They do not exceed the norms of an average monastic lifestyle. While her penitential practices could have been suitable for a young strong farmhand in monastic garb, whether male or female, they were imposed on an already exhausted and spent body. Even while still a lay woman, her life force was sapped and exploited. She gave birth to three children in the first bloom of youth while following the severe fasting rules as mandated by Konrad. In Marburg, she continued systematic fasting as a special exercise of her own. She lived on the worst type of nutritious food, cabbage and legumes cooked in water without fat or salt. She denied herself fish, which was a permitted source of nourishment during lent. Once, people sent several especially beautiful and large fish to her house. She sold them immediately to get money on behalf of the poor and to not be tempted to dine on the fish herself. If the hospital kitchen served something better, she made sure that not she but only the sick would eat it.

Weak and worn down by chronic malnutrition, Elisabeth became sickly and was frequently confined to her bed. Her nocturnal penitential activities must have been even more grueling and painful while in Marburg. Initially, she tried to lie down at night without a covering and sleep on the bare ground even in the winter. It depleted her so much that she placed two cushions next to her to ward off the cold, yet without allowing herself to lie on either one of them. She vehemently rejected any kind of hygiene. Once, her maternal aunt, an abbess in Kitzingen, tried to force her to take a bath. When she was let into the bathroom, she merely splattered some water with her feet so it would sound on the outside as if she were submerged in the water. She then pronounced with satisfaction, "Now I have bathed." This disregard for her own body speaks to her self-contempt and self-hatred.

Elisabeth was fully aware of her asceticism's destination. Several sources have recorded her prophecies of her impending death. They testify to the fact that her strength had left her to the point of near death. When she asked a doctor to what limit she could extend her fasting and remain alive, she must have feared committing the mortal sin of suicide. The illness that she suffered in her third year at Marburg in the late fall of 1231 found little left to destroy.

The onset of her final sickness churned up all the explosive subterranean ties with her foster father. Konrad himself fell so ill that he expected loss of life. He as well was close to capitulation. If illnesses carry symbolic meaning on the psychological level, his illness appears as a last effort to win Elisabeth's love by blackmailing her through an appeal to her compassion. All other attempts to secure her submission through fear had failed. When he felt sick and on the brink of dying, he sent for Elisabeth and asked her how she would arrange her life without him. With guileless confidence, she reacted contrary to what he expected. According to the *Epistola*, she did not give the anticipated answer for him to get well quickly so they could share a blessed life in service to the divine. She simply answered, "I will die, but not you." She beat him to it with her own death. She became ill on the fourth day following their conversation and died after having been bedridden for fifteen days. She might have become infected when visiting Konrad. Konrad on the other hand convalesced and was left behind.

Everybody who dies is a saint, because all humans become unworldly and dignified when they undergo this great transformation. This is true for the former landgravine, who lived her final years as a downtrodden woman deprived of her rights. Dying, she regained her freedom and her dignity. She died fully conscious; as heavy as her life had become, as light and free of conflict was her dying. "I feel that I am weak, but not that I am sick," she even said three days before her end. It is commonly said the dying first lose their eyesight, but that not infrequently, their sense of hearing sharpens. Despite the dimming of her senses, Elisabeth still experienced a moment of deep happiness on one of her last days. According to the *Libellus*, she was lying with her face turned to the wall, when the maidservant who sat by her bedside suddenly heard her sing. When asked about it after an hour had passed, Elisabeth answered that a bird had sat between her and the wall. The bird sang so sweetly that she had to join in. A barely audible sound from the outside grew into a joyful dream. The song thrush that she saw at her bed's headboard likely fulfilled and symbolized everything in her life that was once tender and full of unselfconscious freedom and joie de vivre. Once more, spring was on its way and her life began anew. She became as happy and free as she was when still a child. The dream of the singing bird and her own spontaneous swan song constitute the most authentic and psychologically accurate report of her last days on earth. Without question, all utterances were omitted that expressed the human desires of a woman, such as the wish to see her children once again or the hope to be reunited with her husband before too long. Such statements would have run counter to the purpose of the report. Only one small detail reveals what her fading consciousness clung to. The young, orphaned boy with a severe skin disease, adopted and cared for by Elisabeth, sat at her bedside when she died.

While her last hours seem to have been harmonious and peaceful, the fear of death assaulted her nonetheless, at least briefly. Suddenly, she spoke to those sitting at her bedside, "What shall we do if the devil will arrive now?" Then she shouted in a loud voice as if she wanted to drive something frightening away, "Go away, go away!" One more time, her life's anxieties and burdens threatened to overwhelm her. She soon calmed down. The comforting image of the Christ child born in a stable at midnight frequently strengthened the childless mother during her last days. Her fears at bay, she returned to being cheerful and serene.

Three days before her death, she became so tired that she refused visitors. One day before her death, Konrad, now healthy again, heard her confession and celebrated the Eucharist with her. According to the *Libellus*, he was preoccupied with more urgent concerns, however. Since he knew that his ward was on the brink of death, he asked her after confession whether she would want to create a testament regarding the ownership of the hospital. He expected that as the legal owner, she would designate him as her heir. In her innocence, Elisabeth did not understand the suggestive questions of the old fox. In her view, the hospital was "the fortified tower of the most holy poverty." With confidence in this point of view, she offered him an embarrassing answer: "I wonder why you ask this question. Following your orders, I sacrificed everything: my life, my children, my free will. I have become nothing but a part of you. Whatever I still own legally, I own because you did not want me to go begging. And now I should make a testament?" In the last moments of her life, the dying young woman, a Franciscan to her core, and the nonreligious male politician clashed once more in all their contrariness. Everything that Konrad himself recounts about the last conversation with his spiritual daughter is, as always, carefully edited. Naturally, it omits his dying daughter's reproach, but it confirms Elisabeth's views. Whatever she still owned was to be distributed among the poor. Only the grey smock that she usually wore should be wrapped around her corpse.

According to Konrad, she was still mentally alert on the day preceding the night of her death. She spoke about the best that she heard in a sermon (of course, it was his sermon). She was comforted knowing that Christ had cried out three times. As is typical of premodern cultures, those who were by her bedside had already begun their lamentations and dirges. It seemed like a rejection of these grieving brothers and sisters' tears, when she referenced the bible by saying, "Do not shed tears for me but for yourselves." At dusk, she became quiet. She tried once more to sing without being able to move her lips and remained peaceful throughout the night. Awakening at dawn, she felt the birth of a new state of being arising within. Her last words were,

"Now the hour arrives when the Virgin gave birth." In the early morning hours of November 17, 1231, Elisabeth fell asleep without a struggle.

The patient sufferer of Marburg left a precious legacy to the world. Her corpse would soon attract the attention and reverence of her contemporaries. It became the actual cause of her posthumous fame in the Middle Ages. Bodily incorruptibility was one of the initial supernatural proofs that the deceased was not an ordinary human being but a saint. This belief characterizes the popular cult of saints in the Middle Ages as straightforward magic. The primary sources, while silent about Elisabeth's states of mind, offer detailed reports about the state of decay and appearance of her cadaver. The steely man, who never showed any tenderness for his ward, describes at the end of his biography that the dead woman's limbs did not stiffen but remained soft and flexible, that while pale, her skin did not exhibit signs of decomposition, such as spots and discoloration, and exuded a pleasant scent.[32]

According to the *Libellus*, the fetishism of her mourning companions took ever darker turns. The hospital's inner circle, who had access to the unclothed corpse, removed not only hair and fingernails but an entire finger, the ears, and her nipples as substantial mementoes. The dead body was then clothed with the grey frock, the head was wrapped with fabrics, and the corpse was displayed for the customary four days in the hospital's chapel. A large crowd gathered and as if to immortalize the generosity of the popular benefactress and maternal founder of the hospital, common people cut small pieces from her tunic and the headscarf to serve as relics. Unrecognized at the time, they created the foundation of her fame as a saint with the cultic elevation of these material objects.

In contrast, the few ideals and contributions that the deceased left as her legacy for the world turned into nothing. The Marburg hospital, in which she devotedly cared for the sick and old, was soon repurposed as a pilgrim's hostel. The infirmary at the bottom of the Wartburg castle had already been dismantled immediately after her departure from the castle. Doomed by unusual circumstances, her Thuringian homeland became destitute. As landgravine, she and her spouse saw their life's work as easing the Thuringian people's suffering, which was caused by Landgrave Hermann's many wars. Through her radical break with the world, however, Elisabeth brought a devastating war to Thuringian lands.

---

32 The *Libellus* also notes the lack of decaying odors. Since the sick woman died in the winter season, was of a young age, and had suffered for only a short time, the intact condition of her corpse is a natural phenomenon.

When Elisabeth retired to Marburg, she left crown prince Hermann, her only son, in the care of her brother-in-law Heinrich Raspe, who served as Thuringia's regent until Hermann's adulthood. A persistent allegation, legendary but ahistorical, claims that he was St. Elisabeth's enemy and partially to blame for the death of her only son. Hermann, who died at the age of eighteen at the very beginning of his reign, was rumored to have been murdered by poison. A woman at Raspe's court was named as the perpetrator of the crime, but she was likely only the culprit's assistant. When his nephew began to rule, Heinrich Raspe was relegated back into the shadows. This must have been difficult for someone who ambitiously tried to reach for the emperor's crown. It seems likely that he was the author of the murderous plot even though circumstantial evidence is lacking. Subsequently, folk traditions punished him for his crime against St. Elisabeth's children by interpreting his three childless marriages as divine retribution. It can be ascertained, however, that Heinrich Raspe had a bad conscience concerning the family of his brother, who had died during the crusade. He reveals his secret by a precautionary instruction for the burial of the young prince, who had died suddenly and under mysterious circumstances. Raspe ordered that the young man was not to be buried next to his mother in Marburg with the rationale that she, the miracle worker, could raise him from the dead. Envisioning the continued existence of the rightful young heir to the throne made him uncomfortable. He feared the revenge of the mother. True to the religious views of his era, he believed in her ability to raise the dead.

Tragically, Elisabeth herself was partially guilty of the young man's grim demise. Her radical renunciation of all worldliness and her departure to Marburg destroyed the last protection of her children's destiny. There was no mother to guard the rights and life of a son. The absolute abdication of her temporal and parental rights carried destructive consequences in a social order where family and blood relations signified stability and the protection of life, and where the destiny of dynasties determined the destiny of a people. The demise of the only direct successor to the throne and the childless death of the country's regent Heinrich Raspe triggered the Thuringian war of succession. Experts of eastern Germany's history place the war's brutality above that of the Thirty Years' War. The long war devastated Thuringia. It raged back and forth between the landgraves of Meissen, whose claims were based on their kinship affiliation with Landgrave Ludwig's sister, and one of Elisabeth's daughters, Duchess Sophie of Brabant. The Duchess fought for her son Heinrich's succession to the throne. Wartburg castle, where Elisabeth once had dispensed charity and care for the destitute, turned into the epicenter of military violence. Citizens of Eisenach who joined Sophie of Brabant's party were shackled by the opposition party, tied to the large catapults and, while still alive, hurled down from the castle mountain into surrounding areas. The fierce war destroyed all charitable arrangements created by Landgrave Ludwig and Landgravine Elisabeth. It further disrupted the well-established cultural traditions of the Wartburg castle and concluded with the division of Thuringian lands.

Elisabeth's religious renunciation brought misfortune to her children, her dynasty, and her Thuringian people. There is no positive legacy to balance it. Its excessive stakes are especially tragic considering the calamitous lack of freedom that defined Elisabeth's life. Holy poverty, her core Franciscan-religious goal, always remained out of reach. Nonetheless, a failed life such as hers carries eternity and solemnity. Wholly embedded in Christianity, it stands in contrast to the pragmatic drive for action of other eras. Only this religion taught the truth that those who live unheroic lives and who are without success are of value. Judged from the vantage point of a search for teleological and tangible presence and impact, its values remain invisible. Whatever an individual feels and suffers cannot be accessed objectively. It would be lost and forgotten if not for the emergence of Christianity.

Elisabeth lived at Christianity's medieval zenith; it immortalized the muted struggle of an abandoned woman as religion's proper task. It is impossible to monumentalize what was most unique and personal of Elizabeth's life. She was the real St. Kümmernis.[33] Elisabeth's contemporary Mechthild of Magdeburg captured the timeless significance of such quiet fortitude, which stands in contrast to the heroism of pragmatic activists. Mechthild wrote, "Life without sorrow is the foolishness of fools."

Konrad of Marburg's Psychological Development after Elisabeth's Death

Elisabeth's appalling relationship with her confessor was enabled by the unquestioned authoritarianism that formed the uppermost moral and intellectual principle of medieval society. Under its spell, the former landgravine believed that she acted in the service of a higher morality. She sacrificed everything only to die with a broken sense of self. Her confessor was not an ordinary human being but the representative of an era's highest code of religious conduct. This fact barred her from recognizing the true nature of the relationship and the roles both partners assumed in it.

---

33   Translator's note: This is a wordplay on the bearded female folk saint St. Wilgefortis *alias* St. Sorrowful, a medieval patron saint of women who have experienced spousal abuse.

Even while Elisabeth was still alive, Konrad, the male partner, seems to have felt some doubt in the poorly rationalized justification of his tyrannical supervision. His doubts intensified after her death. Previously, the spiritual guidance of his victim sufficed to legitimize his subjective and egotistical needs as objective aims. In his eyes and the world's, he also could act without qualms as the advocate of a woman who needed support in worldly matters. No doubt, she would have made foolish decisions without his guardianship: rambling through the country, begging for handouts, and perishing somewhere as a pathetic nobody. Most importantly, in his view, she would have recklessly waived her share of assets instead of enriching the church. His mentorship thus carried an appearance of selflessness. The pope himself had entrusted him with the woman's custody. In Pope Gregory's view, Konrad had sacrificed himself in service to the woman's fraught situation.

His pupil's death removed the pretensions of his flattering role as her guardian and spiritual guide. With his legal responsibilities gone, he could not deny or whitewash the fierce subconscious forces at work in his relationship to the recently deceased. Not able to endure this growing insight into his own character, he numbed his bad conscience with two unsurprising interventions. They occupied most of his two remaining years. He lobbied for the canonization of his ward, the former landgravine of Thuringia, with zeal and haste, and he searched to substitute the lost but irreplaceable role of her tormentor. Protected by his status as inquisitor, he murdered anybody within reach.

The intense need for justification drove him to gain approval not only for the results but also for the reasons of his pedagogical methods. With the public recognition of Elisabeth's life as exemplary, his personally motivated violence and arbitrariness could be admired as strategic and necessary to reach an objectively valuable goal, sanctity. Even what he himself had to acknowledge as dubious brutality would thus become justified as the expression of pious devotion. Konrad did not aspire to such self-sanctification as an act of ascetic arrogance but as a measure of moral self-preservation. He could justify tormenting himself and her for as long as his erotic asceticism balanced his jailer's despotism. After her death, his asceticism and the rationalization of his abusive guardianship became pointless. His pedagogy lost its higher purpose despite agonizing self-discipline and addictive sadism. It demanded a revisionist interpretation.

To quiet his self-doubt, Konrad tried to complete Elisabeth's canonization process as quickly as possible. He lobbied the pope with all the means available to him. His perplexity remained, however, and so he searched for new ways to compensate. If he was fully aware of his dilemma, Konrad could only make one of two choices: either self-punishment and dejection or the escalation of his long-established pedagogy. If self-destruction was not his preference, the only solution remaining for him was to destroy the world around him. Following Elisabeth's death, he chose the second option, that of unmitigated mass violence. He shifted from the murder of one to the murder of many. Once again covered by the ruse of legalized proceedings, he projected his previously private cruelties outward. Intensified to an excessive degree, his new activities far surpassed his former deeds.

Konrad's initiation of Elisabeth's canonization process and the burgeoning of his inquisitional pursuits, which made him a central actor in medieval German history, albeit for a short time only, are psychologically interdependent. He could find redemption only if his female victim gained sainthood and only if heretics died by fire and torture. They replaced the slow-moving and unsuccessful "spiritual" soul murder which he missed. The legal role of confessor and religious teacher veiled his lust for the young woman; his role as judge in heresy trials likewise masked his thirst for wholesale destruction. After a year and a half, a violent death freed Konrad of his conflict-ridden psyche.

A Failed Canonization

When the most radical German Franciscan, a "fortified tower of the most holy poverty," closed her eyes forever, she became the cause of a robust inheritance feud. The Teutonic Order of Wiesenfeld soon claimed rights to the hospital by arguing with little evidence that the deceased had designated them as heirs while still alive.[34] It was clearly a case of legacy hunting. Elisabeth, who rejected the request to make a testament in her final hours, could hardly have prepared such provisions earlier. The appropriate, even if not legal, heir should have been the Franciscan order. The Marburg hospital was dedicated to St. Francis as the first Franciscan settlement of its kind in Germany. The founder was a disciple of St. Francis, and Franciscan lay brothers served in the infirmary.

Instead, the deceased's brothers-in-law, Landgraves Heinrich Raspe and Konrad of Thuringia, announced their strong interest in the inheritance.

---

34 Translator's note: Busse-Wilson incorrectly named the Teutonic Order's monastery location as Wiesendahl; the location was Wiesenfeld. See Olaf Schirmeister, "Die Niederlassungen der Johanniter in Breuna, Hiddensee und Warburg durch die Kommende Wiesenfeld," *Zeitschrift des Vereins für hessische Geschichte und Landeskunde* 93 (1988): 49–54.

They emphasized that their former sister-in-law's properties, which provided income for the hospital, were only given to her with a widow's user right, but not an ownership clause. In other words, they were fully entitled to a lay claim to the estate. Not acting on their own claims right away, they first protested the Teutonic Knights' demands before the pope. Master Konrad of Marburg deftly negotiated with the two parties. The pope installed a court of arbitration following of course Konrad's suggestion to resolve the inheritance dispute. The Teutonic Order was advised to submit to Konrad's verdict. They renounced their claims, and the hospital became the property of the Franciscans rather than Elisabeth's kin or any other monastic order. In practical terms, the decision meant that Konrad, although not a Franciscan, remained Elisabeth's true and sole heir as the institution's founder and prefect. He was invested with the ecclesiastical power to censor all enemies of the hospital. Konrad convinced the deceased's brothers-in-law not only to forego the inheritance but also to provide significant new endowments. According to a letter they sent to the pope, the landgraves came to believe that they were the ones who had outfitted the hospice.

Soon after her death, Elisabeth's guardian built or rebuilt close ties with her younger brother-in-law. According to Chaplain Berthold, an eyewitness, Konrad had educated the young man at the Wartburg castle. They must have become estranged, since Elisabeth's extended family did not seem to have favored Konrad of Marburg after Ludwig's death. He had violated custom and the family's interests first by legally securing the widow's property, which the family would have liked to keep for itself, and then, without any scruples, he accompanied Elisabeth to Marburg. Now that Elisabeth was dead, the two men seem to have initiated a rapprochement. The obvious reason was Master Konrad's role as mediator between Marburg and Wartburg inheritance interests. Later, he proved to be a skilled envoy and judge in another affair important to the landgrave. Authorized by the pope, he alone was able to achieve an inheritance settlement between the Thuringian ruler and the bishop of Mainz in February of 1233. The acrimonious inheritance hostilities had flared up with fierce battles and the bishop's excommunication of the aristocrat.

Konrad seems to have transferred his pedagogical efforts at least in part onto Elisabeth's brother-in-law, albeit in greatly weakened measure. It is likely that he encouraged him to join a monastic order. This would have been an especially shrewd step, since the young landgrave chose Hesse as his special territorial focus after Elisabeth's death. In any case, the young man fell under Konrad's influence. The Poverella's guardian turned out to be the winner in both political and ecclesiastical domains. He remained the publicly acknowledged hospital prefect. To improve Elisabeth's relatively paltry foundation—hospital, living quarters, and chapel were half-timbered buildings—he immediately began with the construction of a large church, the public memorial of his success. The undertaking was financed with the recent endowments by Elisabeth's brothers-in-law. The cost of the church construction absorbed funds set aside for the destitute and thus ran counter to Elisabeth's original wishes for her institution. While an ascetic in his personal life, Konrad deemed a lavish church to house her grave indispensable and prestigious. Furthermore, he intended the church as a stage for his sermons. Once completed, the hospital's foundation, transferred with such foresight to his Hessian home territory, would turn into a site-specific magnet. But one piece was still missing to cement his claim to power at the hospital: the pious and charitable founder Elisabeth needed to become a saint.

Elisabeth's canonization was intended to initiate the cult of her grave and to augment the hospital's reputation. Its halo would make it rise above other religious endowments of its era. Most of all, Konrad could shore up his own reputation in tandem with his ward's highest honors. He wished it to be recognized that Elisabeth was truly a candidate for sainthood. As her spiritual father and teacher, he had molded her life so that it became holy. What a consecration of his paternity. Mary was a plain young woman and commoner yet became the mother of God. In the view of the people, she almost surpassed Christ for this reason. Like Mary, Konrad, a harsh and sober man, disliked by all, could thus become at least half a saint. The pope and common people alike should think, he might have wished, that his pedagogical talents were remarkable because he brought forth such a spiritual daughter. Indirectly, the canonization process afforded him a piece of God's creative energy. Nobody but him generated and augmented the foundation's upright reputation. Now that Elisabeth had died, this is how he planned to become the heir of his ward's reputation of holiness.

This scenario explains why Konrad pursued his goal with tenacity even when the pope rejected his schemes and even though he knew that his pupil did not meet the ecclesiastical criteria for its highest rank. Like nobody else, he knew her life, her volatile aimlessness, the mix of heroic stubbornness and weakness. He knew that she had not been popular, and that she attracted unjustified as well as justified hostility. On the other hand, she was capable of utmost self-sacrifice and virtuous humility. Nonetheless, it was not sufficient to qualify for the highest status the church could bestow.

According to the *Epistola*, Elisabeth's corpse was buried for just one day when a Cistercian monk declared to Konrad and others under oath that he had regained his mental health while at her grave. He had been mentally ill for forty years. Women and children living nearby followed the encouraging and suggestive example. Within a year, the number of miraculous healings at Elisabeth's grave grew to sixty. Indeed, Hessian peasant women were the first to gather the stones that built the church in Elisabeth's honor. To this day, the church building has remained above her grave. The miracles at Elisabeth's grave would have dissipated and been forgotten much like those that occurred at her husband's grave in Reinhardsbrunn if not for the circumstance that someone discovered shrewdly and prudently that they were useful.

Konrad immediately reported these incidents to the pope. He requested bluntly that Elisabeth should join the ranks of the saints. This obvious lack of caution could have only been caused by the compulsive haste that propelled him at the time. As was customary then and is also true today, the church only bestows this highest honor after a certain length of time has passed following the death of the candidate and only when unusual ethical and mental traits have been proven. Gregory IX responded by demanding validation of the miracles. Konrad obliged with a speed that could not have been welcomed by the pope. His report gives the impression that he was aware of the issue and tried to excuse the haste. He related that the bishop of Mainz sojourned in Marburg on St. Laurentius Day while in the company of other high-status ecclesiastics to consecrate two altars in the new church building. The presence of these high-ranking church officials turned into a large public festival that attracted people from across Hesse. Even Caesarius of Heisterbach, whom Konrad had already recruited for his canonization activities, was a witness to the hoopla. Konrad himself presented the commemorative homily. And with some degree of cunning and innocence, he reported that while preaching, he suddenly had the thought to take advantage of the opportunity and use the bishop's visit for a formal hearing of witnesses. At the end of his sermon, he asked those in his audience who had experienced a miraculous healing to reassemble with available witnesses at one o'clock the next day. It seems, however, that the bishop of Mainz did not display much interest in the cases. He ordered only the most notable cases to be recorded. Having more important things to do than to pay attention to a few unremarkable healings, he departed as soon as possible. These events occurred on August 10, 1232, nine months after Elisabeth's death. Without delay, Konrad sent the abridged transcripts of the miracles to the pope even though they were not notarized correctly since most of the church officials did not have their seals with them. Furthermore, half of the miracle accounts did not include the names and reports of witnesses.

He added a sketch of Elisabeth's life, titled *Summa vitae* and now known as the *Epistola*, which eventually became one of the two main sources for Elisabeth's work and life.

The pope responded to Konrad's canonization papers as early as October 14, 1232, noting that "not everything is gold that shines, and not all is ivory that looks white. We may proceed with speed in perfectly certain situations but must be cautious when in doubt." This was undoubtedly a rejection of Konrad's hasty proceedings. It communicated that the enclosed biography and everything else known to the pope was insufficient to canonize her. Her virtues were undeniably as white as snow, but they were not ivory. Her merits were admirable, but not pure gold. At the same time, Konrad was irreplaceable as Rome's crucial and most loyal support of the controversial inquisition in Germany. The pope did not want to say no outright. To replace the improper and shoddy testimonials, he asked for a second proceeding, which was tasked to document miracles with juridical precision.

Konrad fanatically continued to pursue his goals. In October 1232, he had received the Roman Curia's objections, that is, the whitewashed rejection of the canonization proceedings. As soon as the beginning of the following year, a new commission began its work. It consisted of the bishop of Mainz, the abbot of Eberbach, and Konrad himself, who now conducted a flawless interrogation of witnesses. It formed the basis for the *Epistola examinatorum miraculorum sancte Elyzabeth*. The documentation met the demands of a legitimate canonization process except that the application inconvenienced the pope. He expressed his sentiments quite openly by demanding that the new miracle accounts be sealed and stored until a special papal envoy brought them to Rome. It was apparently his wish to delay the matter temporarily. Nonetheless, Konrad rushed to send a copy to Rome immediately. The pope returned the miracle accounts and biography to the commission through the Teutonic Knights to Master Hermann of Salza, thus signaling that a canonization was out of the question. When he commented in a letter that even the new protocols were not sufficient, he was most likely searching for formal faults to rid himself of Konrad's intrusive request or at the very least to postpone a decision. He sent another set of instructions. The primary sources do not reveal whether Konrad continued his efforts. In any case, they remained unsuccessful.

Konrad's obtrusiveness placed the pope in an awkward position. He had already been troubled by a precedent, the early canonization of Francis, which took place a mere two years after his death. Francis' religious intensity, however, ignited all of Europe. And now he was asked to canonize the widow of the landgrave of Thuringia only a few months after her death without being convinced that she was a candidate for sainthood. He could not concede this matter, even to his most faithful servant and political deputy.

Konrad did not even notice that his request disturbed the pope. He pursued his project with such blind zeal that he abandoned political savviness, which was his earlier trademark. It is proof that he was guided more strongly by irrational than rational motivations, which resemble the disturbing impulses that propelled his inquisitorial purges. In the deepest layers of his unconscious mind, his actions were compelled by a barely acknowledged bad conscience and the irredeemable damage he had inflicted on the now dead woman.

The Roman Curia tabled Konrad's canonization requests for his ward. A few months after the proceedings, Konrad was murdered. The canonization appeared to have failed. Elisabeth of Thuringia was in danger of sinking into obscurity, the fate of many who had lived a life of suffering. Caused by a surprising turn in family politics, she achieved official sainthood after a few years nonetheless.

Konrad of Marburg as Grand Inquisitor

In the early decades of the thirteenth century, the church fought a life-or-death struggle for her survival. Even the Reformation did not pose a threat of that magnitude. From Scotland to Spain, so-called heretics, in other words, religious sects, had formed conventicles that resisted the authority of the church. The abundance of heretical efforts to become spiritually and organizationally independent reveals how much the loss of the church's moral and psychological creative energies had grown. Despite a public position of power and the global reach for influence, the papacy's inner core never looked worse than at this time. The fanatical intensity with which heretics were persecuted must be understood against the background of an ecclesiastical sense of existential threat.

The most significant of the movements that embraced poverty and stirred the minds of Western Europe since the beginning of the thirteenth century was Francis of Assisi's. Luckily, it could be channeled into the calm waters of official churchdom. The Poverello, however, was Italian. He lived and worked under Rome's eyes. The church could therefore assimilate his evangelical movement without a fight. The situation in Germany and France was more difficult. Located in southern France, with a reach all the way to the Rhine region, Albigensians and Waldensians had turned into a dangerous illegal counterforce. Vernacular bibles were secretly passed from hand to hand.

Today, we like to think of the movements as folk religion and spontaneously arising Protestant predecessors.

These movements attempted a return to ancient Christianity. A great many other religious sects were rooted in gnostic traditions, so, for example, the Cathars, Manichees, and Montanists all the way to the pseudo-pagan secret societies, which regressed to a barbarized Germanic paganism.[35] Everywhere, these groups grew and drew libidinal strength from Catholicism's mental atrophy, which the church leadership was unable to eradicate. In a state of conscious rejection of the church, these underground sects operated on different levels of sophistication. The church did not care to take note of such diversity. It was always a mortal sin, because a foreboding of emancipation, to distance oneself from her authority. There was only one remedy: not education and elucidation but persecution and draconic punishment.

The institution of the inquisition was tailor-made for Konrad of Marburg. The system chose him. Here, he could utilize all his virtues: a talent for analysis, a cold bent for destruction, and ruthless determination. It is not clear what kind of heretics stood in Konrad of Marburg's way. As his report to the pope reveals, he only worked with the belief in a barbaric agrarian cult of the devil. For example, he accused the Count of Sayn, the victim of a denunciation, that "the Count was said to have been riding on a crawfish."

In medieval Catholic countries, inquisitional tribunals were considered initially as legal and just. Heresy was a mortal sin. Indeed, secret religious communities outside of the church were considered disreputable and unlawful by ecclesiastics and lay people alike. With an instinct honed by obedience and powerlessness, members of oppressed social groups persecute first and foremost those who refuse to abide by what is officially sanctioned. Historians are wrong to reproach Konrad of Marburg for holding heresy tribunals as such. All primary sources testify that despite the formal legality and a general acceptance of heresy trials at the time, he was a cruel despot; his tribunals were marked by arbitrariness. His abuse of authority was

---

35   Translator's note: The author seems to refer here to the Cathari mentioned originally at the First Ecumenical Council of Nicaea in 325. In the eighth century, John of Damascus also refers to an older heretical group called the Cathari. See Roelof Van den Broek, *Studies in Gnosticism and Alexandrian Christianity*, Nag Hammadi and Manichaean Studies, vol. 39 (Leiden, Netherlands: Brill, 1996). Busse-Wilson's choice to label these developments as "barbarized regression" is rooted in her comparative evolutionary methodology, which studied polytheism not as existing parallel to monotheism, but preceding it in unilinear fashion. See the discussion of her methodology in the introduction. As in other sections of her study, the author subverts the common evolutionary scheme by pointing to a supposedly "more advanced" stage's internal contradictions and flaws.

pronounced and terrifying. It reduced the inquisition in Germany to absurd-ity. Konrad established a reign of terror through a system of denunciations and executions that lost all resemblance to legal proceedings. It lasted for almost two years until an assassination removed him.

It seems like a strange historical accident that Konrad's appointment as grand inquisitor coincided with the death of his penitent. In May 1232, four heretics were burned in Erfurt in Konrad's presence. The Erfurt chronicle noted that "countless" others in Thuringia and Hesse ended at the stake. In Marburg, the Ketzerbach, or Heretics' Creek, is said to have been given its name because the ashes of those burned at the stake were thrown into it. The creek is located behind Elisabeth's hospital. Precisely at the place of Elisabeth's suffering and death, his desire for revenge demanded human sacrifices. Until her death, Konrad ordered hardly any executions despite his far-ranging powers and his undisputed and frequently acknowledged "zeal" in finding and punishing heretics. In 1227, Pope Gregory IX author-ized him as Germany's inquisitor in the same momentous document that granted him the right of patronage in Thuringia before the landgrave left for the Holy Land. However, it is only in the year of Elisabeth's death, 1231, that fierce persecutions of heretics by Bishops Dietrich of Trier and Konrad of Hildesheim begin in Germany. Master Konrad became the bishops' executive arm. Politically, the inquisitorial escalation was enabled by Emperor Friedrich II's heresy laws, ratified in Ravenna in 1232. The law permitted the pope to install the infamous Dominican inquisition in Germany, which operated independently of all secular and ecclesiastical judicial systems.

Activating the basest instincts, Konrad's trial proceedings were exac-erbated in such a way that everybody was admitted as a witness to the prosecution, including personal enemies of the accused and even persons of ill repute. In principle, every Christian was obligated to inform on everybody suspected of heresy without a summons. This duty could be used to ruin people one personally disliked. It created dangerous legal instability. The descendants of heretics lost all titles, ranks, and honors except those who had denounced their own parents. Even more insidious was the treatment of the accused. They were refused access to legal support. The insistence on their innocence could be interpreted as proof of their guilt. It led to the use of torture and the death penalty. When admitting guilt, however, they could only save themselves by turning in other heretics. Konrad of Marburg topped such cruel legal practices. He promised those who went to the stake insisting on their innocence that they would receive the crown of innocent martyrdom in the afterlife.

Konrad tried to surpass the "Dogs of the Lord" (*Domini canes*) and their perfidious proceedings. On October 11, 1231, shortly before Elisabeth's death, a papal missive urged him to intensify his inquisitorial work. To make him feel secure in his position, he only had to report to the papal seat and received the privilege that his decisions could not be appealed by another court. According to the missive, he was not to concern himself with any examination of the legality of his cases. Konrad was granted the right to impose ecclesiastical penalties on whoever would try to threaten him on account of such arbitrary and specious legal procedures. German inquisitors were placed above the law and in adition, protected by the German Empire.

All of this indicates that the pope granted Konrad the absolute right to institute courts that operated outside of secular and ecclesiastical jurisdiction. The privilege gave him permission to act like a despot. Indeed, after 1231, all his trials resulted in the death penalty, which was carried out on the same day that the verdict was pronounced. The tribunals ceased to qualify as proper trials. If the accused could not point out other heretics in their deeply unsettled state of mind and mortal fear, Konrad himself provided names and thus forced new incriminations. He was so keen on rounding up new victims that he fell for crude fraud. For example, while in Bingen, he interrogated Adelheid, a twenty-year-old woman of dubious reputation, who declared herself a heretic. Since her husband had died, she, too, wished to die. But, she added cunningly, if she was allowed to live, she would be willing to name a great number of other heretics. At that, she denounced all in-laws with whom she was at odds. Since Konrad did not see through her ruse, he condemned many innocent persons to a painful death. In a letter to the pope, the archbishop of Mainz, while a supporter of the inquisition, noted, "and thus, brother accuses brother, the wife her husband, the lord his indentured servants. Some offered money to those who were already shorn [as a sign of being condemned as heretics] so that they could offer advice on how to escape danger. All of this caused unheard of confusion."[36]

Konrad created a climate of paralyzing dread. In the grip of a fear-based collective psychosis, which insinuated that one could be imprisoned and condemned to death at a moment's notice due to as little as a trivial observation by others, everybody tried to deflect even the shadow of a suspicion.

---

36 Those who confessed to be heretics had their hair cut above their ears as a kind of branding. Next, they were publicly flagellated in the church. At the beginning of the inquisition, these punishments seemed sufficient until Innocent III declared "The fear of a death sentence is a beneficial means to heal the soul." Spiritual authorities, such as St. Bernard and St. Hildegard did not approve of the death sentence except in rare cases.

Whenever Konrad preached against heretics, his audience collected wood and straw to burn their very own neighbors. In inciting the masses, which he knew how to do well, Konrad attempted to justify his arbitrariness. He did not even refrain from staging lynchings. This is proof that the persecution of heretics was not a judicial matter but a series of pogroms. In German history, witch trials paralleled his method.

Konrad tried to preempt opposition among secular and ecclesiastical ruling elites by eliciting their support or by sowing division among them. He made the corrupt offer to confiscate the property of heretics on behalf of regional rulers, with half of it given to secular, and the other half to religious leaders in the region. Until his proposal, royal law had decreed that the property had to either be returned to the lawful heirs or to their feudal lords. While Konrad bribed the secular and religious powerful with material goods, he also leveraged the inquisition against his political enemies, a suspicion that has been voiced in the case of the Count of Sayn.[37]

Historians have rarely acknowledged Konrad's diabolical actions and the inquisition's monstrosities. A decidedly Protestant historiography has frequently pointed the finger at the system as such, and exonerated Konrad as a result. Yet given his intellectual and political powers, it is not enough to simply assign Konrad the role of a minion of the law. Rather, as evidenced in the earliest chronicles, which considered heresy worthy of punishment, he was considered from the start a cruel fiend who exceeded any permissible limits set by even radical papal contemporaries.

Konrad's rejection of any political rationality while allowing himself to be guided by his frightening instincts is fully confirmed by his pact with two dreary companions, who had already undertaken heresy persecutions of their own in the Rhine region. These were a lay brother of the Dominican order named Konrad Tors and a secular priest named Johannes. They claimed to "possess the gift to recognize a heretic by mere sight." In other words, they captured and burned whoever took their fancy. They also incited common people to sniff out heretics. According to the Worms Chronicle, their activities "did not conform to Holy Scripture, and clerics everywhere were very distressed." Not only lay people but clerics also grumbled against these "judges without skill or mercy."

When the situation for these two criminals became too hot, they tried to seek the protection of Konrad, who enjoyed papal authorization and was

---

37   Count Heinrich III von Sayn was an influential personality in the archbishopric of Mainz, Thuringia's long-standing rival. Konrad, however, represented Thuringian interests as demonstrated in his negotiations between Landgrave Ludwig and the archbishop of Mainz. The latter had also criticized Konrad's inquisitorial proceedings and submitted complaints to the pope.

licensed "to take on assistants from anywhere." One of them, Johannes, was a "totus nequam," an entirely good for nothing. Missing an eye and a hand, he was one of those shady figures who searched for revenge for their own disfigurement by mutilating others, in this case, executing as many victims as possible. In collusion with such pogrom-hungry criminals, Konrad built his reign of terror with a frightening death squad driven by asocial cruel instincts. "In towns and villages, they asked to arrest whomever they liked, and handed them without proof to [secular] judges, who were forced to burn them." In the end, even the appearance of legal proceedings was abandoned. According to the Sponheim Chronicle, Konrad merely pronounced, "Send the wretched heretic to his fiery death" when a suspect was presented to him, since "the number of the condemned gave him greater pleasure than the number of the innocent." His victims' fear of death, their pleas and screams at the stake only provoked his need for increasingly vicious pleasures. For two years, he and his uncanny companions ran amok through Germany. The Worms Chronicle recorded,

> The people saw this and moved by fear and compassion, asked, "Why do you proceed in this manner?" They however gave the horrifying answer, "We will burn a hundred innocent persons if only one among them is guilty." Thus, the country trembled in fear of them. Even those in power were helpless.

Even if we consider that Konrad received repeated encouragement to use any means available, and that Germany's political situation favored the rise of a dictatorship, his nearly maniacal drive to stir up hatred, to condemn, and to murder cannot be merely explained by his legal omnipotence. All factors point to the conclusion that the loss of his penitent with whom he had bonded so strongly, had hardened him and changed him deeply. Cohabitation with his abject ward had barely contained his destructive energies. Now, having become psychologically homeless and "without work," he directed them without restraint toward other targets. She had ceased to exist whose fear and tears constituted his raison d'être. Other deaths, and as many as possible, had to compensate him for hers. An absence of 'quality' was filled with 'quantity.' Konrad had a vague sense that he was guilty of the landgravine's destruction. The unscrupulous and excessive progression of his cruelty became the means by which he diffused the threat of retrospective moral doubt.

This kind of escape is not possible for modern humans. The victory of critical nonauthoritarian thinking does not permit the religious cover-up of our emotional lives. In the Middle Ages, a religious cover-up still provided self-assurance and encouraged unscrupulousness for all those who could lay claim to a higher authority.

Konrad of Marburg's Death of Atonement

All dictators in history fall because they become too self-assured. They lose a sense of reality, that is, an ability to recognize danger, because of a lack of resistance from the outside and a lack of self-control from within. In the case of Konrad, his lack of self-awareness and attentiveness to the impact of his actions are even more notable, because he was once able to pursue practical and rational goals with circumspection and success. In the past, this included a peaceful resolution of the conflict between the archbishop of Mainz and the landgrave of Thuringia; the management of inheritance quarrels regarding the Marburg hospital property and its economic stability; initiating the construction of a large church; and his extensive activities as a preacher, which attracted a growing number of people to Marburg. All of this testifies to his previous prudence and presence of mind. It proves that for Konrad, the inquisition's excess signified not an administrative judicial incompetence but the discharge of his most frightening instincts.

In the frenzy of his need to numb himself, Konrad lost any measure of the limits to his power. Even thoughtful admonitions did not bring him to his senses. The archbishop of Mainz warned him to proceed with restraint and moderation. He later reiterated his disapproval together with the bishops of Trier and Cologne. As a final measure, the ecclesiastical dignitaries, who were self-professed and eager supporters of the inquisition, submitted formal complaints to the pope. They sensed that Konrad's arbitrariness undermined the reputation of the church rather than affirming it. The tribunals also curtailed their own judicial authority as bishops. Yet growing ecclesiastical resistance only provoked Konrad to increase his fury of wanton destruction. According to the Trier Chronicle, "Filled with personal recklessness, he became so bold that fearing nobody, a king and bishop counted for as little as a poor lay person."

The persecutions of heretics in the thirteenth century and those of witches in subsequent centuries share one substantial similarity. The objects of these pogroms were almost exclusively people of the lower classes and those who were without social influence and protection. In most cases, witches were proletarian women without family. They were harmless and old. Likewise, initially only peasants and burghers were the heretics of the thirteenth century who climbed onto a pyre. Made to feel secure by a lack of opponents, Konrad eventually dared to attack members of high noble rank, the leaders among aristocrats. It was to be his downfall.

At the beginning, it appears that he was able to generate a psychotically fearful atmosphere among some members of this rank, such as the counts of Solms, Arensberg, and Looz. Even though innocent, Count Henry of Solms professed himself a heretic and like many others, was thus able to save his life. Yet merely the suspicion of heresy was considered an absolute dishonor. It destroyed a man who lived a public life in full view of his peers and the population at large.

Finally, Konrad's despotism was shattered by one of the aristocrats. Konrad had summoned the count of Sayn to his tribunal. Belonging to the Hessian nobility, the count was known as a good Catholic and loyal son of the church. He neither capitulated nor allowed himself to be intimidated. It was the first time that someone opposed Konrad's terror. Blinded by his authority, Konrad went to extremes. He insisted on the count's summons. The case was referred to the royal assembly of noblemen at Mainz.

Konrad of Marburg's appearance at the assembly, which was called to order by King Henry on July 25, 1233, revealed a violent anarchist's self-assurance. The assembly's collective strength counted for nothing if someone like him had permission to challenge secular and religious rules with calm insolence. Since papal authority backed him, his ability to get his will turned into a contest of power between the inquisitor's camp and the rest of the ecclesiastical caste. Even though one of the main tasks of the assembly was to fight heresy, the mood turned against Konrad the inquisitor. He had gone too far. He appeared as plaintiff, but in the eyes of the people and the religious and secular authorities, he was the accused.

The count of Sayn defended himself courageously against the accusation of heresy and asked for an acquittal. The witnesses of the prosecution abandoned Konrad and retracted their statements. Konrad was put to shame, and his case was revealed as a farce. According to the Trier Chronicle, the archbishop of Trier took the side of the duke. Protecting him from Konrad, he demanded, "My Lord and King desires that the trial will be postponed." Turning to the assembly, he emphasized," The count of Sayn will leave as a respected Catholic man and not as a man proven guilty." He thus removed him from Konrad's judicial powers. Yet the latter insisted on keeping his victim and declined to drop his accusations. He could not prevail against the collective might of an aristocratic assembly and was left to gripe, "If the count would have been convicted, matters would be quite different." Immediately thereafter, the count of Sayn travelled to Rome to submit complaints to the papal court furnished with letters from the king and the archbishops of Mainz and Trier. This was the first time that Konrad's dictatorship had collapsed. The contemporary authors of the Trier Chronicle commented, "The count of Sayn became a fence so that the godless rampage could not spread any further."

Konrad suffered a damaging public defeat in full view of all of Germany. His rage nearly boiled over. To get even, at least in his own eyes, he immediately began to preach crusades against heretics while still in Mainz and with the aristocratic assembly still in session. His aim was to incite the people and encourage denunciations. It was hinted that he should leave for his own security. King Henry and the archbishop of Mainz offered him armed escorts. He either did not suspect that he was in danger or, defiantly, rejected the overture. This sealed his death. He left to return home but never reached the Marburg hospital. A few miles outside of Marburg, he was attacked and murdered. The assassins consisted of the duke of Dörenbach and other supporters of the count of Sayn. The vigilantes also included the relatives of those executed by Konrad who were eager for a vendetta and others who were afraid to become the inquisition's next victims. Caesarius of Heisterbach notes that Konrad was accompanied by the Franciscan lay brother Gerhard of Lützelkolb. In a later source, twelve religious and secular companions are mentioned.

Konrad's last moments reveal much of the character of this strange man. Facing death, the violent judge of heretics in Germany broke down. He is said to have tearfully begged for mercy. For the first time in this life, but too late, he abandoned a posture of masculine authority. He is afraid, he begs. He who never cried and who was not softened by Elisabeth's death, he who without compassion condemned many to a violent death, collapsed and became submissive when he was threatened with violence. He experienced what he had dodged before. His assassins' answer to his pleading was "Beat him to death, the cruel man. He showed mercy to none." In death, Konrad lost everything, even the blessing of a death without struggle. He lived through panic and fear of death in the verbal exchange with his executioners. He experienced the lethal blows while being fully conscious. The Trier Chronicle concluded, "Thus Germany was freed of this egregious and cruel judge in accordance with divine counsel." While Konrad's final moments lacked honor and heroism, Elisabeth's death triumphed over suffering and sorrow.

Yet one person truly loved the ogre, whose death elicited prayers of gratitude. The assassins intended to spare Gerhard so as not to spill innocent blood, since Gerhard had nothing to do with the executions. He embraced the master's body with such desperate force that the two could not be torn apart. Caesarius of Heisterbach wrote, "Because they loved each other their whole lives, they could not be separated in death." This is all that tradition has to say about the man who remained faithful to Konrad unto death. It was the same man who was ordered to beat Elisabeth and Irmingard at the Altenberg monastery while Konrad sang the Miserere. Elisabeth's humiliation at Altenberg was now atoned for. The lives of three people linked in a ghastly tragedy came full circle. To symbolize their connection, Konrad and Gerhard were buried next to Elisabeth in the hospital chapel. After a few years, their remains were transferred to the magnificent new church, which was built above the old chapel by the Teutonic Knights. In death, the former landgravine of Thuringia does not rest at the side of her husband but next to the owner of her soul, who followed her after two years of blind and fanatic rage.

Despite all his uncanniness, Konrad is a tragic figure. Though he culti-vated the art of suffering like many great historical personalities, his type of affliction was diametrically opposed to Elisabeth's. He was already hardened and incapable of salvation when he met the woman with whom he became obsessed. In a case of libidinous attraction between two complementary personality types, he was and remained void of erotic feeling. In this heart-less union, he lived with the fear of having to change. To avoid becoming gentle and humane, forgiving, and courteous, he destroyed what should have redeemed him. Yet the loss of his aristocratic victim threw him even more off course. Her death plunged him into actions of nearly unlimited destruction. Elisabeth was able to save herself through an early death. Konrad could redeem himself only through the murder of others. In his life of St. Ludwig, Chaplain Berthold wrote about Konrad of Marburg, "Following the saying of the wise Salomon, who can know whether one has deserved divine friendship or divine hatred? All things of this earth will be weighed in the life to come and will be fully known at that time."

In all of Germany, Konrad's assassination was experienced as liberation. A nightmare had ended. At the Frankfurt assembly, which listed Konrad's murder on its agenda, a high-ranking church official even dared to state, "Konrad deserves that his corpse be exhumed and burned." An uprising threatened to take place when Bishop Konrad of Hildesheim and a Domini-can by the name of Otto, two unreformed supporters of the hated man, dared to defend him. They had to flee for their lives. Soon, the one-eyed and one-armed Johannes and Konrad Tors, Konrad's two other assistants, were disposed of. One was stabbed to death in Alsatia, the other hanged in Hesse. The slack persecution of these two crimes by secular authorities proves how much Konrad's activities as inquisitor were hated by the laity. Only the pope bemoaned the deaths. He issued letter upon letter detailing the continuation of the inquisition, yet no German ecclesiastical authorities followed suit except for Bishop Konrad of Hildesheim. The pope excommunicated Konrad's executioners and declared an interdict for every citizen or town that would harbor them. Yet these were protestations in name only. It is not known whether his heavy penances were ever enforced.

Nonetheless, the assassins presented themselves to a secular court. Half a year later, in February of 1234, the royal assembly in Frankfurt decided their case. No secular punishments were issued, but they received the advice to seek ecclesiastical absolution. All of Germany thus approved of their deed. In addition, the assembly rehabilitated the count of Solms and other victims of Konrad who had confessed to be heretics under mortal duress. The heresy laws as such remained in force and were applied in years to come. Trials, however, now followed legal regulations. According to the Trier Chronicle, "Since then, the terrifying persecutions ended. The horrific era, which was without precedent since the days of the heretical emperor Constantius and the apostate Julian, began to give way to friendlier times."

Achieving Sainthood Through Politics

Two years after Konrad's murder, Elisabeth attained sainthood. In part, it was a posthumous success of Konrad's efforts to garner the highest honor for his ward. However, it could come about only because of new political circumstances in Marburg. With Konrad's death, the local hospital had lost its leader and representative. Although it was orphaned, Konrad's sound political strategies came to bear fruit. Likely because of his advice and recommendation, Thuringian landgrave Konrad entered the Order of the Teutonic Knights one year after the inquisitor's death. The landgrave's avid pursuit of heretics even after Konrad's execution testifies to his dependence on his religious mentor. At the time, the Teutonic Knights were dedicated to hospital care, originally for wounded and sick crusaders, as a kind of chivalric Red Cross. No other religious order was as qualified to take over the Marburg hospital as the Teutonic Knights. In July 1234, the third year after Elisabeth's peaceful death, the hospital became officially transferred to the order. A papal decree ordered the Franciscans, the previous owners of the hospital, to recognize the Teutonic Knights as the new masters. The Thuringian landgraves made numerous rich donations to the newcomers. In the fall, the now definitive heirs of the Poverella of Marburg began to build their new settlement. Their convent was erected near the hospital. When Landgrave Konrad joined the order, his sister-in-law's property and funds served as his dowry—a clever combination, since a family member benefitted from Elisabeth's inheritance, which was invested in the hospital, yet without withdrawing it from the church.

The new foundation required one important asset to increase its monastic reputation and income. The hospital's founder had to be canonized. Before his official entry into the order, Landgrave Konrad traveled to the pope in Rieti. Like Elisabeth's foster father, he had no luck in advancing her case. Even though he was honored and taken under papal protection as a zealous persecutor of heretics, the highest ecclesiastical authority remained unmoved and rejected the canonization of a pious and charitable widow, one among many like her. Although Konrad II returned to Germany with a rejection, he joined the Teutonic Knights with nine aristocratic companions in commemoration of the anniversary of Elisabeth's death, on November 18, 1234. In the meantime, healing miracles at her grave site multiplied.

There was hope that their official recognition would eventually be successful since the Teutonic Knights enjoyed political influence and were imperial protégés. The pope must have had a certain interest in seeking the order's loyalty precisely because of their imperial allegiance. By granting the substantial favor for one of its members, the pope could thus pull the Thuringian dynasty on his side. Furthermore, the canonization process was expensive. The Teutonic Knights were wealthy. This ensured that unofficial fees did not need to be paltry. On the other hand, the Thuringian landgravine's house could not accept a rejection of the canonization. If the pope turned down Landgrave Konrad, he turned down an eminent family of the highest aristocratic rank in German lands. The success of Elisabeth's canonization would double the prestige for a monastic order and a dynasty. After Landgrave Konrad joined the order, he traveled to Italy once more, but now accompanied by aristocrats of the Teutonic Knights. He believed that he could justify the canonization of his deceased sister-in-law with stronger church political reasons and pursued the matter with every emphasis possible. Finally, after long negotiations and with access to key officials, the canonization process was reinstated apace.

In January 1235, only two months after that journey, Bishop Konrad of Hildesheim ordered a new procedure to document the miracles at Elisabeth's grave and to interrogate four persons who had lived with Elisabeth, primarily to garner the required proof of the candidate's Christian virtues. This is the origin of the *Libellus*. As noted, it contains statements by Elisabeth's female friends Guda and Isentrud and by her two female servants in Marburg, Elisabeth and Irmingard. Done correctly, Elisabeth's family ought to have been interrogated as well. However, since Elisabeth had been much too controversial in her husband's family, Konrad likely suggested omitting this step.

With the formal inquiries concluded, a delegation departed to submit the documents to the pope. The delegation was led by the former landgrave and now Teutonic knight Konrad and Abbot Bernhard of Buch. As early as Pentecost of the same year, on May 27, 1235, the former landgravine of Thuringia was officially declared a saint. Elated about the result of much labor and effort, Brother Konrad organized a splendid celebration. He donated precious chandeliers to the church and distributed thick wax candles among the people to be burned in honor of the new saint. He invited three hundred clerics as guests. In turn, the pope admitted him to his table as a special honor. The declaration of sainthood was staged, with no expenses spared, in the Dominican church at Perugia, a town near Assisi where the pope was staying at the time.

The canonization was accomplished by the mutually beneficial interplay between the landgraves of Thuringia and Hesse, whose lands were adjacent to each other, and the power politics of a prominent monastic order. Yet modern literary authors and scholars have always reasoned that it derived from its object. How overwhelming must the deceased Elisabeth's charitable work have been in the eyes of her own contemporaries that she was canonized a mere four years after her death. The gist of this argument has in effect never been abandoned. At most, modern writers might have seen an effort on the part of the landgravine's dynasty to right posthumously the wrongs Elisabeth suffered through their actions. In truth, at least as far as her two brothers-in-law were concerned, the family had only one opinion of her. In their letter to the pope, they intimated that she was a simpleton who caused them plenty of grief. Lacking a bad conscience, it seemed all the more necessary for their family honor to rehabilitate her status. Elisabeth had embarrassed them too many times to forget that she had renounced home and hearth and behaved scandalously while in Eisenach.

In contrast, medieval religious authors such as Caesarius of Heisterbach thought it necessary to posit exceptional motivations for the hurried zeal with which the brother of the Teutonic Knights lobbied for his sister-in-law's canonization. Naturally, he too reversed cause and effect. After her death, Elisabeth's miraculous healings were so widespread, objectively real, and apparent to all that her brother-in-law Konrad felt compelled to demand her canonization. And when he fell sick while in Rome, Elisabeth herself appeared to him and promised to bring him back to health through her prayers. In this manner, she proved herself to be a saint even while he was still lobbying for her canonization—it was as if she had personally confirmed his mission.

Elisabeth's life and death did not leave a big impression on the wider public for the simple reason that she died young. Nobody beyond Thuringia and

Hesse's borders knew of her. And in those regions, as already noted, she did not count for much. As a young woman and landgravine, she had provoked her aristocratic peers. She often fought and argued with her extended family. There was also the peculiar relationship with her confessor. Although she seemed to desire personal poverty like St. Francis, her confessor had to take legal action against her relatives and forcefully retrieve her widow's inheritance. When he succeeded, she took off with her defender. While she obeyed him in all matters, she failed in her duty to submit to her mother-in-law and brothers-in-law more than once. She could not even keep house. As a widow and as a landgravine, she lavished money on the poor but neglected her peers and kin.

In short, the conspicuously rushed canonization process, which was not even preceded by a customary beatification, surprised contemporaries. Some observers were even forced into a stance of critical disapproval. The *Libellus* closes with the words of its compiler, Brother Nikolaus: "May there be peace at her grave and all slander silenced." The statement suggests that even ecclesiastical circles found her canonization controversial. It alienated religious groups who championed their own candidates for sainthood. They interpreted the Landgravine Elisabeth's preferential treatment, a woman nobody had heard of before, as an unjustified, or at least disproportionate honor for a woman who, in a religious sense, had not been overly productive. Only the visionary Mechthild of Magdeburg, who lived in contemplative tranquility and far removed from ecclesiastical politics, saw the canonization as cause for meditation. She wrote in a chapter about five new saints:

> I feel as if I lose my senses, because I am so astonished when looking at the noble character of saintliness and the sick and fallen humanity. I wonder why it happened so quickly that St. Elisabeth became a saint and died. Our Lord instructed me and said, "It is the right and virtue of a messenger to act swiftly."

Yet God's messengers would not have been that swift if Elisabeth had been not the landgravine of Thuringia but a peasant girl. Despite the undeniable merits that she possessed in terms of medieval religiosity, as a peasant woman, Elisabeth would never have been discovered or if so, only with much delay. And she certainly would not have become the most popular German saint. Sanctity follows the same rules as secular fame. Whoever got a good start in life based on birth and lines of succession has more of a chance that their actions will find recognition than those who first must find a way out of the anonymous majority. Much touted endeavors in religion and politics would perhaps not even be noted as top achievements if accomplished by members of a lower social class.

This explains why numerous highly significant religious personalities never achieved official sainthood. No order, no dynasty, in short, nobody powerful rose to show interest in the renown that their protégé could add to their reputation. Mechthild of Magdeburg, Elisabeth's most distinguished female contemporary, never achieved sainthood. Also numbered among the forgotten and disregarded is Landgrave Ludwig, Elisabeth's spouse. His grave in Reinhardsbrunn was the cause of miracles and extraordinary healings as well, but his status has remained that of a folk saint. Nobody was willing to pursue an official canonization process. Yet his unhappy wife, whose religious and personal autonomy was crushed in a master-slave relationship, achieved the aura of highest Catholic prominence with outrageous speed.

Landgrave Konrad, her confessor, the Teutonic Knights, and even the pope did not act entirely without faith in Elisabeth's remarkable extraordinariness. One argument weighed too strongly in favor of her saintly status: the miracles that took place at her grave and which continued without interruption to advertise her case. They lifted the unknown and unnoticed woman to the rank of a female visionary and miracle worker who lived in close relationship with the divine. No doubt, as was required, it was also examined whether Elisabeth had lived a virtuous and pious life. Yet her person, life, and works only attracted attention once the miraculous cures at her grave became known. Her oldest admirers and devotees approached her canonization merely as believers in miracles.

In preparation for the celebration of her newly gained fame in German lands, Elisabeth's miracle-working corpse had to be arranged and displayed properly. It was her cult's most precious substance. Three days before the feast day, Brother Ulrich, the prior of the Teutonic Knights, and seven other monks, went to the church in the dark of night. They locked the church door and began to dig up the ground. When they removed the stone slab—Elisabeth was laid to rest in a burial chamber—the cadaver suddenly emitted such a pleasant fragrance that they stood in awe and praised the Lord. They knew that the sacred body had not been embalmed or buried with aromatic spices. And yet, it was not decomposed. And still, her hands were crossed over her chest. Even though the corpse had been buried for five years! Caesarius of Heisterbach concludes his biography by proposing, "While still alive, the humble servant of the Lord, ignited by her love for Christ, did not eschew the stench and grime of the poor. For this reason, her corpse was free of any type of impurity and the odor of putrefaction."

The monks proceeded to prepare the cadaver. Skin and hair were removed from the skull. With all likelihood, the corpse was then treated as was customary for deceased secular and religious dignitaries, including the preservation of Elisabeth's dead spouse in Italy. According to Landgrave Ludwig's hagiographic biography, "They dug up the noble corpse and cooked it until the bones separated. The skeleton was as white as new snow." As a dreadful transaction in the service of generating a saint's cultic veneration, the preparation of the valuable carcass was doubly gruesome given the meager technical means and anatomical knowledge of the time. Nonetheless, the saint rewarded her devotees. It was reported that her bones exuded tears of sweat, "an aromatic oil" that pilgrims to her shrine poured into small flasks to take with them. Who could still doubt that the woman was exceptional? Finally, the skeletal remains were wrapped in red silk and placed into a sumptuous reliquary that still exists today, for Elisabeth was now tasked with adding a numinous dignity to the hospital's church.

On May 1, 1236, a group of high social rank gathered for the so-called translation. It included the Hessian and Thuringian aristocracy, all in-laws of the canonized Elisabeth, such as her mother-in-law Sophie, Landgrave Heinrich Raspe, and the Teutonic Knight Konrad, who was the actual host and master of ceremonies, and likely also her three children, who were fourteen, twelve, and nine years of age at the time. Nobody of her own family in Hungary attended, which proves the narrow local political interests at play in the canonization process.

However, there was one more guest. Immediately after Elisabeth's sainthood became official, and as a finishing touch, Landgrave Konrad, now a Teutonic Knight, hurried to the imperial diet in Mainz to ask Emperor Friedrich II for his appearance at the translation ceremony. The emperor agreed, but not because of the deceased herself and her extraordinary significance. He intended to demonstrate his devotion to the official canonization of a pious Christian woman. The relationship between the fully Latinized and enlightened emperor, the papacy, and German vassals was difficult enough. Only recently, in a major ritual murder lawsuit, he did not side against the Jews. An act of flagrant religious laxity, it annoyed secular as well as religious circles. His participation was even more disarming and necessary because of it, and he could bestow highest honors on the landgravine's family.

In recognition of the deceased's Franciscan lifestyle, the emperor attended the ceremony barefoot and clad in undyed garments. He donated jewels for the pitiful remains of the emaciated and careworn woman, a precious crown for Elisabeth's skull, and placed a chalice in the skeleton's hand. Caesarius noted that never did such a large crowd gather as at that celebration. It was almost impossible to enter the church because of the congestion caused by the arrivals and departures of visitors. Masses were sung. Sermons were given. The Teutonic Knights commissioned Caesarius to compose a commemorative text, the *Vita S. Elisabeth*, which would offer an account of the saint's life and virtues. He had some experience in this genre, having written a biography of a Rhenish saint who also did not convince everybody of his claims to such ecclesiastical honors.[38]

It is a historical paradox that this canonization, which succeeded because of political maneuvering, was driven by local politics and dynastic interests on a national level on one hand and fed by a naïve-atavistic folk fetishism on the other.[39] Nonetheless, it concerned itself with an authentically holy person in the absolute and timeless sense of the word. As is true of the greatest representatives of sainthood in Christianity, Elisabeth paid for her religious ideal with her life. She endured a martyrdom only a few had experienced. Mentally dependent and not entirely free of critical character deficits, her human stature is more devastating than that of many other, more important medieval personalities. She had won the palm of a true martyr because of the many reasons for her personal suffering, the self-aware sacrifice of her femininity, and her deliberate choice of self-annihilation. Her advocates and champions, whether they were sly politicians or artless fetishists, could not apprehend what monstrous battles she had to fight to reach such timeless sanctity.

The second historical irony of the posthumous translation lies in the fact that those who now celebrated Elisabeth, and as such themselves, were hated with such passion by the deceased while she was still alive. Her life was lived

38 Translator's note: The saint was the murdered St. Engelbert, Archbishop of Cologne, whose life, death, and miracles Caesarius collated in a hagiography entitled *Actus, passio et miracula domini Engelberte*. See Jacqueline E. Jung, "From Jericho to Jerusalem: The Violent Transformation of Archbishop Engelbert of Cologne," in *Last Things: Death and the Apocalypse in the Middle Ages*, ed. Caroline Walker Bynum and Paul H. Freedman (Philadelphia: University of Pennsylvania Press, 2000), 60–82.

39 Translator's note: Folk religion is not defined in these pejorative terms today, which are now understood as a discursive, epistemologically violent means to justify Western domination of the global South. The "superior" and "civilized" West and its Christian missionaries rationalized imperial violence and extractive economic exploitation in part as the spread of Christian monotheism among "primitive" and less "advanced" peoples. Busse-Wilson's Catholic audience, even and especially if they believed in Western imperial hierarchization of global religions, were tasked to rethink Christianity's presumed apex status where it must have been the most contrarian, at the 700-year celebration of the death of Germany's most revered female saint. Her relics were central to its liturgical commemorations.

as a protest of an aristocratic society that saw her canonization as nothing but a brilliant social spectacle. After only a few decades, the Hohenstaufen dynasty was extinct, and the culture of chivalric high aristocracy ebbed away little by little.

Materiality and the Emergence of a Cult

Elisabeth's fame illuminated three centuries—not because of the ethos of her works or the pathos of her suffering but because of her body's earthly remains. The Teutonic Knights safeguarded this most precious treasure at her grave. It provided them with an influx of religious prestige and substantial prosperity. The character of medieval religiosity is revealed with much greater clarity by the cult of relics than by its much-evoked transcendentalism. Only a minority of theologians and religiously gifted lay people were schooled in the esoteric knowledge of the mind and nature duality that defined a human being. In general, people today vastly overestimate the religious sophistication of medieval society. Unperturbed by official cultic practices, most lay people and clergy subscribed to an ingenuous type of magic. It was this kind of medieval folk religion that propelled the mute sufferer of Marburg to fame.

The veneration of relics and graves is rooted in an archaic pre-Christian cult of materiality. Wood from the cross or from Christ's manger, iron chains, coagulated blood, and the tactile remains of organic life—hair, bones, and scraps of garment—turned into objects of desire and reverence. Medieval magic could change any material object into a simple token of a hero cult. Shreds, scraps, and rags of any kind were embellished with precious artistic trimmings. Aristocrats and monasteries would trade them as gifts.[40] Even wars were waged to own the skeletal remains of holy men and women, because such ownership ensured the economic existence of a monastery or church.

For medieval people, such deification of materiality did not signify a sacrilege but signified the dynamic center of an innocent religiosity. The majority still believed in the unity of body and mind with the church as the custodian of such simple magic. A study of the Franciscan movement

---

40 By necessity, the result of such collectors' passion was the constant forgery of relics. It is comparable to today's counterfeits in the trade of fine art. Translator's note: In this section, Busse-Wilson loops back to her graduate work in art history at the University of Leipzig and the evolutionary theory of ornaments in global context.

is quite instructive in this type of materially minded medieval worldview. St. Elisabeth was not revered in any intellectual fashion. Her fame spread solely because of an archaic folk fetishism. Already a few weeks after her burial, people had scraped a hole next to her grave to use the earth for healing purposes. Yet it would be wrong to interpret the increase of her cult as superstition or mass hysteria or even purely as a perversion and regression of religiosity. As is true for the arts, it is not always the most sophisticated and intellectualized manifestation of religiosity that can convey the deepest experiences of the numinous. A chapel in the countryside that may house an artistically unsophisticated icon, perhaps even only an archaic or barbaric statue of a deity, frequently causes a stronger *tremendum fascinosum* and deeper awe than the invisible concepts of highly abstract theology.[41]

The divine itself is and will remain something frightening and sublime we are afraid to approach. In contrast, saints are demigods and goddesses and protectors with whom we can share our daily concerns. Christian or pagan, humankind needs protection and support. It therefore populates fields and houses, forest, and village with a cadre of sympathetic and powerful beings. In Christian theology, Mary and the saints never reached the status of divinities. Their function is merely that of mediators and confidants. If one does not dare share with the divine that one would like to get rid of gout, that a sick cow should eat again, or that a thunderstorm causes no harm, the semi-human saints will certainly lend their ear.

At an age when civilization had not yet managed to tame natural forces, human vulnerability was greater than we can imagine today. The abstract divinity of modern theology is entirely useless to a farmer who is defenseless against bad luck, bad weather, and bad health. His trinity consists of his farm animals, his hearth, and his fields. For this reason, he erects wayside shrines with the patron saints of farm animals. Medieval religious history is saturated with the miracles of these male and female saints. They exemplify a medieval powerlessness to undo an unbreakable causality through prayers. They demonstrate the degree to which medieval humanity felt overwhelmed and intimidated by experiences and events that are no longer threatening to us today.

41 Translator's note: Busse-Wilson references the German theologian Rudolf Otto (1869–1937) and his still widely read study *Das Heilige: Über das Irrationale in der Idee des Göttlichen und sein Verhältnis zum Rationalen* [*The Idea of the Holy: An Inquiry into the Non-Rational Factor in the Idea of the Divine and its Relation to the Rational*], 1st ed. (Breslau, 1917); current ed. (Munich: C.H. Beck, 2014). Leveraging Otto's theological notion of the divine as *tremendum fascinosum* in discussing "archaic" and "barbaric" stages of religion undermines once again the hierarchical evolutionary model en vogue in bourgeois German circles.

The greatest threat was a multitude of popular diseases. Physical suffering that today's medical arts can cure quickly caused fear and despair among medieval people who lacked any understanding of causality in the natural sciences. For that reason, humans created a host of folk saints for every type of physical unease, among them the saints Vitus, Blasius, Ottilie, Apollonia, and others. Human afflictions thus elected the quiet woman in Marburg's hospital as a healer. Due to well-connected and shrewd protectors such as her successors, the Teutonic Knights, her cult was soon sanctioned by the highest authorities even though the needs of illiterate farming women gave birth to it. To direct feelings of powerlessness, dependency, and privation to standard Christian practices, the medieval church had to acknowledge a developmental stage of faith it had long left behind in its doctrinal deliberations. For this reason, to put it bluntly, the church opted for the veneration of the bodily remains of their greatest men and women as one of its didactic tools.

Thus began the pilgrimages to Elisabeth's mortal remains. Pilgrimages focus on destinations known for unusual events or extraordinary denizens. The secret that shrouded Elisabeth's life turned her grave into a place of mystery and destiny. At the beginning, she was a royal daughter from a country with an unknown language. Then she turned into a lavish benefactress and friend of the poor who drew attention during her short time at Marburg's hospital. She was a foreigner, since Thuringia seemed far away from Hesse; she was not a nun but lived the life of a recluse. Yet none of this would have been sufficient to attract crowds to the hospital church if people had not also been riled up by the psychotic heresy mania in the years following Elisabeth's death. Konrad preached his incendiary sermons at the hospital. To do his bidding, people searched for sinister enemies, accused them, and burned them. Stirred up by the fanatic's suggestive sermons, people also visited the nearby chapel with the deceased's grave. The miracles at the tomb were crafted from a climate of dread and fear.

The first miracle is recorded as early as the spring following Elisabeth's death. A boy is healed who was born blind. According to the *Epistola examinatorum miraculorum*, the miracle occurred during one of Konrad's sermons after the boy's eyes were moistened with a mixture of water and earth taken from her grave, thus highlighting the connection between anti-heretical sermons and burial cult. God stood with orthodox believers against the menacing enemies of the Church and used the poor and weak to prove it. Those who were honored with a miracle gained at least a little bit of pious dignity themselves.

We are thus able to draw a rather precise picture of the medieval dynamics of St. Elisabeth's cult. The pagan magical elements of medieval Christianity survived into the nineteenth century because of the tremendous endurance of popular agricultural mentalities. Until only a few generations ago, rural communities in remote regions, in the Alpine valleys, and especially in Romanophone European countries, practiced a form of religiosity that was quite different from the spiritually abstract Christian type. If members of an archaic-agricultural community seek assistance or healing for themselves or a family member, they 'commit' or 'engage' themselves to the Mother of God or to a saint who works miracles at a specific location.

The relationship between the petitioner and the miracle-working icon is very straightforward. "Lady Elisabeth, if you help me, I will undertake a pilgrimage to your grave and make an offering." ("If not, it will hurt your reputation"). This is the meaning of almost all invocations of the saints. The applicants offer themselves to the saints by consecrating a small wax figure of that part of the body which is diseased and in need of a cure. Arms, hands, legs, also the ears and eyes, lungs, heart, and face were submitted as simple sculptures made of wood or wax.[42] The walls of the Marburg pilgrimage church that surrounded Elisabeth's grave were covered with such votive offerings. A woman offered a wax candle with the length of her sick child's body to ask for a healing. A pilgrim, whose eyelids and face suffered from nervous twitching, gave a mask made of wax. These expressions of Elisabeth's cult testify to the original unity of religion and the healing arts, and the even older double identity of priest and healer. As is still true for contemporary Catholic pilgrimage churches in southern regions, Elisabeth's grave was also surrounded by discarded crutches, intended to testify to the miraculous powers of the holy remains, and small folk paintings representing requests or gratitude that depicted an accident or illness.

Every miracle generates another one. According to the *Epistola examinatorum miraculorum*:

> Gertrudis of Buttla saw how a miracle took place at the grave of Sister Elisabeth. Then she thought of her paralyzed daughter, whom she had left behind at home. She began to cry bitterly and asked a pious woman to join her in a vow to go on pilgrimage.

It would be mistaken to interpret miraculous healings such as those taking place at Elisabeth's grave as conscious or unconscious fraud by patients or pilgrimage administrators, in this case the Teutonic Knights. Most likely,

---

42 Sick women offered turtles, votive offerings that represented the uterus. Spheres had a similar function and were called "little birthing mothers."

all healings were authentic. Frequently, these were only slight cases. People living simple lives in stressful life circumstances tend to overestimate the severity of their physical suffering. Pain and bleeding might be prematurely interpreted as symptoms of serious illness. Today, the reverse is true as well. It is difficult to convince the economically insecure that their health might be in great danger even though a sick person might not look unwell and be without pain. The following miracle story illustrates our point.

A woman was in tears because her three-year-old child could not yet walk. The guardian at St. Elisabeth's grave, a lay brother, asked her to make the child stand on the ground. He showed the child an egg and began to talk to it. The child began to walk a few steps toward the egg along the side of the sarcophagus. The guardian then moved to the other side of the grave and showed the child the egg once more. This ordinary nursery trick was the cause for the "miracle" of the child being able to walk.

Those who are desperate and considered incurable are ready for miracles and invocations. From the inception, their assumptions about their illness and signs of healing are misguided if combined with a lack of careful observation and scientific insight. This explains why resurrections of the "dead" and the healing of blind and deaf-mute people in the name of Elisabeth occurred with such frequency. In the guileless affective worlds of medieval peasants, a boy who lay pale and motionless after a fall into a body of water, or a baby that did not breathe right after birth, immediately were assumed to be dead. In the case of serious illness, even small improvements were a source of contentment. A mother of a hopelessly paralyzed boy who was covered with sores and permanently bed-ridden took a vow to go on pilgrimage to Marburg. As a result, the boy could lift his arm! No mention was made of a full recovery.[43]

Another contributing factor—still observable today—is a simple-minded subjective selectivity to measure the success of a pilgrimage. As is true for fortune telling, only positive results are counted. The much larger number

43 Catholicism after the Middle Ages would not have accepted any of the nearly one hundred miracles that took place at Marburg's grave as divine intervention operating independently of scientific causality. The contemporary church has become extremely cautious and demands the most careful medical and legal protocols and analyses of a case. Already Benedict XIV's (1740–1755) rules for canonization demanded the assessments of five physicians who had to prepare statements about the gravity of an illness (severe, incurable, curable only with great difficulty), whether the illness was in the process of a "crisis" that could turn it around, that no medicines were administered before the miraculous healing, that the patient was healed immediately, and that no regressions occurred, which tended to be kept a secret. None of the miraculous healings at Elisabeth's grave measured up to these criteria. Indeed, they are evidence for anything but a meticulous *probatio miraculorum*.

of negative outcomes were kept secret because they did not noticeably change the previous degree of suffering. It remained the same. The miracle accounts did not report any failures. Even those healings that were registered did not always take place at the first pilgrimage. Frequently, they had to be repeated two or three times in a row.

Once, a man stayed in Marburg for four weeks without any success. A woman with a sick child prayed for twelve days at the grave. Only on her way home could a change be observed in the child's condition. It speaks volumes that a separate graveyard was built nearby for pilgrims who died empty-handed. Nonetheless, the site remained immensely popular. Pilgrims arrived not only from Hesse but also from the Rhön mountains and environs, even from Koblenz and Wiesbaden. It merely proves that human misery and hopelessness were large enough to grasp for any straw available. It matched the degree to which people believed in miracles.

The terrifying fate of pregnant women in the Middle Ages propelled such feelings of helplessness and, implicitly, the belief in miracles. For centuries, human population numbers remained stagnant even though every wife had ten to fifteen births on average. Children died like mayflies. "Oh God, eight children are with you. Please leave the ninth with us," wrote a couple on a prayer votive in a village in the Alps. A woman's labor was made even more frightening by ignorance and brutality. The *Epistola examinatorum miraculorum* offers an example in a story about a woman delivering twins, who asked Elisabeth for help. For a long time, Elisabeth's skull, her girdle, and her bag served as a birthing fetish for women expecting their delivery. In a reactivation of archaic pagan sympathetic magic, women drank wine from her skull. In an exchange of letters dated to the year of 1474, electoral prince Albrecht Achilles of Brandenburg thanked Duke Wilhelm of Weimar for lending him the Elisabeth relics since "they seemed to have brought about a happy and quick birth of a daughter."[44]

Eighty percent of all those reported to have been healed in the *Epistola miraculorum* are children. They were either brought to Marburg by their parents or were promised a visit to Marburg in the future. Frequently, the children's spine was bent forward to such a degree that the head hung down to the knees and the child was forced to crawl like a four-legged animal. It was the dreadful final stage of poliomyelitis, a pediatric illness that is rare today. The second most frequent health issue were sores that covered the whole body, likely as a symptom of scrofula. A pilgrimage to Marburg also

---

44   See Emmy Wilson, "Die Reliquien der Heiligen Elisabeth," *Bayerische Hebammenzeitung* (December 1928).

healed or relieved nervous disorders—whether light or heavy—paralysis, and epilepsy.

The "therapy" consisted of intensive and frequent prayers, placing the sick person on the tomb slab, touching the reliquary with Elisabeth's skeletal remains, and earth scratched from the area surrounding her gravestone, which would also be drunk when dissolved in water. Drinking the solution three times aided in a man's recovery from dysentery. The dream of a woman who suffered for years from paralysis and an inability to walk offers additional insights. The woman dreamt that she was in the Marburg hospital and extended her hand into Elisabeth's grave. After moving her hand across the dead woman's moist body, she touched her own rigid knees, broke out in a sweat, and was able to walk again. Without delay, she turned her dream into reality, thus doubling a wishful dream and its miracle.

All pilgrims arrived on foot. It was essential that the pilgrimage vow included sacrifice and physical discomfort. Walking for many days in fresh air and a change of scenery could often offer a temporary improvement of symptoms, which was ultimately ascribed to the holy site itself. Today, a medical operation frequently includes a risk for the patient; taking refuge in miraculous cures still offers an attractive alternative. The risk factor of pilgrimages differs from that of modern medicine. If a pilgrimage does not help, it also does not harm. We may assume that at least indirectly, a pilgrimage usually brought some physical benefit. Its physiological and psychological effects perhaps resemble most of those of contemporary travel to a health spa or resort. In a scientific era, medical doctors prescribe such trips to patients when they run out of medical solutions.

Besides a radical temporary separation from professional and family responsibilities, the most successful factor in facilitating healing now and then is the will and readiness to get well again. A twelve-year-old sick boy said, "I will not rest until I have seen Marburg," when his parents asked him to sit down while on pilgrimage. Having arrived at the hospital chapel and been placed on the tomb, he feels truly healed. Another pilgrim prayed at Elisabeth's grave in Marburg for a long time, but without success. His own summoning of strength—"I want to walk without a walking stick and crutches"—was triggered by a fellow pilgrim's order, who had obviously learned something by being in Marburg. The entirely natural causality of such successful curative pedagogy cannot be obfuscated by artificial rationalization. The now healed pilgrim did not return immediately home but hurried to the chapel at Marburg. Filled with gratitude, he hung his crutches on the chapel wall.

Social and medical hopelessness still turns miracles into faith's best-loved children. Yet it has often been not only the cause of miraculous healing but also of the illness itself. The dream-based healing of a young Cistercian monk from Amelungsborn, who suffered greatly from epilepsy, offers insights into the depth psychology of medieval people. One night, a woman in white clothing appeared to him. She said that he would be healed if he made a pilgrim's vow to Elisabeth in Marburg. He did not dare to make the vow since his superiors were absent at the time. He also felt that his desire was illicit. The apparition appeared again and repeated her suggestion. As was to be expected, his abbot and prior expressed concerns about the pilgrimage upon their return. Despairing, the young man succumbed to a fierce epileptic seizure. The woman appeared once more, telling him that he would never be healed if he refused to leave on pilgrimage. The seizure was an unconscious effort to pressure his superiors, and achieved the desired result. The abbot granted him permission to leave and equipped him with the necessary provisions, including wax for a votive. From that hour on, the young brother was "healthy, happy, and strong."[45] The seizures disappeared even before he began the long journey from Weser Bergland to Marburg. Unconsciously, his understanding of his illness was accurate: if I can escape the constraints of monastic rule to be outdoors and free, I shall get better. As the simultaneous agent and object of his desire for freedom and contact with women, he allowed himself to visualize an alien "Goddess" who appeared in conjunction with his painful seizures.

The recurring vision proves the dim force of conscience, which sends life's natural desires on a collision course with lifelong monastic vows. Only miracles can shatter these bonds. Indeed, the illness signified perhaps his protest of the highly esteemed and thus inescapable, but nonetheless cursed, lack of freedom. As its cause is removed, the illness disappears as well. The young monk became well merely by the prospect of "holiday travel," that is, by his success in getting his wish and with that gaining a sense of freedom despite his vow of monastic obedience. Arriving in Marburg, he considered the tomb with its holy remains to be the cause of his healing for more reasons than he was aware of. He likely commissioned a small tablet with the inscription "St. Elisabeth helped with a miracle".

In this fashion, most medieval people practiced a Christianized fetishism. Although unable to help herself, the unfortunate Landgravine Elisabeth could come to the assistance of others who subscribed to a magical worldview. For centuries, the pagan enchantment of her relics worked through

45   Huyskens, *Epistola examinatorum miraculorum* (1908).

the force of suggestion. Nobody in the Middle Ages was interested in the true nature of her holiness.

The vow to visit Elisabeth's grave, taken by someone in distress for themselves or their relatives, always included a donation for the tomb. Every pilgrim contributed money or natural produce, including highly coveted beeswax. Some offered Marburg an annual church tax. Donations for a Mass were paid for in cash. A man who at first only donated a wax hand on behalf of his sick daughter returned the following year to Marburg with another wax hand and the vow to bestow two denars annually. A mother who believed her son to be dead and had begun preparations for his funeral invoked Elisabeth of Marburg as a last resort. She vowed to bequeath bread, corn, frankincense, myrrh, silver, money, and wax of equal weight as the boy's body.

The pilgrims' donations were received and managed by the Teutonic Knights. The initiators of her canonization process calculated accurately. Even in the early years of the pilgrimages to Marburg, the hospital could fund and feed thirteen priests. Elisabeth chose voluntary poverty. Her heirs saw a literally golden era flourish for centuries. The religious community at Marburg grew rich, and its daily operations had to be expanded.

Any trace of its female founder became quickly obscured. The simple timber-framed hospital in which Elisabeth fasted and shed tears during her lifetime made room for an extensive new building, the so-called Firmanei, as early as twenty-five years later. Originally envisioned as an asylum for the differently abled and sick, for old and frail men and women, it pivoted gradually toward becoming a pilgrim hostel. The Teutonic Knights monopolized board and lodging for the pilgrim crowds, including, for example, the sale of wine. Like the economic development of a remote valley through industrialization, the small town of Marburg attracted tourism as a rapidly growing pilgrim destination. A steady flow of pilgrims arrived and departed. An independent small pilgrimage town emerged at the Ketzerbach. Marburg, a settlement unknown to most of Germany, and which did not even have its own parish during Elisabeth's lifetime, became famous near and far. It attracted several monasteries and could eventually boast a handsome parish church.

Growing rich so quickly, the Teutonic Knights designed an even larger religious building, with the foundation stone already being laid in the year of Elisabeth's canonization. Four years earlier, Elisabeth's foster father had begun to build a plain yet spacious stone church at the same location, which was perhaps just completed at that time.[46] One new building replaced

46 Translator's note: Busse-Wilson follows Huyskens (1909) here; recent archeological research has rejected the existence of Konrad's stone church; see Maxi Maria Platz, "Archäologische

another. Nothing provides greater proof of Marburg's pilgrimage politics, its greed for power and prestige, than this construction mania. The pretext for the new building was the claim that a church was needed to accommodate the growing number of Teutonic Knights with a special section separate from the common worship area. However, medieval churches were not built to meet specific needs. Rather, they were built with surplus funds which in turn generated new desires. The magnificent cathedral was begun in the most "modern" style, Gothic architecture, which was barely known in Germany. It was completed after a mere fifty years. It is an unusually short period of time, since to build a medieval cathedral typically took centuries, and most have remained incomplete to this day.

Available funding could not match the size of the architectural design. However, financial resources at Marburg's pilgrimage monastery never ran dry. Over the years, exquisite artworks began to fill the church interior. A mausoleum was erected above Elizabeth's shrine as if the heirs were intent on obliterating any memory that the patron saint sought "a fortified tower of the most holy poverty" in a dilapidated farmhouse right on this spot. The superb cathedral of the Teutonic Knights swallowed up Konrad's church much as his church had replaced Elisabeth's Franciscan half-timbered chapel.[47]

From a contemporary view, the magnificent early Gothic cathedral represents the triumph of spirit over matter, since the building seems to manifest Gothic spirituality at its best. However, its genesis had as little to do with spirituality as Elisabeth's canonization. The building's purpose was never to represent a highly refined religiosity but to cater to the archaic fetishism of an illiterate agrarian population. Built upon the foundation of its mentality, the Gothic spirit rises all the more victorious. The tension between the cathedral's formal designs and its true purpose symbolizes the medieval era as a whole, including the life of the woman to whom the church is dedicated—a life defined by a terrifying lack of freedom and yet also by a radical spirituality.

The Elisabeth cathedral served as a pilgrimage church for almost 300 years. Finally, in the year 1539, Landgrave Philip of Hesse terminated the pilgrimages abruptly and brutally, likely because visitor numbers had weakened substantially over time. He tore open the reliquary that housed

Untersuchungen im Umfeld der Elisabethkirche in Marburg an der Lahn," *Mittelalter. Interdisziplinäre Forschung und Rezeptionsgeschichte,* May 22, 2017, https://mittelalter.hypotheses.org/10417 [Accessed December 2, 2023].

47   Huyskens appears to have confused Konrad's church with the east wing of the Gothic cathedral.

Elisabeth's precious bones to bar "pagan idol worship" but certainly also because he was interested in the objects accompanying the sacred bones: her crown, chalice, and jewels. Since that time, the location of Elisabeth's skeletal remains has remained a mystery.[48]

The Teutonic Order, strategically invited to his spiritual daughter's hospital by Magister Konrad, remained at the location of Elisabeth's work and suffering until 1817, the year of its dissolution as an order.

As a substitute for the pilgrimages, Landgrave Philip provided the city with a university and envisioned it as an incubator for the new Protestant movement. In the age of humanism, the sciences were liberated from religious oversight. In contrast to an earlier era of miraculous healing, the study of medicine ceased to be subordinate to theology. University clinics were built behind the Elisabeth cathedral. A modern children's clinic is located adjacent to the church choir where the ill-fated friend of children was once buried.

The veneration of Elisabeth survived the birth of Protestantism. It moved back to the Wartburg castle in Thuringia, the site of Elisabeth's rule as landgravine and home to today's Elisabeth cult, where she is venerated as a local saint. In this region, which is Protestant to its core, schoolgirls are taught Luther's catechism in tandem with Elisabeth's acts of Christian charity, her Seven Works of Mercy. The late nineteenth century turned Elisabeth into a benevolent lady of the manor and thus obliterated the truth of her tragic life. It has been the goal of our study to uncover this truth. Elisabeth's most recent incongruous metamorphosis demonstrates the damaging impact of pseudo-romanticism. Once the locations of her deepest suffering, Wartburg castle and Eisenach have turned into major tourist attractions. The "Patroness of Thuringia," her official ecclesiastical title today, had to add to her beneficial functions that of being a patroness of tourism. At an earlier time, when Wartburg castle was barely known and Romanticism was kept a secret among a handful of poets and artists, Elisabeth and her castle's veneration had not yet been at its worst.

---

48 Landgrave Philip of Hesse was forced to return the stolen skeletal remains at a later point. However, it is doubtful whether what he returned was authentic since her bones were buried anonymously in a graveyard after the theft. As early as the thirteenth century, Dietrich of Apolda was forced to admit that the sacred bones were torn apart and dispersed. Today, a cathedral in Breslau houses an Elisabeth skull that the prince bishop Friedrich of Breslau, who converted to Catholicism in 1668, received as a gift from the Teutonic Order. A monastery of the Order of the Sisters of St. Elisabeth in Vienna also claims to be in possession of the saint's skull.

Appendix

Chronology

1207	Elisabeth is born in Hungary.
1211	Relocation to Landgrave Hermann of Thuringia's palatinate in Germany.
1221	Marriage with Landgrave Ludwig IV of Thuringia and Hesse.
1222	Birth of son Herrmann.
1224	Birth of daughter Sophie.
1225	Konrad of Marburg becomes the confessor and spiritual guide of Landgravine Elisabeth.
1227	Landgrave Ludwig dies on September 12 in Otranto, Italy.
1227, Fall	Birth of daughter Gertrude.
1227/28, Winter	Departure from Wartburg castle and days of misery in Eisenach. Sojourn in Bamberg.
1228, Spring	Return to Thuringia. Konrad of Marburg officially becomes the legal guardian of the widowed landgravine. On Good Friday, Elisabeth vows to Konrad to relinquish her children and personal freedom.
1228, Summer	Relocation to Marburg. Elisabeth chooses to dwell in a nearby village. Construction of the hospital commences.
1228, Fall	Opening of the hospital.
1231	Elisabeth dies on November 17.
1233	Konrad of Marburg is assassinated on July 30.
1234	Teutonic Knights settle in Marburg in July and begin to manage the hospital and church.
1234	Landgrave Konrad, Elisabeth's brother-in-law, enters the Order of the Teutonic Knights on November 18 and begins to lobby for her canonization.
1235	Landgravine Elisabeth of Thuringia is canonized in Perugia on May 27.
1235	The foundation stone of today's Elisabethkirche (Elisabeth Church) is laid on August 14.
1236	Elisabeth's remains are exhumed in Marburg and translated with a large celebration in her honor on May 1.

1289   The Elisabethkirche is completed. Dietrich of Apolda writes
               the first popular biography of Elisabeth.
1855   Moritz of Schwind paints the Elisabeth frescoes in the
               Wartburg castle.

Annotated Bibliography (Organized According to Date of Publication)

Primary Sources[1]

a) The canonization files include the *Libellus de dictis quattuor ancillarum*,
   the *Epistola examinatorum miraculorum*, and two lists of miracles
   that occurred at the grave, which were edited by Albert Huyskens,
   Quellenstudien zur Geschichte der Heiligen Elisabeth. Jahrbuch der
   Görresgesellschaft, 1907 and Marburg: Elwerth Publisher, 1908.
b) Konrad of Marburg *Epistola*, also known as *Summa vitae*. Edited by
   Albert Huyskens, Quellenstudien.
c) Caesarius of Heisterbach, *Vita S. Elisabeth*. Edited by Albert Huyskens,
   Annalen des Historischen Vereins für den Niederrhein, Köln 1908, Nr. 86.
d) Fragment of a Franciscan Vita. S.E. Koblenzer Staatsarchiv. Abt. 701, Nr. 122.
e) *Das Leben des Heiligen Ludwig, des Gemahls der Heiligen Elisabeth.*
   Edited by H. Rückert, Leipzig 1851.

As for the sources' credibility, please consult the chapter "Legend and
History." Caesarius of Heisterbach (c), prior of the Cistercian monastery
of Heisterbach in the Siebengebirge, composed the first *Vita S. Elisabeth*
in 1236 as requested by Prior Ulrich of the Teutonic Knights in Marburg.
Konrad of Marburg had suggested this project to him a few years earlier.
For the most part, Caesarius merely copies the *Libellus*, but besides a few
embellishments and theological flourishes, his *Vita* contains several very
valuable biographical additions. We learn more about Konrad of Marburg,
whom he knew personally, Elisabeth's mother, and events after Elisabeth's
death. Besides the *Vita*, he composed a "Sermo de translatio Beate Elisabeth,"
a sermon which was preached on the first anniversary of the ceremonial

---

1   Our study cites primary sources according to the following editions: the *Libellus* and the
Epistola as edited by Albert Huyskens, Marburg 1908; the legends according to the *Volksbuch von
der Heiligen Elisabeth*, edited by Lulu von Strauß und Torney, Verlag Diederichs, 1927; *Heinrich
Seuse's (Suso's) Schriften*, edited by Lehmann, Verlag Diederichs, 1922.

translation of her remains. His two works are thus a kind of *Festschriften*, which were edited in celebration of her successful canonization.

Berthold, the landgrave's chaplain, composed part of St. Ludwig's Life (e). He was always by the landgrave's side and without a doubt accompanied him across the Alps to Italy. He also guided the transfer of his earthly remains back to Germany. The biographical sections about Landgrave Ludwig and Landgravine Elisabeth up until this point, that is, the spring of 1228, thus constitute a contemporary eyewitness account.

Medieval Biographies of St. Elisabeth

Dietrich of Apolda, *Vita S. Elisabeth*, is edited by Mencken, Scriptores rer. germ., and Canisius, Thesaurus eccles., tome II, p. 119 (not published in a German translation). The author, a monk in Erfurt's Dominican monastery, composed the most popular and extensive biography of the saint between 1289 and 1291. His *Vita* became the foundation for every legend and conventional image of St. Elisabeth. The author wrote the history of his royal landgravine as a Thuringian and composed it with obvious sympathy. He identified his sources as the *Libellus* and the *Epistola*, adapted them without any major changes according to their overall meaning, but added literary embellishments. He also diluted any statements in his sources that reference St. Elisabeth's relationship with Konrad. Besides the two primary sources, Dietrich of Apolda notes that he consulted two sermons written around the time of her translation. Furthermore, the diligent and, by medieval standards, conscientious historian personally examined all oral traditions and met persons who had known St. Elisabeth face-to-face.

However, Dietrich does not list Caesarius of Heisterbach in his sources, possibly because of the rivalry between Dominicans and Cistercians, nor does he mention Chaplain Berthold's *Life of St. Ludwig*. This omission caused a controversy among historians about dating the manuscripts, because Dietrich includes all biographical episodes of St. Elisabeth's spouse, including those of a presumably more recent tradition. In *Die Entstehung der Reinhardsbrunner Geschichtsbücher* (Halle 1878), Karl Wenck has argued that St. Ludwig's biographer used Dietrich of Apolda as a source. In his study *Zur Kritik der Quellen der Heiligen Elisabeth*, Börner assumed on the other hand that Dietrich relied on an already completed *Life of St. Ludwig*. Dietrich of Apolda is the first to present a collection of miracle stories and literary tales that had sprung up around the lives of Landgravine Elisabeth and her spouse.

About two years after the completion of Dietrich of Apolda's *Vita*, a monk at the Reinhardsbrunn monastery embellished Dietrich's work with several miracle stories and minor details of Ludwig and Elisabeth's lives. These might have always been a part of the Reinhardsbrunn oral tradition since the monastery was one of Ludwig's most favored foundations. All late medieval and popular biographies and accounts of St. Elisabeth depart only rarely from Dietrich of Apolda's account, including the work of Johannes Rothe, a canon at the Collegiate Church of St. Mary in Eisenach, where Rothe died in 1434. He is the author of the *Thuringian Chronicle*, written in German, which describes in great detail and literary fashion all biographical episodes of the Thuringian royal couple. Johannes Rothe contributed greatly to the Thuringian landgravine's popularity.

The so-called auctor rhythmicus who is assumed by some to be identical with Johannes Rothe, composed a short biographical sketch of Landgravine Elisabeth.[2] A type of rhymed chronicle, it offers a pared down version of her life but adds several previously unknown episodes which might have circulated in the Wartburg town of Eisenach as local oral traditions.

The canonized landgravine of Thuringia and Hesse's popularity led to an extensive biography as early as the Reformation era. Written in German and illustrated with woodcuts, the *Cronica St. Elisabeth* was published in Erfurt in 1520. It was reissued by Lulu von Strauß und Torney in the series Deutsche Volksheit by Eugen Diederichs Verlag in Jena. Emphasizing her royal bloodline and aristocratic milieu, the *Cronica* completes a 300-year process of turning the historical Elisabeth into a fairytale figure embedded in fictional events and miraculous stories.

Elisabeth's story is recounted in abbreviated form in the *Legenda Aurea*, the monumental collection of all hagiographies known in the thirteenth century. It was created by the Dominican Jacobus de Voragine at the end of the thirteenth century and was printed in German around 1470 as one of the earliest books in print. A new edition was prepared by Richard Benz in Jena in 1912 and 1915.

Source Criticism

Gustav Börner. *Zur Kritik der Quellen der Heiligen Elisabeth*. Neues Archiv der Gesellschaft für ältere deutsche Geschichtskunde, 1888, 13:433.

Hellmut Mielke. "Zur Biographie der Heiligen Elisabeth." PhD diss., Universität Rostock, 1888.

Albert Huyskens. *Quellenstudien zur Geschichte der Heiligen Elisabeth*. Marburg: Verlag Elwerth, 1908.

---

2   See August Witzschel, *Über das Leben der Heiligen Elisabeth* (Jena 1869). The text is printed in Mencken, *Scriptores rerum Germanorum* (Leipzig 1728).

Historiographical Studies of the Nineteenth Century

A. Romantic Literature

Moving beyond theological inquiries, a literary interest in St. Elisabeth awakened with Romanticism's rediscovery of the Middle Ages. The best-known publication in this genre is Count Charles Forbes Montalembert's *Leben der Heiligen Elisabeth von Ungarn, Landgravine of Thuringia and Hesse* (1829), translated into German by Städtler, 3rd edition, Regensburg, 1862. The novel exemplifies a romantic-idyllic historiographical approach to the Middle Ages. The young French author did not write with the objective distance of a modern historian but with a (re-)discoverer's enthusiasm and personal preferences. In his defense of a Christian-Catholic Middle Ages, he whitewashed his admired heroine's life. Despite his biases, he has collated and evaluated all primary sources, including the legends and late medieval traditions, with a remarkable attention to detail. His work remains an outstanding scholarly achievement, because the critical study of medieval manuscripts was in its early stages at the time of his writing.

Moritz Schmerbauch, *Die Heilige Elisabeth* (Erfurt 1827) and Joh. H. Mey, *Charakterzüge und Lebensumstände der Heiligen Elisabeth* (Eisenach 1822) are also motivated by the desire to defend the "dark Middle Ages" and to recover its lighter attributes, but not without a thorough critical and scholarly stance.

A.F. Vilmar's *Die Landgräfin Elisabeth von Thüringen* (new edition published by Elwerth, Marburg), first appeared in print in 1852 after a presentation by the author at the Wartburg castle in 1850, an era shaped by Grand Duke Karl Alexander's promotion of late Romanticism.

B. Historiographical Research

Despite an eighteenth-century style, which treats historical materials in a literary rather than scholarly fashion, Karl Wilhelm Justi's *Elisabeth, die heilige Landgräfin von Thüringen* (Zürich, 1797), offers at least in part a critical approach to the saint's life. The short text is noteworthy for being among the first to thoroughly examine known primary sources, chronicles, and medieval traditions about the saint's life.

Karl Heusinger, *Das Hospital St. Elisabeth*, Marburg 1860.

Franz X. Wegele, "Die Heilige Elisabeth," Historische Zeitschrift, vol. 5 (1861): 351 ff. This historical study hovers on the boundary between critical scholarship and literary description. With intuition and psychological acumen, however, the author uncovered key relational contexts in the saint's life.

Winkelmann's biography of Konrad of Marburg, published in Deutsche Rundschau, ed. Rodenberg, vol. 28, 1881, also includes a study of St. Elisabeth. Although the author relies extensively on primary sources, his analysis is based on a narrow rationalism.

Critical historical research about Elisabeth's life reached a new level in the following scholarly studies.

Karl Wenck. "Die Heilige Elisabeth." *Historische Zeitschrift* 69 (1892): 209.

Karl Wenck. "Die Heilige Elisabeth und Papst Gregor IX." *Hochland* 5 (1907).

Karl Wenck. "Die Heilige Elisabeth." *Die Wartburg*. Edited and published under the authority of Grand Duke Karl Alexander. Verlag Baumgärtle: Berlin, 1907.

Karl Wenck. "Die Heilige Elisabeth." *Sammlung gemeinverständlicher Vorträge und Schriften aus dem Gebiet der Theologie und Religionsgeschichte* 52. Tübingen (1908). (Includes a translation of the *Epistola*).

Karl Wenck has sifted through Elisabeth traditions of varying quality and extracted the core of what should be considered the historical aspects of her life.

Helmut Mielke. *Die Heilige Elisabeth*. Hamburg, 1891 (Sammlung gemeinverständlicher Vorträge).

G. Küch. "Elisabeth die Heilige." *Beiträge zur Geschichte Eisenachs* (1907).

Paul Braun. "Studien zur Geschichte der Heiligen Elisabeth und die erste Wallfahrtskirche zu Marburg." *Zeitschrift des Vereins für hessische Geschichte und Altertumskunde, Neue Folge* 9, no. 1 (1913): 1–12.

Albert Huyskens. "Der Hospitalbau der Heiligen Elisabeth und die erste Wallfahrtskirche zu Marburg." *Zeitschrift des Vereins für hessische Geschichte und Altertumskunde, Neue Folge* 33 & 43 (1909): 130–43.

Albert Huyskens. "Die Heilige Landgräfin Elisabeth von Thüringen." *Korrespondenzblatt des Gesamtvereins der deutschen Geschichts- und Altertumsvereine* 77, no. 10-12 (1929).

Maria Maresch. *Ein altes Heiligenleben im Lichte moderner Forschung*. München-Gladbach, 1918.

Studies of Konrad of Marburg

Unsurprisingly, historical studies of Konrad of Marburg must be divided according to Protestant and Catholic points of view. This concerns not only the evaluation of inquisitorial courts, but also Konrad of Marburg's relationship with his penitential daughter St. Elisabeth. The studies were published in the seventies and eighties of the nineteenth century. Still missing is a type of scholarship that employs the standards of modern character analysis that would do justice to his personality, which is at least as significant and problematical as St. Elisabeth's. As is true for St. Elisabeth scholarship, writers of the first half of the nineteenth century, considered perhaps to have been the last representatives of an interdisciplinary humanist era, intuitively grasped the truth of their relationship. This is not the case among scholars at the end of the nineteenth century, who were trained in narrowly defined scholarly disciplines.

Karl Wilhelm Justi. "Konrad von Marburg, Beichtvater der Heiligen Elisabeth und erster Inquisitor in Teutschland [sic]." *Jahrbücher der Geschichte und Staatskunst* 1 (1829).

Henckel, *Konrad von Marburg*. Marburg, 1854. Includes a bibliography of primary sources.

Adolf Hausrath, *Konrad von Marburg: Der Ketzerrichter von Marburg*. Dissertation, 1861. Printed in *Kleinere Schriften religionsgeschichtlichen Inhalts*. Leipzig, 1881.

Josef Beck. *Konrad von Marburg: Inquisitor in Deutschland*. Dissertation, Breslau, 1871.

Includes an extensive bibliography of primary sources.

Balthasar Kaltner. *Konrad of Marburg und die Inquisition in Deutschland*. Prague, 1882.

Winkelmann, "Konrad von Marburg." *Deutsche Rundschau*. Edited by Rodenberg. Vol. 28, 1881.

L. Ranke. "Konrad von Marburg." *Allgemeine deutsche Biographie*. 1882.

Paul Braun. "Der Beichtvater der Heiligen Elisabeth und deutsche Inquisitor Konrad von Marburg." *Archiv für Hessische Geschichte und Altertumskunde*. Neue Folge, Ergänzungsband IV, Heft 4. *Beiträge zur hessischen Kirchengeschichte*, 248–300, Darmstadt 1910. Part Two in Heft 5, 33-1363, Darmstadt 1911. Both studies include an exhaustive bibliography.

General Literature

Richard Benz. *Die Legenda Aurea*. Eugen Diederichs Verlag, 1912 and 1915.

Schmoll, *Die Heilige Elisabeth in der bildenden Kunst des 13. bis 16. Jahrhunderts*. Verlag Elwerth, Marburg, 1918.

P. Diodor Henniges. "Die Heilige Messe zu Ehren der Heiligen Elisabeth," *Franziskanische Studien* 1 (1919).

P. Meffert. *Charitas und Volksepidemien*, 1925.

P. Meffert. *Charitas und Krankenwesen bis zum Ausgang des Mittelalters*, 1927.

William James. *Die religiöse Erfahrung in ihrer Mannigfaltigkeit*. German translation. Leipzig, 1907.

Karl Birnbaum. *Grundzüge der Kulturpsychopathologie*. Verlag Bergmann: München, 1924.

Translator's Introduction: Select Bibliography

Angulo, Inure. "The Unnamed Presence: Abuse of Power in Consecrated Life." *Magistra* 28, no. 1 (2022): 3–29.

Bäumer, Gertrud. *Adelheid, Mutter der Königreiche*. Tübingen: Rainer Wunderlich Verlag Hermann Leins, 1936.

Barthlow, Arley. "The New Culture-History in Germany." *History Teacher's Magazine* 4 (1913): 215–21.

Beckmann, Emmy, and Irma Stoss, eds. *Quellenhefte zum Frauenleben in der Geschichte*. 26 Vols. Berlin: F.A. Herbig, 1927–1936.

Bernhart, Joseph. "Hildegard of Bingen." *Archiv für Kulturgeschichte* (December 1930): 249–60.

Busse-Wilson, Elisabeth. *Das Leben der Heiligen Elisabeth von Thüringen: Das Abbild einer mittelalterlichen Seele*. Munich: C.H. Beck, 1931.

Busse-Wilson, Elisabeth. "Eine Franziskanerin des Nordens: Zur Heiligsprechung der heiligen Elisabeth Pfingsten 1235." *Die Wartburg* 34 (1935): 203–206.

Busse-Wilson, Elisabeth. "Die Wunder am Grabe der Heiligen Elisabeth in Marburg: Ein Beitrag zur Erhebung ihrer Gebeine im Jahre 1236." *Beiträge zur Hessischen Kirchengeschichte* 11 (1939): 184–209.

Chickering, Roger. *Karl Lamprecht: A German Academic Life (1856–1915)*. Atlantic Highlands, N.J.: Humanities Press, 1993.

Cocks, Geoffrey. "Repressing, Remembering, Working Through: German Psychiatry, Psychotherapy, Psychoanalysis, and the 'Missed Resistance' in the Third Reich." *Journal of Modern History* 64 (1992): 204–16.

De Robeck, Nesta. *St. Elizabeth of Hungary: A Story of Twenty-four Years*. Milwaukee: Bruce Publishing Company, 1954.

Elliott, Dyan. "Elisabeth of Hungary: Between Men." In Dyan Elliott, *Proving Woman: Female Spirituality and Inquisitional Culture in the Later Middle Ages*. Princeton: Princeton University Press, 2004, 85–119.

Elliot, Dyan. "Sexual Scandal and the Clergy: A Medieval Blueprint." In *Why the Middle Ages Matter: Medieval Light on Modern Injustice*, edited by Celia Chazelle, Simon Doubleday, Felice Lifshitz, and Amy G. Riemensnyder, 90–106. London: Routledge, 2012.

Eulenburg, Albert. *Sadismus und Masochismus*. Wiesbaden: Verlag von J.F. Bergmann, 1902.

Eulenburg, Franz. *Die Entwicklung der Universität Leipzig in den letzten hundert Jahren: Statistische Untersuchungen.* Leipzig: S. Hirzel, 1909.

Fischer, Hermann. *Die heilige Hildegarde von Bingen, die erste deutsche Naturforscherin und Ärztin: Ihr Leben und Werk.* Munich: C.H. Beck, 1927.

Großmann, Britt. *Elisabeth Busse-Wilson (1890–1974): Eine Werk- und Netzwerkanalyse.* Weinheim: Benz-Juventa, 2017.

Huyskens, Albert. *Quellenstudien zur Geschichte der Heiligen Elisabeth.* Marburg: N.G. Elwert, 1908.

Huyskens, Albert. *Der sogenannte Libellus de dictis ancillarum s. Elisabeth confectus.* Kempten: Verlag der Josef Kösel'schen Buchhandlung, 1911.

Huyskens, Albert. *Die Schriften des Caesarius von Heisterbach über die heilige Elisabeth von Thüringen.* Bonn: Publikationen der Gesellschaft für Rheinische Geschichtskunde 43, 1937.

Illemann, Regina Marianne. "'Abbild einer mittelalterlichen Seele'? Das Bild der heiligen Elisabeth bei Busse-Wilson." Unpublished Diplomarbeit. Katholische-Theologische Fakultät, Rheinische Friedrich-Wilhelm-Universität Bonn, 2008.

James, William. *Die religiöse Erfahrung in ihrer Mannigfaltigkeit.* Leipzig, 1907. German translation of James, *The Varieties of Religious Experience: A Study in Human Nature,* 1902.

Kienzle, Beverly Mayne, and Nancy Nienhuis. "Battered Women and the Construction of Sanctity." *Journal of Feminist Studies in Religion* 17, no. 1 (2001): 33–61.

Klönne, Irmgard, ed. *Elisabeth Busse-Wilson: Die Frau und die Jugendbewegung.* Hamburg: Freideutscher Jugendverlag Saal, 1920; reprint Münster: Lit Verlag, 1989.

Krebs, Stefan and Werner Tschacher. "Im Sinne der rassischen Erneuerung unseres Volkes – Albert Huyskens, die Westdeutsche Gesellschaft für Familienkunde und das Aachener Stadtarchiv im Nationalsozialismus." *Zeitschrift des Aachener Geschichtsvereins* 109 (2007): 215–38.

Mansager, Eric, and Marina Bluvshtein. "Adler and Maslow in Collaboration: Applied Therapeutic Creativity." *Journal of Humanistic Psychology* 60, no. 6 (2020): 1–21.

Melman, Billie. "Gender, History and Memory: The Invention of Women's Past in the Nineteenth and Early Twentieth Centuries." *History and Memory: Studies in Representation of the Past* 5, no. 1 (1993): 5–39.

Miller, Julie B. "Eroticized Violence in Medieval Women's Mystical Literature: A Call for a Feminist Critique." *Journal of Feminist Studies in Religion* 15, no. 2 (1999): 25–49.

Musial, Magdalena. "Jugendbewegung und Emanzipation der Frau: Ein Beitrag zur Rolle der weiblichen Jugend in der Jugendbewegung bis 1933." Dissertation, Universität Essen, Fachbereich 2, 1982.

Pfister, Oskar. "Hysterie und Mystik bei Margaretha Ebner (1291–1351)." *Zentralblatt für Psychoanalyse* 1 (1911) 468–85.

Pieper, Lori. "A new Life of St. Elizabeth of Hungary: The Anonymous Franciscan." *Archivum Franciscanum historicum* 93 (2000): 29–78.

Pieper, Lori. *The Greatest of These is Love: The Life of St. Elizabeth of Hungary*. Second Revised Edition, New York: Tau Cross Books and Media, 2013.

Pieper, Lori. *The Voice of a Medieval Woman: St. Elizabeth of Hungary as a Franciscan Penitent in the Early Sources for Her Life*. Second Edition, New York: Tau Cross Books and Media, 2016.

Scholz, Hans-Jürgen. "Elisabethforscher von Justi bis Busse-Wilson." In *St. Elisabeth – Kult, Kirche, Konfessionen*, edited by Brigitte Rechberg. Marburg: J.A. Koch, 1983, 39–43, 146–156.

Smith, Jennifer. *Women, Mysticism, and Hysteria in Fin-de-Siècle Spain*. Nashville: Vanderbilt University, 2021.

Stange-Fayos, Christina. "Die erste Kaiserin. Ein Mythos zum 'geistigen Zusammenhalt' der Frauenbewegung." *Cahiers d'Études Germaniques* 76 (2019): 251–64.

Thalmann, Rita. *Frausein im Dritten Reich*. Munich: Carl Hanser Verlag, 1984.

von Strauss und Torney, Lulu. *Das Leben der heiligen Elisabeth: Nach den alten Quellen erzählt*. Jena: Eugen Diederichs Verlag, 1926.

von Strauss und Torney, Lulu, ed. *Volksbuch von der Heiligen Elisabeth*. Jena: Verlag Diederichs, 1927.

Tatar, Maria. *Lustmord: Sexual Murder in Weimar Germany*. Princeton: Princeton University Press, 1995.

Werner, Matthias. "Elisabeth of Thüringen, Franziskus of Assisi und Konrad von Marburg." In *Elisabeth von Thüringen: Eine Europäische Heilige*, edited by Dieter Blume and Matthias Werner. Petersberg: Michael Imhof Verlag, 2007, 109–137.

Wiethaus, Ulrike. "The German Historian Elisabeth Busse-Wilson (1890–1974): Academic and Medieval Hagiography 1914–1931." In *Women Medievalists and the Academy*, edited by Jane Chance. Madison: University of Wisconsin Press, 2005, 353–67.

Wiethaus, Ulrike. "Naming and Un-naming Violence against Women: German Historiogaphy and the Cult of St. Elisabeth of Thuringia." *Studies in Medievalism* 1, no. 9 (1997): 187–202.

Wiethaus, Ulrike. "Who is Hrotsvit of Gandersheim?" In Ulrike Wiethaus, *German Mysticism and the Politics of Culture*. New York: Peter Lang, 2014, 57–75.

Wolf, Kenneth Baxter. *The Life and Afterlife of St. Elizabeth of Hungary: Testimony from Her Canonization Hearings*. Oxford: Oxford University Press, 2011.

Young, Kathleen Zuanich. "The Imperishable Virginity of St. Maria Goretti." *Gender and Society* 3, no. 4 (1989): 474–82.

Translator's Acknowledgments

I extend my heartfelt gratitude to Lucy Bregman and E. Ann Matter, who sparked my interest in the psychology of religion and medieval women mystics so many years ago; Jane Chance, who always believed that women medievalists have a genealogy worth celebrating; Robert Beachy, Britt Großmann, and Regina Marianne Illmann for their insights into Weimar Republic cultural themes and Elisabeth Busse Wilson's work and context; Gale Sigal and Gillian Overing for lively conversations about the project; Lori Pieper for her support; Sally Barbour and Duncan G. Lewis for their close readings; Wake Forest University for providing me with a Reynolds Faculty Research leave and travel funds to explore St. Elisabeth's presence in Marburg and Eisenach; the Archiv der deutschen Jugendbewegung Burg Ludwigstein for their sharing of archival materials; the librarians at the Z. Smith Reynolds Library who worked their magic in finding obscure sources, especially Kaeley McMahan for her expertise in religious studies; Jeff Nichols for his gracious support in all technical matters; Zac Zuber-Zander for his generosity, acumen, and wholehearted support for the project; Shannon Cunningham for her extraordinary patience and belief in the project; and Nicole Busse for her enthusiasm and deep appreciation of her grandmother's work.

Note on the Translator

Ulrike Wiethaus is Professor Emerita in the Department for the Study of Religions at Wake Forest University. Her research interests focus on the history of Christian spirituality with an emphasis on gender justice and political history, and most recently, historic trauma, religion, and the long-term impact of US colonialism. As the inaugural director, she has guided the creation of the Religion and Public Engagement concentration in Religious Studies at Wake Forest University. Her Medieval and Early Modern Studies monographs include *German Mysticism and the Politics of Culture* (New York: Peter Lang, 2014), *American/Medieval: Nature and Mind in Cultural Transfer*, co-edited with Gillian R. Overing (Göttingen: Vandenhoeck & Ruprecht, 2016); *American/Medieval Goes North: Earth and Water in Transit*, coedited with Gillian R. Overing (Göttingen: Vandenhoeck & Ruprecht, 2019); and *Moravian Americans and Their Neighbors, 1772–1822*, coedited with Grant P. McAllister (Leiden: Brill, 2023).